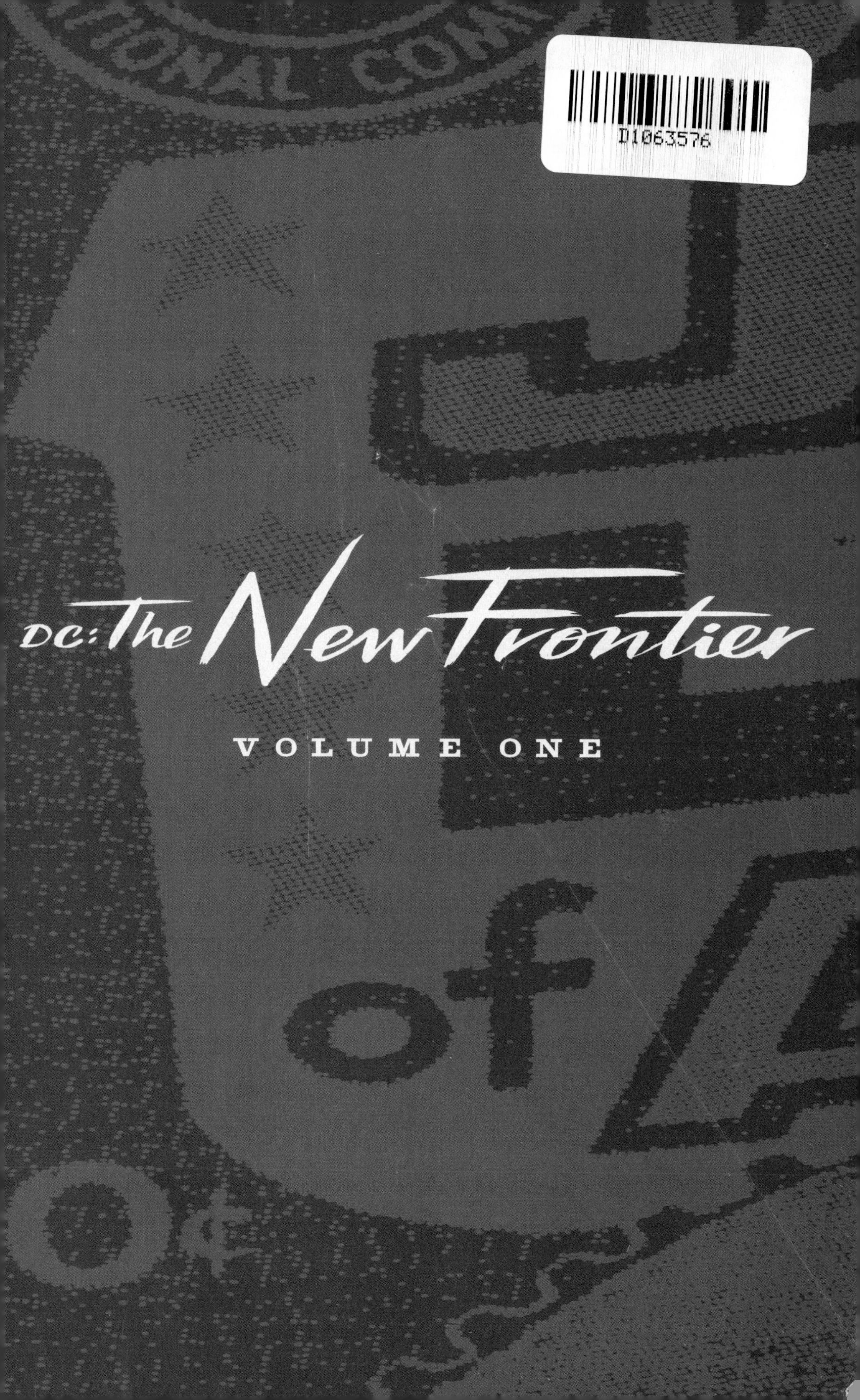

DC: The New Frontier

VOLUME ONE

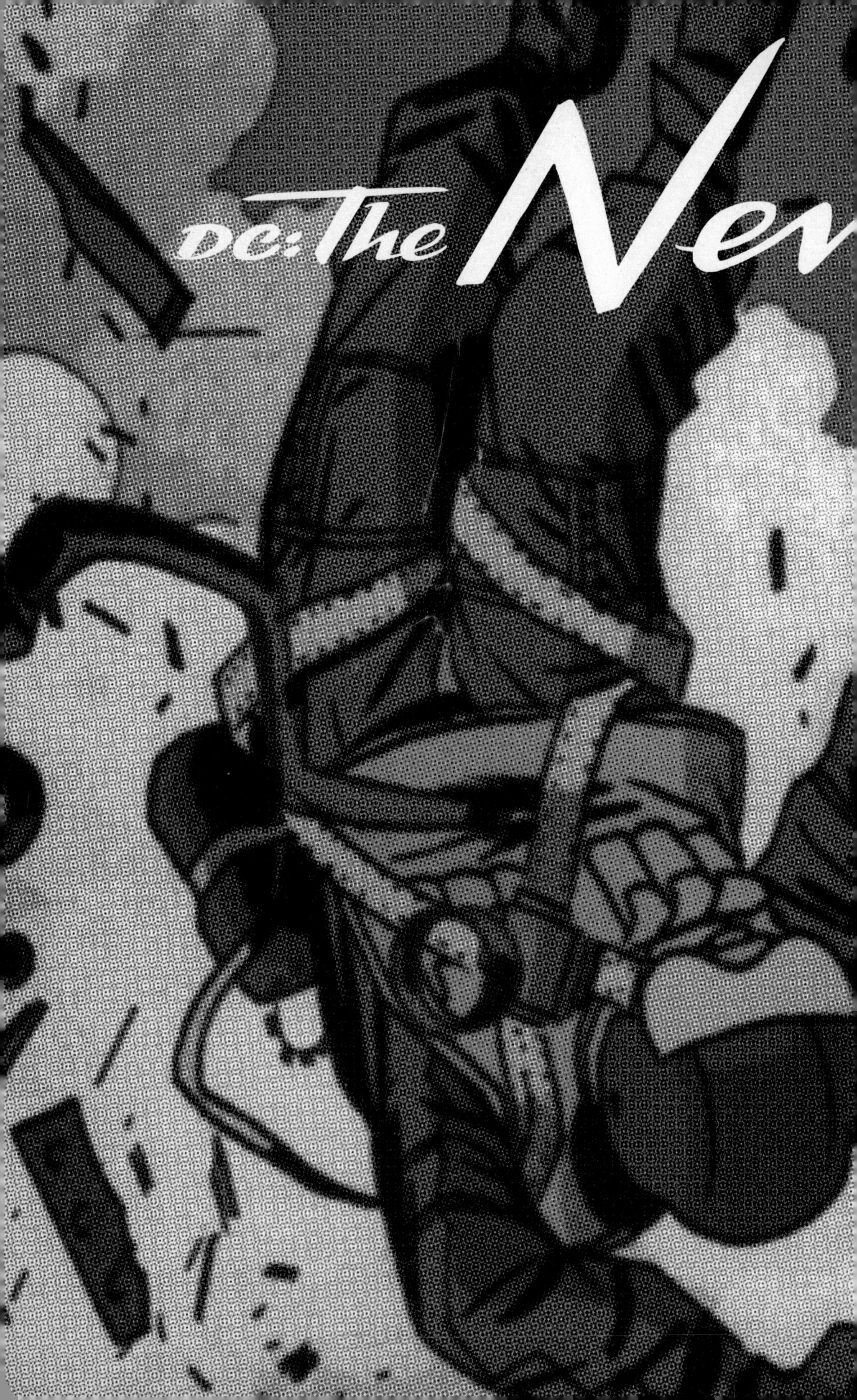
DC: The Ne

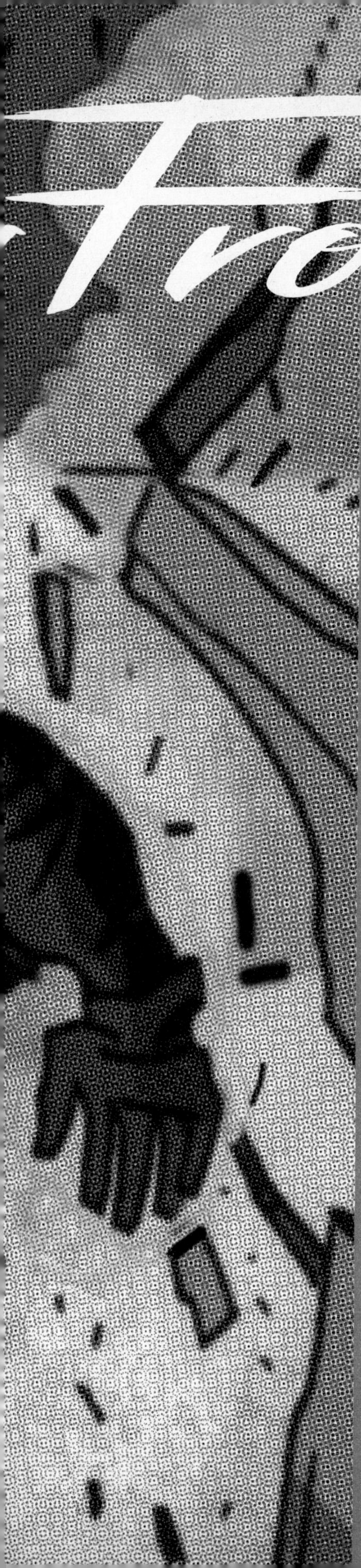

Frontier

VOLUME ONE

DARWYN COOKE
WRITER AND ILLUSTRATOR

DAVE STEWART
COLORIST

JARED K. FLETCHER
LETTERER

Dan DiDio
VP-EXECUTIVE EDITOR

Mark Chiarello
EDITOR-ORIGINAL SERIES

Valerie D'Orazio
ASSISTANT EDITOR-ORIGINAL SERIES

Anton Kawasaki
EDITOR-COLLECTED EDITION

Robbin Brosterman
SENIOR ART DIRECTOR

Amie Brockway-Metcalf
ART DIRECTOR

Paul Levitz
PRESIDENT & PUBLISHER

Georg Brewer
VP-DESIGN & RETAIL PRODUCT DEVELOPMENT

Richard Bruning
SENIOR VP-CREATIVE DIRECTOR

Patrick Caldon
SENIOR VP-FINANCE & OPERATIONS

Chris Caramalis
VP-FINANCE

Terri Cunningham
VP-MANAGING EDITOR

Alison Gill
VP-MANUFACTURING

Rich Johnson
VP-BOOK TRADE SALES

Hank Kanalz
VP-GENERAL MANAGER, WILDSTORM

Lillian Laserson
SENIOR VP & GENERAL COUNSEL

Jim Lee
EDITORIAL DIRECTOR-WILDSTORM

David McKillips
VP-ADVERTISING & CUSTOM PUBLISHING

John Nee
VP-BUSINESS DEVELOPMENT

Gregory Noveck
SENIOR VP-CREATIVE AFFAIRS

Cheryl Rubin
SENIOR VP-BRAND MANAGEMENT

Bob Wayne
VP-SALES & MARKETING

DC: THE NEW FRONTIER VOLUME ONE

Published by DC Comics. Cover, introduction and compilation copyright © 2004 DC Comics. All Rights Reserved.

Originally published in single magazine form in DC: THE NEW FRONTIER #1-3. Copyright © 2004 DC Comics. All Rights Reserved. All characters, their distinctive likenesses and related elements featured in this publication are trademarks of DC Comics. The stories, characters and incidents featured in this publication are entirely fictional. DC Comics does not read or accept unsolicited submissions of ideas, stories or artwork.

DC COMICS
1700 Broadway, New York, NY 10019
A Warner Bros. Entertainment Company

Printed in Canada. Third Printing.
ISBN: 1-4012-0350-7
ISBN 13: 978-1-4012-0350-4

Cover painting and publication design by DARWYN COOKE

INTF

Heroes walked the Earth then. It was a simpler time, and every child of my generation knew their names. We laboriously made models out of plastic and as-yet-unmaligned glue, building their craft. We had their pictures on our bedroom walls. It was the moment when man broke the bounds of our eternal home on this world, and soared through sky and space like gods. From the flight of the X-15 on, the impossible became real.

Imagination was rich then, too. The new medium of television was linking the globe's distant corners in new ways, and the old media felt the need to respond. For comics, it was a time of experimentation with both the concept of what it was to be a hero, and with the seemingly thousands of environments for heroism. The writers at DC placed men in danger in every possible situation: war, peace, crime, space, time, in skies and under seas, and even improbable combinations like an island where dinosaurs survived to battle 20th-century soldiers.

This was clearly the world of Darwyn Cooke's childhood, and having grown to maturity with a mastery of storytelling and image honed in the art of animation, he chose to return to the twin iconographies of his childhood, and combine them. THE NEW FRONTIER is assertively set in America as the '50s fade into the '60s, and brings together the changes in our culture with the stories in our comics in a way that was impossible at the time. The writers and artists working on comics during those years saw the changes as current events, swaying to and fro, not as the clearer pattern that emerged from the perspective of history. And even for those who wanted to play a part in that cultural change (and there were many within the world of comics), the fear of speaking out was great in the years just after witchhunts became a national pastime with comics bearing scars from the lightest of brushes wielding tar and feathers.

So Darwyn chose to go back to revisit

ODUCTION

this world with the freedoms of the 21st cen-
tury, and tell a tale that was fundamentally
of the mid-20th.

The first freedom he exercised was
the ability to cross the invisible boundaries
that rigidly divided comics in those years:
the stark walls of editorial offices that were
often prisons for characters and talent alike.
It was inconceivable in the DC comics of
1960 to have characters from Bob Kanigher's
war comics meet the super-heroes who populated the Justice League, or to have either
exist in the same world as the Blackhawks.
There were creative advantages to this
approach: you didn't have to build complex
reasons into every story why another hero
wouldn't come in and help solve your pro-
tagonist's problems, for one, and the need to
tell story after story set in a single character's fictional world pushed writers to invent
richer casts of villains and supporting characters for each hero than is the case today.
Darwyn went back to the beginning, and
structured a story that allowed the heroes and
their casts to mingle, and look at what some of
the likely touch points would have been. The
results of the exercise are fascinating.

The second freedom he exercised was
to retell stories without being bound by the
way they were first told. The last few years
of comics have opened up the serial medium
to alternate versions of characters' origins or
canonical adventures, in ways that a generation of comics fans-turned-writers (myself
included) shunned. For THE NEW FRONTIER,
this became a vital catalyst to allow the
mixing of mythology between the characters, and the creation of common themes of
great importance.

The final freedom was the modern
ability to add issues from the real world into
the fictional worlds of our characters. THE
NEW FRONTIER touches lightly on the great
dilemmas of its period as it moves from
McCarthy to Kennedy, but each deft touch
brings the story onto a very large stage with

echoes of the challenges we faced. It is a
very special gift of comics, with their ease at
transcending space and time, to mix reality
with fiction seamlessly, and Darwyn does it
especially well. Each nugget gives a
moment of archetype, and sets the stage for
what the reader can fill in from his or her
knowledge of the time . . . or merely move
quickly past, if the knowledge isn't there.
These anchors can be enduring additions to
the myths of our characters: I smiled to see
the echo of a story I wrote over 25 years ago,
in a scene alluding to the Justice Society's
break-up being caused by a Congressional
investigation. When I added that bit to the
history of our characters at a time already
two decades past when it was "supposed"
to have happened, I didn't expect to find it
being used so many years later.

Nor, I suspect, does Darwyn know
what of this work will show up in another
storyteller's tales of our heroes, years down
the road. A visual trick, perhaps, like his
sense of the Flash in motion. Or a line, that
just fits a character so well. There are many
such within, and only time will tell what
endures. The story of our heroes is a mosaic,
intricately built by many talents over many
decades, and often we don't know which
tiles will become keystones for a new ele-
ment in the design. But a wise man taught
me that the reader can tell which are placed
in the mosaic with sincerity, and only those
can endure.

So come back to a time of heroes, and a
tale that Darwyn Cooke needed to tell, of how
they came to walk the Earth and reach beyond
it. And whether you lived in those times or not,
as you turn the pages, you will now...

Paul Levitz
2004

CHAPTER ONE
ANALOG HEROES

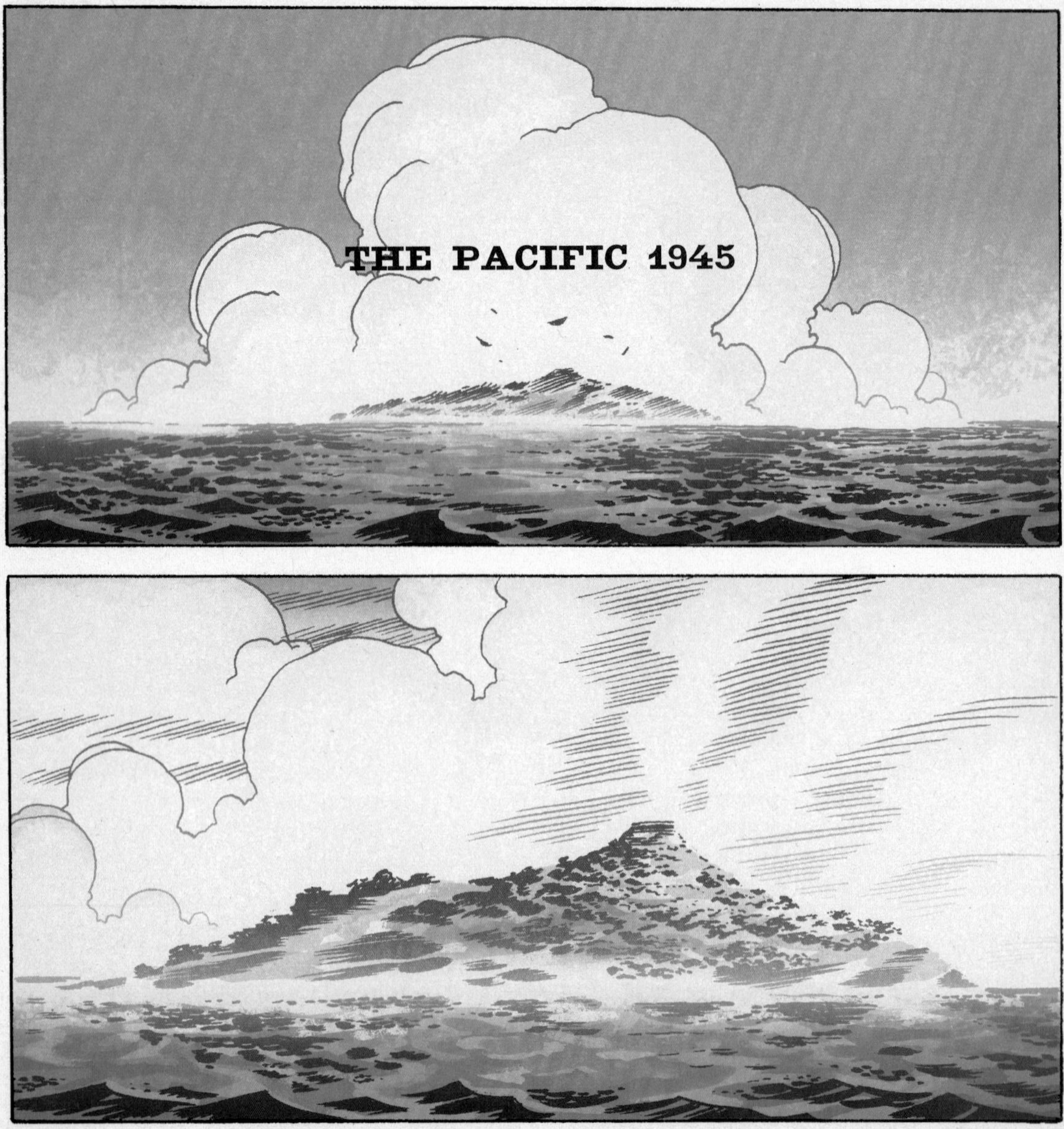
THE PACIFIC 1945

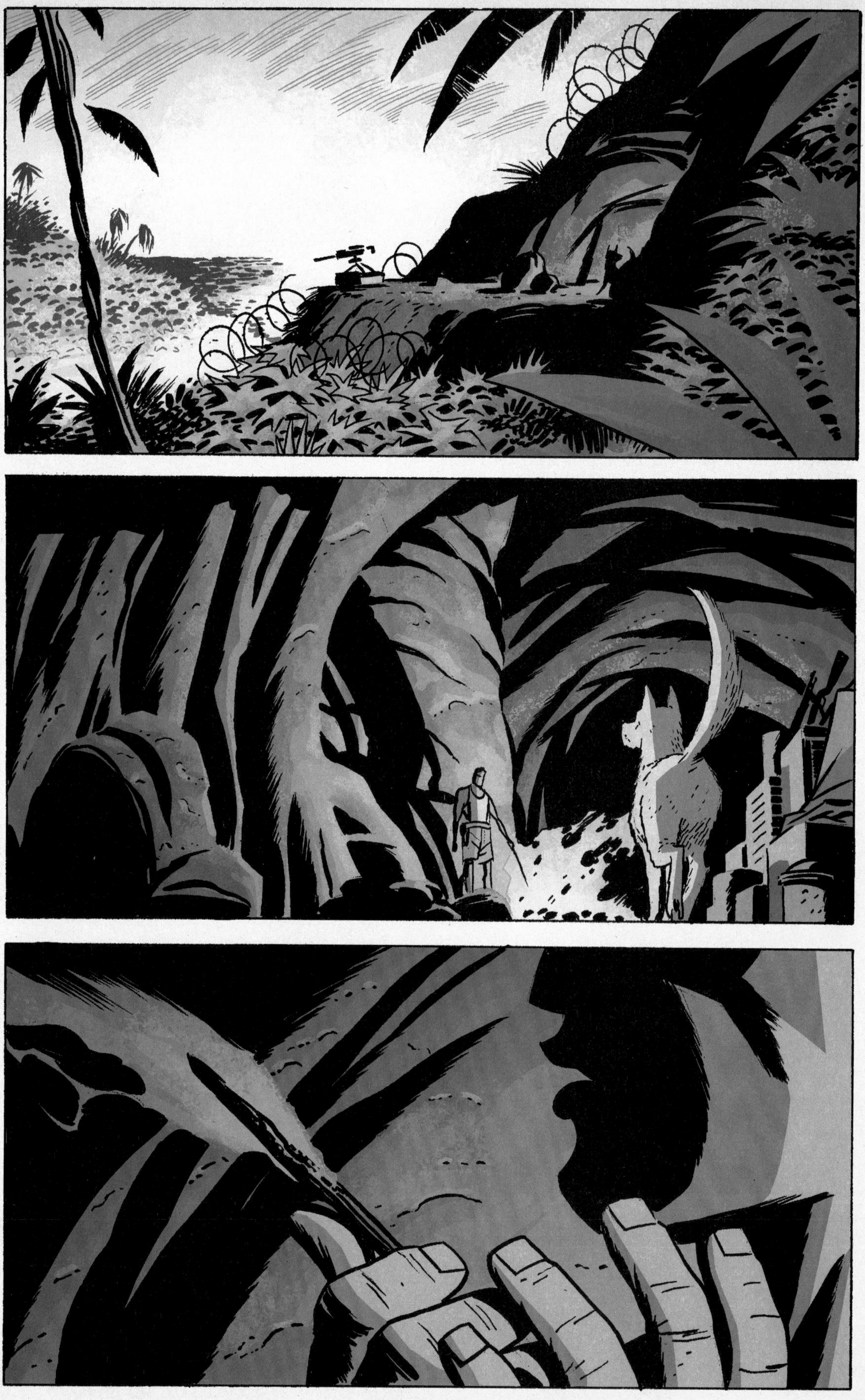

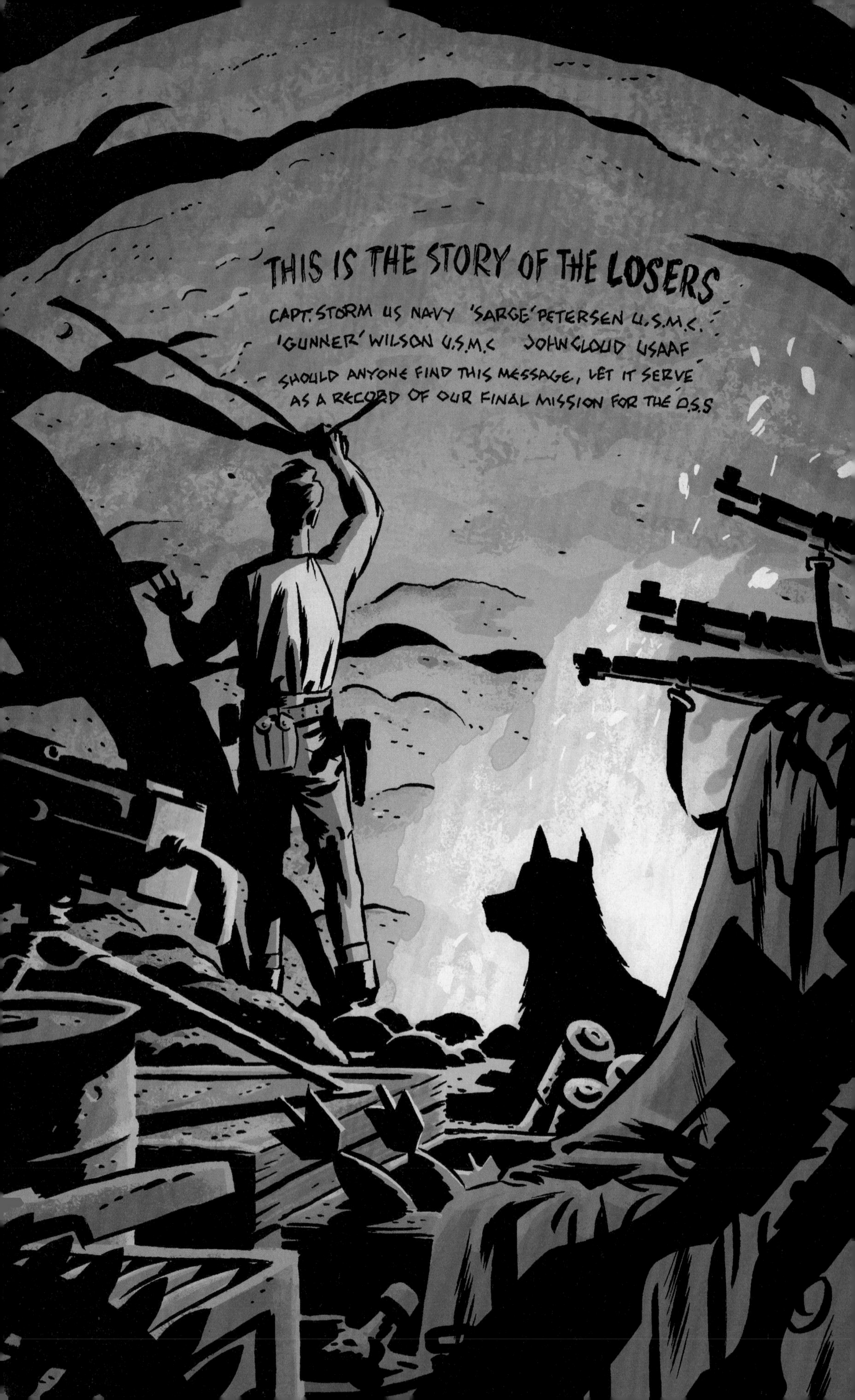
THIS IS THE STORY OF THE LOSERS
CAPT. STORM US NAVY 'SARGE' PETERSEN U.S.M.C.
'GUNNER' WILSON U.S.M.C JOHNCLOUD USAAF
SHOULD ANYONE FIND THIS MESSAGE, LET IT SERVE
AS A RECORD OF OUR FINAL MISSION FOR THE O.S.S

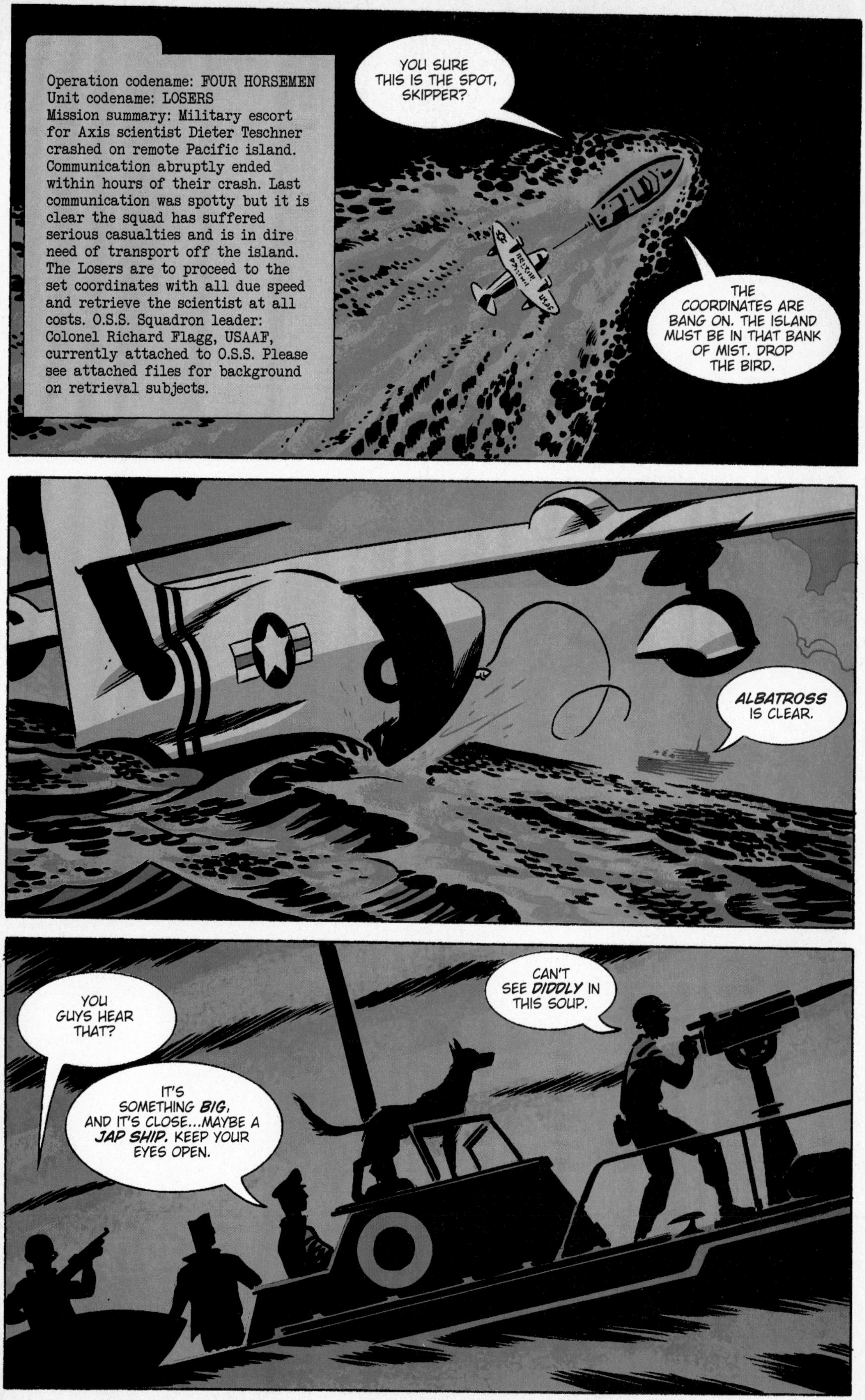
Operation codename: FOUR HORSEMEN
Unit codename: LOSERS
Mission summary: Military escort for Axis scientist Dieter Teschner crashed on remote Pacific island. Communication abruptly ended within hours of their crash. Last communication was spotty but it is clear the squad has suffered serious casualties and is in dire need of transport off the island. The Losers are to proceed to the set coordinates with all due speed and retrieve the scientist at all costs. O.S.S. Squadron leader: Colonel Richard Flagg, USAAF, currently attached to O.S.S. Please see attached files for background on retrieval subjects.
YOU SURE THIS IS THE SPOT, SKIPPER?
THE COORDINATES ARE BANG ON. THE ISLAND MUST BE IN THAT BANK OF MIST. DROP THE BIRD.
ALBATROSS IS CLEAR.
YOU GUYS HEAR THAT?
CAN'T SEE *DIDDLY* IN THIS SOUP.
IT'S SOMETHING *BIG*, AND IT'S CLOSE...MAYBE A *JAP SHIP.* KEEP YOUR EYES OPEN.

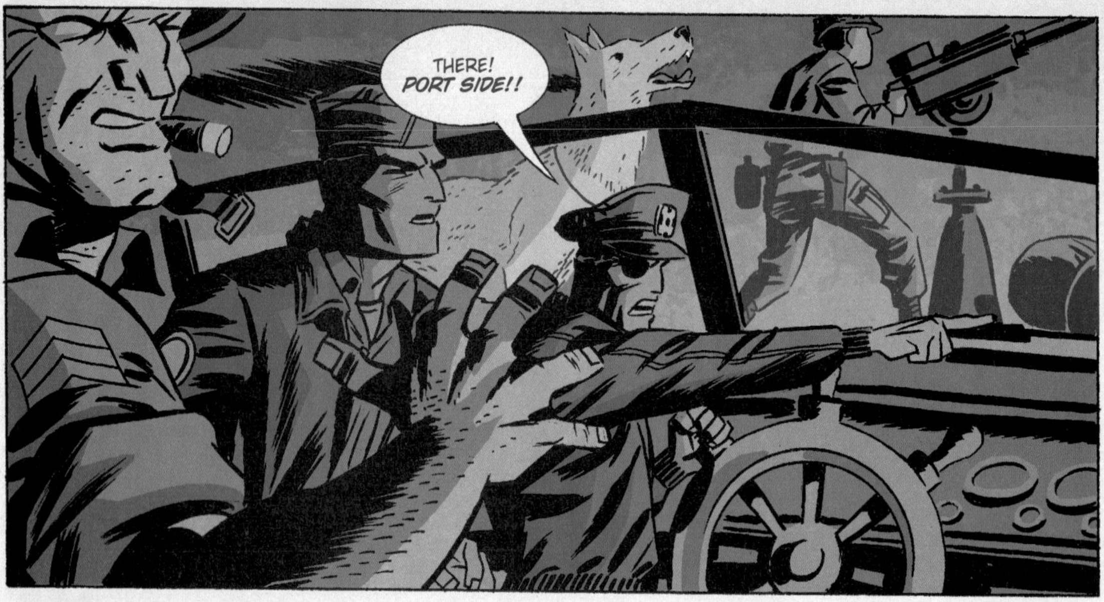
THERE!
PORT SIDE!!

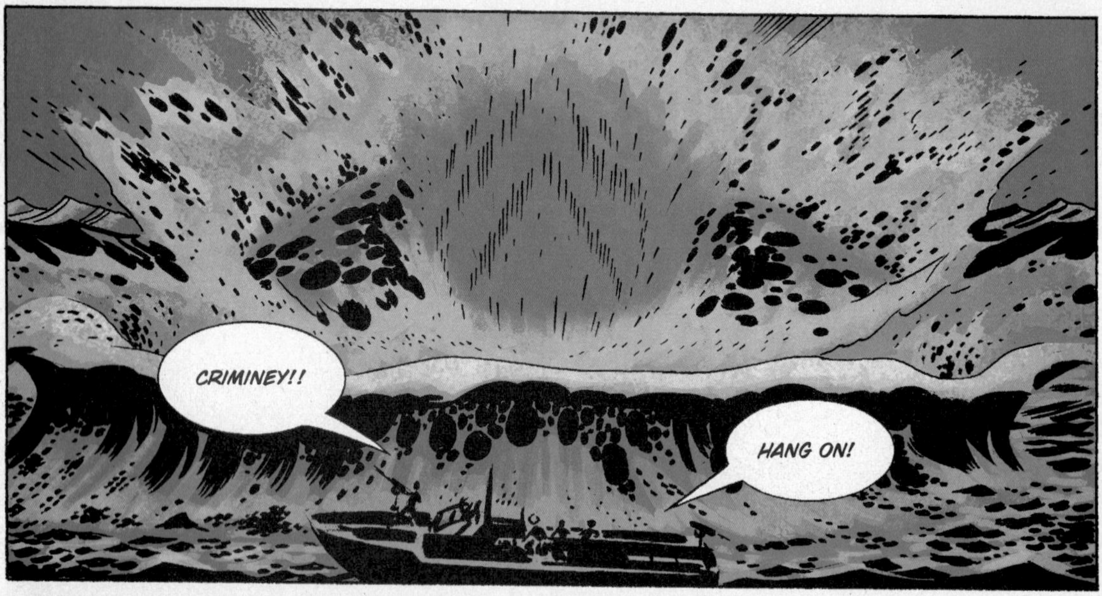
CRIMINEY!!
HANG ON!

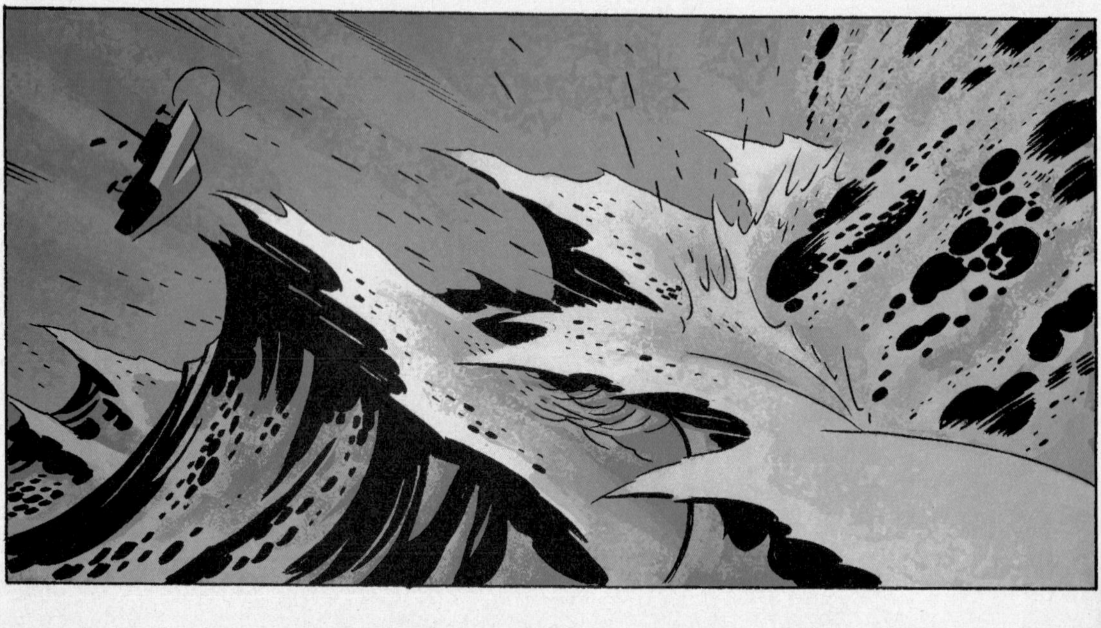

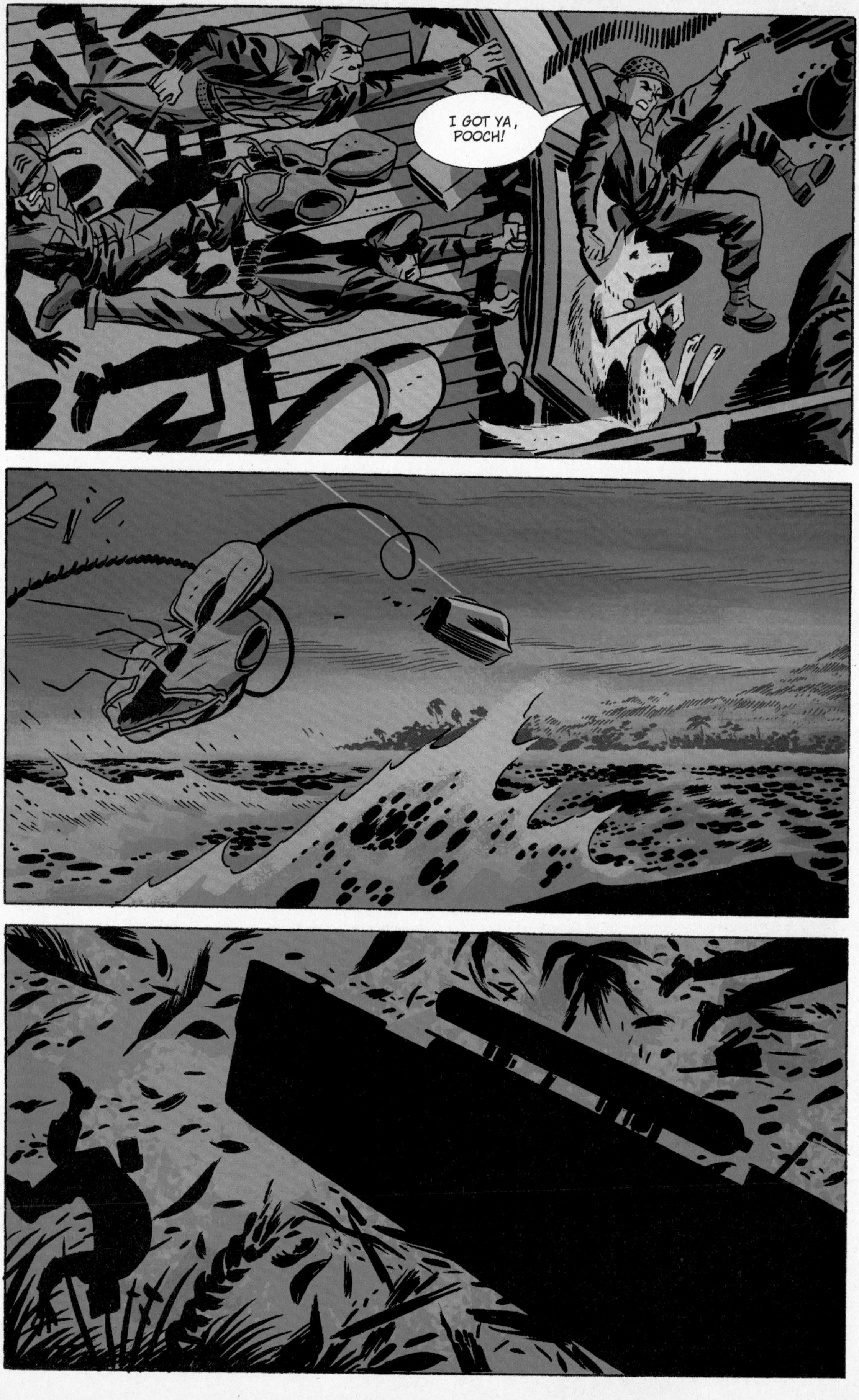
I GOT YA, POOCH!

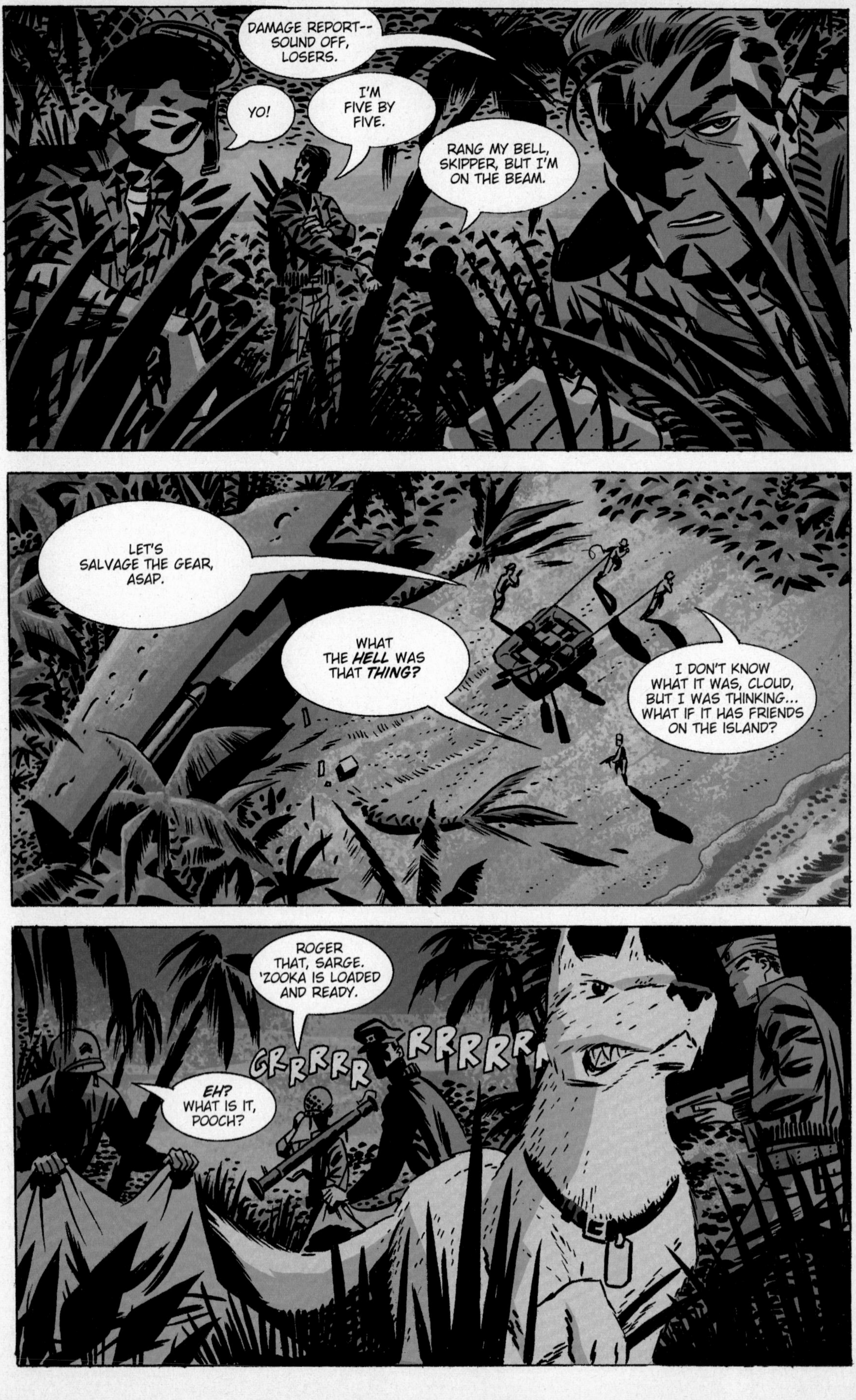
DAMAGE REPORT-- SOUND OFF, LOSERS.
YO!
I'M FIVE BY FIVE.
RANG MY BELL, SKIPPER, BUT I'M ON THE BEAM.
LET'S SALVAGE THE GEAR, ASAP.
WHAT THE *HELL* WAS THAT *THING?*
I DON'T KNOW WHAT IT WAS, CLOUD, BUT I WAS THINKING... WHAT IF IT HAS FRIENDS ON THE ISLAND?
ROGER THAT, SARGE. 'ZOOKA IS LOADED AND READY.
GRRRRRRRRRRR
EH? WHAT IS IT, POOCH?

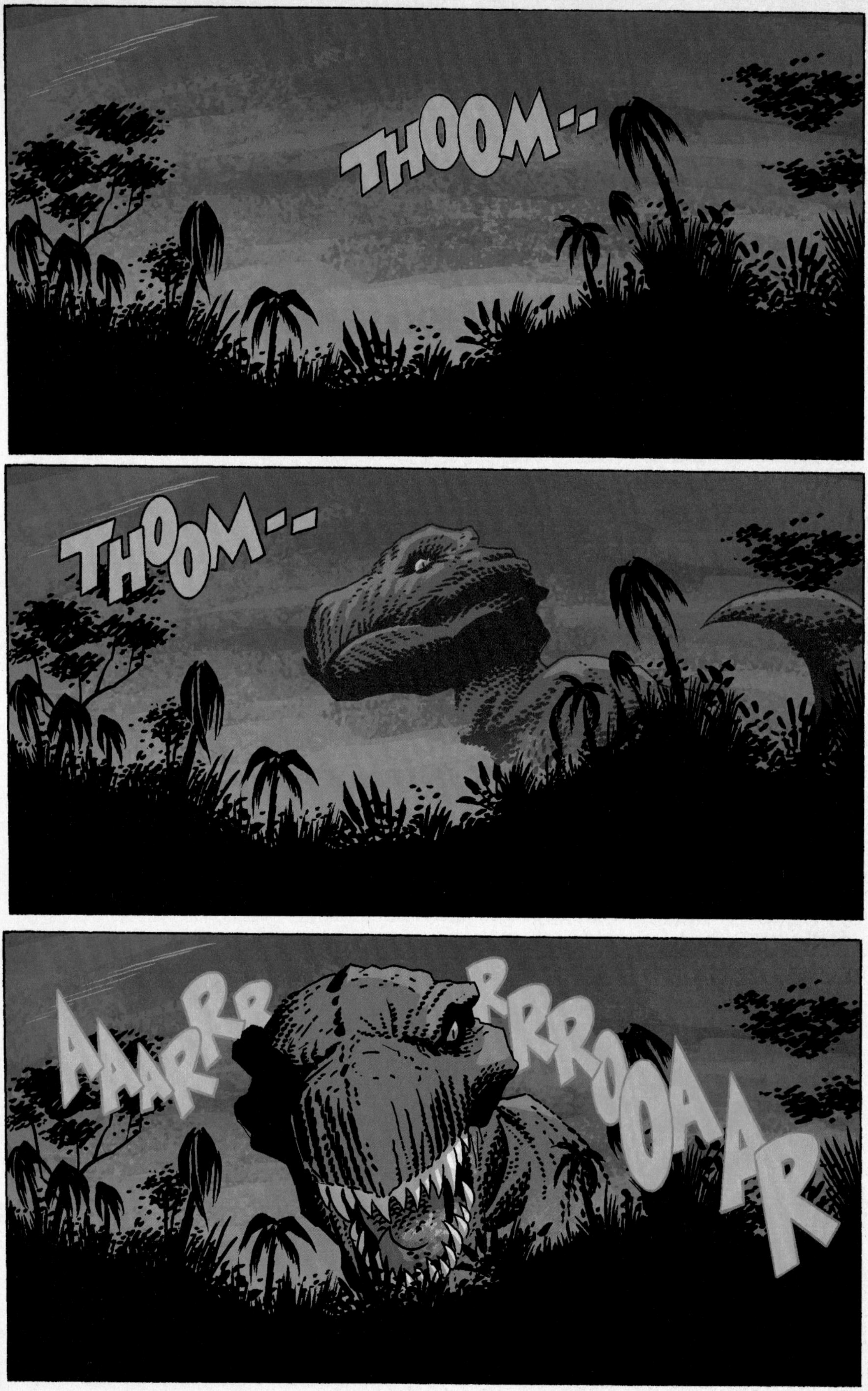
THOOM--
THOOM--
AAARRR
RRRROOAAR

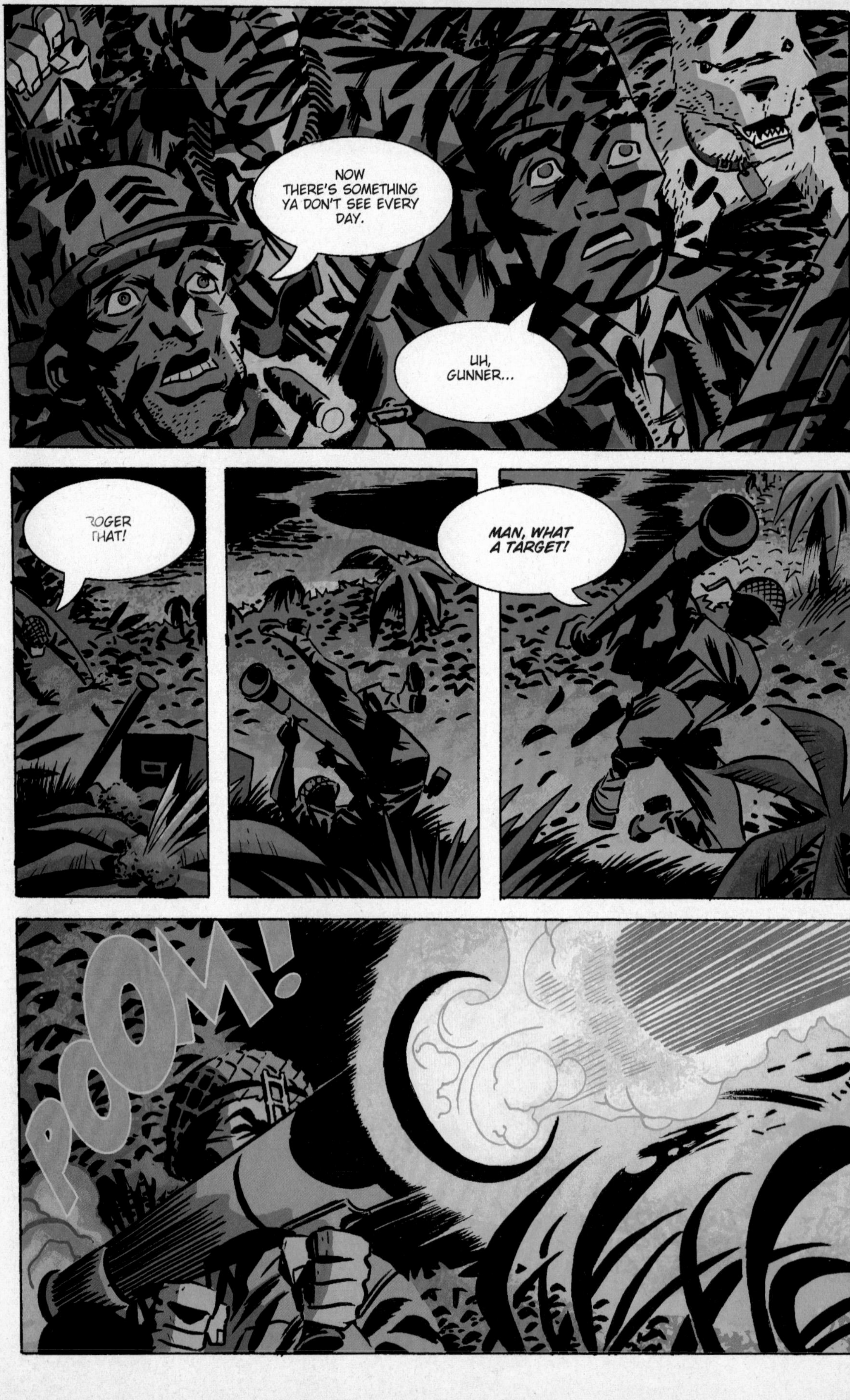
NOW THERE'S SOMETHING YA DON'T SEE EVERY DAY.
UH, GUNNER...
ROGER THAT!
MAN, WHAT A TARGET!
POOM!

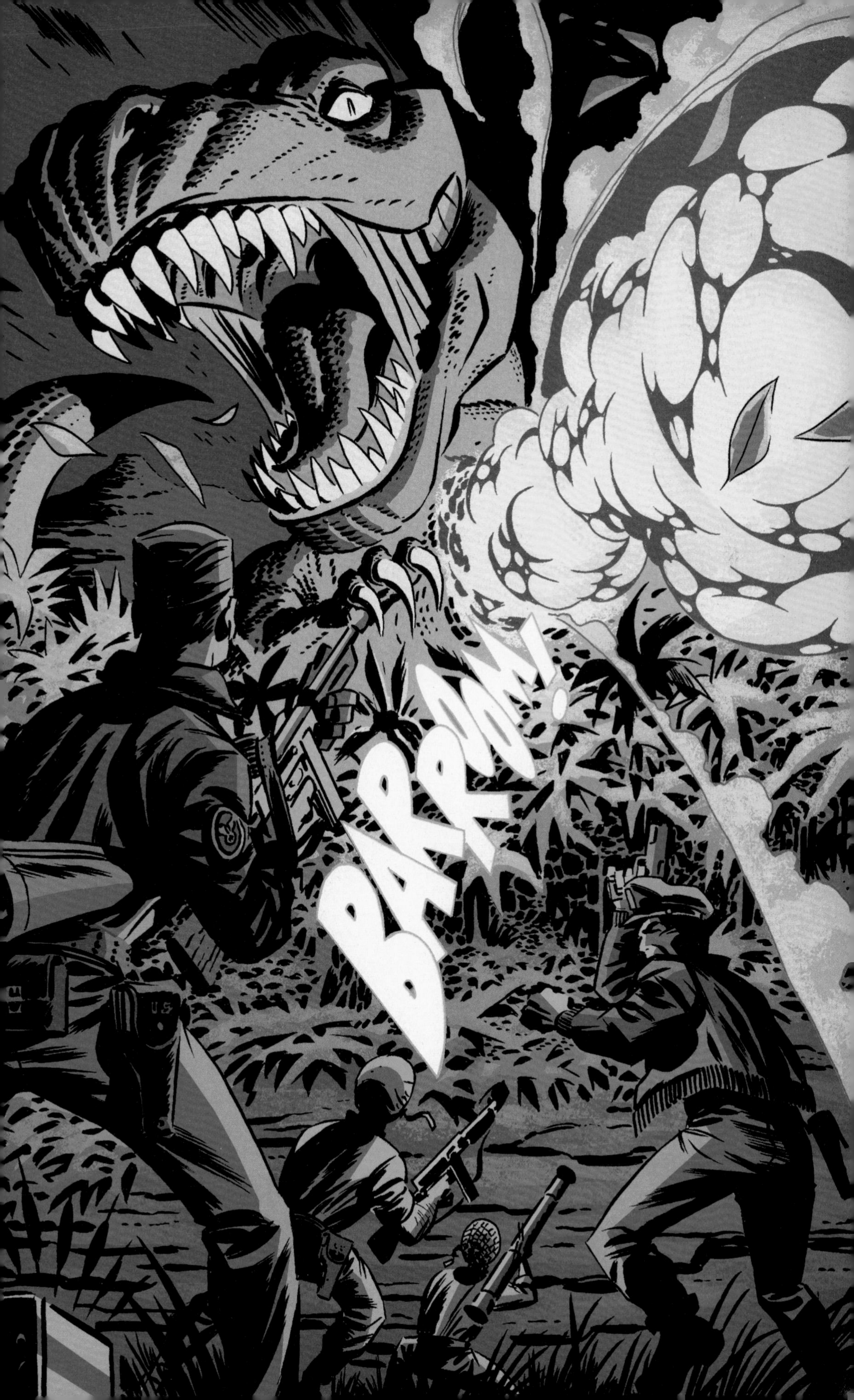
BARROOM!

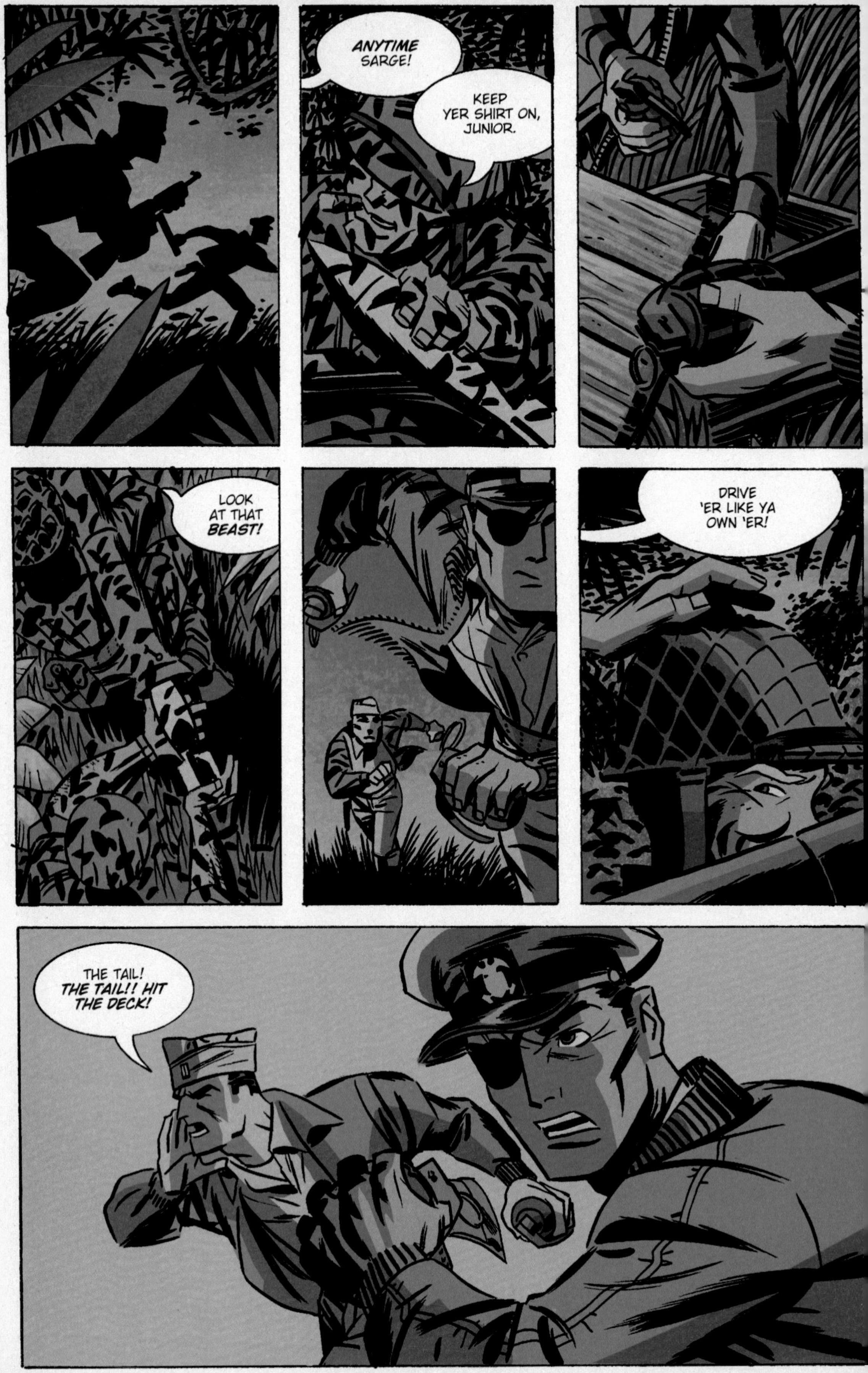

ANYTIME SARGE!
KEEP YER SHIRT ON, JUNIOR.
LOOK AT THAT BEAST!
DRIVE 'ER LIKE YA OWN 'ER!
THE TAIL! THE TAIL!! HIT THE DECK!

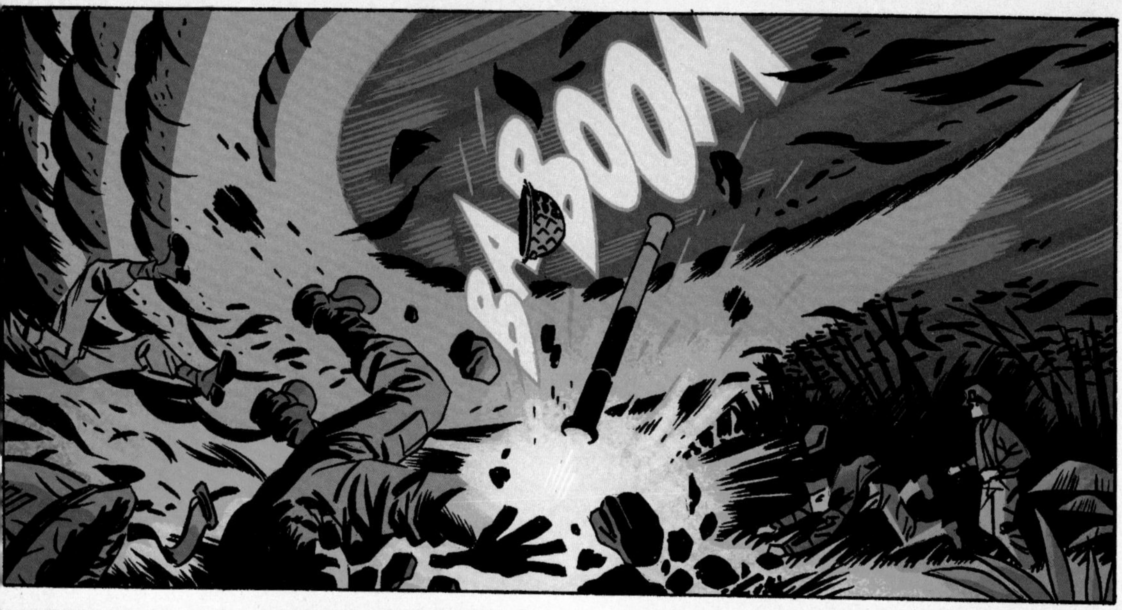
BABOOM

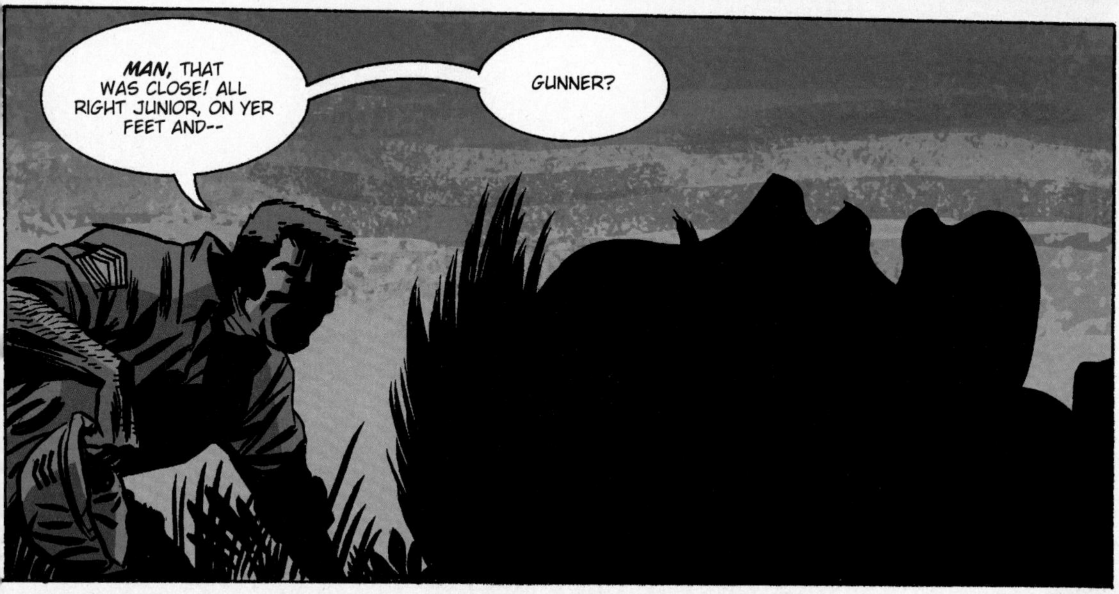
MAN, THAT WAS CLOSE! ALL RIGHT JUNIOR, ON YER FEET AND--
GUNNER?

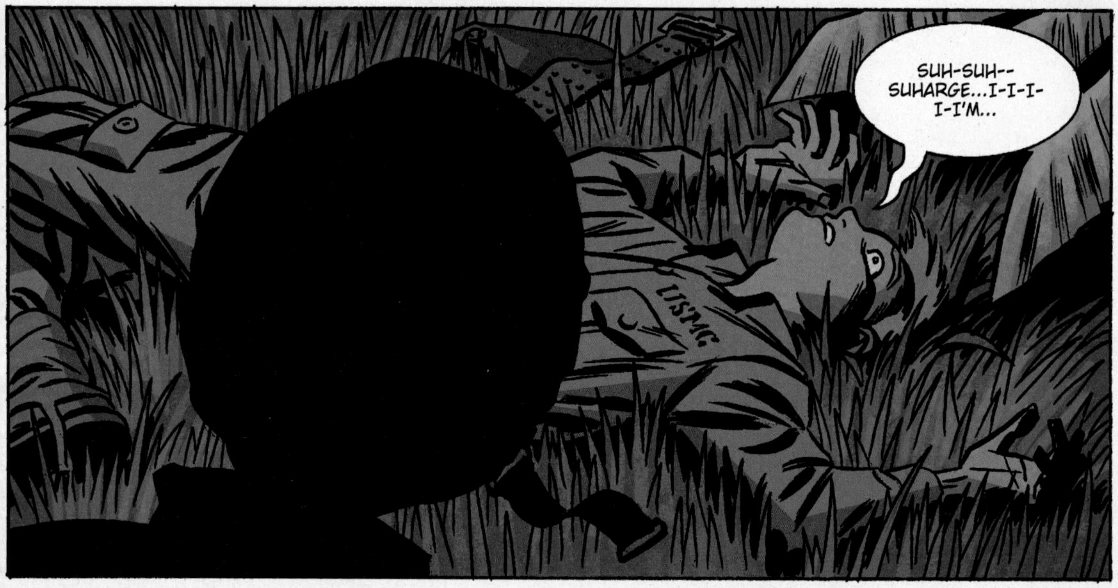
SUH-SUH--SUHARGE...I-I-I-I-I'M...
USMC

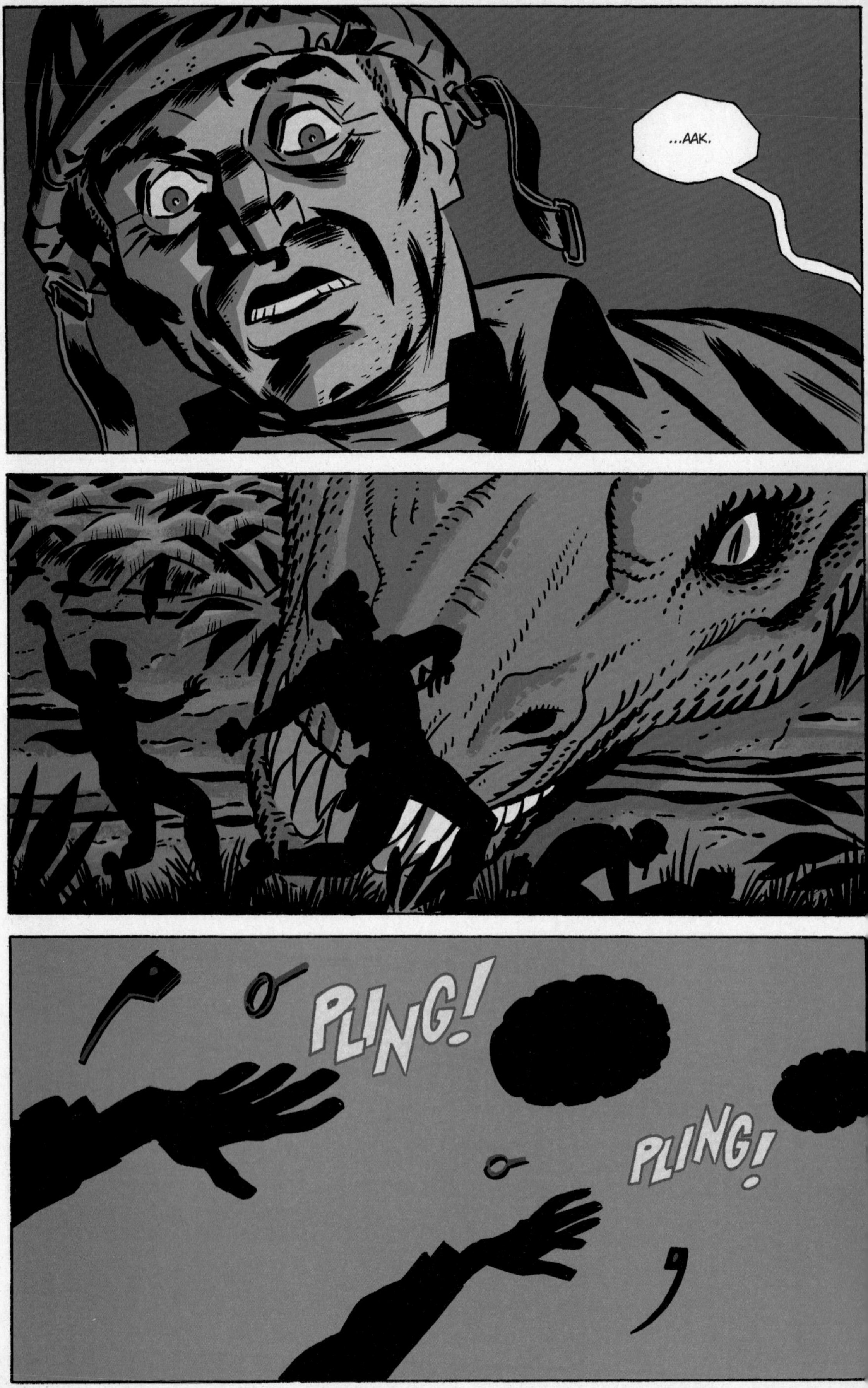
...AAK.
PLING!
PLING!

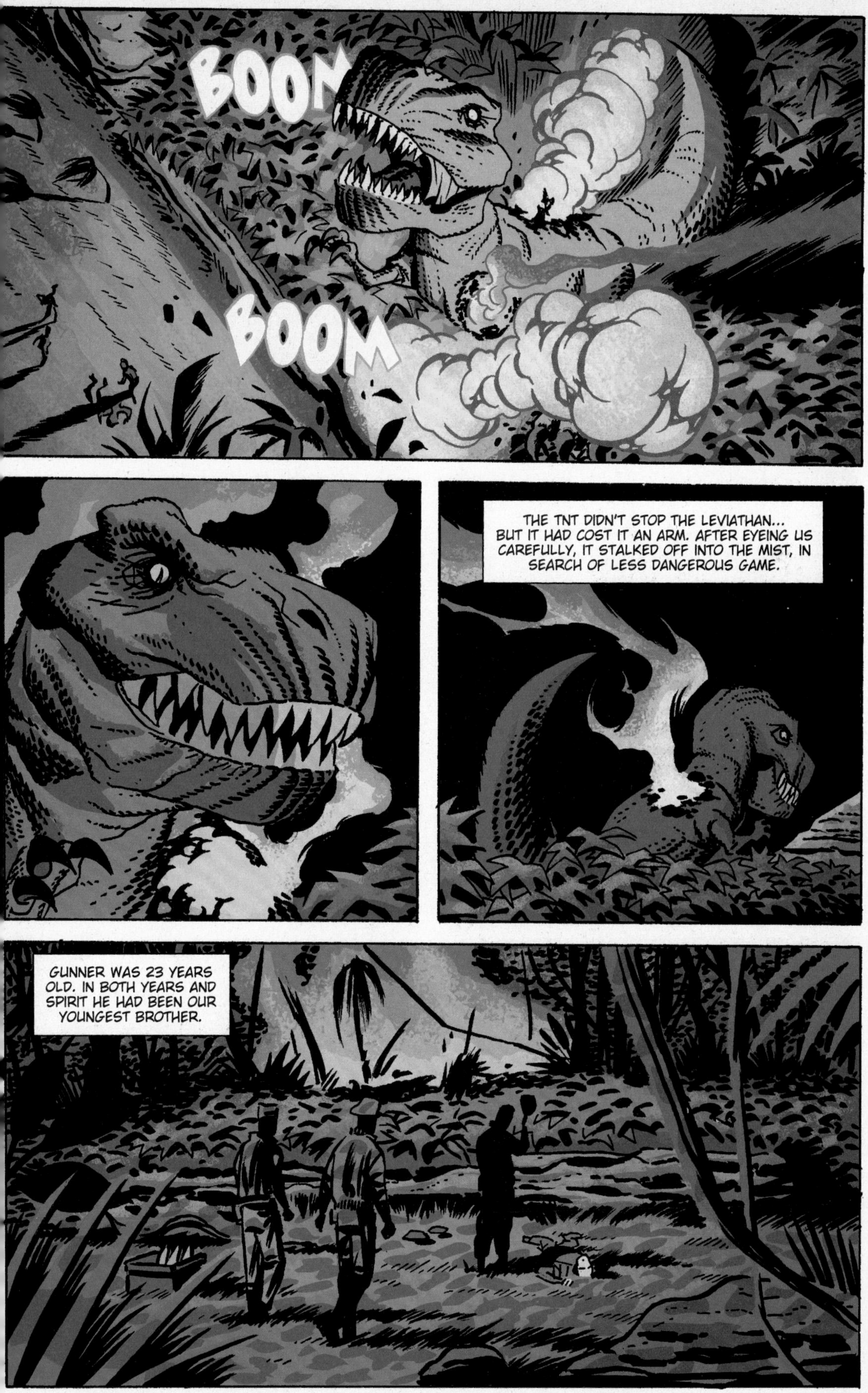
BOOM
BOOM
THE TNT DIDN'T STOP THE LEVIATHAN... BUT IT HAD COST IT AN ARM. AFTER EYEING US CAREFULLY, IT STALKED OFF INTO THE MIST, IN SEARCH OF LESS DANGEROUS GAME.
GUNNER WAS 23 YEARS OLD. IN BOTH YEARS AND SPIRIT HE HAD BEEN OUR YOUNGEST BROTHER.

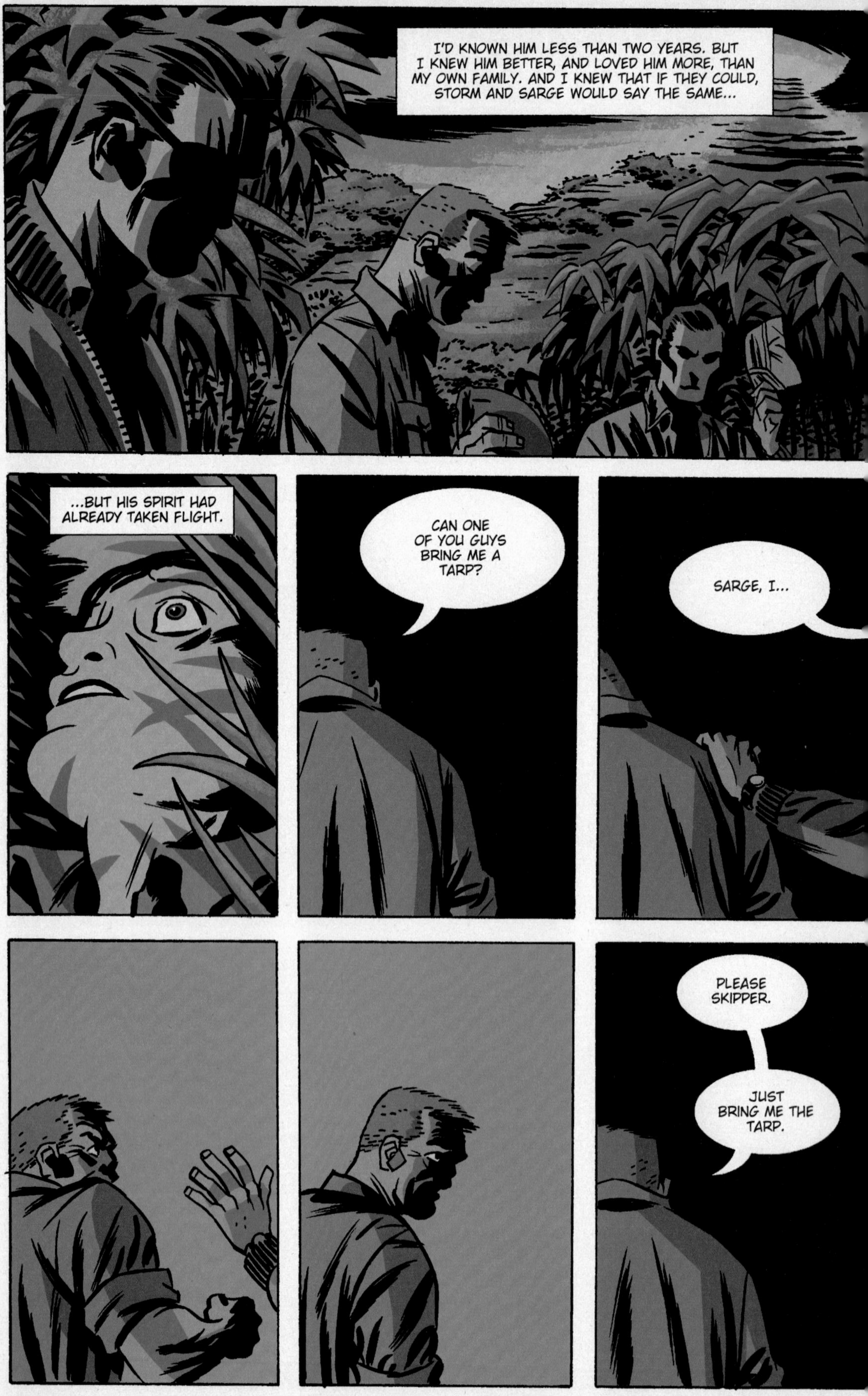
I'D KNOWN HIM LESS THAN TWO YEARS. BUT I KNEW HIM BETTER, AND LOVED HIM MORE, THAN MY OWN FAMILY. AND I KNEW THAT IF THEY COULD, STORM AND SARGE WOULD SAY THE SAME...
...BUT HIS SPIRIT HAD ALREADY TAKEN FLIGHT.
CAN ONE OF YOU GUYS BRING ME A TARP?
SARGE, I...
PLEASE SKIPPER.
JUST BRING ME THE TARP.

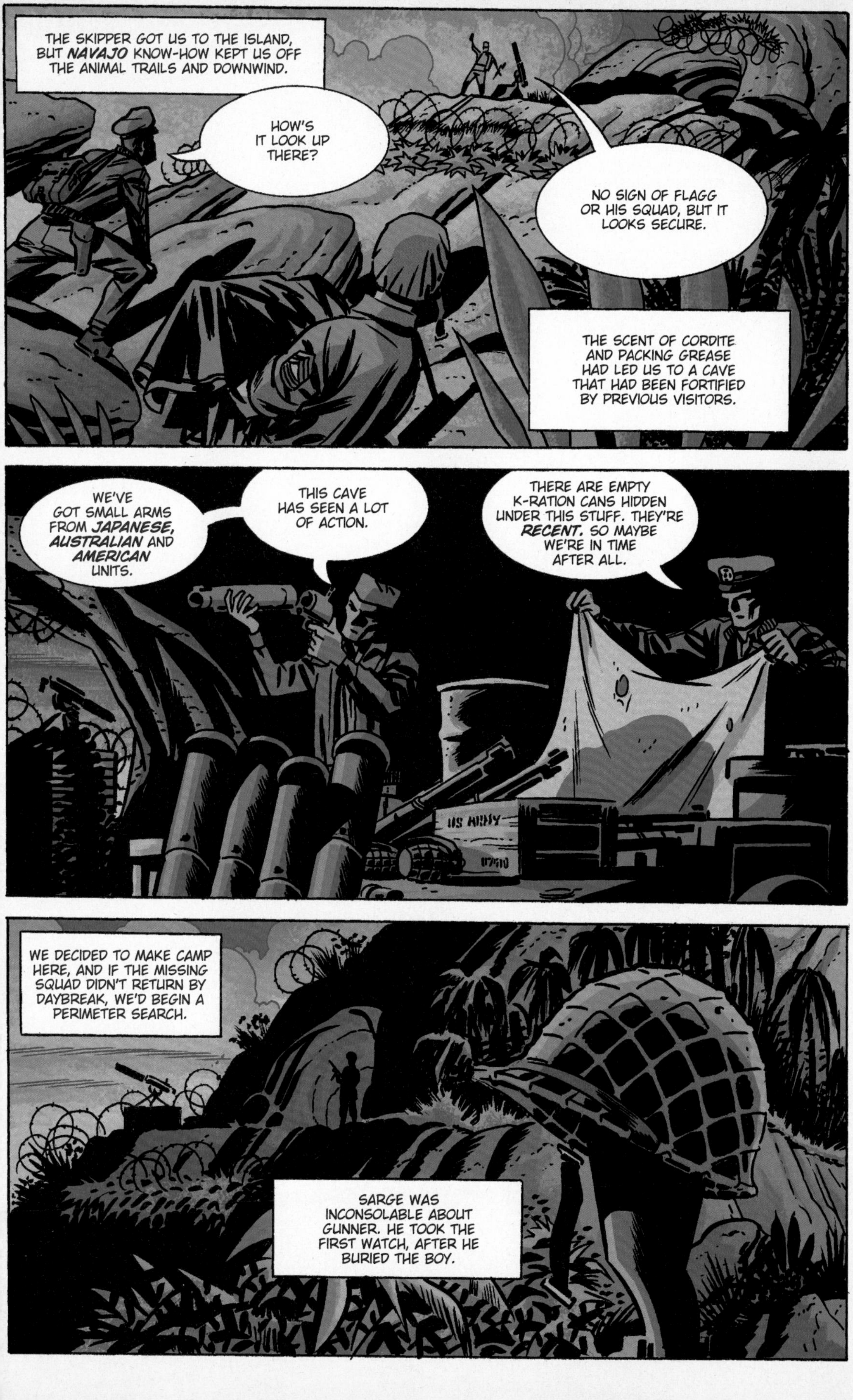
THE SKIPPER GOT US TO THE ISLAND, BUT NAVAJO KNOW-HOW KEPT US OFF THE ANIMAL TRAILS AND DOWNWIND.
HOW'S IT LOOK UP THERE?
NO SIGN OF FLAGG OR HIS SQUAD, BUT IT LOOKS SECURE.
THE SCENT OF CORDITE AND PACKING GREASE HAD LED US TO A CAVE THAT HAD BEEN FORTIFIED BY PREVIOUS VISITORS.
WE'VE GOT SMALL ARMS FROM JAPANESE, AUSTRALIAN AND AMERICAN UNITS.
THIS CAVE HAS SEEN A LOT OF ACTION.
THERE ARE EMPTY K-RATION CANS HIDDEN UNDER THIS STUFF. THEY'RE RECENT. SO MAYBE WE'RE IN TIME AFTER ALL.
US ARMY
WE DECIDED TO MAKE CAMP HERE, AND IF THE MISSING SQUAD DIDN'T RETURN BY DAYBREAK, WE'D BEGIN A PERIMETER SEARCH.
SARGE WAS INCONSOLABLE ABOUT GUNNER. HE TOOK THE FIRST WATCH, AFTER HE BURIED THE BOY.

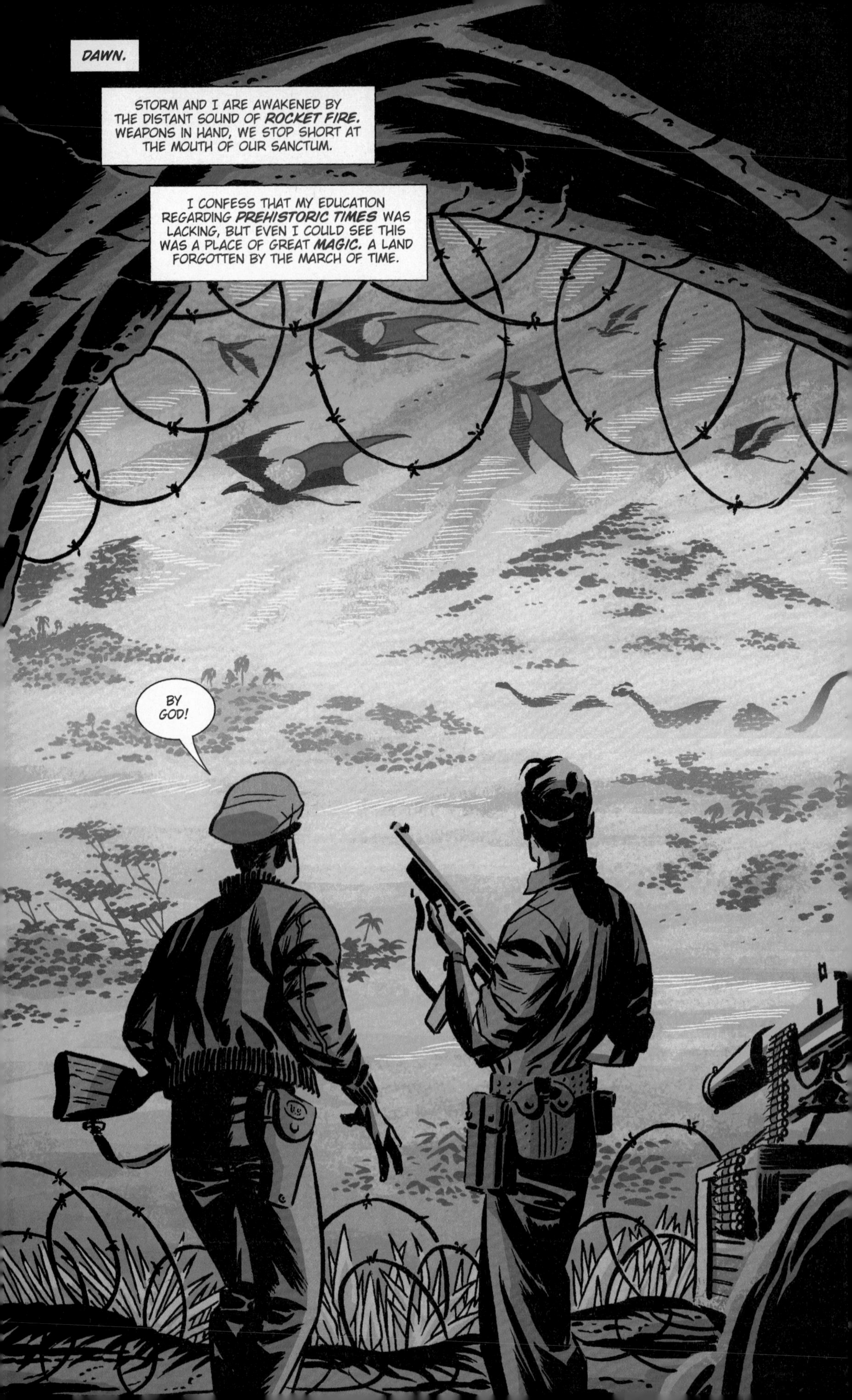
DAWN.
STORM AND I ARE AWAKENED BY THE DISTANT SOUND OF ROCKET FIRE. WEAPONS IN HAND, WE STOP SHORT AT THE MOUTH OF OUR SANCTUM.
I CONFESS THAT MY EDUCATION REGARDING PREHISTORIC TIMES WAS LACKING, BUT EVEN I COULD SEE THIS WAS A PLACE OF GREAT MAGIC. A LAND FORGOTTEN BY THE MARCH OF TIME.
BY GOD!

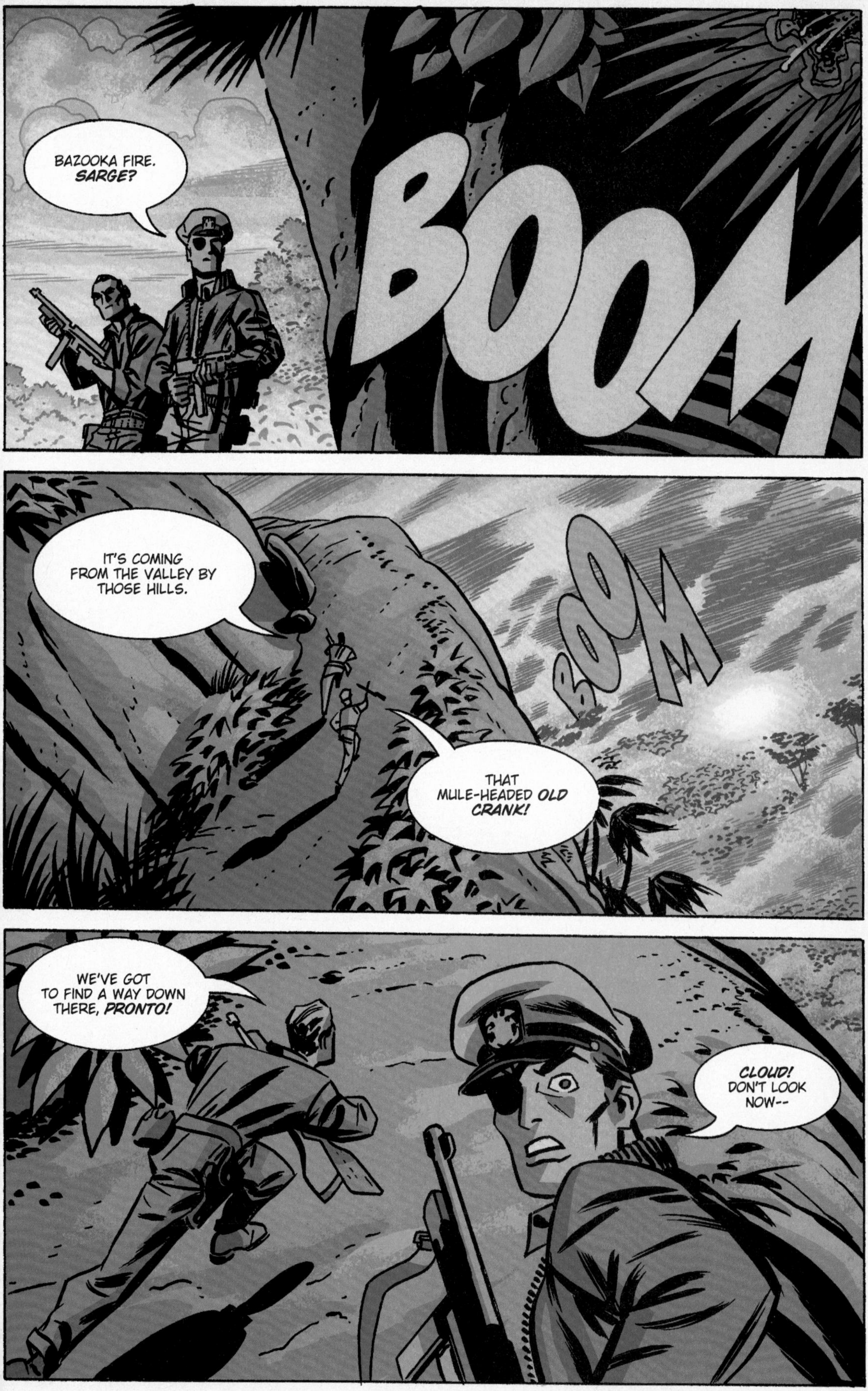
BAZOOKA FIRE. SARGE?
BOOM
IT'S COMING FROM THE VALLEY BY THOSE HILLS.
BOOM
THAT MULE-HEADED OLD CRANK!
WE'VE GOT TO FIND A WAY DOWN THERE, PRONTO!
CLOUD! DON'T LOOK NOW--

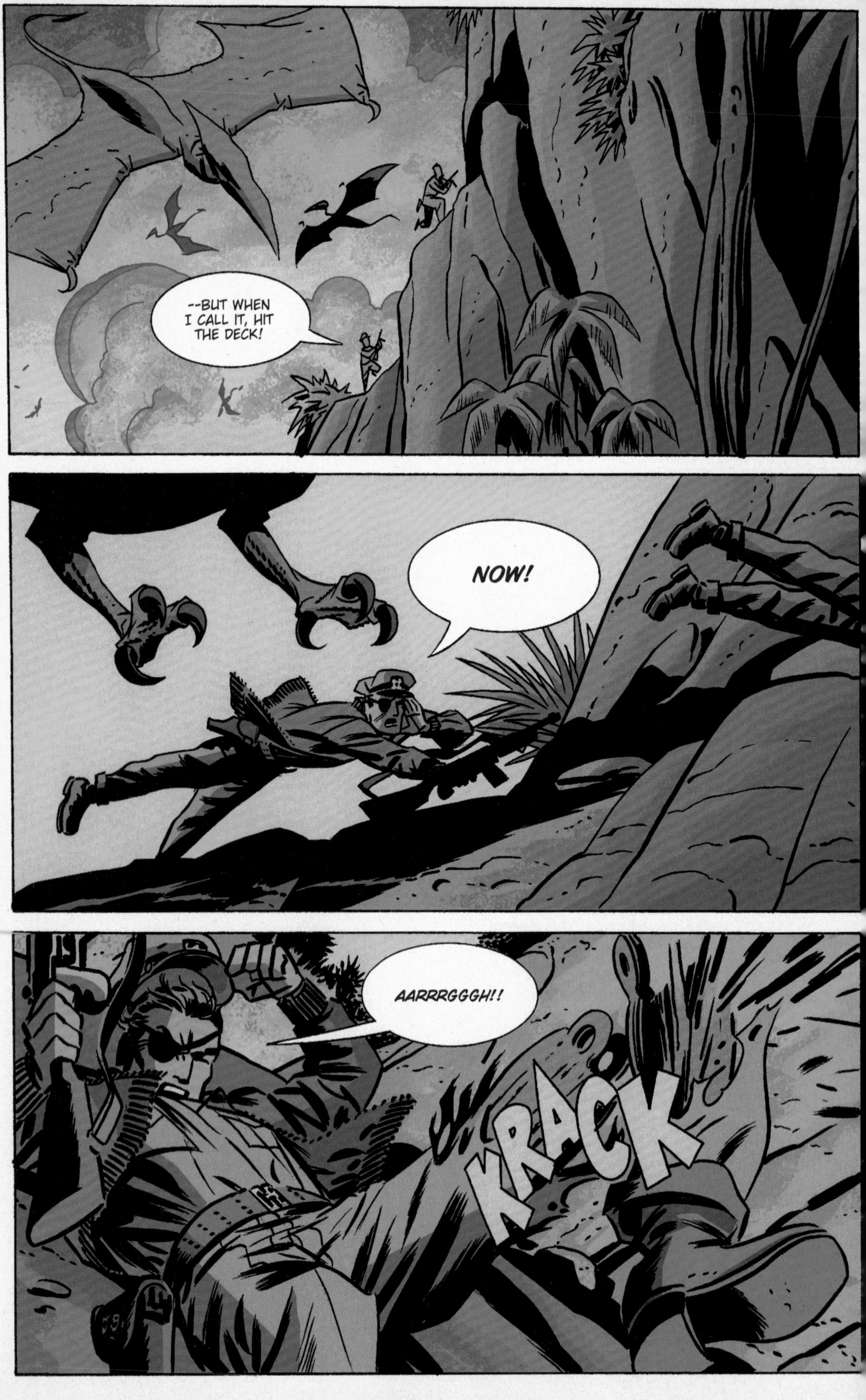
--BUT WHEN I CALL IT, HIT THE DECK!
NOW!
AARRRGGGH!!
KRACK

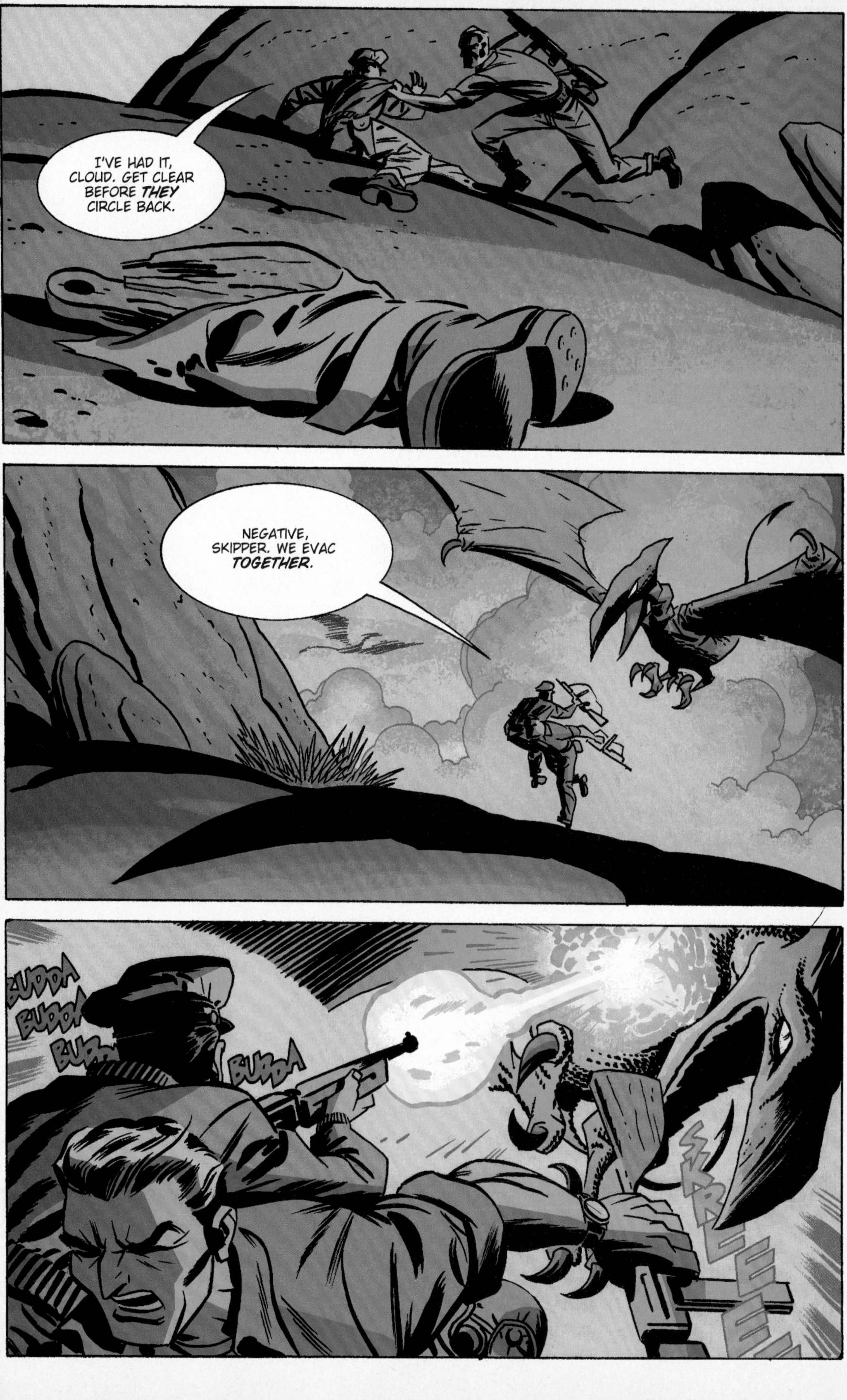
I'VE HAD IT, CLOUD. GET CLEAR BEFORE *THEY* CIRCLE BACK.
NEGATIVE, SKIPPER. WE EVAC *TOGETHER*.
BUDDA
BUDDA
BUDDA
SKREEE

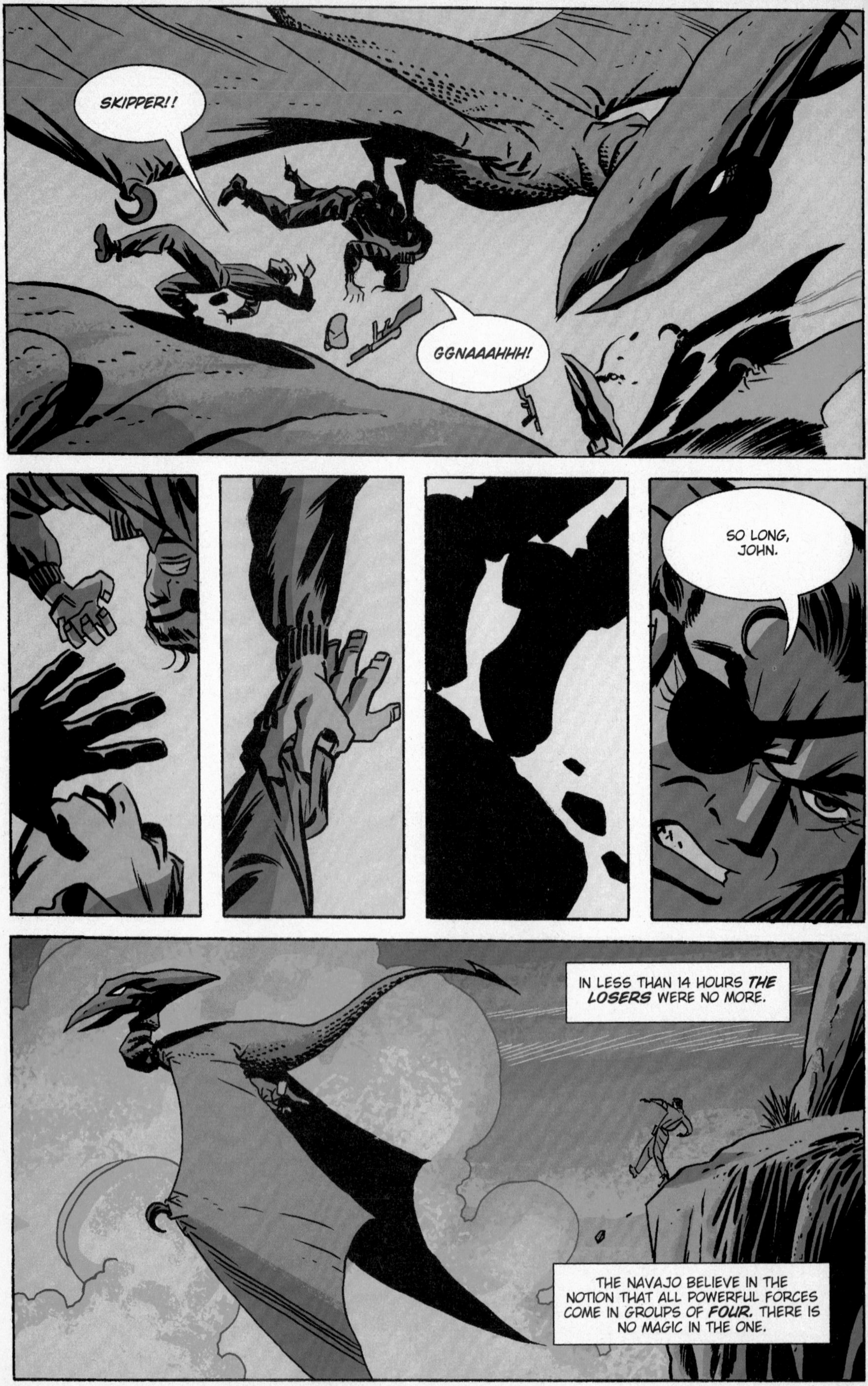
SKIPPER!!
GGNAAAHHH!
SO LONG, JOHN.
IN LESS THAN 14 HOURS THE LOSERS WERE NO MORE.
THE NAVAJO BELIEVE IN THE NOTION THAT ALL POWERFUL FORCES COME IN GROUPS OF FOUR. THERE IS NO MAGIC IN THE ONE.

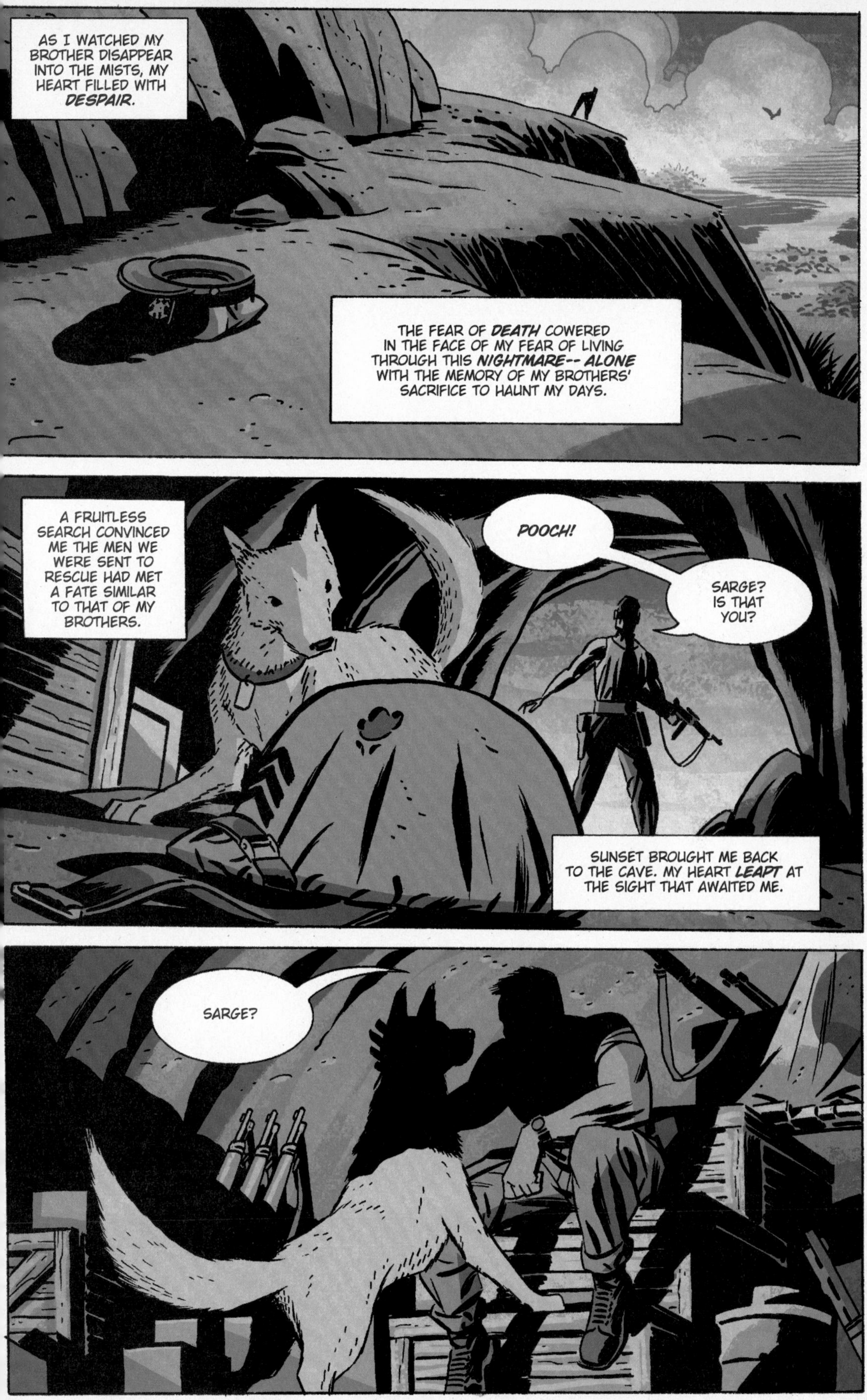
AS I WATCHED MY BROTHER DISAPPEAR INTO THE MISTS, MY HEART FILLED WITH DESPAIR.
THE FEAR OF DEATH COWERED IN THE FACE OF MY FEAR OF LIVING THROUGH THIS NIGHTMARE-- ALONE WITH THE MEMORY OF MY BROTHERS' SACRIFICE TO HAUNT MY DAYS.
A FRUITLESS SEARCH CONVINCED ME THE MEN WE WERE SENT TO RESCUE HAD MET A FATE SIMILAR TO THAT OF MY BROTHERS.
POOCH!
SARGE? IS THAT YOU?
SUNSET BROUGHT ME BACK TO THE CAVE. MY HEART LEAPT AT THE SIGHT THAT AWAITED ME.
SARGE?

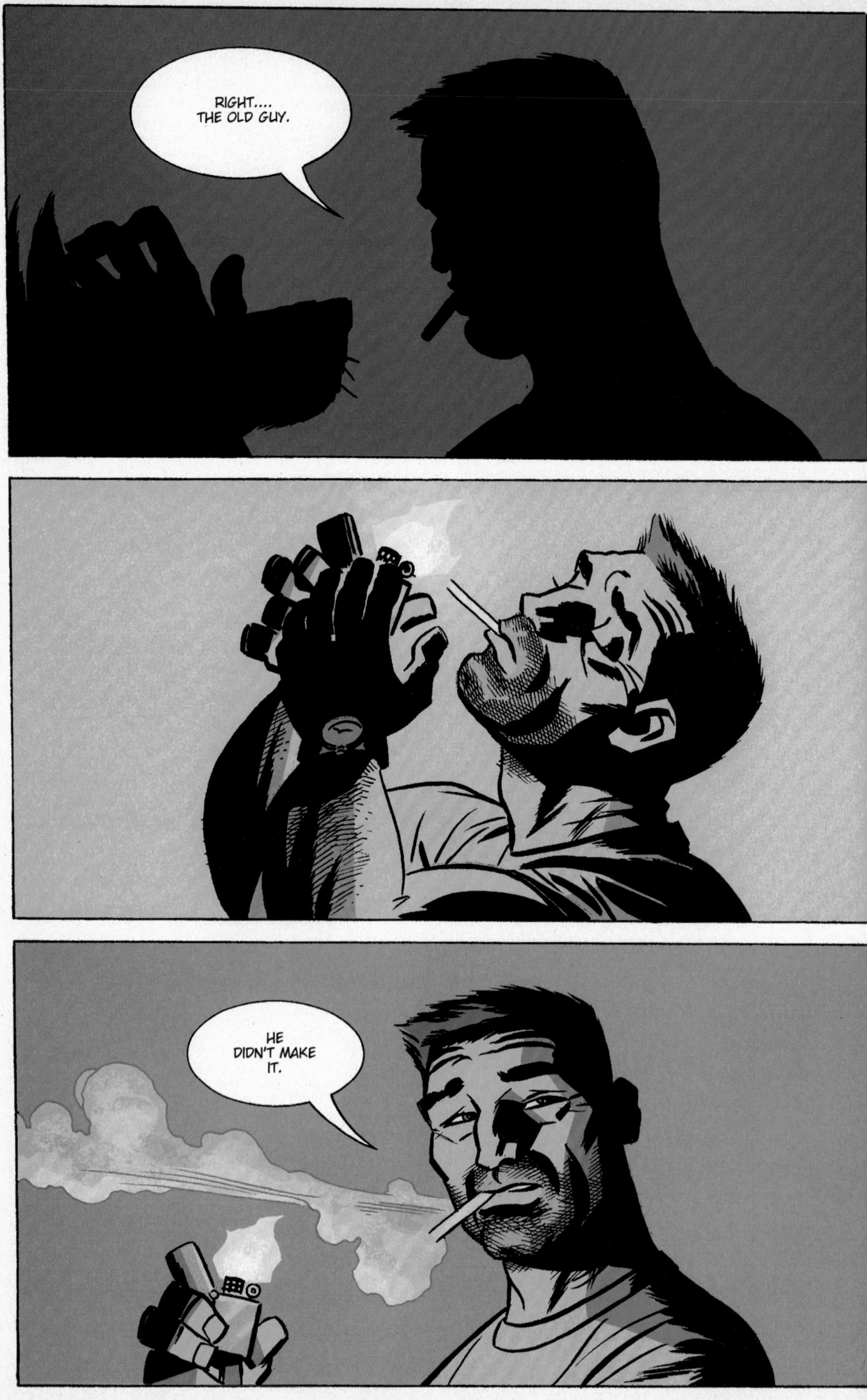
RIGHT.... THE OLD GUY.
HE DIDN'T MAKE IT.

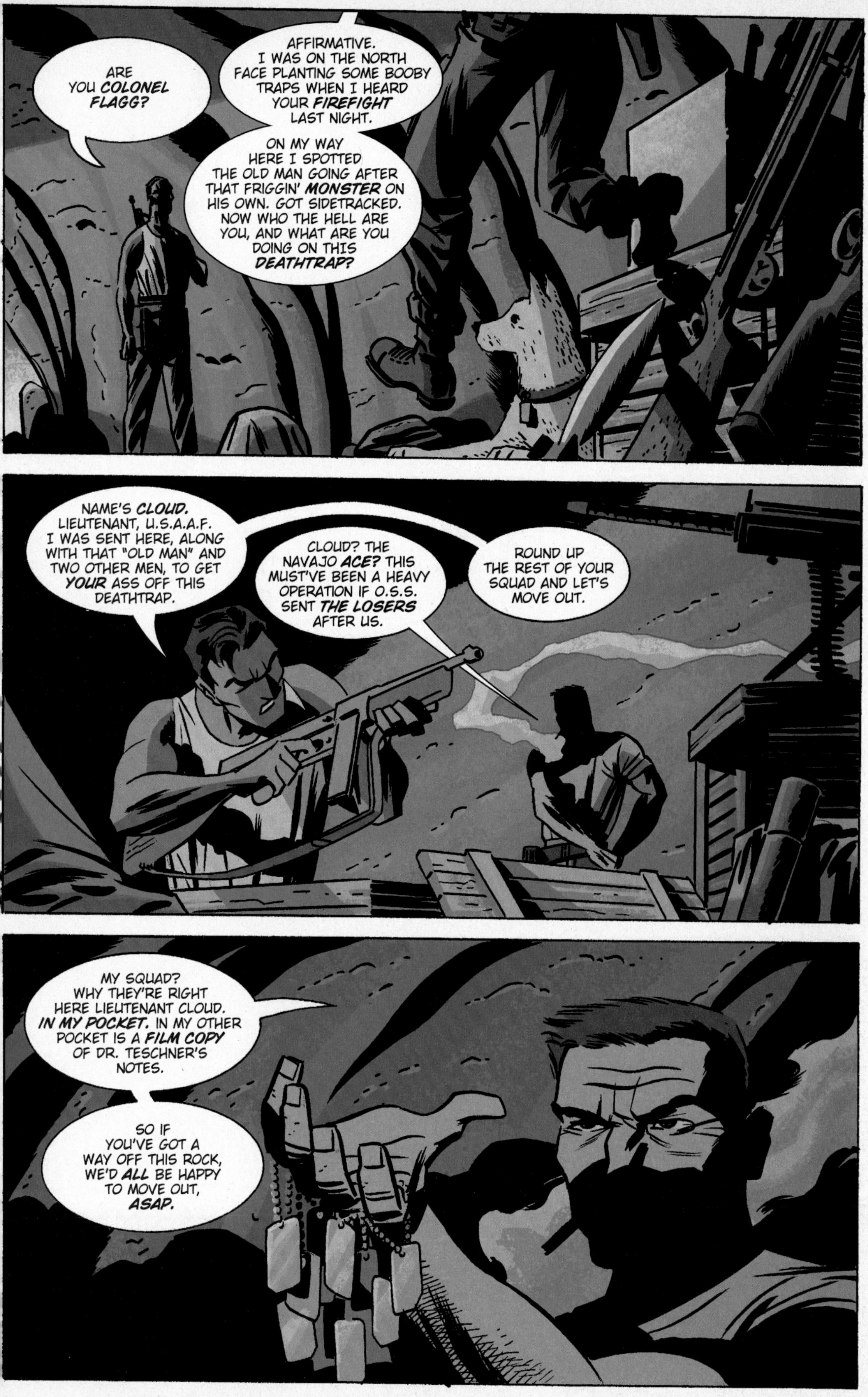
ARE YOU COLONEL FLAGG?
AFFIRMATIVE. I WAS ON THE NORTH FACE PLANTING SOME BOOBY TRAPS WHEN I HEARD YOUR FIREFIGHT LAST NIGHT.
ON MY WAY HERE I SPOTTED THE OLD MAN GOING AFTER THAT FRIGGIN' MONSTER ON HIS OWN. GOT SIDETRACKED. NOW WHO THE HELL ARE YOU, AND WHAT ARE YOU DOING ON THIS DEATHTRAP?
NAME'S CLOUD. LIEUTENANT, U.S.A.A.F. I WAS SENT HERE, ALONG WITH THAT "OLD MAN" AND TWO OTHER MEN, TO GET YOUR ASS OFF THIS DEATHTRAP.
CLOUD? THE NAVAJO ACE? THIS MUST'VE BEEN A HEAVY OPERATION IF O.S.S. SENT THE LOSERS AFTER US.
ROUND UP THE REST OF YOUR SQUAD AND LET'S MOVE OUT.
MY SQUAD? WHY THEY'RE RIGHT HERE LIEUTENANT CLOUD. IN MY POCKET. IN MY OTHER POCKET IS A FILM COPY OF DR. TESCHNER'S NOTES.
SO IF YOU'VE GOT A WAY OFF THIS ROCK, WE'D ALL BE HAPPY TO MOVE OUT, ASAP.

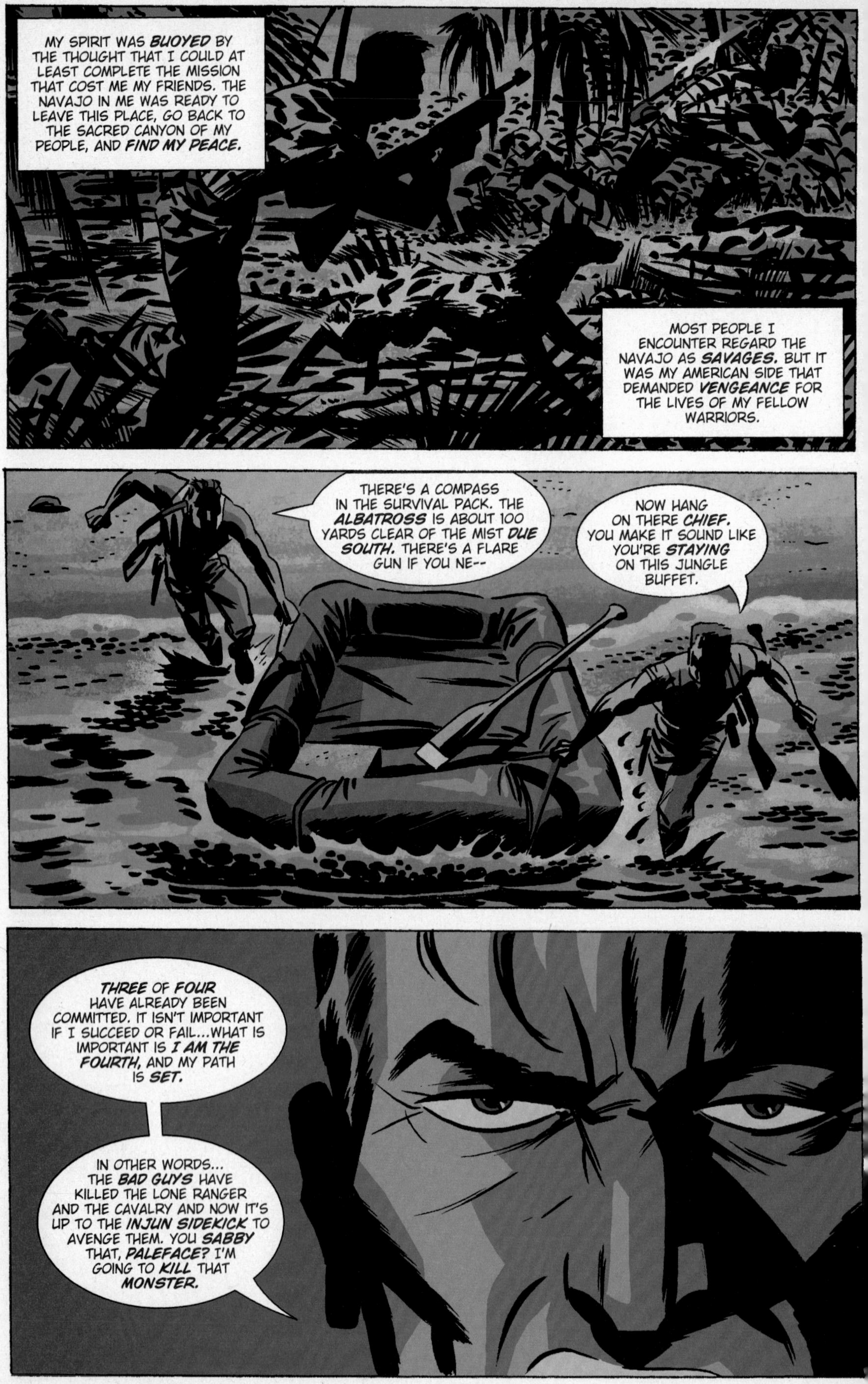
MY SPIRIT WAS BUOYED BY THE THOUGHT THAT I COULD AT LEAST COMPLETE THE MISSION THAT COST ME MY FRIENDS. THE NAVAJO IN ME WAS READY TO LEAVE THIS PLACE, GO BACK TO THE SACRED CANYON OF MY PEOPLE, AND FIND MY PEACE.
MOST PEOPLE I ENCOUNTER REGARD THE NAVAJO AS SAVAGES. BUT IT WAS MY AMERICAN SIDE THAT DEMANDED VENGEANCE FOR THE LIVES OF MY FELLOW WARRIORS.
THERE'S A COMPASS IN THE SURVIVAL PACK. THE ALBATROSS IS ABOUT 100 YARDS CLEAR OF THE MIST DUE SOUTH. THERE'S A FLARE GUN IF YOU NE--
NOW HANG ON THERE CHIEF. YOU MAKE IT SOUND LIKE YOU'RE STAYING ON THIS JUNGLE BUFFET.
THREE OF FOUR HAVE ALREADY BEEN COMMITTED. IT ISN'T IMPORTANT IF I SUCCEED OR FAIL...WHAT IS IMPORTANT IS I AM THE FOURTH, AND MY PATH IS SET.
IN OTHER WORDS... THE BAD GUYS HAVE KILLED THE LONE RANGER AND THE CAVALRY AND NOW IT'S UP TO THE INJUN SIDEKICK TO AVENGE THEM. YOU SABBY THAT, PALEFACE? I'M GOING TO KILL THAT MONSTER.

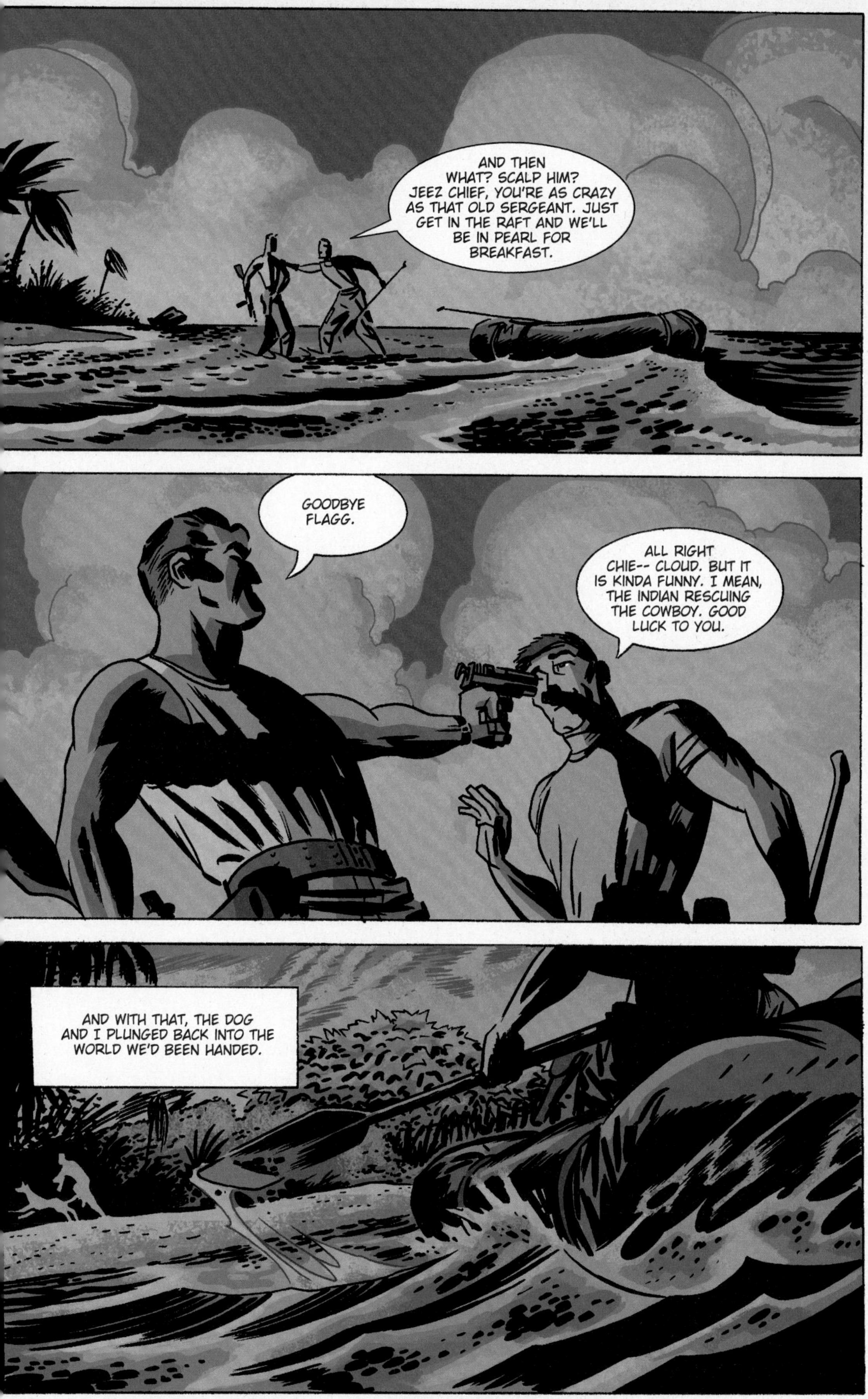
AND THEN WHAT? SCALP HIM? JEEZ CHIEF, YOU'RE AS CRAZY AS THAT OLD SERGEANT. JUST GET IN THE RAFT AND WE'LL BE IN PEARL FOR BREAKFAST.
GOODBYE FLAGG.
ALL RIGHT CHIE-- CLOUD. BUT IT IS KINDA FUNNY. I MEAN, THE INDIAN RESCUING THE COWBOY. GOOD LUCK TO YOU.
AND WITH THAT, THE DOG AND I PLUNGED BACK INTO THE WORLD WE'D BEEN HANDED.

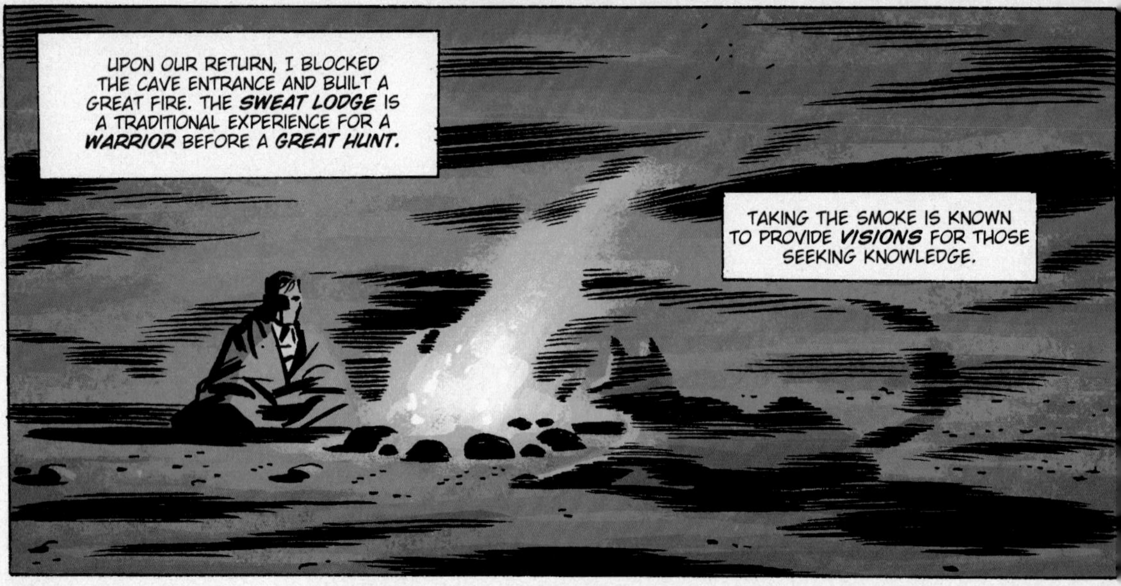
UPON OUR RETURN, I BLOCKED THE CAVE ENTRANCE AND BUILT A GREAT FIRE. THE ***SWEAT LODGE*** IS A TRADITIONAL EXPERIENCE FOR A ***WARRIOR*** BEFORE A ***GREAT HUNT.***
TAKING THE SMOKE IS KNOWN TO PROVIDE ***VISIONS*** FOR THOSE SEEKING KNOWLEDGE.

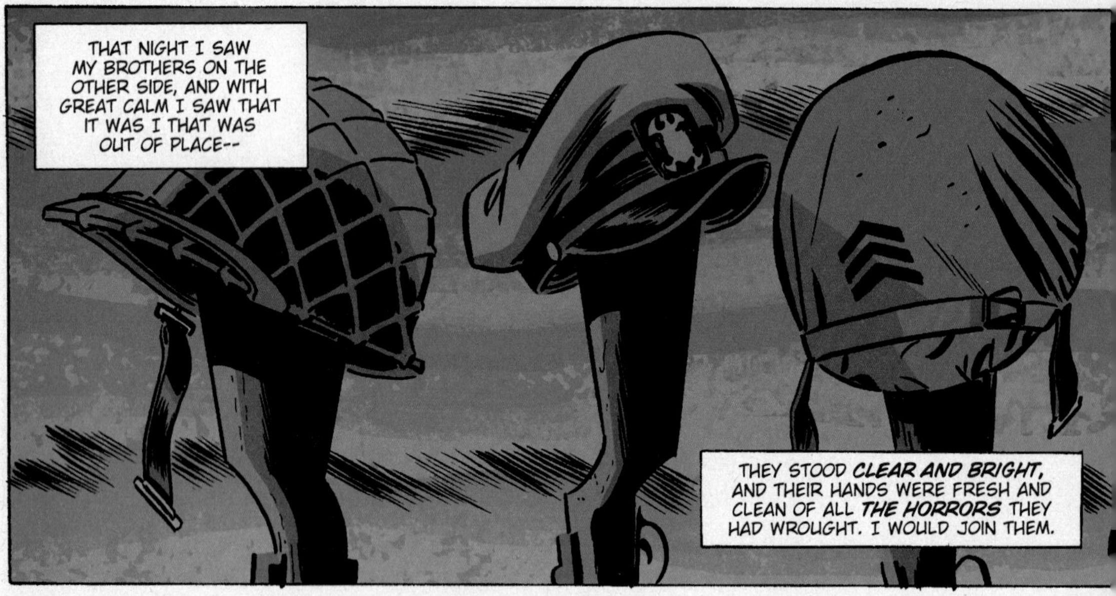
THAT NIGHT I SAW MY BROTHERS ON THE OTHER SIDE, AND WITH GREAT CALM I SAW THAT IT WAS I THAT WAS OUT OF PLACE--
THEY STOOD ***CLEAR AND BRIGHT,*** AND THEIR HANDS WERE FRESH AND CLEAN OF ALL ***THE HORRORS*** THEY HAD WROUGHT. I WOULD JOIN THEM.

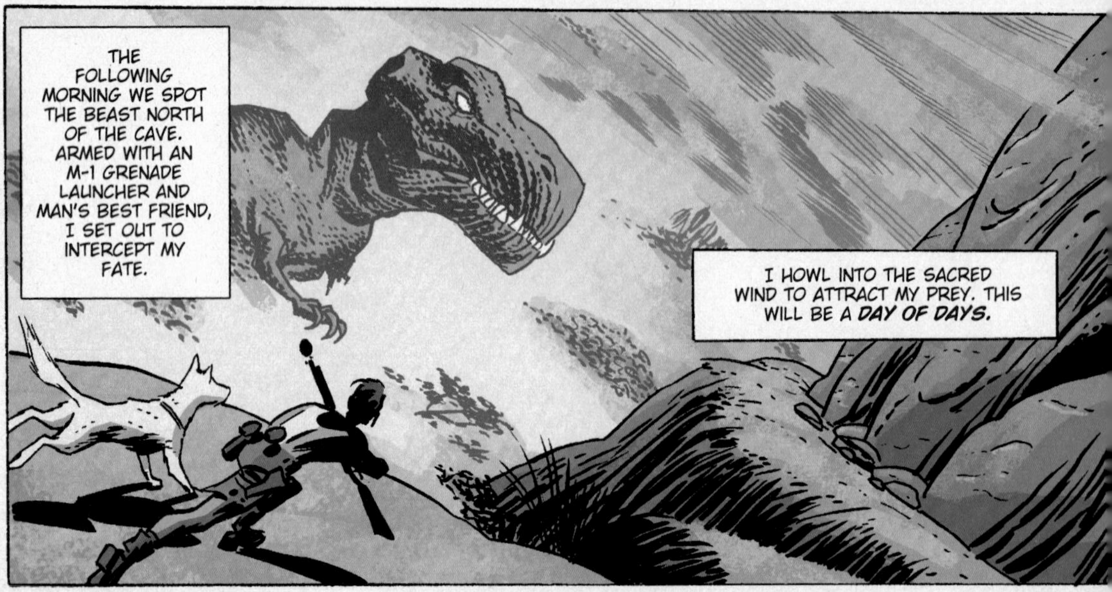
THE FOLLOWING MORNING WE SPOT THE BEAST NORTH OF THE CAVE. ARMED WITH AN M-1 GRENADE LAUNCHER AND MAN'S BEST FRIEND, I SET OUT TO INTERCEPT MY FATE.
I HOWL INTO THE SACRED WIND TO ATTRACT MY PREY. THIS WILL BE A ***DAY OF DAYS.***

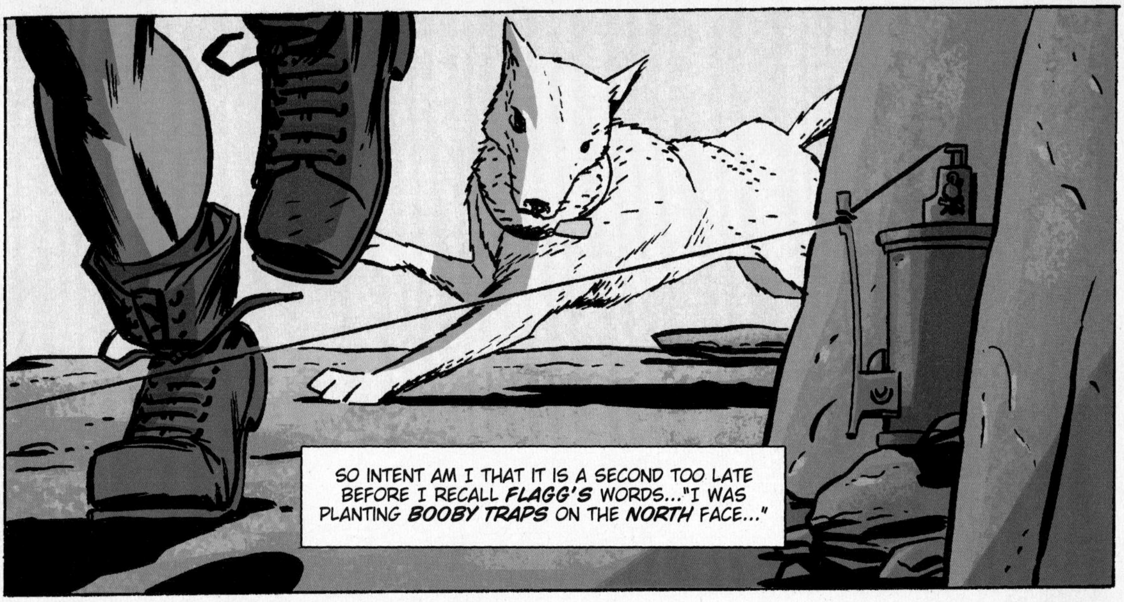
SO INTENT AM I THAT IT IS A SECOND TOO LATE BEFORE I RECALL ***FLAGG'S*** WORDS..."I WAS PLANTING ***BOOBY TRAPS*** ON THE ***NORTH*** FACE..."

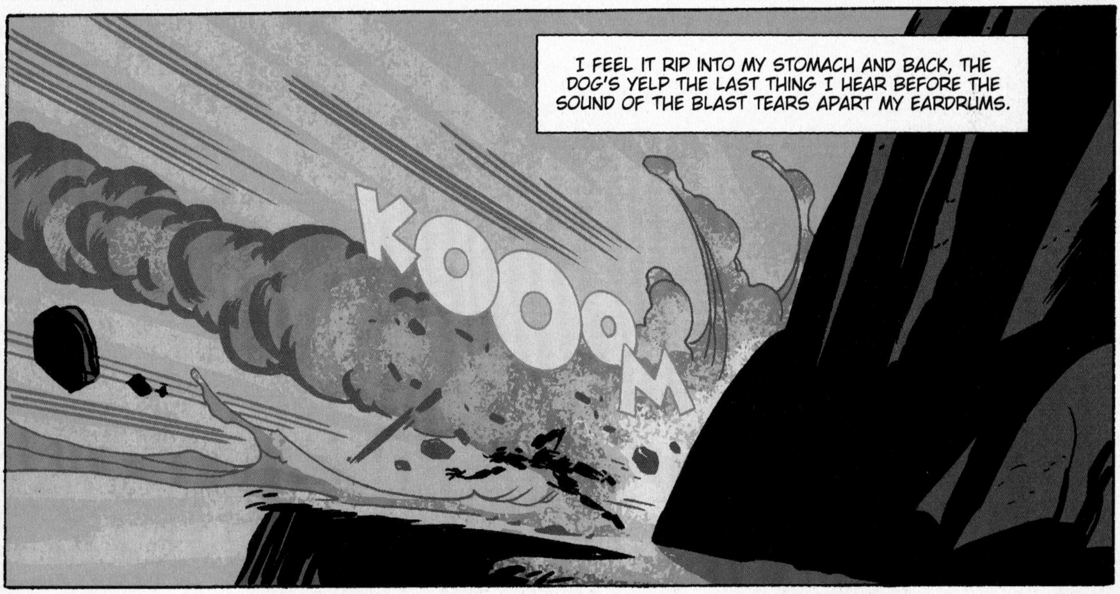
I FEEL IT RIP INTO MY STOMACH AND BACK, THE DOG'S YELP THE LAST THING I HEAR BEFORE THE SOUND OF THE BLAST TEARS APART MY EARDRUMS.
KOOOM

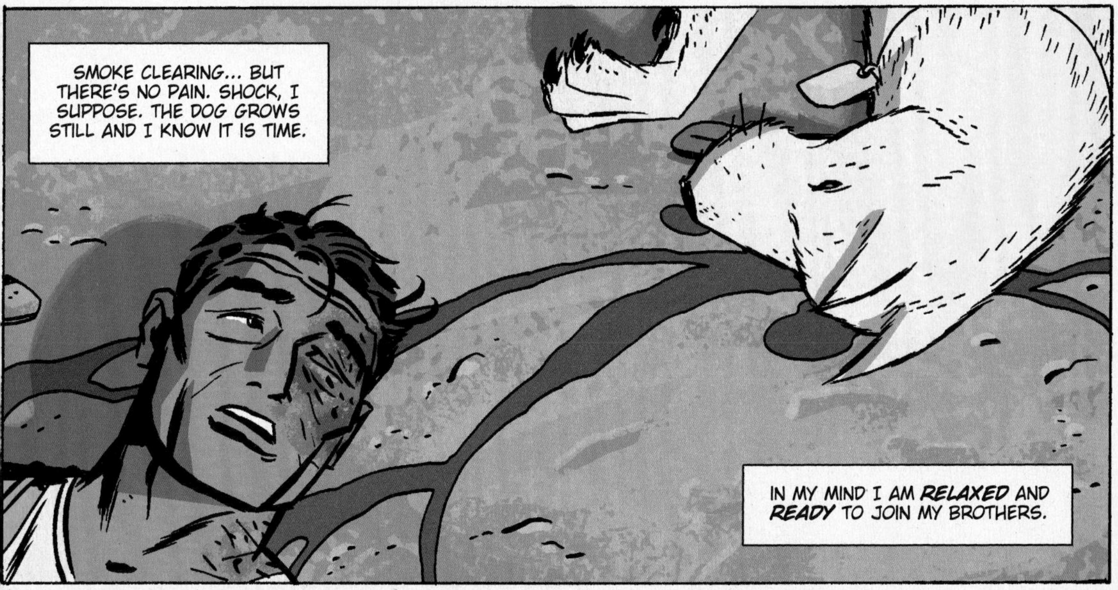
SMOKE CLEARING... BUT THERE'S NO PAIN. SHOCK, I SUPPOSE. THE DOG GROWS STILL AND I KNOW IT IS TIME.
IN MY MIND I AM ***RELAXED*** AND ***READY*** TO JOIN MY BROTHERS.

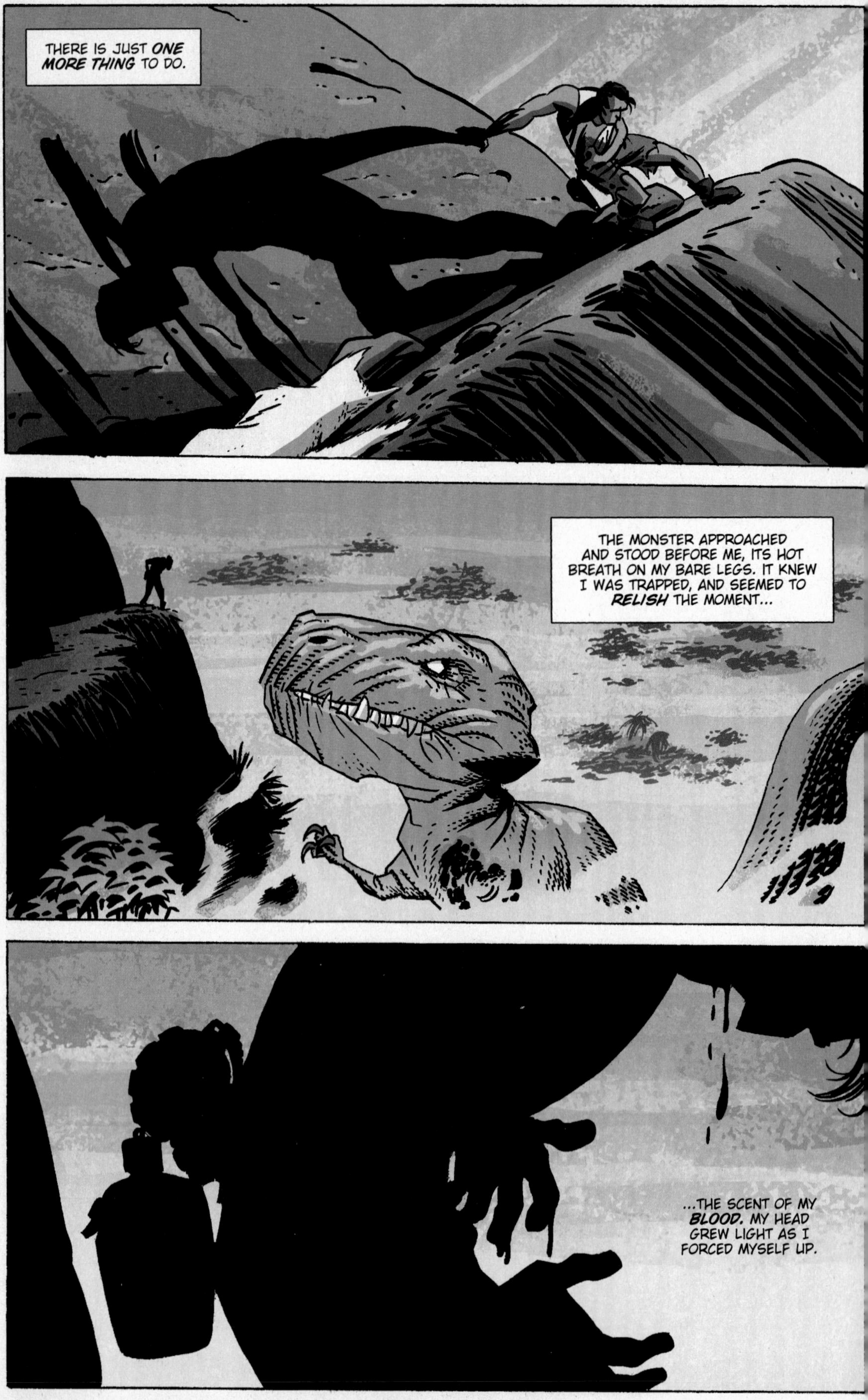
THERE IS JUST *ONE MORE THING* TO DO.
THE MONSTER APPROACHED AND STOOD BEFORE ME, ITS HOT BREATH ON MY BARE LEGS. IT KNEW I WAS TRAPPED, AND SEEMED TO *RELISH* THE MOMENT...
...THE SCENT OF MY *BLOOD.* MY HEAD GREW LIGHT AS I FORCED MYSELF UP.

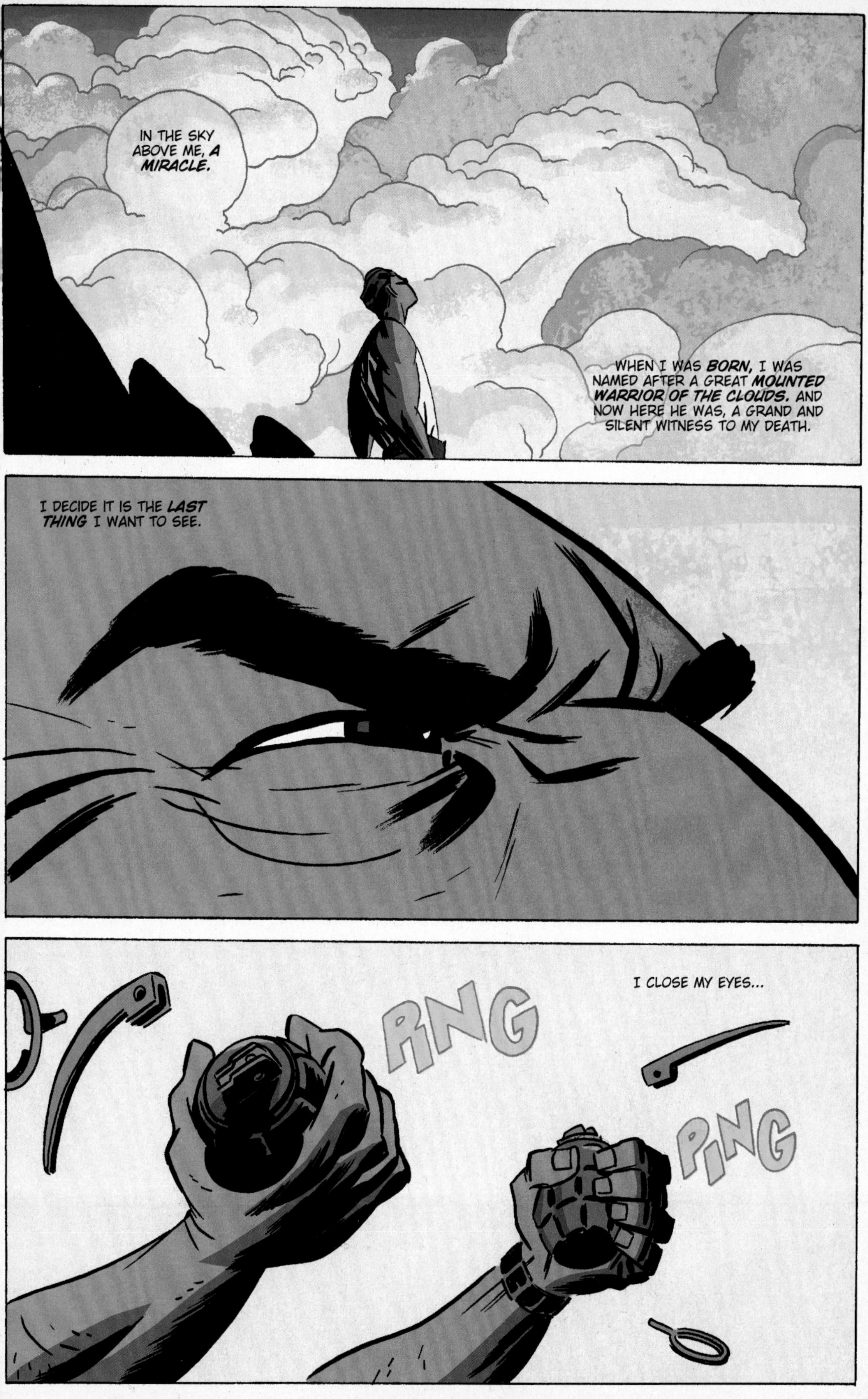
IN THE SKY ABOVE ME, A MIRACLE.
WHEN I WAS BORN, I WAS NAMED AFTER A GREAT MOUNTED WARRIOR OF THE CLOUDS. AND NOW HERE HE WAS, A GRAND AND SILENT WITNESS TO MY DEATH.
I DECIDE IT IS THE LAST THING I WANT TO SEE.
I CLOSE MY EYES...
RNG
PING

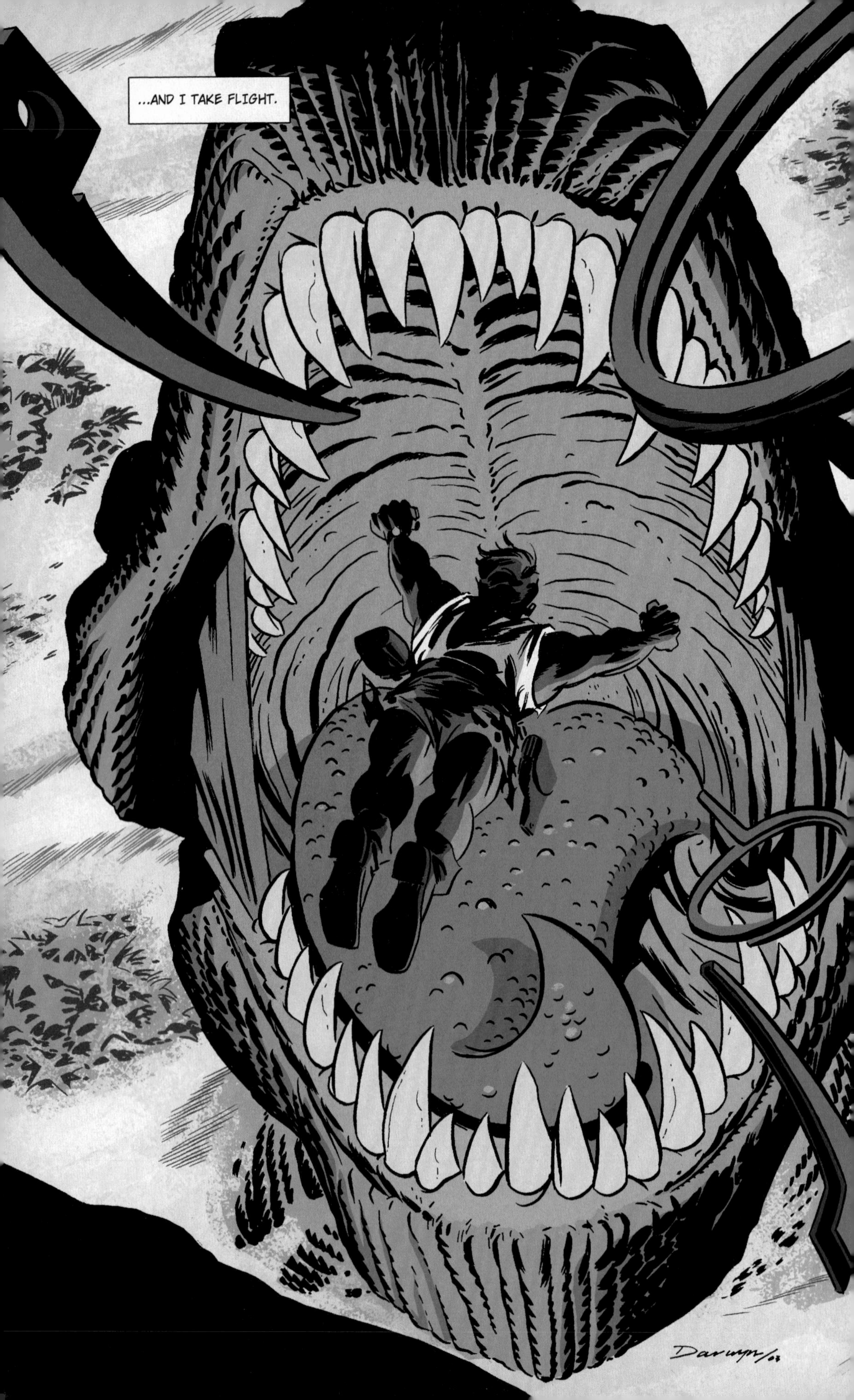
...AND I TAKE FLIGHT.
Darwyn/03

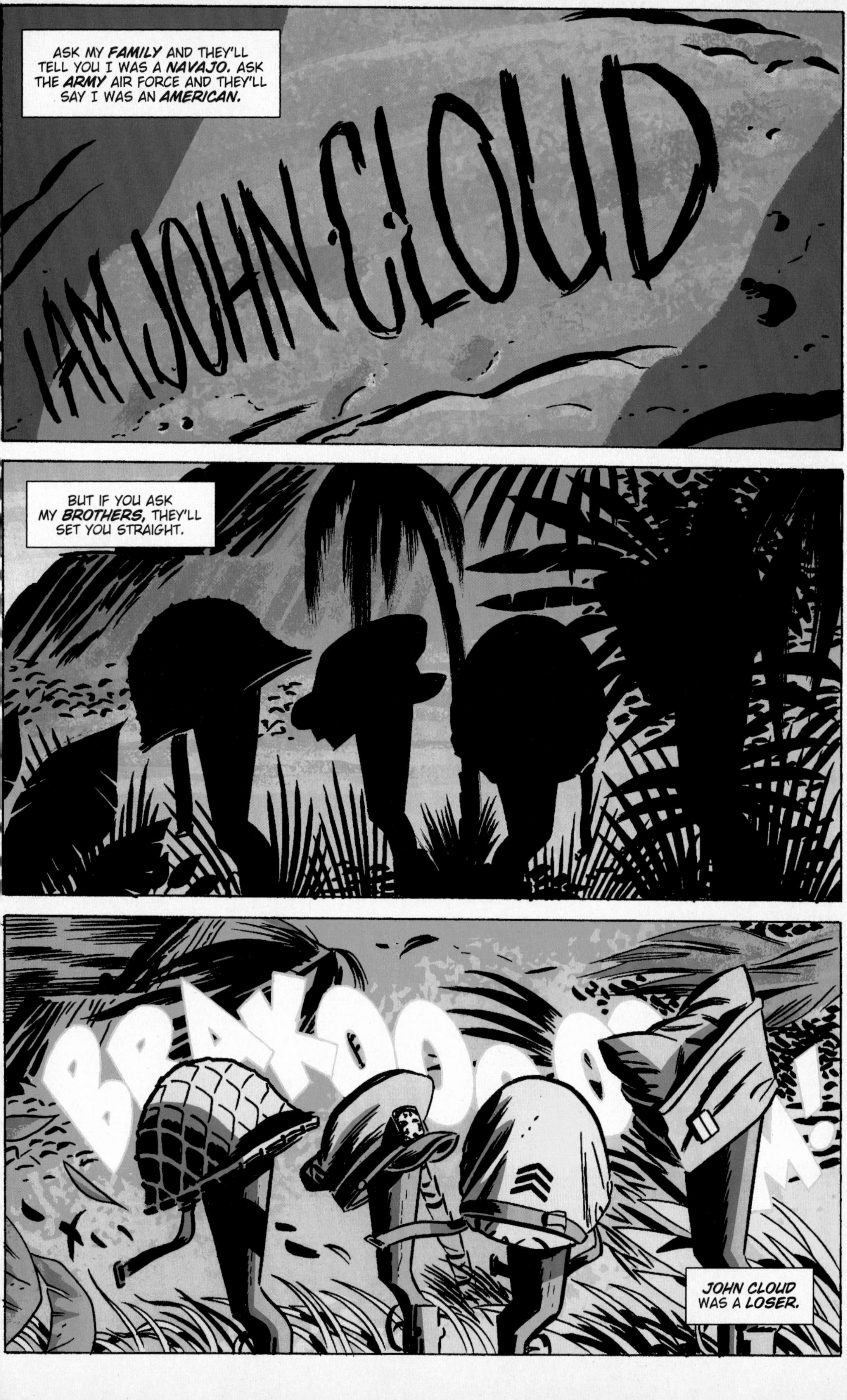

ASK MY *FAMILY* AND THEY'LL TELL YOU I WAS A *NAVAJO.* ASK THE *ARMY* AIR FORCE AND THEY'LL SAY I WAS AN *AMERICAN.*
I AM JOHN CLOUD
BUT IF YOU ASK MY *BROTHERS,* THEY'LL SET YOU STRAIGHT.
BRAKOOOOOM!
JOHN CLOUD WAS A *LOSER.*

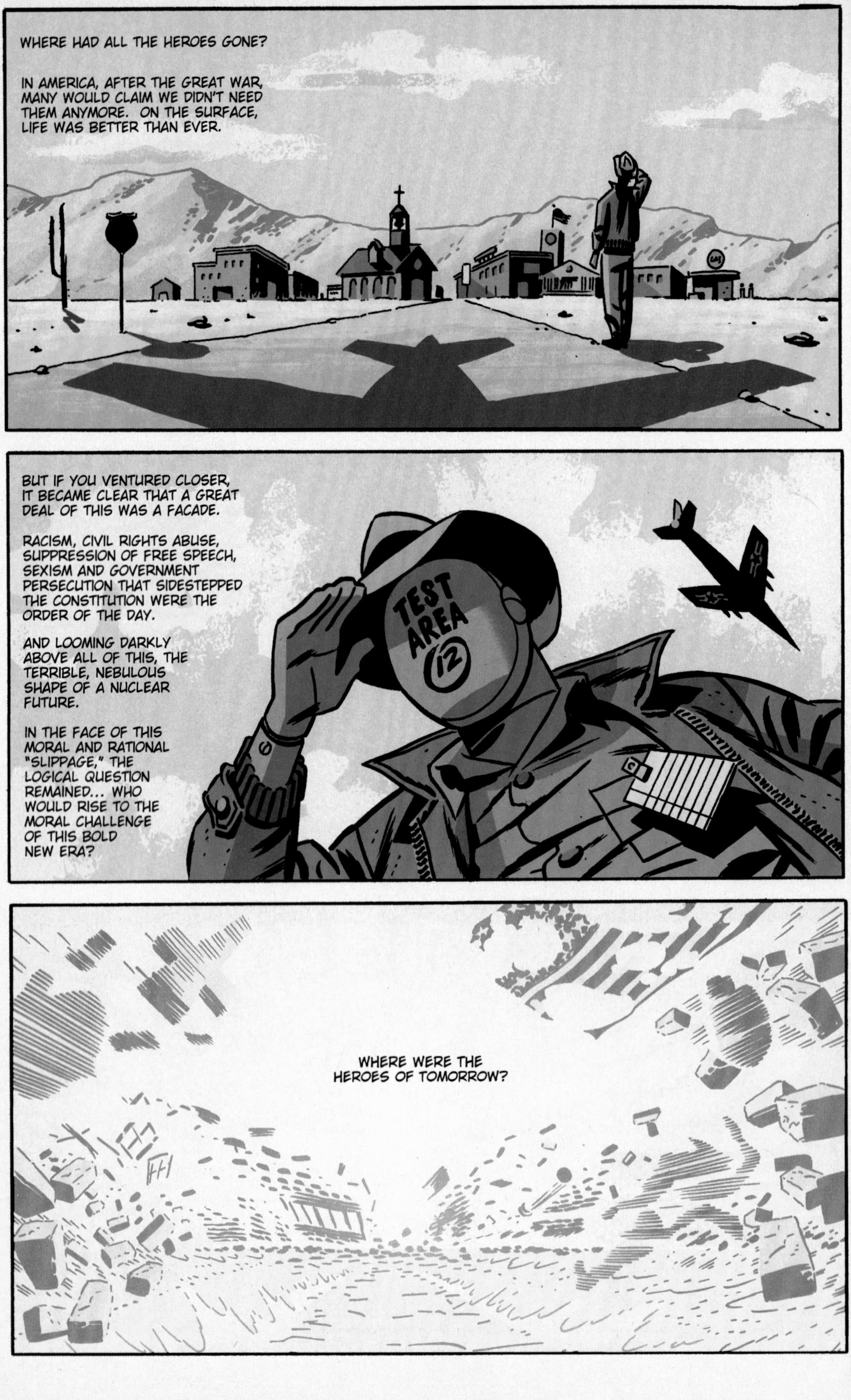
WHERE HAD ALL THE HEROES GONE?
IN AMERICA, AFTER THE GREAT WAR, MANY WOULD CLAIM WE DIDN'T NEED THEM ANYMORE. ON THE SURFACE, LIFE WAS BETTER THAN EVER.
BUT IF YOU VENTURED CLOSER, IT BECAME CLEAR THAT A GREAT DEAL OF THIS WAS A FACADE.
RACISM, CIVIL RIGHTS ABUSE, SUPPRESSION OF FREE SPEECH, SEXISM AND GOVERNMENT PERSECUTION THAT SIDESTEPPED THE CONSTITUTION WERE THE ORDER OF THE DAY.
AND LOOMING DARKLY ABOVE ALL OF THIS, THE TERRIBLE, NEBULOUS SHAPE OF A NUCLEAR FUTURE.
IN THE FACE OF THIS MORAL AND RATIONAL "SLIPPAGE," THE LOGICAL QUESTION REMAINED... WHO WOULD RISE TO THE MORAL CHALLENGE OF THIS BOLD NEW ERA?
TEST AREA 12
WHERE WERE THE HEROES OF TOMORROW?

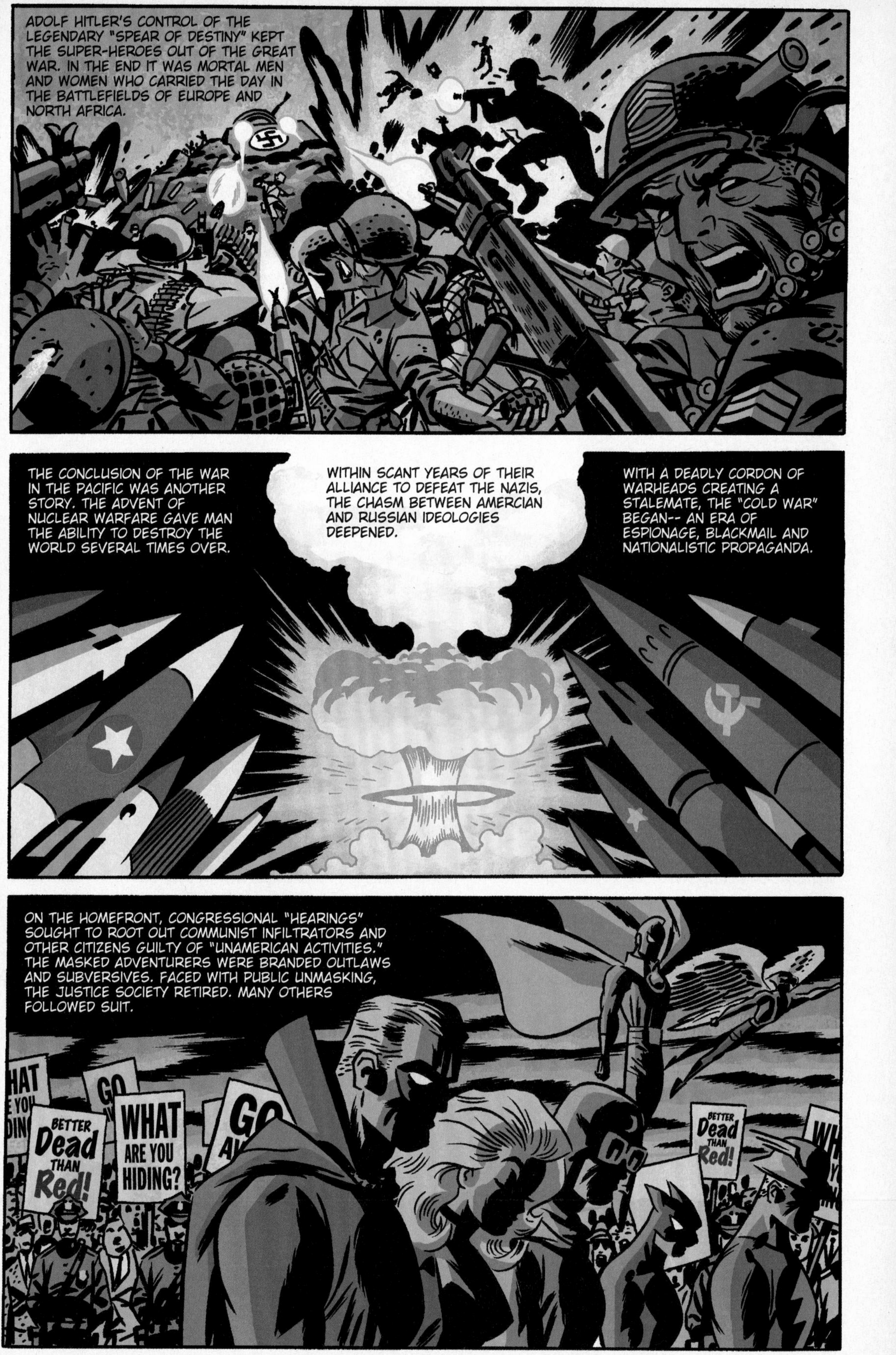

ADOLF HITLER'S CONTROL OF THE LEGENDARY "SPEAR OF DESTINY" KEPT THE SUPER-HEROES OUT OF THE GREAT WAR. IN THE END IT WAS MORTAL MEN AND WOMEN WHO CARRIED THE DAY IN THE BATTLEFIELDS OF EUROPE AND NORTH AFRICA.
THE CONCLUSION OF THE WAR IN THE PACIFIC WAS ANOTHER STORY. THE ADVENT OF NUCLEAR WARFARE GAVE MAN THE ABILITY TO DESTROY THE WORLD SEVERAL TIMES OVER.
WITHIN SCANT YEARS OF THEIR ALLIANCE TO DEFEAT THE NAZIS, THE CHASM BETWEEN AMERCIAN AND RUSSIAN IDEOLOGIES DEEPENED.
WITH A DEADLY CORDON OF WARHEADS CREATING A STALEMATE, THE "COLD WAR" BEGAN-- AN ERA OF ESPIONAGE, BLACKMAIL AND NATIONALISTIC PROPAGANDA.
ON THE HOMEFRONT, CONGRESSIONAL "HEARINGS" SOUGHT TO ROOT OUT COMMUNIST INFILTRATORS AND OTHER CITIZENS GUILTY OF "UNAMERICAN ACTIVITIES." THE MASKED ADVENTURERS WERE BRANDED OUTLAWS AND SUBVERSIVES. FACED WITH PUBLIC UNMASKING, THE JUSTICE SOCIETY RETIRED. MANY OTHERS FOLLOWED SUIT.
BETTER Dead THAN Red!
WHAT ARE YOU HIDING?
BETTER Dead THAN Red!

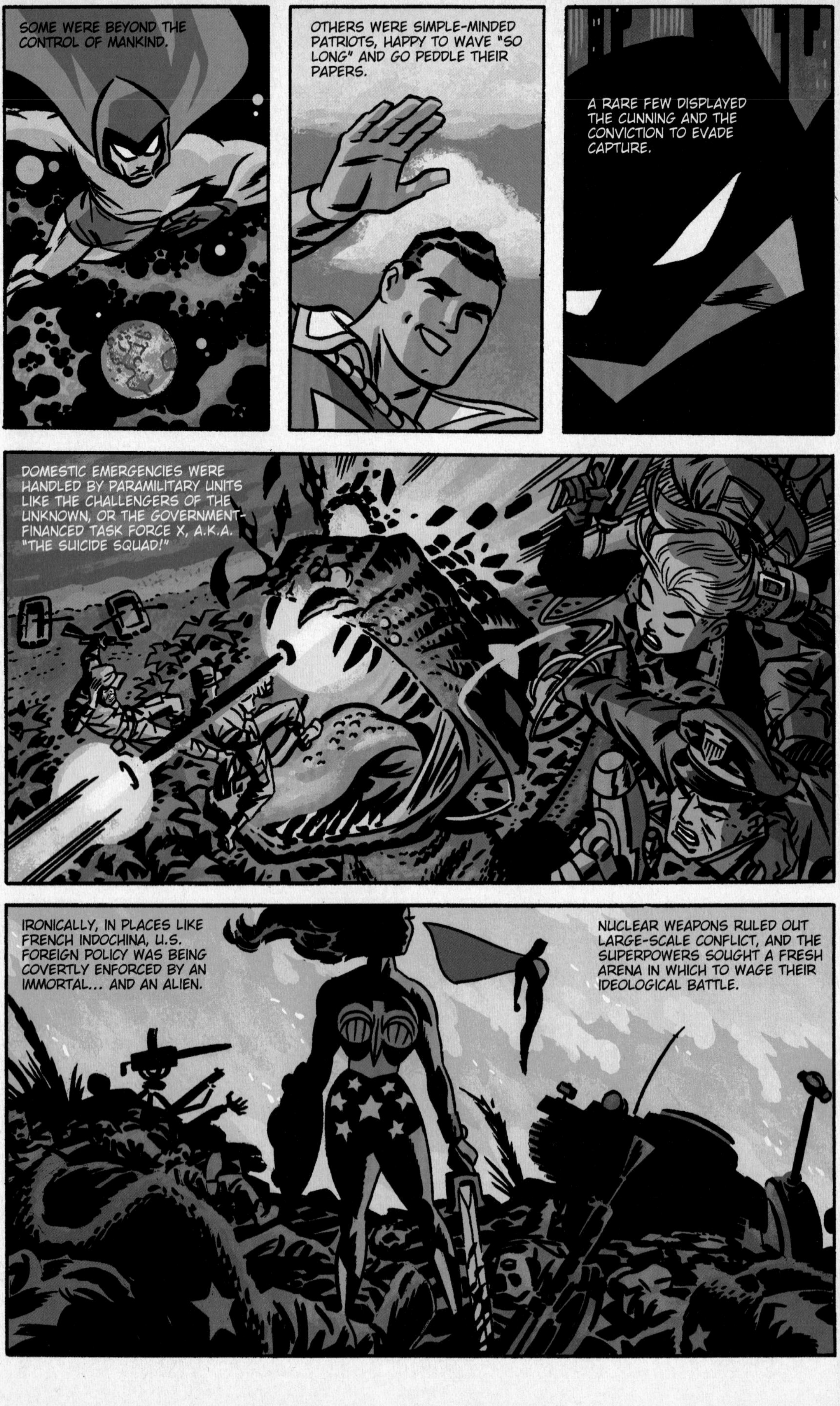
SOME WERE BEYOND THE CONTROL OF MANKIND.
OTHERS WERE SIMPLE-MINDED PATRIOTS, HAPPY TO WAVE "SO LONG" AND GO PEDDLE THEIR PAPERS.
A RARE FEW DISPLAYED THE CUNNING AND THE CONVICTION TO EVADE CAPTURE.
DOMESTIC EMERGENCIES WERE HANDLED BY PARAMILITARY UNITS LIKE THE CHALLENGERS OF THE UNKNOWN, OR THE GOVERNMENT-FINANCED TASK FORCE X, A.K.A. "THE SUICIDE SQUAD!"
IRONICALLY, IN PLACES LIKE FRENCH INDOCHINA, U.S. FOREIGN POLICY WAS BEING COVERTLY ENFORCED BY AN IMMORTAL... AND AN ALIEN.
NUCLEAR WEAPONS RULED OUT LARGE-SCALE CONFLICT, AND THE SUPERPOWERS SOUGHT A FRESH ARENA IN WHICH TO WAGE THEIR IDEOLOGICAL BATTLE.

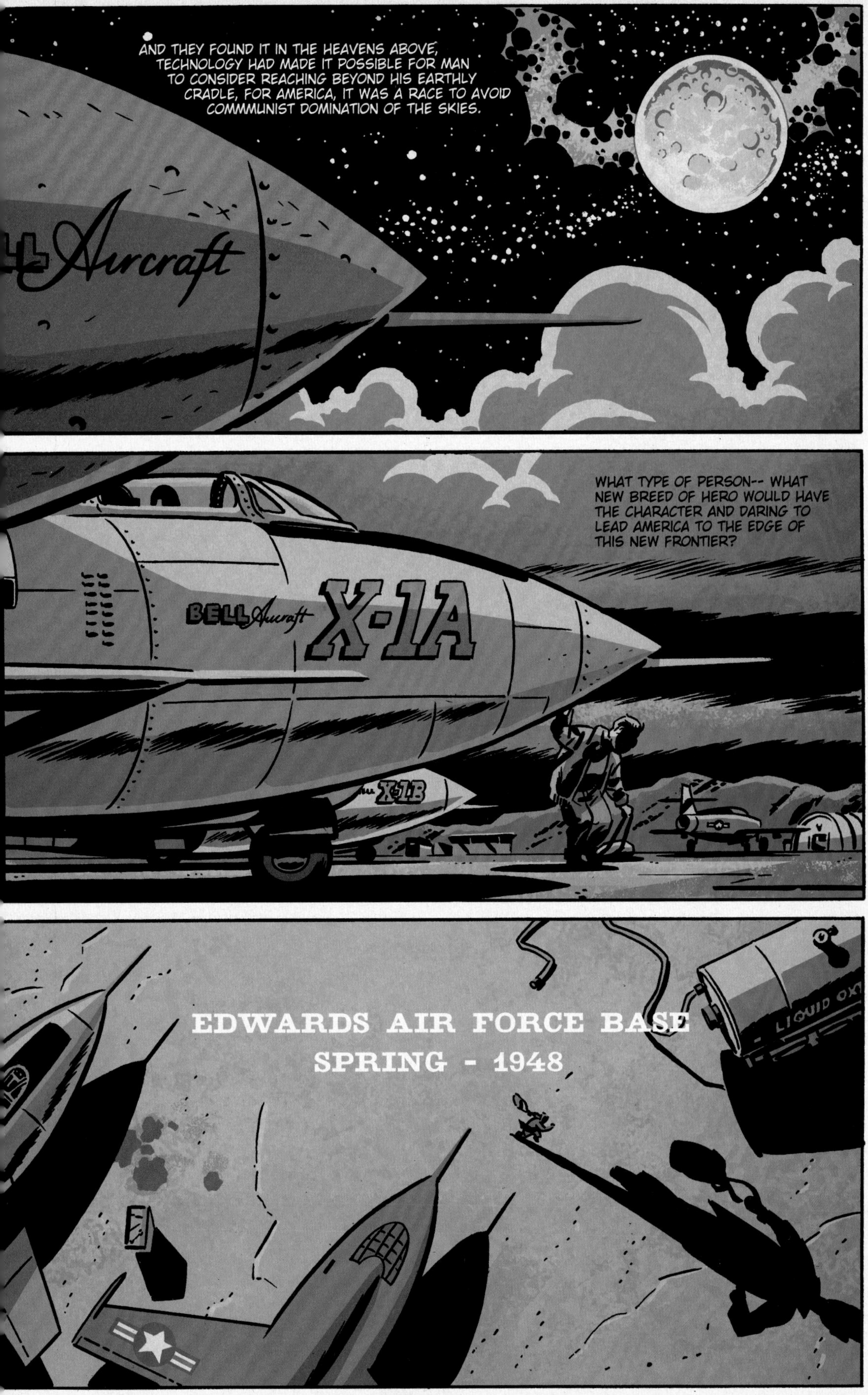
AND THEY FOUND IT IN THE HEAVENS ABOVE, TECHNOLOGY HAD MADE IT POSSIBLE FOR MAN TO CONSIDER REACHING BEYOND HIS EARTHLY CRADLE, FOR AMERICA, IT WAS A RACE TO AVOID COMMMUNIST DOMINATION OF THE SKIES.
BELL Aircraft
WHAT TYPE OF PERSON-- WHAT NEW BREED OF HERO WOULD HAVE THE CHARACTER AND DARING TO LEAD AMERICA TO THE EDGE OF THIS NEW FRONTIER?
BELL Aircraft X-1A
X-1B
EDWARDS AIR FORCE BASE
SPRING - 1948
LIQUID OX

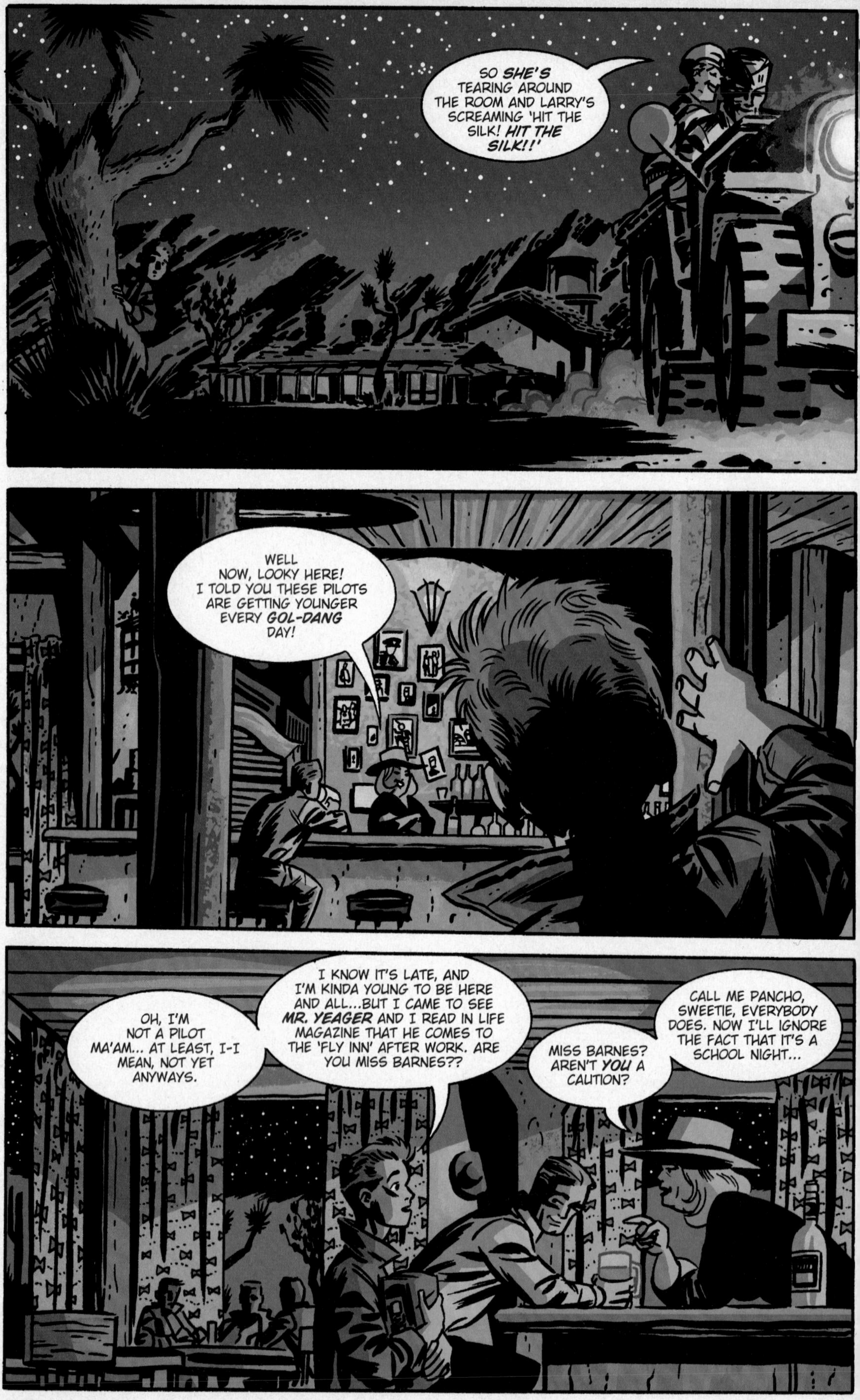
SO SHE'S TEARING AROUND THE ROOM AND LARRY'S SCREAMING 'HIT THE SILK! HIT THE SILK!!'
WELL NOW, LOOKY HERE! I TOLD YOU THESE PILOTS ARE GETTING YOUNGER EVERY GOL-DANG DAY!
OH, I'M NOT A PILOT MA'AM... AT LEAST, I-I MEAN, NOT YET ANYWAYS.
I KNOW IT'S LATE, AND I'M KINDA YOUNG TO BE HERE AND ALL...BUT I CAME TO SEE MR. YEAGER AND I READ IN LIFE MAGAZINE THAT HE COMES TO THE 'FLY INN' AFTER WORK. ARE YOU MISS BARNES??
MISS BARNES? AREN'T YOU A CAUTION?
CALL ME PANCHO, SWEETIE, EVERYBODY DOES. NOW I'LL IGNORE THE FACT THAT IT'S A SCHOOL NIGHT...

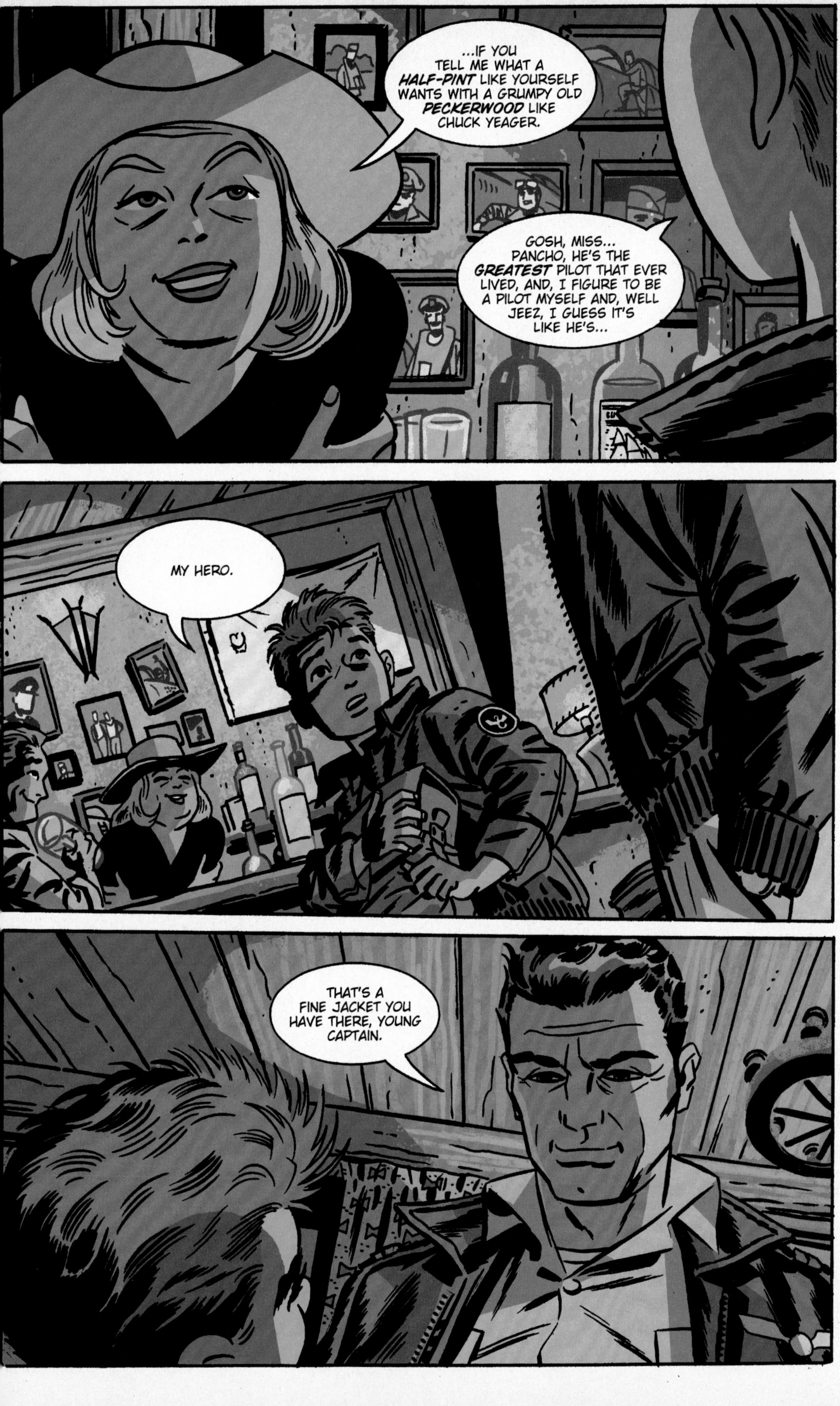
...IF YOU TELL ME WHAT A HALF-PINT LIKE YOURSELF WANTS WITH A GRUMPY OLD PECKERWOOD LIKE CHUCK YEAGER.
GOSH, MISS... PANCHO, HE'S THE GREATEST PILOT THAT EVER LIVED, AND, I FIGURE TO BE A PILOT MYSELF AND, WELL JEEZ, I GUESS IT'S LIKE HE'S...
MY HERO.
THAT'S A FINE JACKET YOU HAVE THERE, YOUNG CAPTAIN.

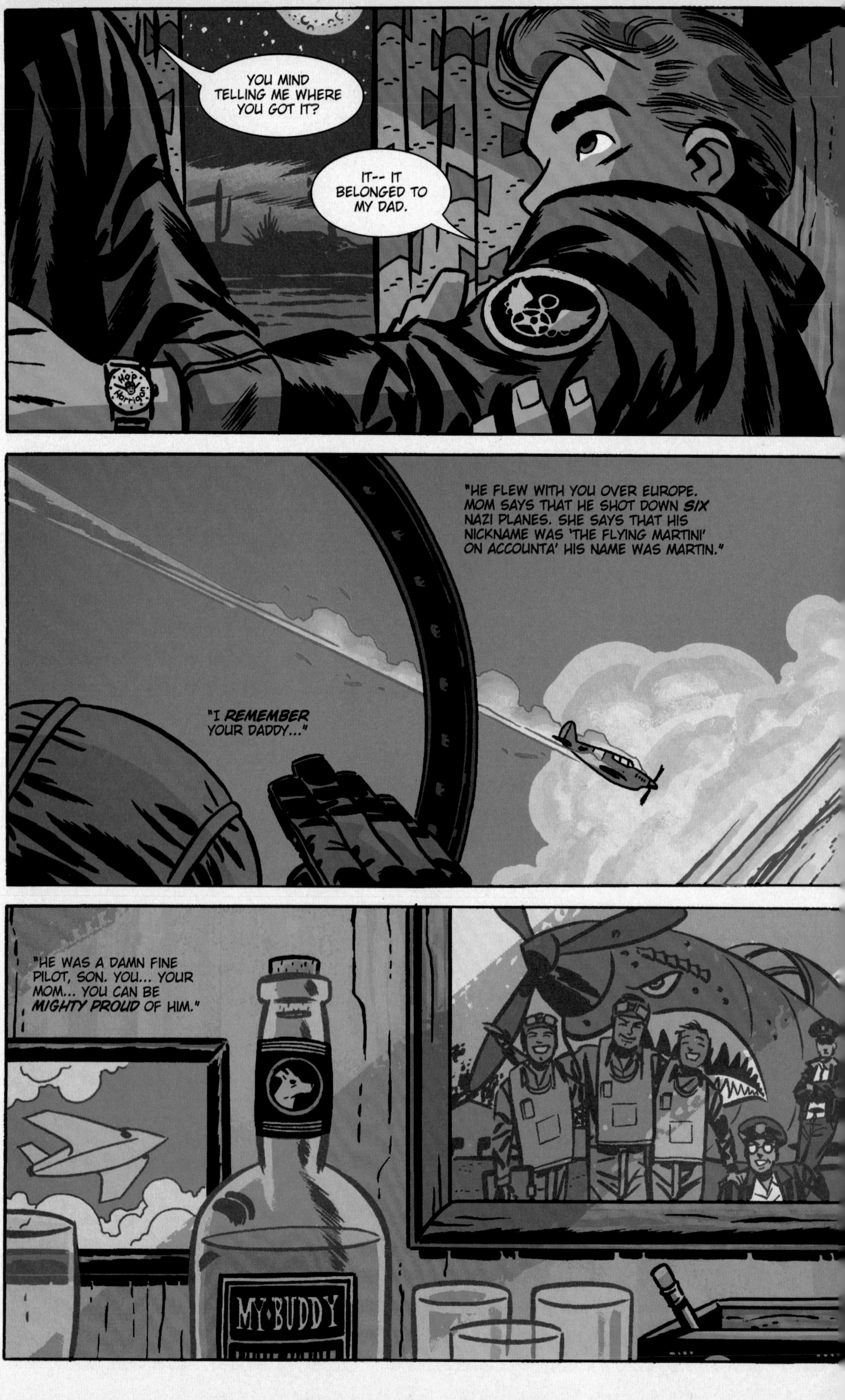
YOU MIND TELLING ME WHERE YOU GOT IT?
IT-- IT BELONGED TO MY DAD.
Hop Harrigan
"HE FLEW WITH YOU OVER EUROPE. MOM SAYS THAT HE SHOT DOWN *SIX* NAZI PLANES. SHE SAYS THAT HIS NICKNAME WAS 'THE FLYING MARTINI' ON ACCOUNTA' HIS NAME WAS MARTIN."
"I *REMEMBER* YOUR DADDY..."
"HE WAS A DAMN FINE PILOT, SON. YOU... YOUR MOM... YOU CAN BE *MIGHTY PROUD* OF HIM."
MY·BUDDY

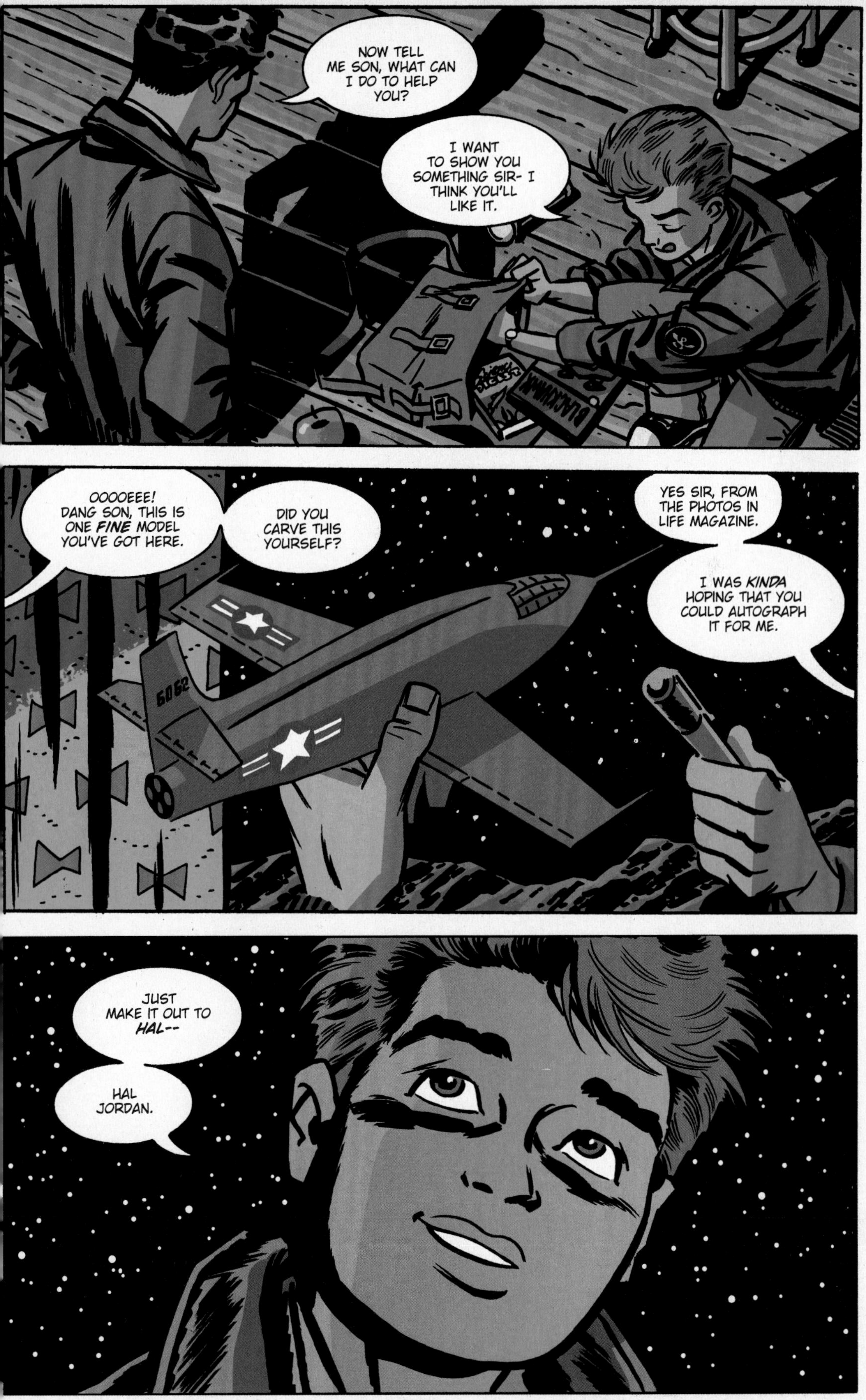
NOW TELL ME SON, WHAT CAN I DO TO HELP YOU?
I WANT TO SHOW YOU SOMETHING SIR- I THINK YOU'LL LIKE IT.
OOOOEEE! DANG SON, THIS IS ONE FINE MODEL YOU'VE GOT HERE.
DID YOU CARVE THIS YOURSELF?
YES SIR, FROM THE PHOTOS IN LIFE MAGAZINE.
I WAS KINDA HOPING THAT YOU COULD AUTOGRAPH IT FOR ME.
JUST MAKE IT OUT TO HAL--
HAL JORDAN.

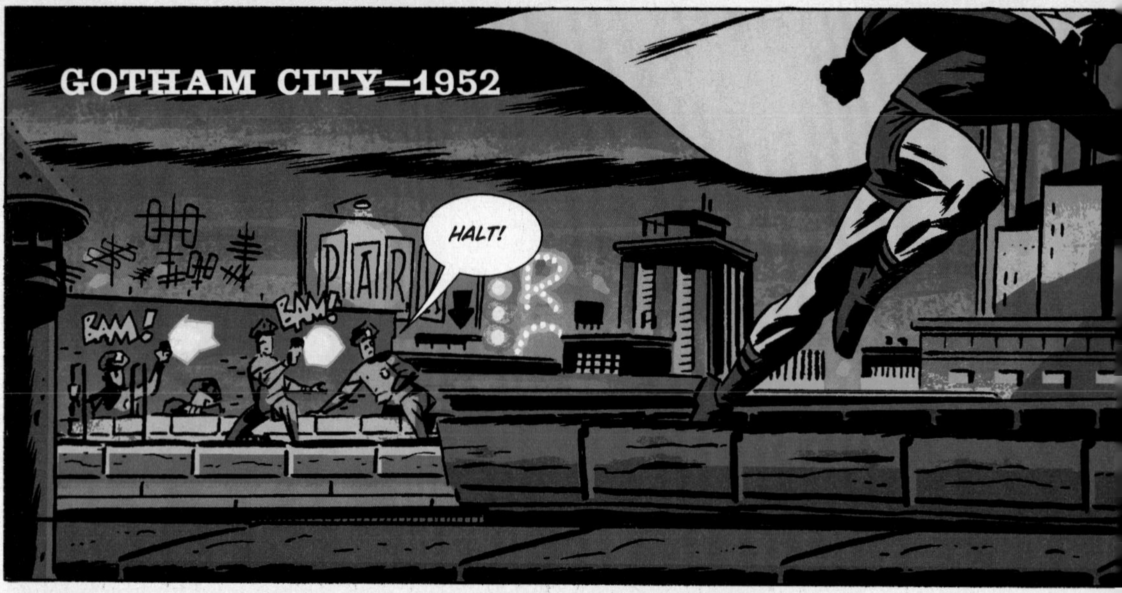
GOTHAM CITY—1952
BAM!
BAM!
HALT!

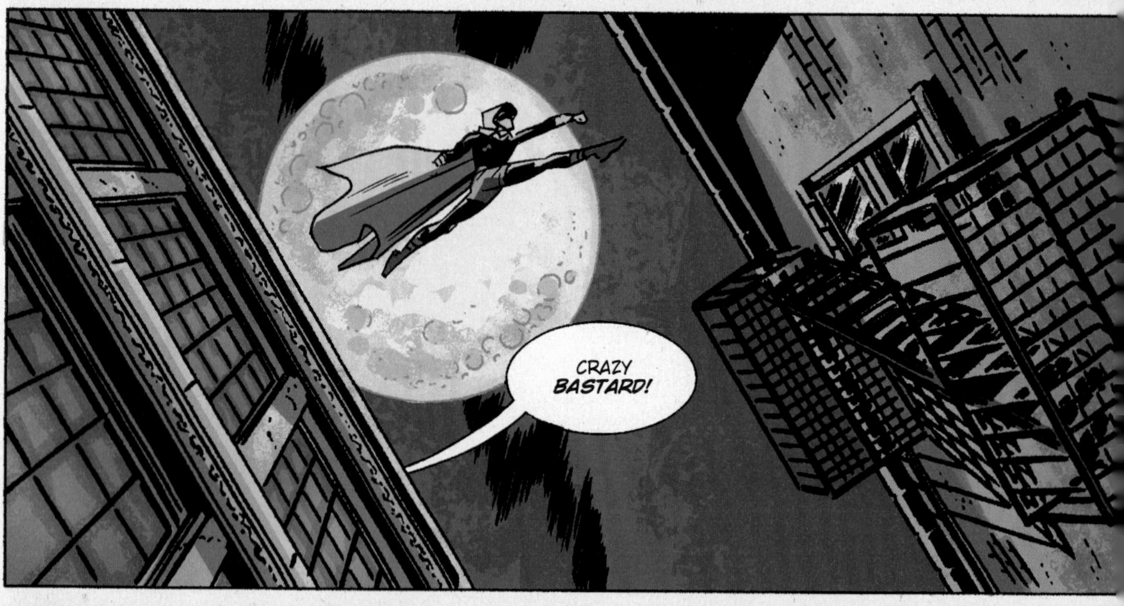
CRAZY BASTARD!

CHAPTER TWO
STATE OF THE UNION SUIT

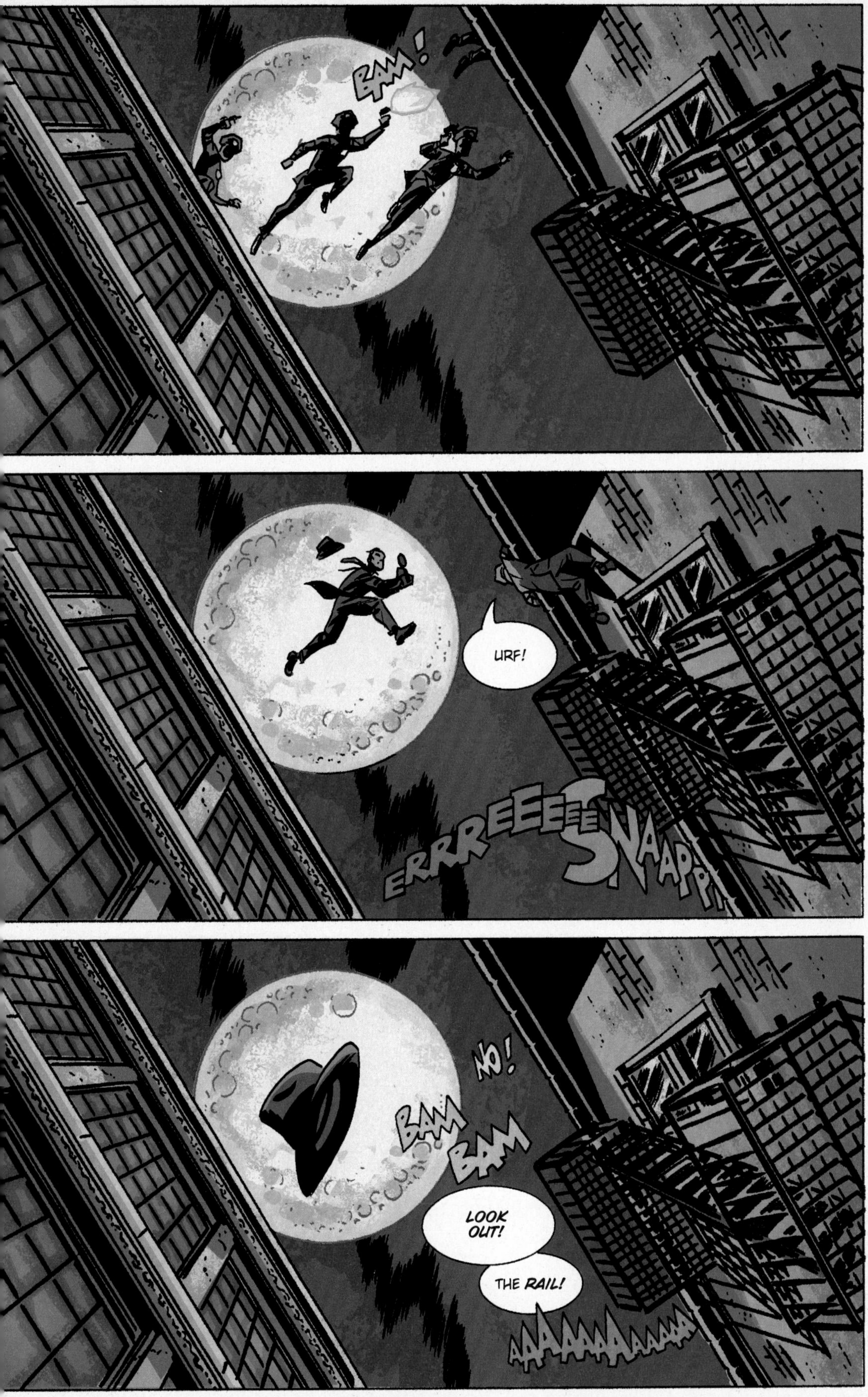
BAM!
URF!
ERRREEEEESNAAPP
NO!
BAM
BAM
LOOK OUT!
THE RAIL!
AAAAAAAAAAAA

**Recent Congressional hearings aimed at purging the nation
of subversive influence target the masked vigilantes of urban America.**

by IRIS WEST

WASHINGTON DECLARES WAR ON THE MYSTERY MEN

ON AN UNCHARACTERISTICALLY BALMY MAY EVENING THE
MASKED ADVENTURER KNOWN AS HOURMAN PLUNGED TO HIS
DEATH, TAKING FOUR COAST CITY POLICEMEN WITH HIM.

It was the latest and most tragic chapter in the Eisenhower Administration's efforts to register and reveal the identities of the Nation's "masked do-gooders".The fallen officers were in pursuit of Hourman for questioning regarding a Federal warrant. Hourman was one of a handful of Vigilantes that refuse to retire or register with the Congressional Commitee on Un-American Activities.

The Federal response has been swift and decisive; last month a bill passed unanimously making vigilantism a federal offense, akin to treason. O nly those registered with the FBI and cleared by Congress are allowed to legally operate in government sanctioned ways.

It was four years ago, in the wake of the Alger Hiss case, that the House

on Unamerican Activities and Senator Joe McCarthy turned their attention to segments of the populace that enjoyed the public spotlight.

Hollywood in particular has been in the headlines of late, as congress sopeonas dozens of actors, directors and screenwriters with known communist associations.

Supporters consider it key to purge Hollywood of "red thinking" that could infest the entertainment world, but critics call it a shameless circus, conducted for publicity .

Whether the hearings are a circus or not, one thing is certain; the repercussions are not. Hollywood insiders relate that even the slightest communist affiliation or refusal to name associates could lead to "blacklisting." Film makers who've been labeled

The Hourman, AKA Rex Tyler, plunges to his death along with
four uniformed police officers. The only attendees at his funeral
were a small clutch of mourners that came to pay their respects
to a man that had saved their lives as Hourman.

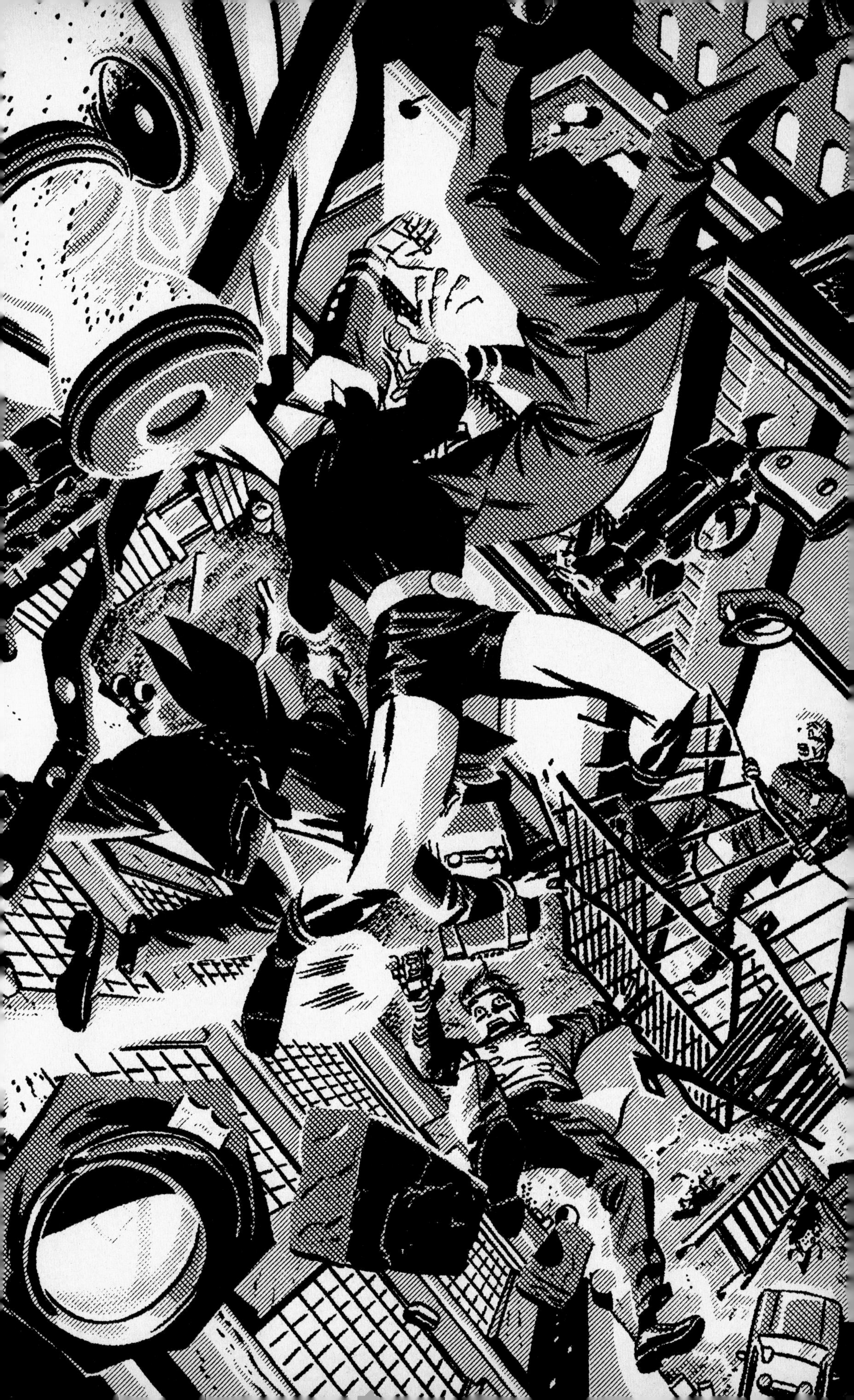

communist sympathizers are unable to find work of any sort.

MAN WITHOUT A COUNTRY

Eight months ago Roy Raymond was on top of the world. A hit television show, radio program and weekly column made him one of America's best known celebrities. When brought before the HUAC commitee, Raymond refused to inform on any friends or associates, and pleaded the Fifth amendment in regards to himself.

He was cited for contempt and branded a communist sympathizer.

"Something has gone horribly wrong with this country." states

Above: the JSA takes a final walk into the sunset. Facing page: Photo taken seconds before the Bat-Man defeated Superman with explosive charge. After several well-placed boots to the solar plexus, the Bat-Man made good his escape. Analysis of the chemical charge used on Superman has been inconclusive.

Raymond. " To imagine that this great nation has somehow allowed muckrakers like McCarthy enough power to degrade and destroy private citizens...I (Raymond pauses, looks away)...I can't stay here anymore. I've lost everything. But I suppose the worst of it is I've lost my home. My faith in my country."

EISENHOWER INTERVENES

"It was Richard Nixon's idea to go after the Masked Marvels" confides Roy Cohn, over drinks in a Beltway cocktail bar. Cohn has been Senator Joe McCarthy's hachet man, or assistant, for several months. He is clearly a man who loves his work.

After hearing a few friendly credentials, Cohn is happy to speak, with a candor that borders on arrogance. He pauses to drink, his eyes darting with the light of the bartop. "Hunting Reds in the entertainment industry sells newspapers- this Masked Freak thing would be a real opportunity.

After all, these people are flagrantly breaking dozens of municipal, state and federal laws, in the pursuit of

their own idea of what's right and wrong." Another drink. "It just isn't American." Finally his eyes come up and the tone is confidential;"This aggression will not stand."

When it came to making an example, HUAC wisely targeted the largest, most visible collective; The Justice Society of America.

Months of public baiting and Federal pressure to appear before the congressional hearing went unanswered by the venerable JSA, until the President himself took public airtime on September 14 to order the Justice Society to support its country and make itself to available to Congress immediately.

After reading a list of allegations that ranged from inarguable to absurd, Congress demanded that the JSA unmask and reveal their identities, and to take an oath of loyalty to the current administration.

The JSA, however, had come prepared with an alternative of their own. They simply vanished. In a statement issued the following day, they refused to recognize Congress' authority, but as patriotic Americans they refuse to break Federal law. Henceforth they were retiring.

This set a remarkable precedent, and in the preceding weeks, dozens of masked adventurers followed suit.

At this date, only a half dozen have registered and taken the loyalty oath, most notably Superman and the Amazon princess, Wonder Woman.

The President himself enlisted the Man of Steel's help to round up the remaining Masked Men who refused to turn themselves in or retire. This was all it took to finish all but the most resourceful of the vigilantes. In a truly fantastic encounter, Superman cornered the legendary Bat-Man that haunts Gotham City's underworld. Eyewitness accounts indicate that Superman's victory seemed assured until he was hit in the face by a chemical explosive of some sort by the Gotham City Bat-Man.

Analysis of the chemical charge has been inconclusive. The Bat-Man is still at large.

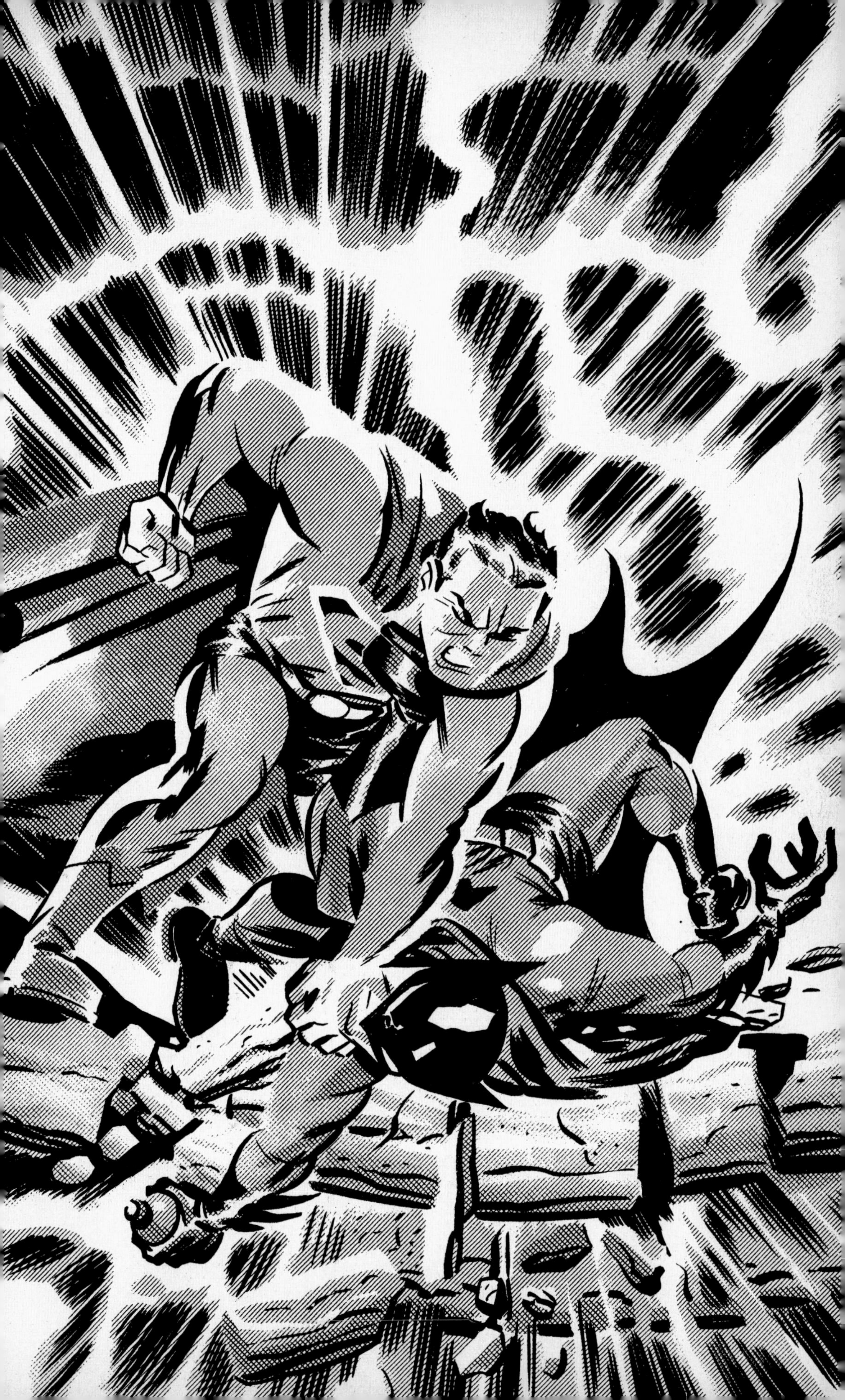

come for Americans to take control of their destiny again." Air Force Colonel Rick Flagg is the field leader of Task Force X.

"Why do we need a bunch of circus sideshow types looking after our well-being? With our drive, and our knowledge and ability, there's nothing Americans can't take care of themselves. Task Force X is here to take charge in situations where the nation's safety and security are jeopardized by unforeseen forces. We've been trained and equipped to react creatively to any challenge, Terran or Alien, scientific or biologic."

AMERICAN TRAGEDY

Although a new order has emerged it is important that whatever our direction in the future, we recognize there is a certain debt owed to these masked loners.

Which brings us full circle to the death of the masked adventurer known as Hourman. Post mortem investigation uncovered he was Pharmaceutical Magnate Rex Tyler.

The autopsy indicated trace elements of several drugs, which are still under analysis. Tyler's journal gives us a glimpse into this troubled soul. His dependence on drugs, his sense of isolation and his pride at doing what he referred to as "good work."

Rex Tyler was a self made millionaire who saw something wrong with society, and acted on his principles.

He was a drug addict and he was wanted for federal crimes.

But corroborating reports indicate he personally had prevented 17 murders, 23 attempted rapes, 9 armed robberies and at least 5 acts of wanton madness that would have resulted in mass destruction.

He was principled and flawed . Loved by those he helped, and vilified by those that sought to control him.

Upon posthumous reflection a tragic irony is revealed. Rex Tyler, AKA the Hourman, was a quintessential American. •

Task Force X's Suicide Squad defeat a commie threat in Paris last month.

TASK FORCE X

Concurrent to the constriction of vigilante activity, the Eisenhower administration broadened its support of paramilitary means to deal with the type of phenomena most often associated with the Mystery Men. Earlier this year the White House introduced Task Force X, a revamped version of Truman's wartime Suicide Squad- A group of highly trained government personnel, with state of the art technology and almost limitless resources.

"We're here because the time has

CHAPTER THREE
HEAVY TRAFFIC IN MIG ALLEY

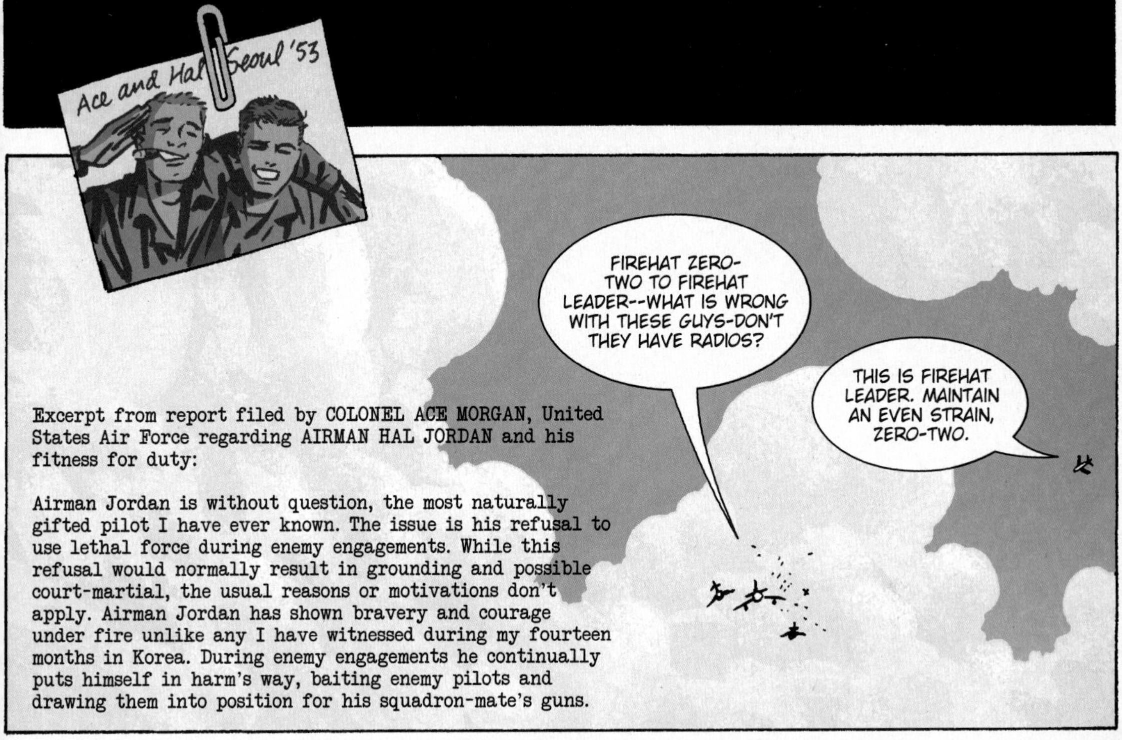
Ace and Hal Seoul '53
FIREHAT ZERO-TWO TO FIREHAT LEADER--WHAT IS WRONG WITH THESE GUYS-DON'T THEY HAVE RADIOS?
THIS IS FIREHAT LEADER. MAINTAIN AN EVEN STRAIN, ZERO-TWO.
Excerpt from report filed by COLONEL ACE MORGAN, United States Air Force regarding AIRMAN HAL JORDAN and his fitness for duty:
Airman Jordan is without question, the most naturally gifted pilot I have ever known. The issue is his refusal to use lethal force during enemy engagements. While this refusal would normally result in grounding and possible court-martial, the usual reasons or motivations don't apply. Airman Jordan has shown bravery and courage under fire unlike any I have witnessed during my fourteen months in Korea. During enemy engagements he continually puts himself in harm's way, baiting enemy pilots and drawing them into position for his squadron-mate's guns.

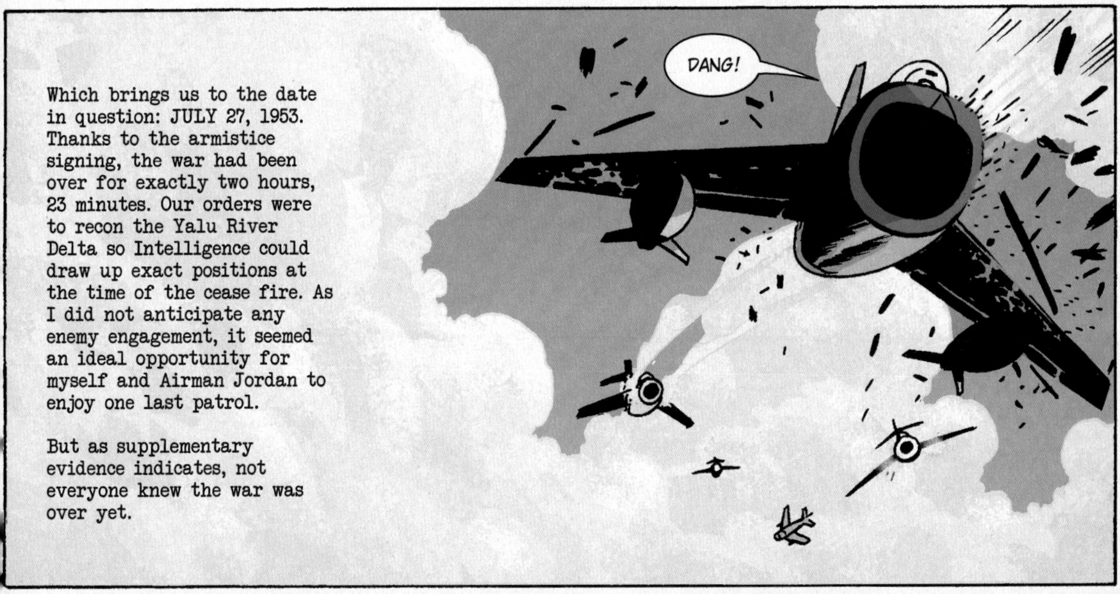
Which brings us to the date in question: JULY 27, 1953. Thanks to the armistice signing, the war had been over for exactly two hours, 23 minutes. Our orders were to recon the Yalu River Delta so Intelligence could draw up exact positions at the time of the cease fire. As I did not anticipate any enemy engagement, it seemed an ideal opportunity for myself and Airman Jordan to enjoy one last patrol.
DANG!
But as supplementary evidence indicates, not everyone knew the war was over yet.

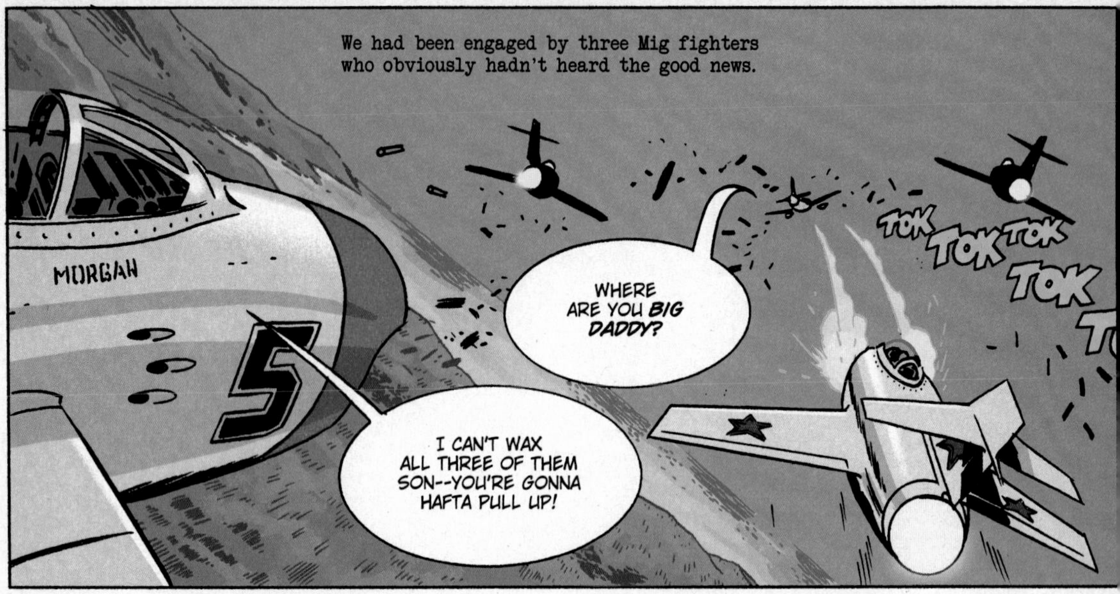
We had been engaged by three Mig fighters who obviously hadn't heard the good news.
MORGAN
5
WHERE ARE YOU *BIG DADDY?*
I CAN'T WAX ALL THREE OF THEM SON--YOU'RE GONNA HAFTA PULL UP!
TOK TOK TOK TOK

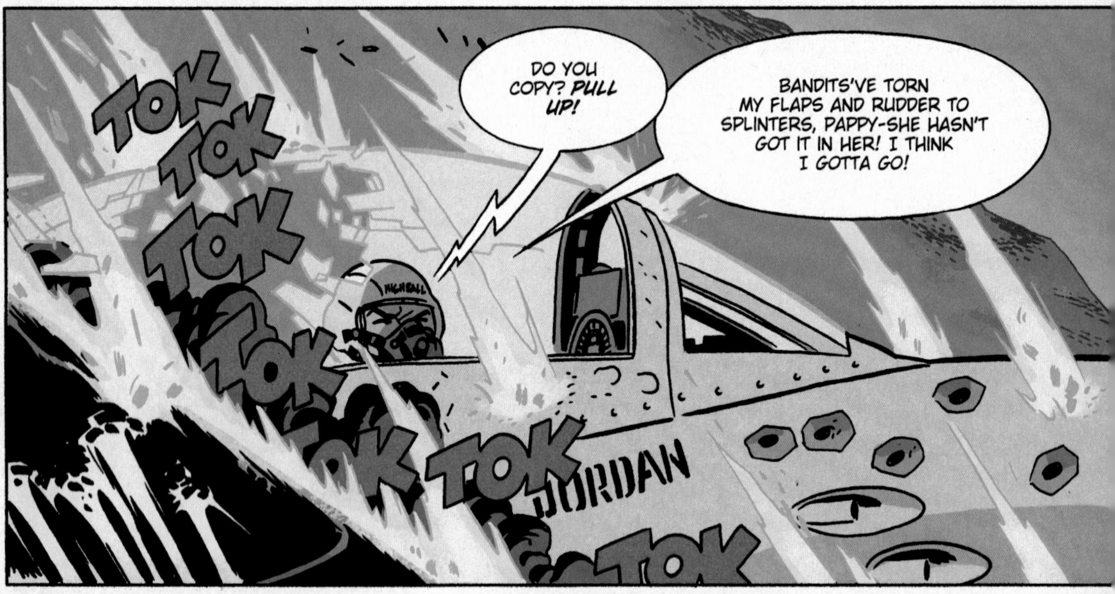
TOK TOK TOK TOK
DO YOU COPY? *PULL UP!*
BANDITS'VE TORN MY FLAPS AND RUDDER TO SPLINTERS, PAPPY-SHE HASN'T GOT IT IN HER! I THINK I GOTTA GO!
TOK TOK
JORDAN
TOK

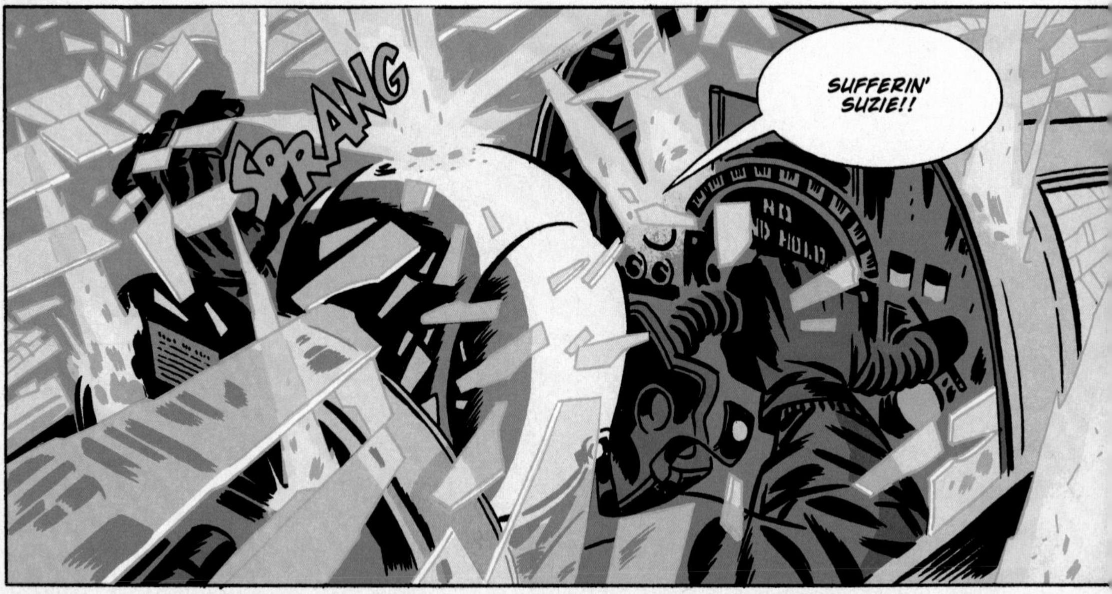
SPRANG
SUFFERIN' SUZIE!!

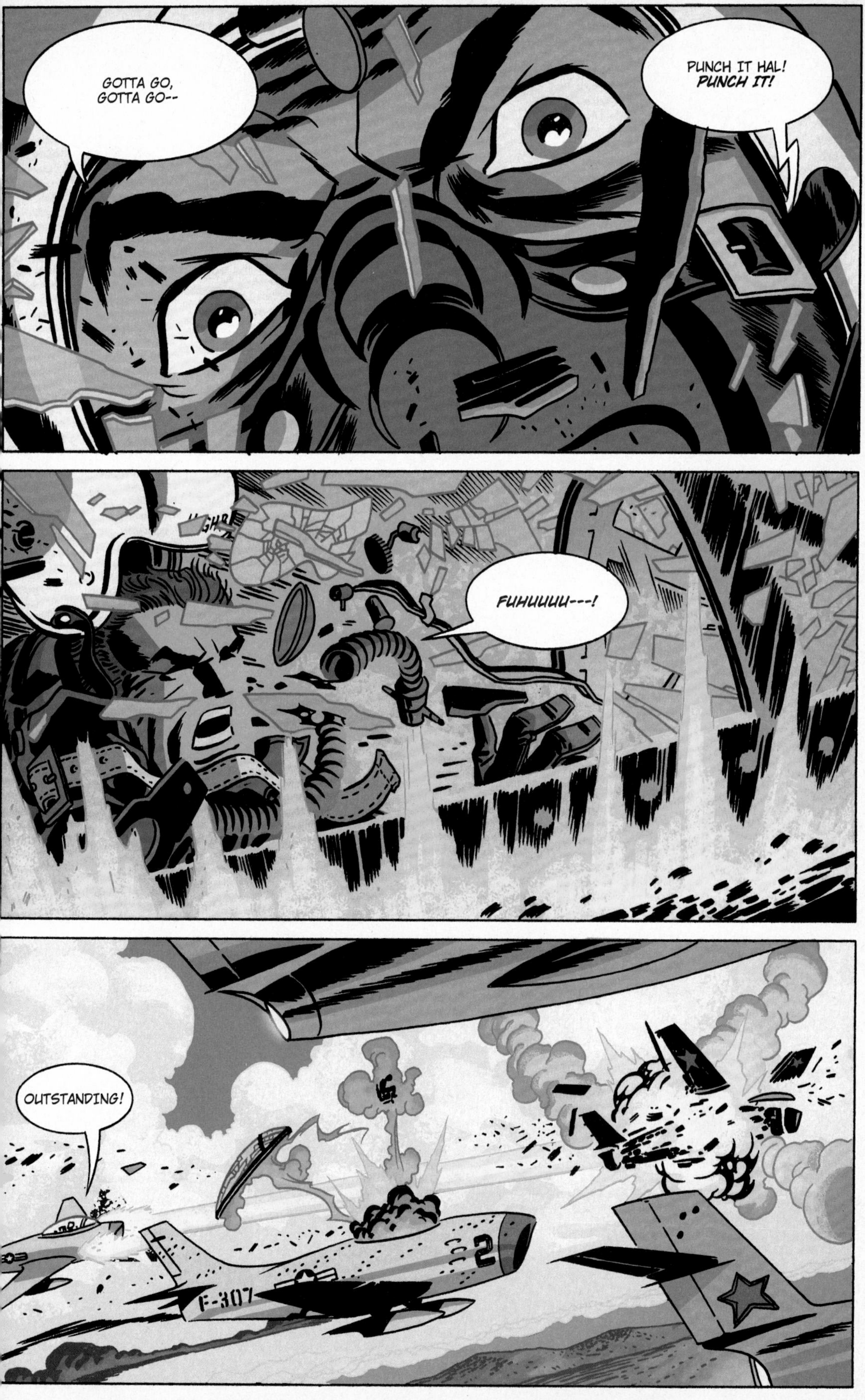
GOTTA GO,
GOTTA GO--
PUNCH IT HAL!
PUNCH IT!
FUHUUUU---!
OUTSTANDING!
F-307

Although Airman Jordan had successfully ejected from his aircraft, he became unable to activate his parachute.

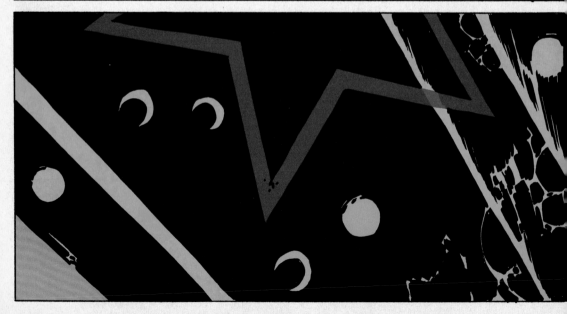

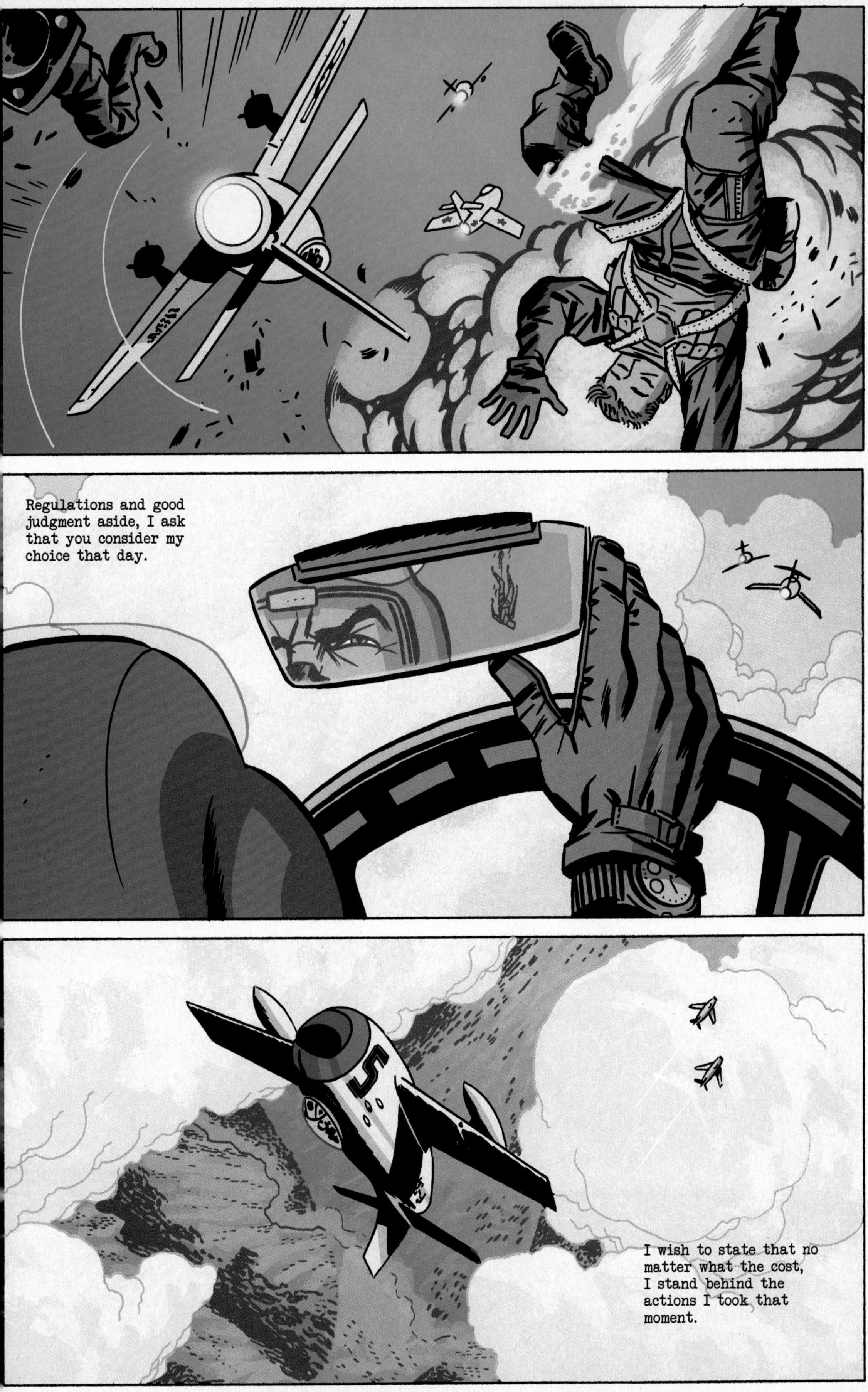
Regulations and good judgment aside, I ask that you consider my choice that day.
I wish to state that no matter what the cost, I stand behind the actions I took that moment.

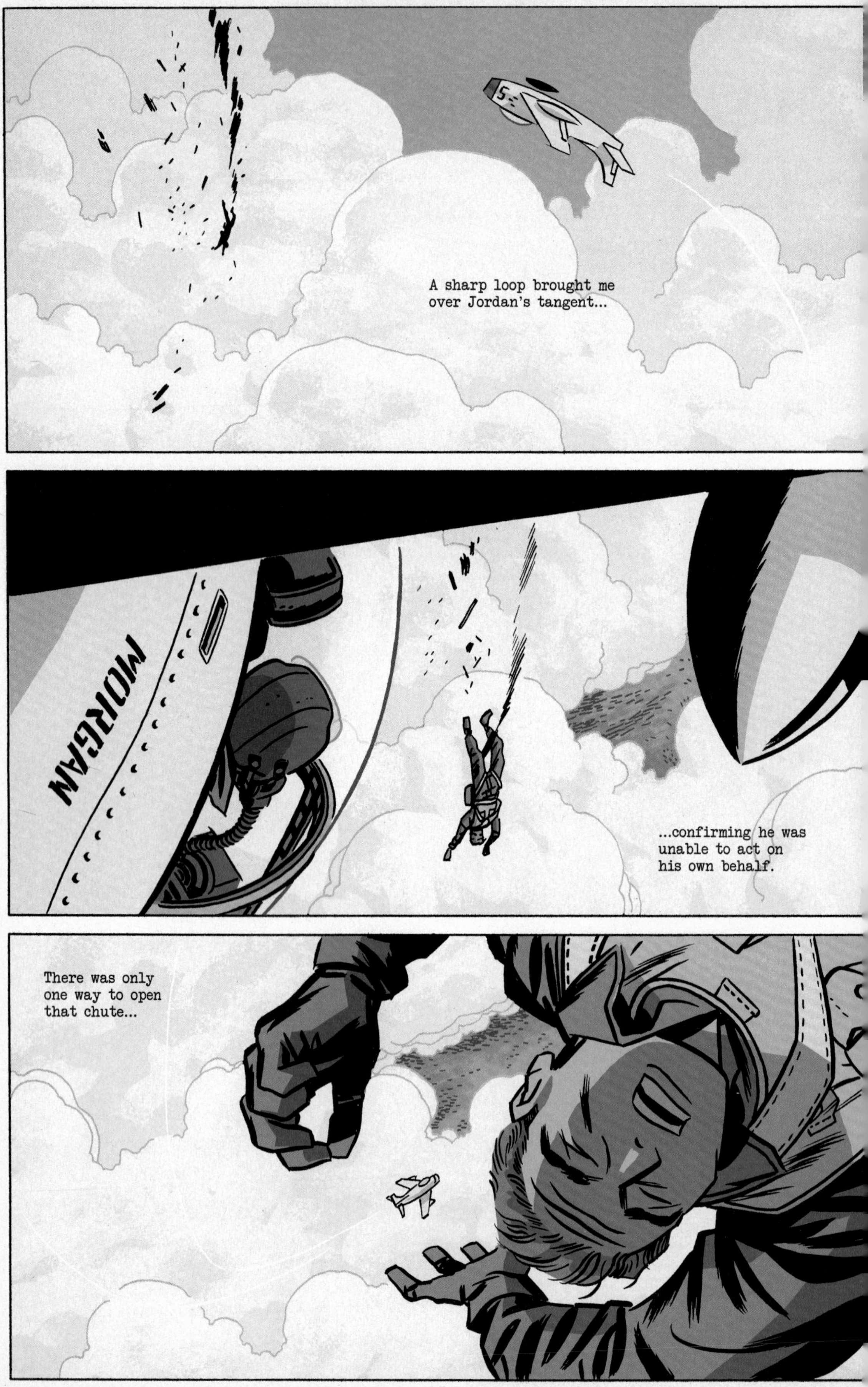
A sharp loop brought me over Jordan's tangent...
MORGAN
...confirming he was unable to act on his own behalf.
There was only one way to open that chute...

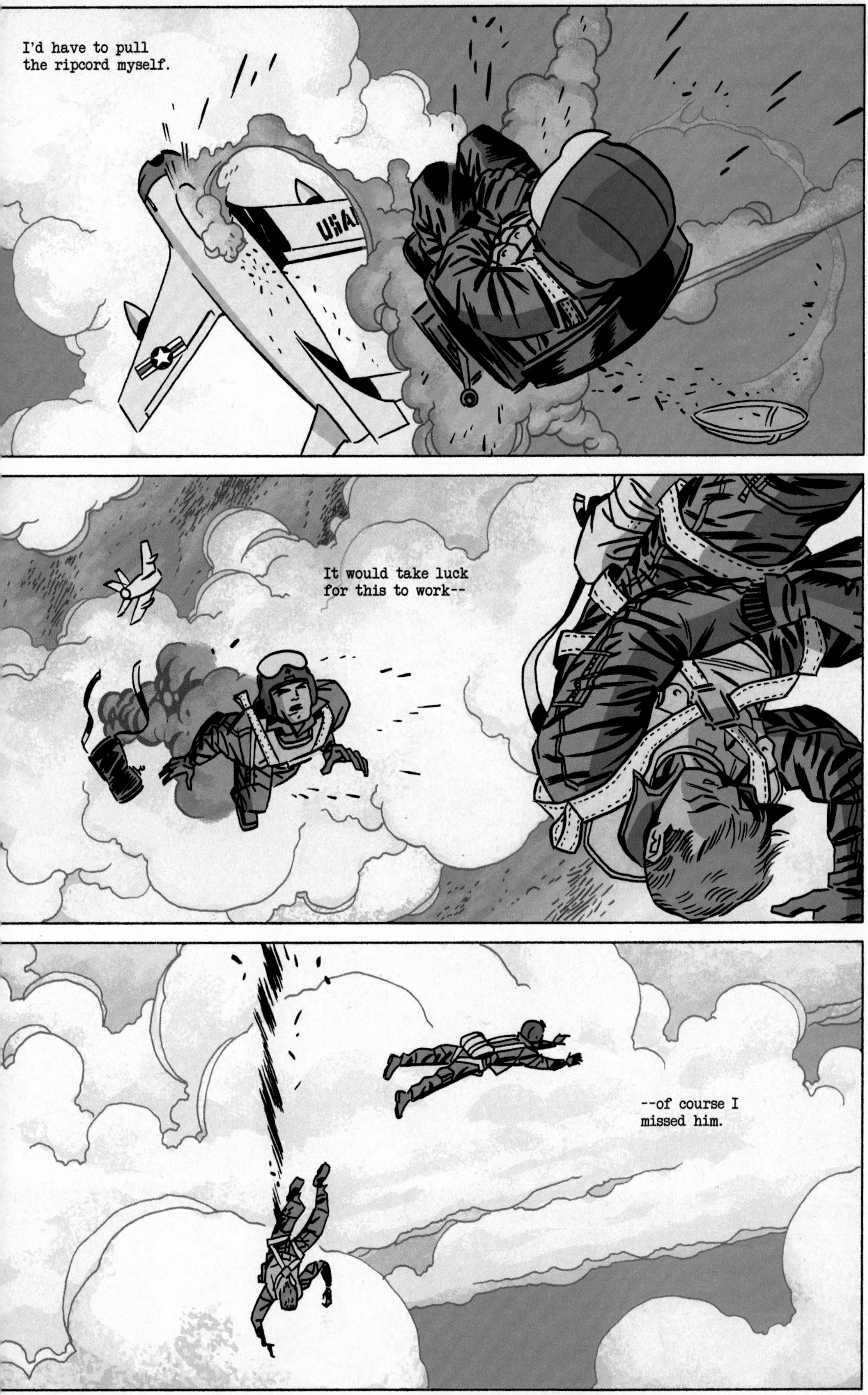

I'd have to pull the ripcord myself.
It would take luck for this to work--
--of course I missed him.

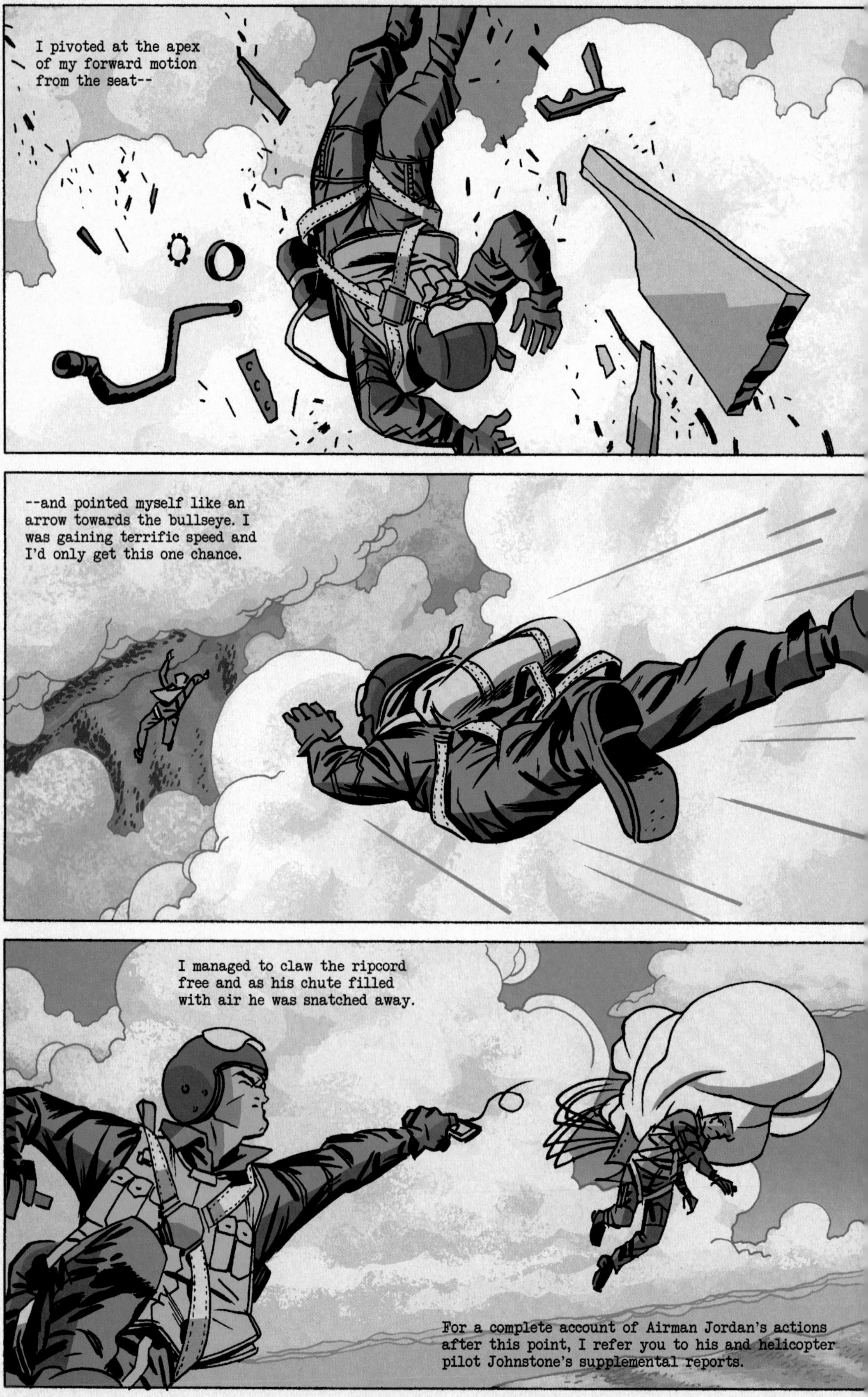
I pivoted at the apex of my forward motion from the seat--
--and pointed myself like an arrow towards the bullseye. I was gaining terrific speed and I'd only get this one chance.
I managed to claw the ripcord free and as his chute filled with air he was snatched away.
For a complete account of Airman Jordan's actions after this point, I refer you to his and helicopter pilot Johnstone's supplemental reports.

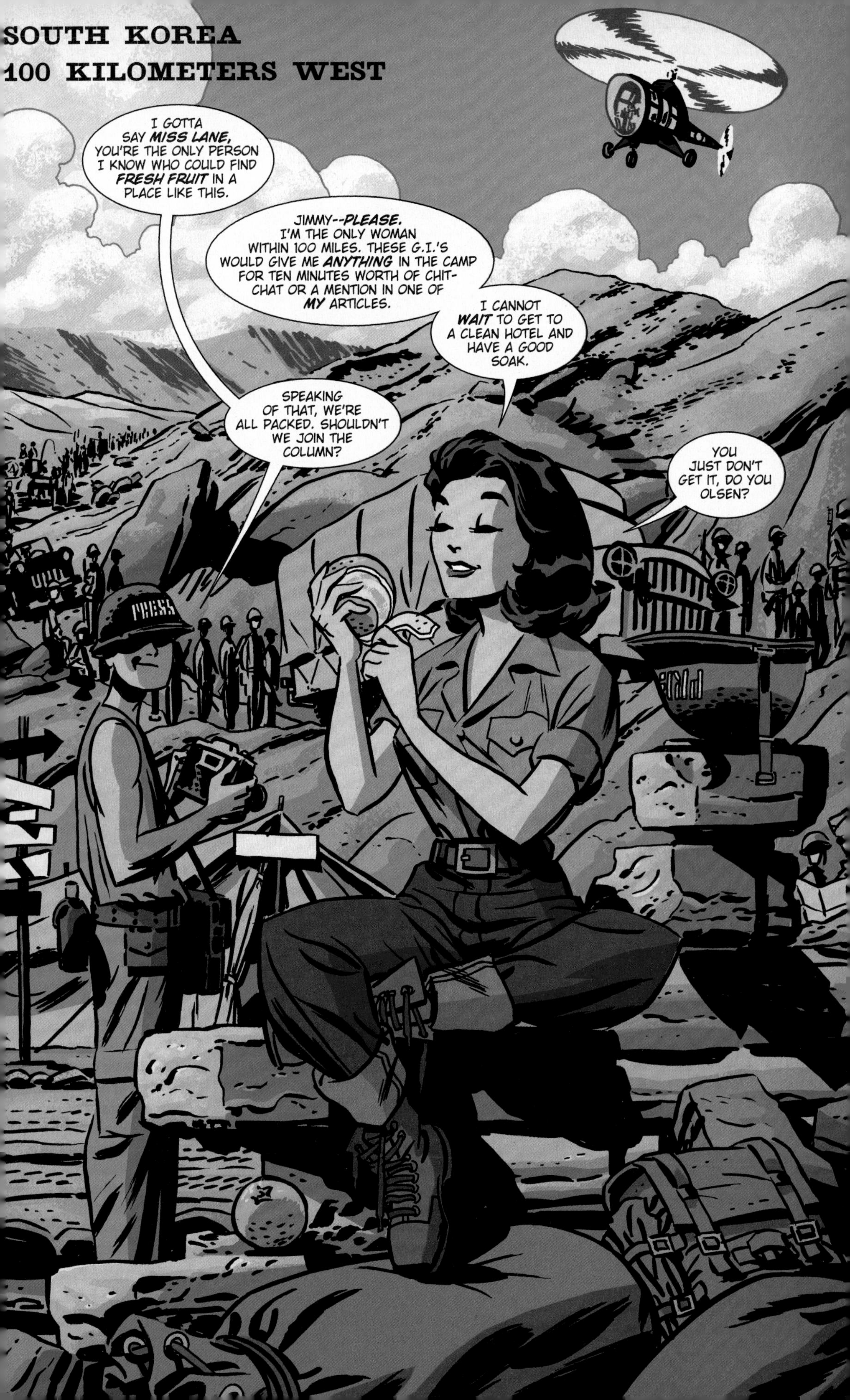
SOUTH KOREA
100 KILOMETERS WEST
I GOTTA SAY MISS LANE, YOU'RE THE ONLY PERSON I KNOW WHO COULD FIND FRESH FRUIT IN A PLACE LIKE THIS.
JIMMY--PLEASE. I'M THE ONLY WOMAN WITHIN 100 MILES. THESE G.I.'S WOULD GIVE ME ANYTHING IN THE CAMP FOR TEN MINUTES WORTH OF CHIT-CHAT OR A MENTION IN ONE OF MY ARTICLES.
I CANNOT WAIT TO GET TO A CLEAN HOTEL AND HAVE A GOOD SOAK.
SPEAKING OF THAT, WE'RE ALL PACKED. SHOULDN'T WE JOIN THE COLUMN?
YOU JUST DON'T GET IT, DO YOU OLSEN?
PRESS

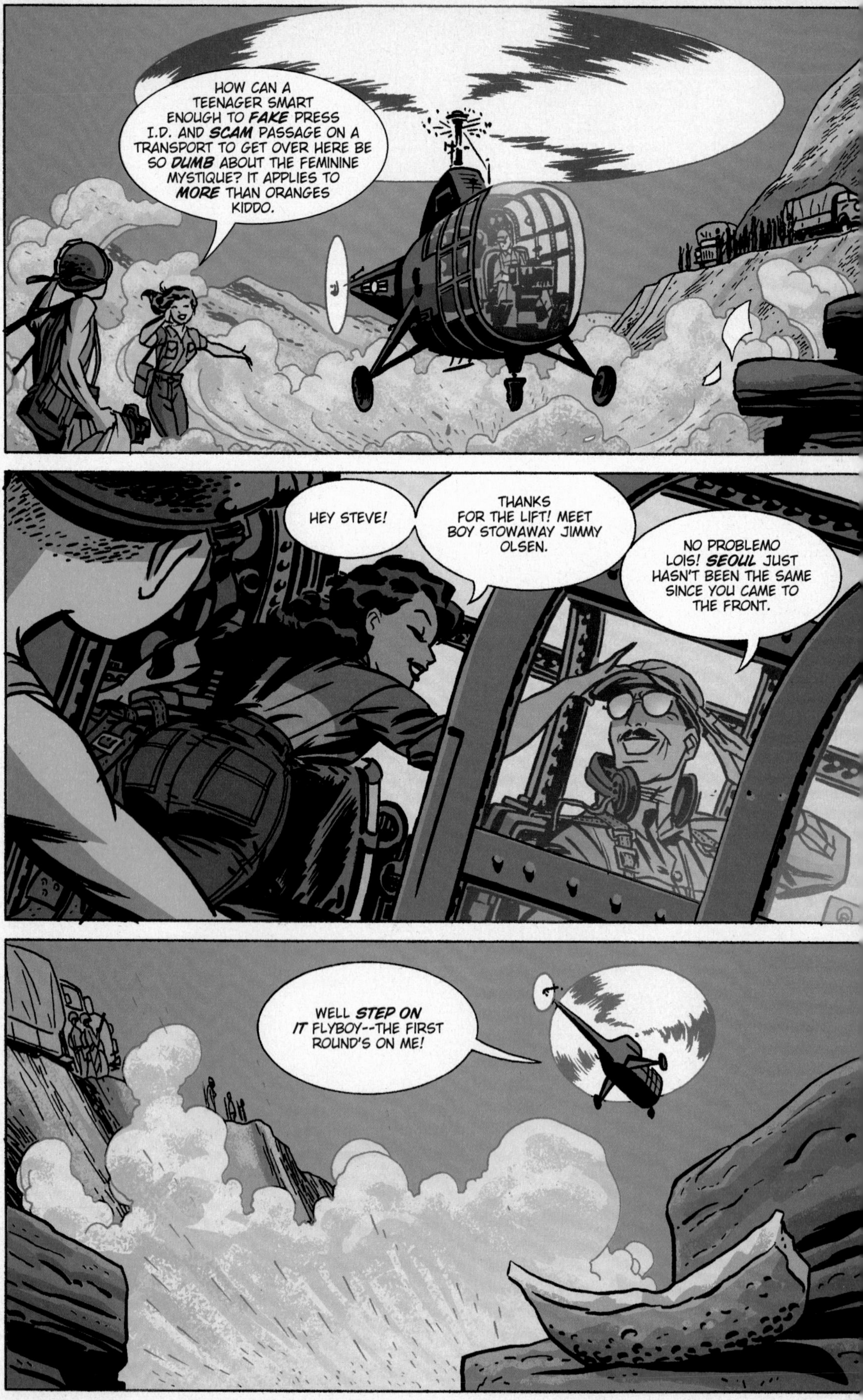
HOW CAN A TEENAGER SMART ENOUGH TO FAKE PRESS I.D. AND SCAM PASSAGE ON A TRANSPORT TO GET OVER HERE BE SO DUMB ABOUT THE FEMININE MYSTIQUE? IT APPLIES TO MORE THAN ORANGES KIDDO.
HEY STEVE!
THANKS FOR THE LIFT! MEET BOY STOWAWAY JIMMY OLSEN.
NO PROBLEMO LOIS! SEOUL JUST HASN'T BEEN THE SAME SINCE YOU CAME TO THE FRONT.
WELL STEP ON IT FLYBOY--THE FIRST ROUND'S ON ME!

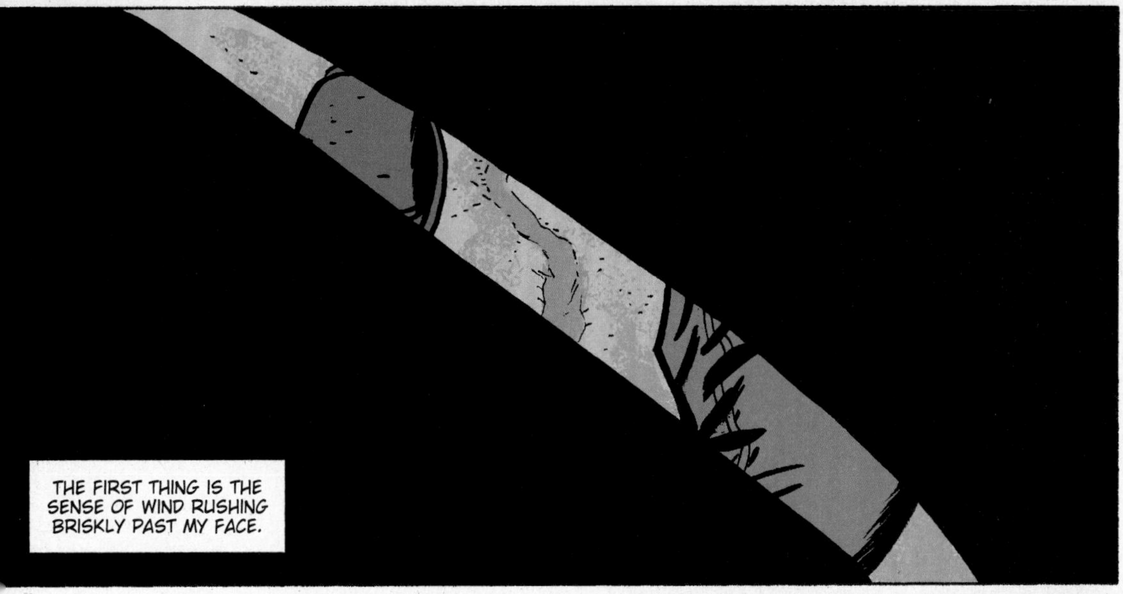
THE FIRST THING IS THE SENSE OF WIND RUSHING BRISKLY PAST MY FACE.

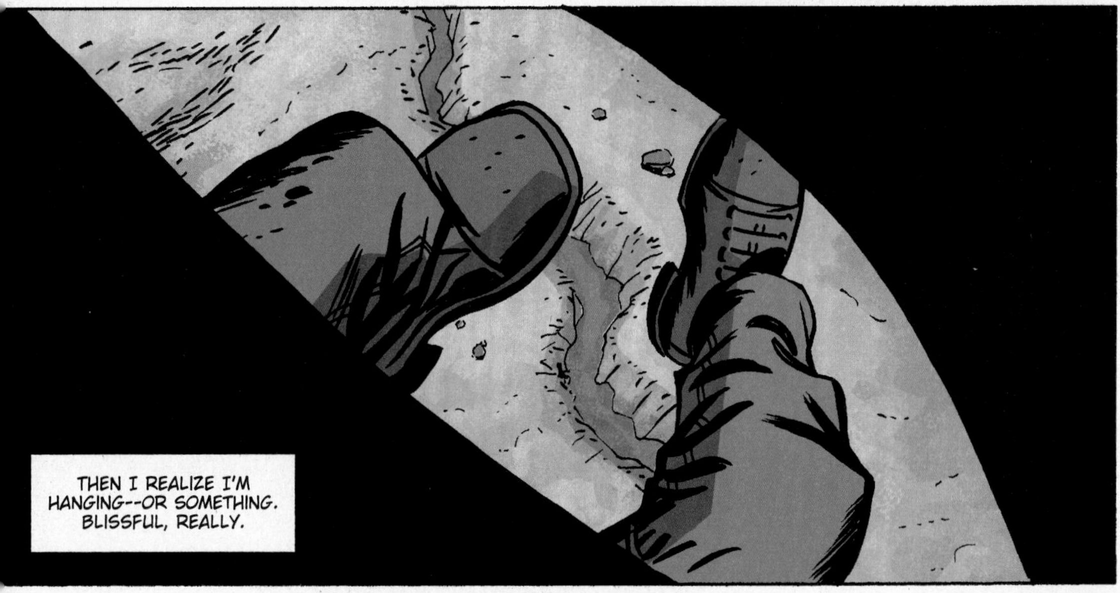
THEN I REALIZE I'M HANGING--OR SOMETHING. BLISSFUL, REALLY.

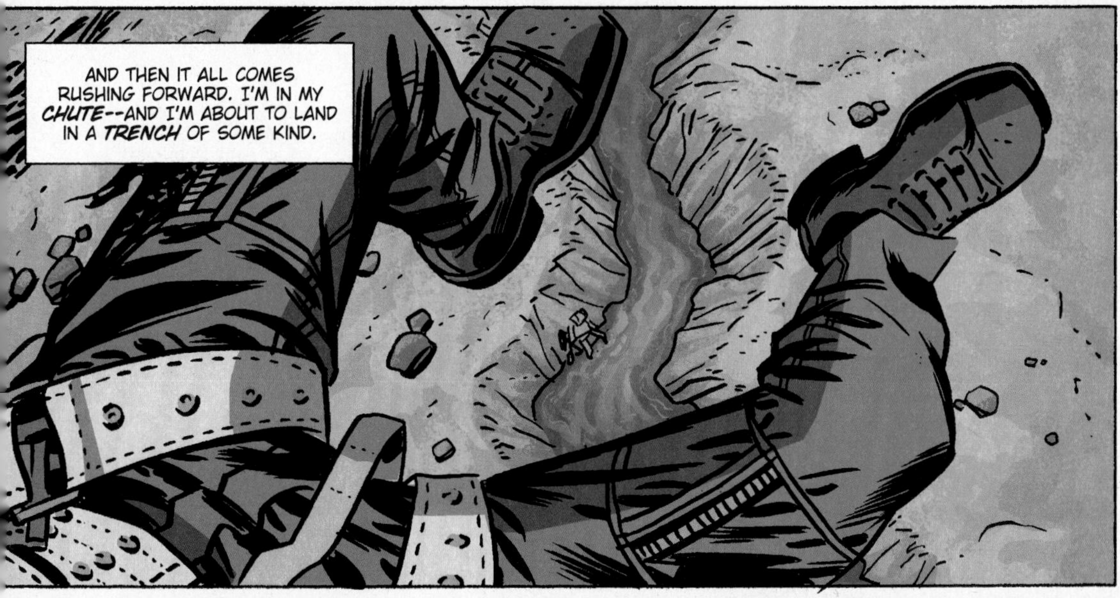
AND THEN IT ALL COMES RUSHING FORWARD. I'M IN MY *CHUTE*--AND I'M ABOUT TO LAND IN A *TRENCH* OF SOME KIND.

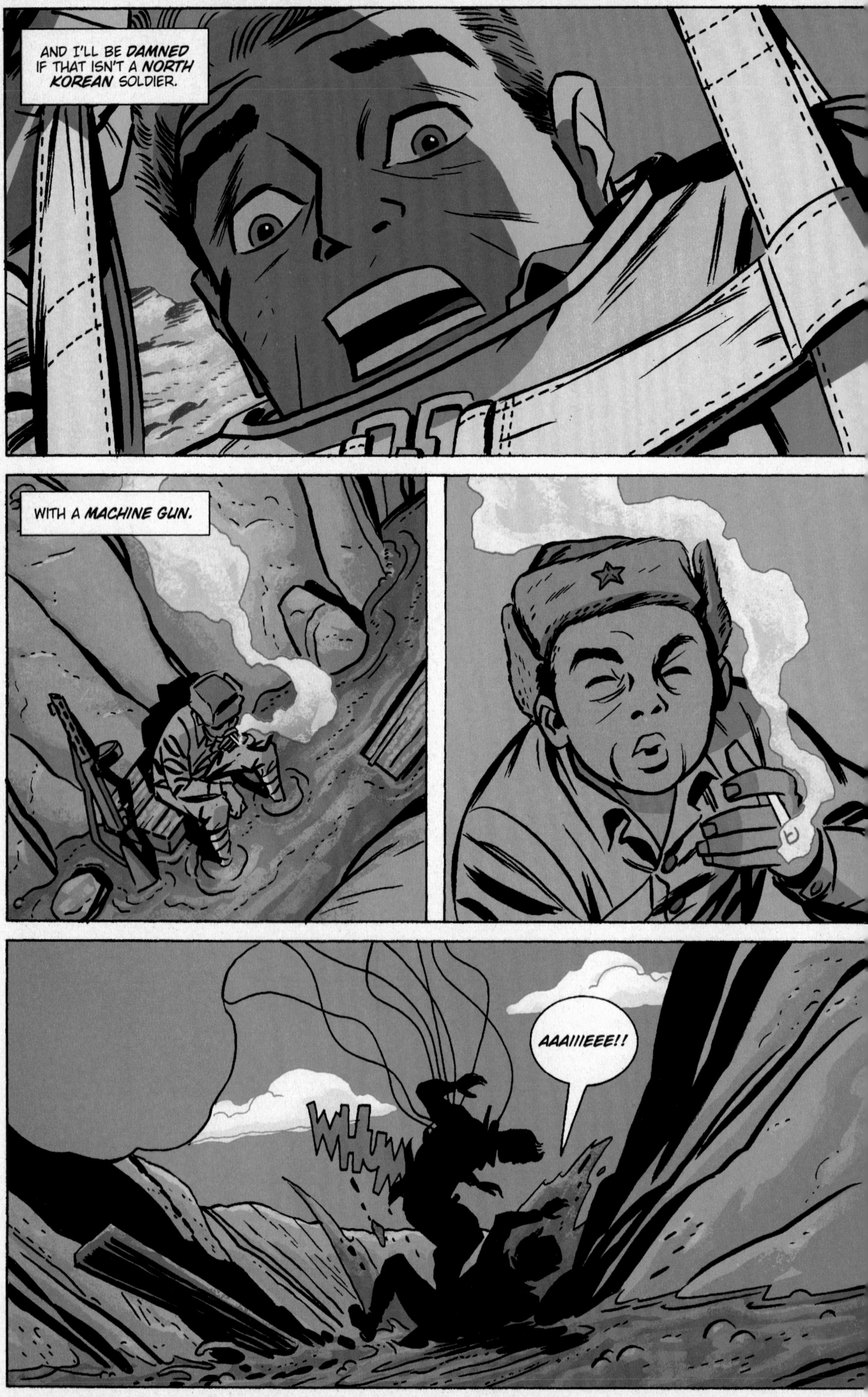
AND I'LL BE DAMNED IF THAT ISN'T A NORTH KOREAN SOLDIER.
WITH A MACHINE GUN.
AAAIIIEEE!!
WHUM

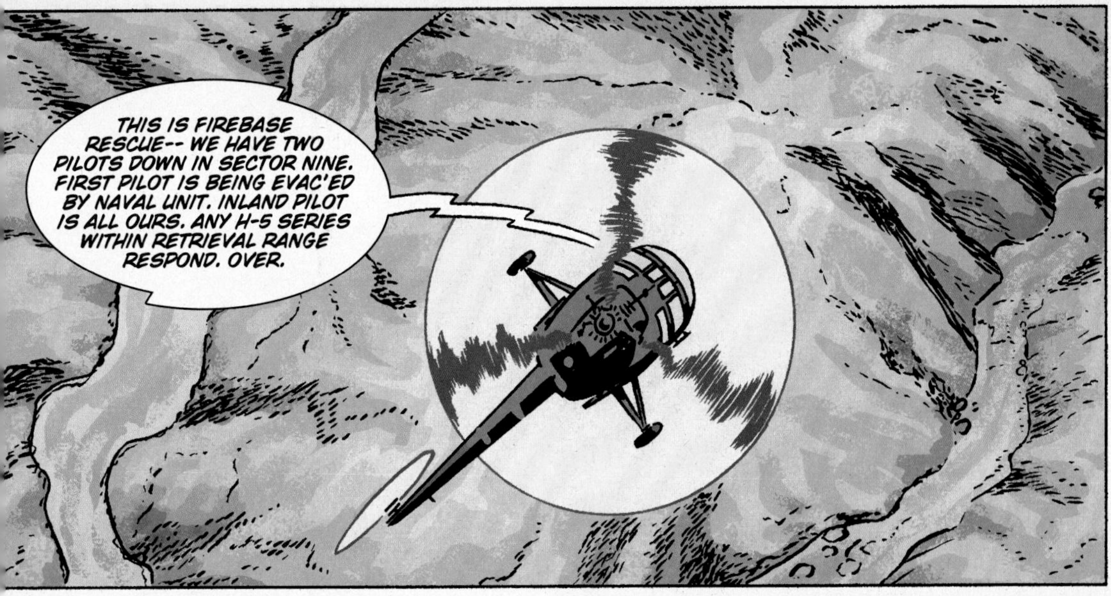
THIS IS FIREBASE RESCUE-- WE HAVE TWO PILOTS DOWN IN SECTOR NINE. FIRST PILOT IS BEING EVAC'ED BY NAVAL UNIT. INLAND PILOT IS ALL OURS. ANY H-5 SERIES WITHIN RETRIEVAL RANGE RESPOND. OVER.

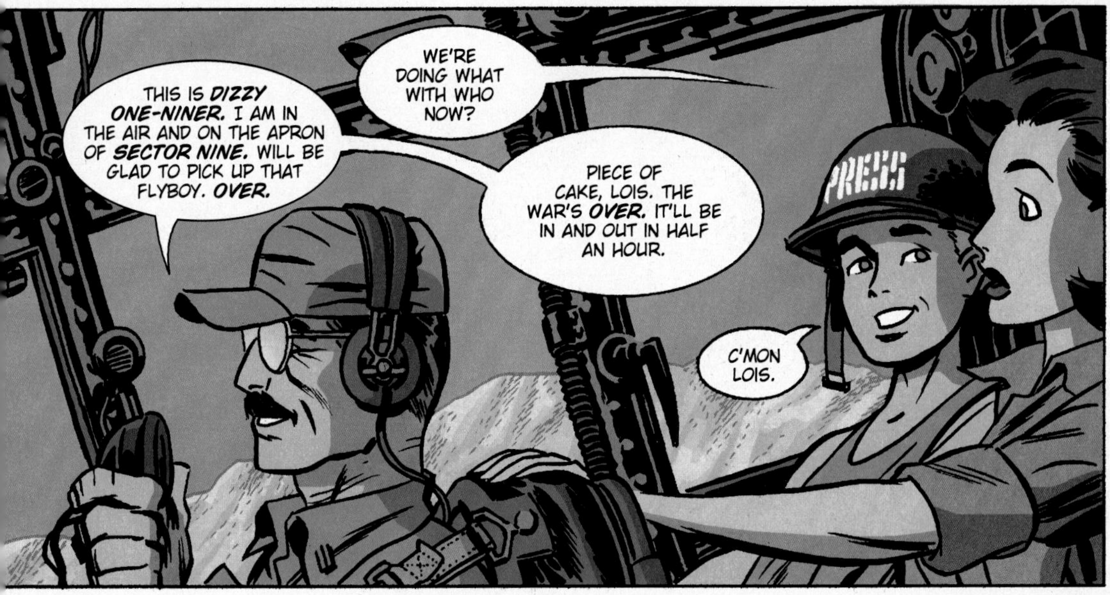
THIS IS DIZZY ONE-NINER. I AM IN THE AIR AND ON THE APRON OF SECTOR NINE. WILL BE GLAD TO PICK UP THAT FLYBOY. OVER.
WE'RE DOING WHAT WITH WHO NOW?
PIECE OF CAKE, LOIS. THE WAR'S OVER. IT'LL BE IN AND OUT IN HALF AN HOUR.
PRESS
C'MON LOIS.

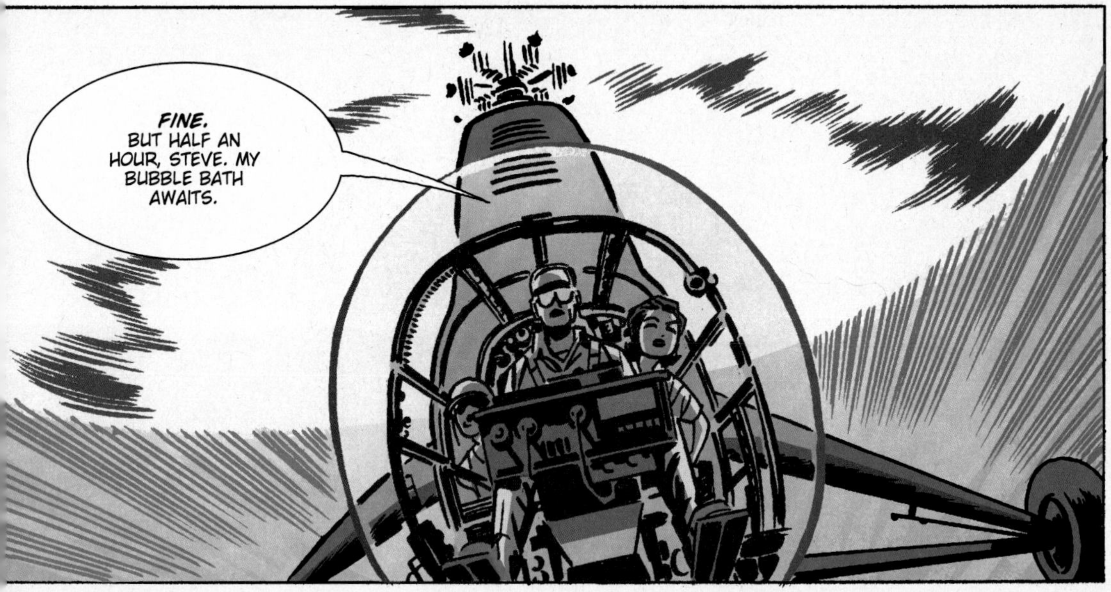
FINE. BUT HALF AN HOUR, STEVE. MY BUBBLE BATH AWAITS.

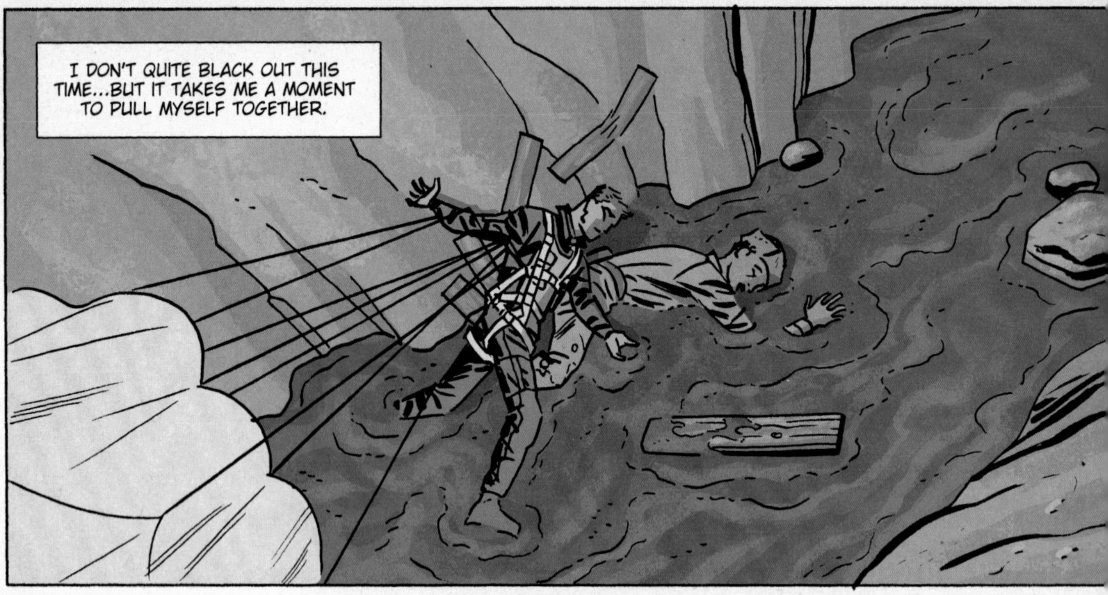
I DON'T QUITE BLACK OUT THIS TIME...BUT IT TAKES ME A MOMENT TO PULL MYSELF TOGETHER.

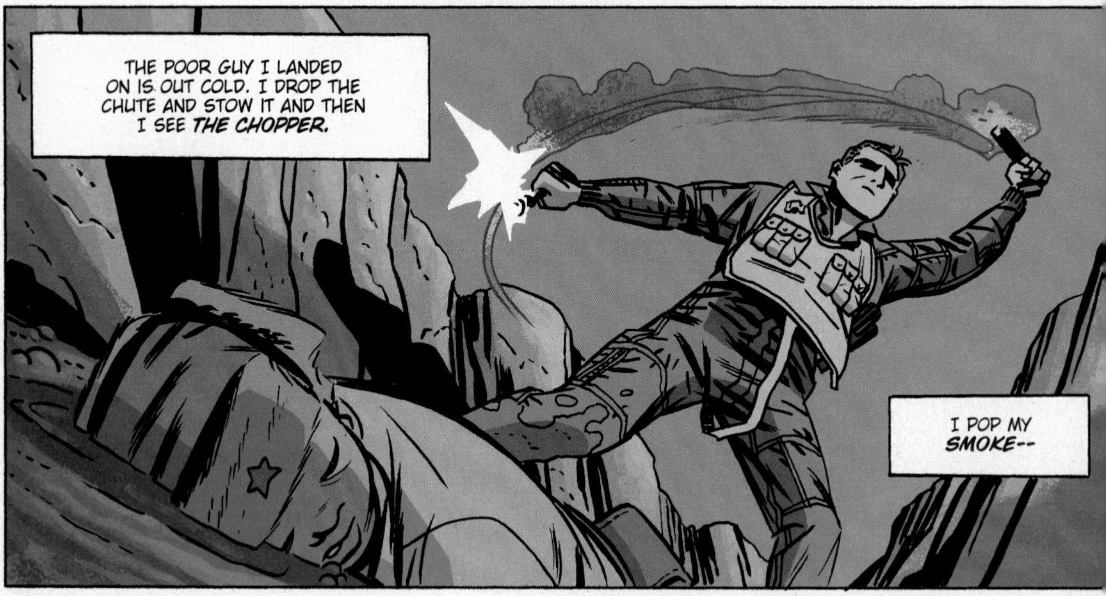
THE POOR GUY I LANDED ON IS OUT COLD. I DROP THE CHUTE AND STOW IT AND THEN I SEE *THE CHOPPER.*
I POP MY *SMOKE--*

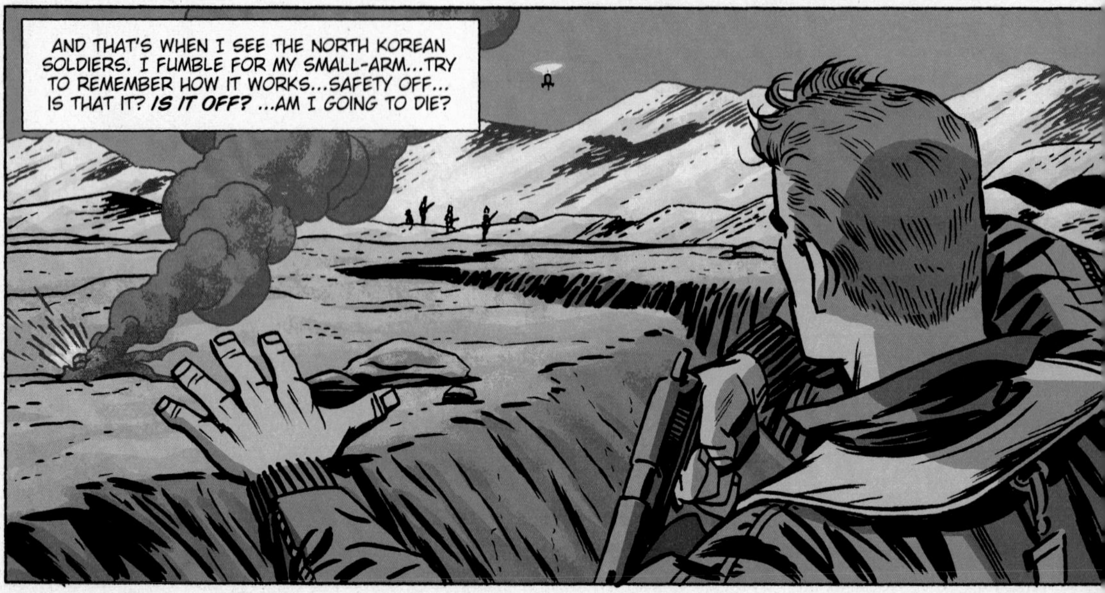
AND THAT'S WHEN I SEE THE NORTH KOREAN SOLDIERS. I FUMBLE FOR MY SMALL-ARM...TRY TO REMEMBER HOW IT WORKS...SAFETY OFF... IS THAT IT? *IS IT OFF?* ...AM I GOING TO DIE?

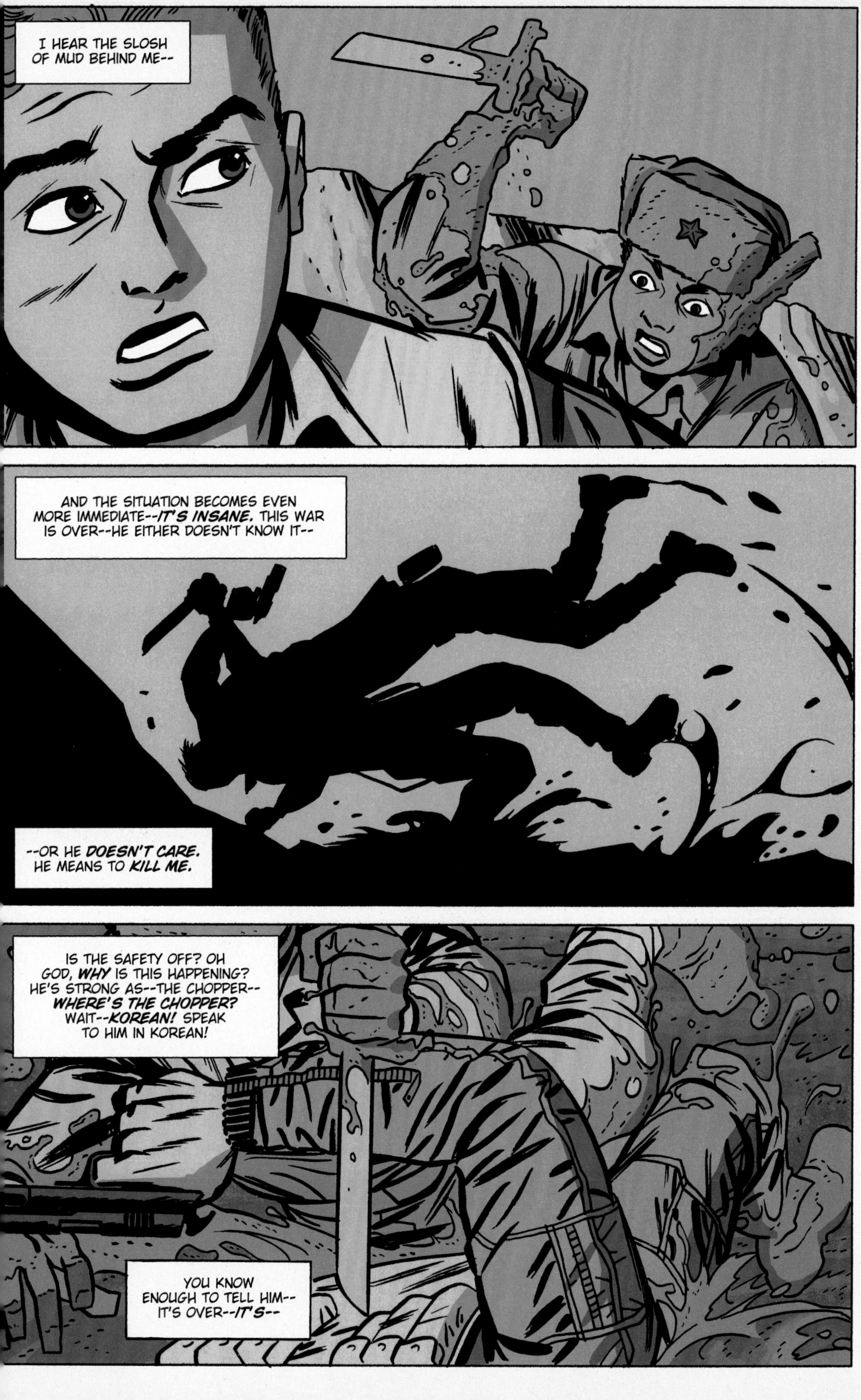
I HEAR THE SLOSH OF MUD BEHIND ME--
AND THE SITUATION BECOMES EVEN MORE IMMEDIATE--*IT'S INSANE.* THIS WAR IS OVER--HE EITHER DOESN'T KNOW IT--
--OR HE *DOESN'T CARE.* HE MEANS TO *KILL ME.*
IS THE SAFETY OFF? OH GOD, *WHY* IS THIS HAPPENING? HE'S STRONG AS--THE CHOPPER-- *WHERE'S THE CHOPPER?* WAIT--*KOREAN!* SPEAK TO HIM IN KOREAN!
YOU KNOW ENOUGH TO TELL HIM-- IT'S OVER--*IT'S*--

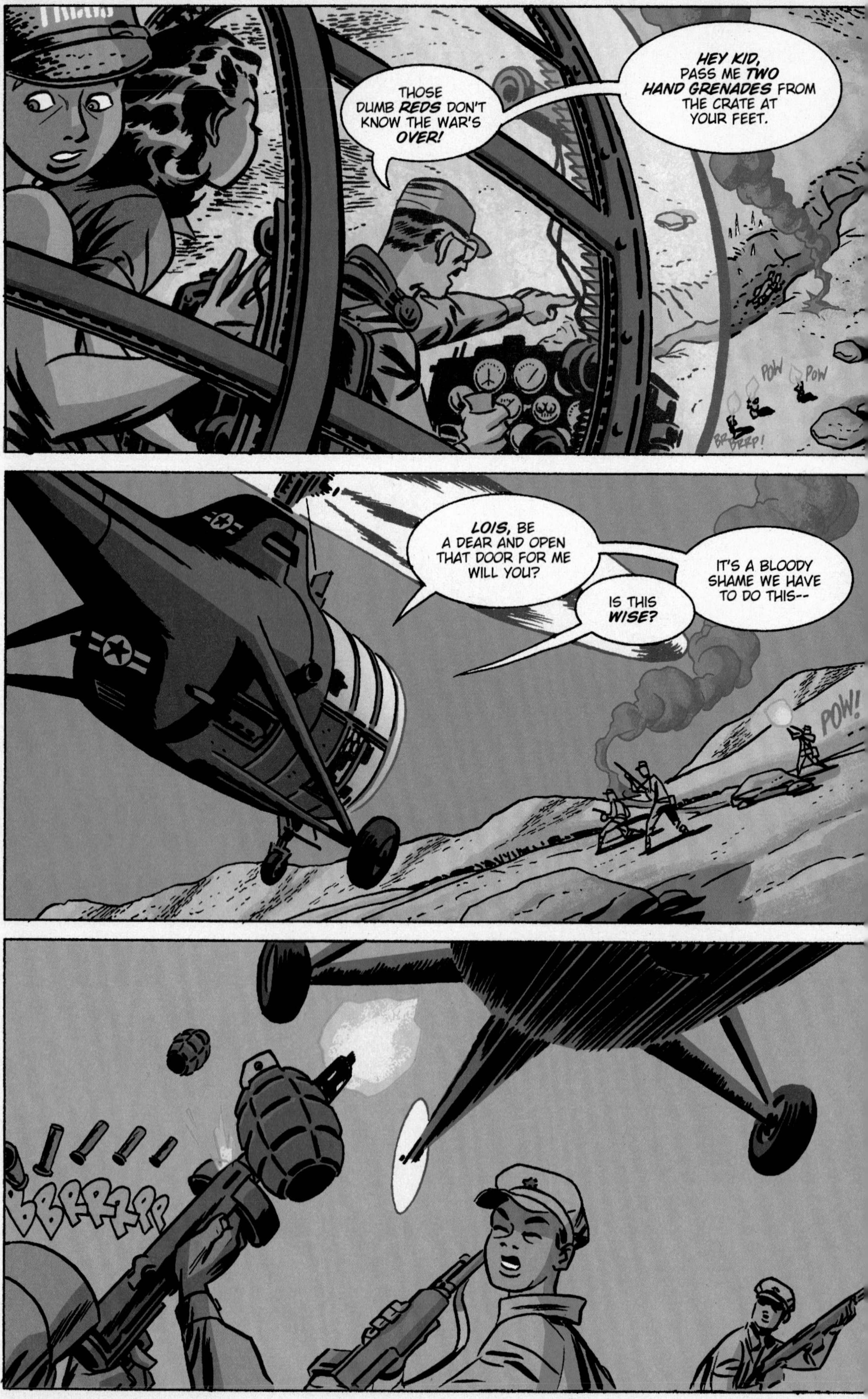
THOSE DUMB REDS DON'T KNOW THE WAR'S OVER!
HEY KID, PASS ME TWO HAND GRENADES FROM THE CRATE AT YOUR FEET.
POW
POW
BR BRRP!
LOIS, BE A DEAR AND OPEN THAT DOOR FOR ME WILL YOU?
IT'S A BLOODY SHAME WE HAVE TO DO THIS--
IS THIS WISE?
POW!

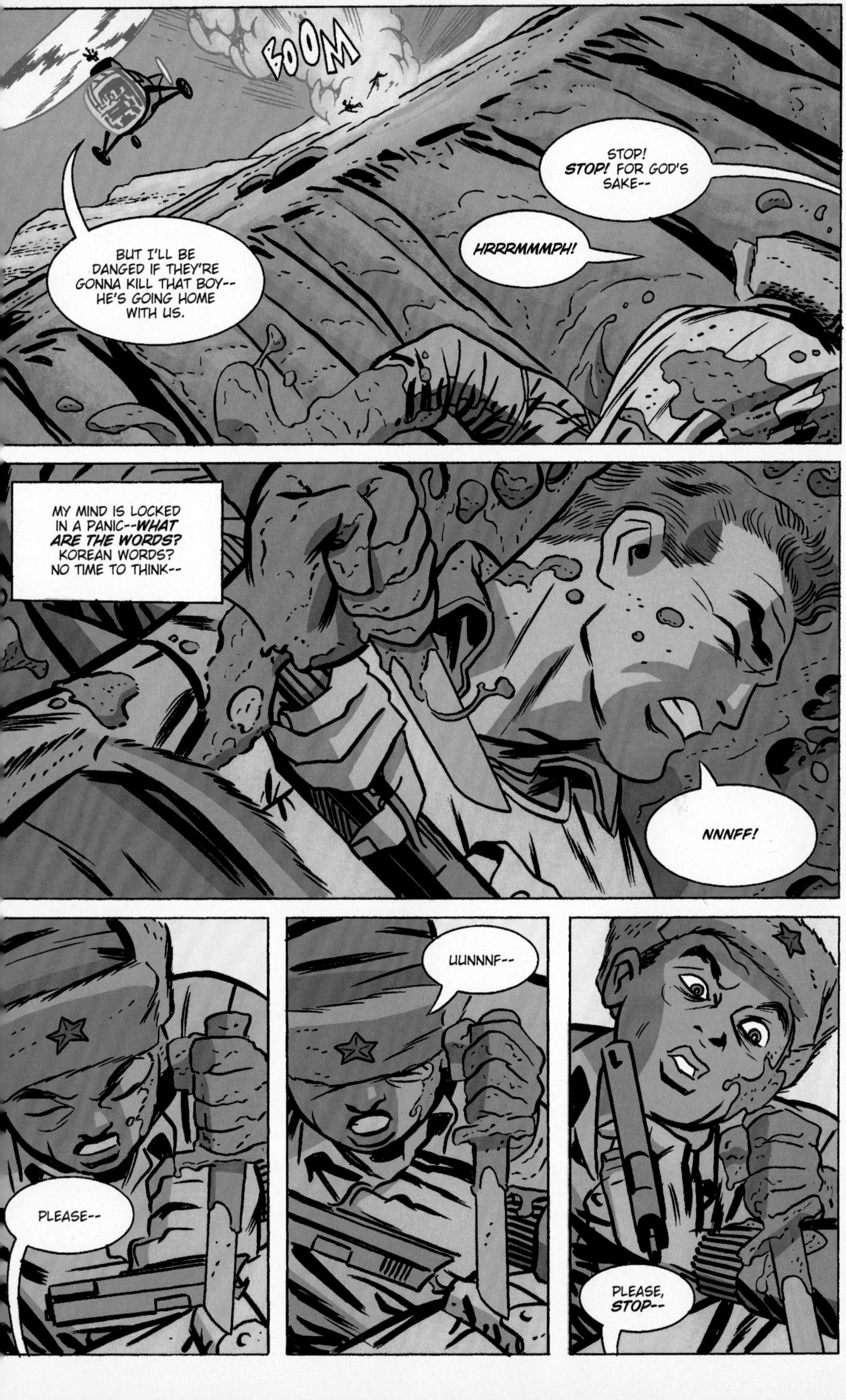
BOOM
STOP! STOP! FOR GOD'S SAKE--
HRRRMMMPH!
BUT I'LL BE DANGED IF THEY'RE GONNA KILL THAT BOY-- HE'S GOING HOME WITH US.
MY MIND IS LOCKED IN A PANIC--WHAT ARE THE WORDS? KOREAN WORDS? NO TIME TO THINK--
NNNFF!
PLEASE--
UUNNNF--
PLEASE, STOP--

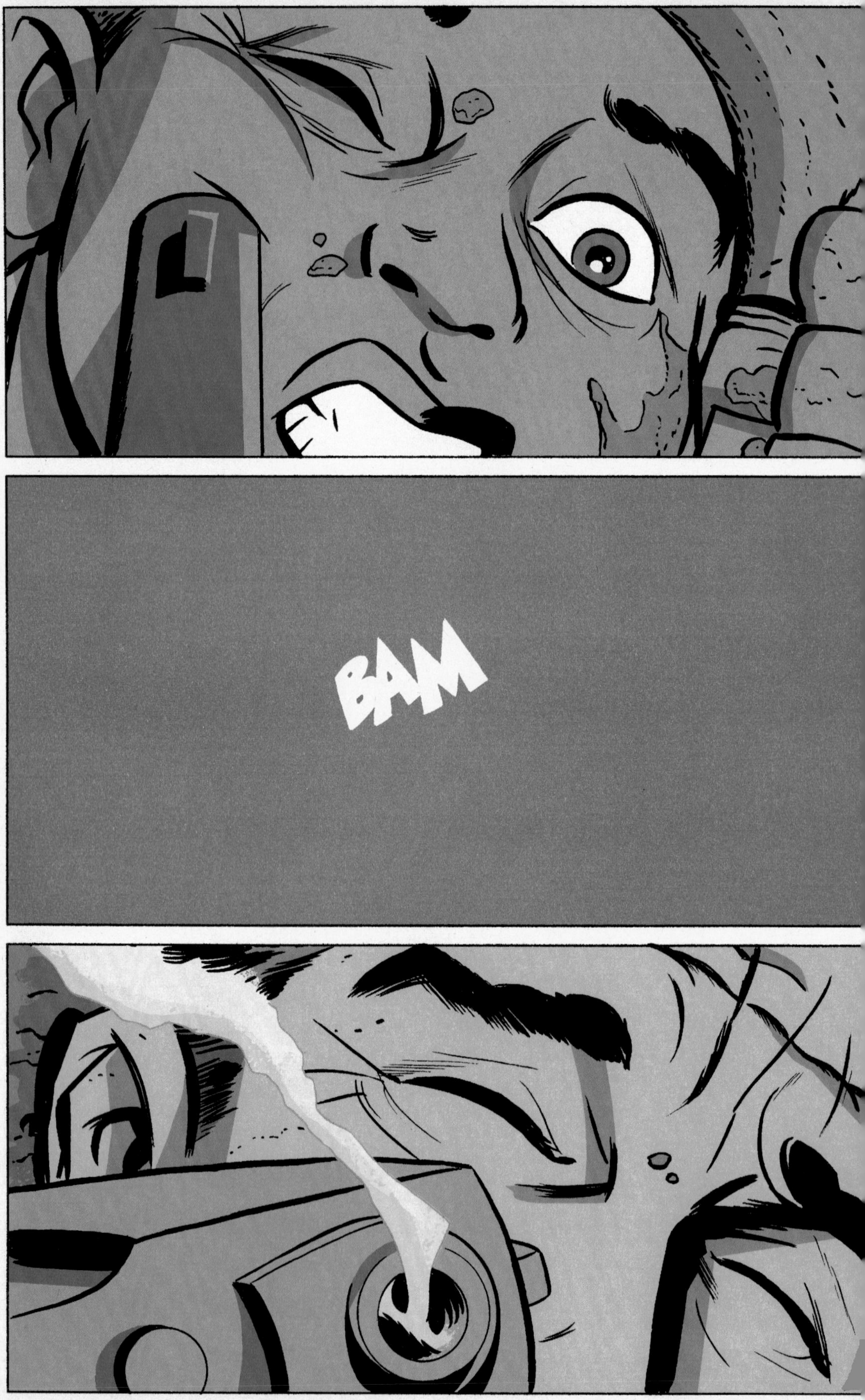
BAM

MY COUNTRY HAS GIVEN ME *EVERYTHING.* FREEDOM, OPPORTUNITY AND THE CHANCE TO *FLY.* I OWE MY COUNTRY *MY LIFE.*

HURRY, JIMMY!

BUT I'VE NEVER FELT I OWE MY COUNTRY THE *LIVES OF OTHERS.* I HAD SWORN TO SERVE MY COUNTRY IN EVERY WAY I CAN *BUT ONE.* I HAVE NOT *KILLED* FOR MY COUNTRY.

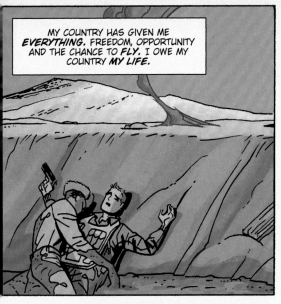

IF ONLY THE KOREAN WORDS HAD COME TO ME--IF ONLY I'D BEEN STRONGER...ALL MY *RIGHTEOUS POSTURING* AND *MORAL CODES...*

BRRRP

ALL OF IT NARROWED DOWN TO THIS FILTHY TRENCH, AND SOMETHING I'D NEVER CONSIDERED.

SURVIVAL.

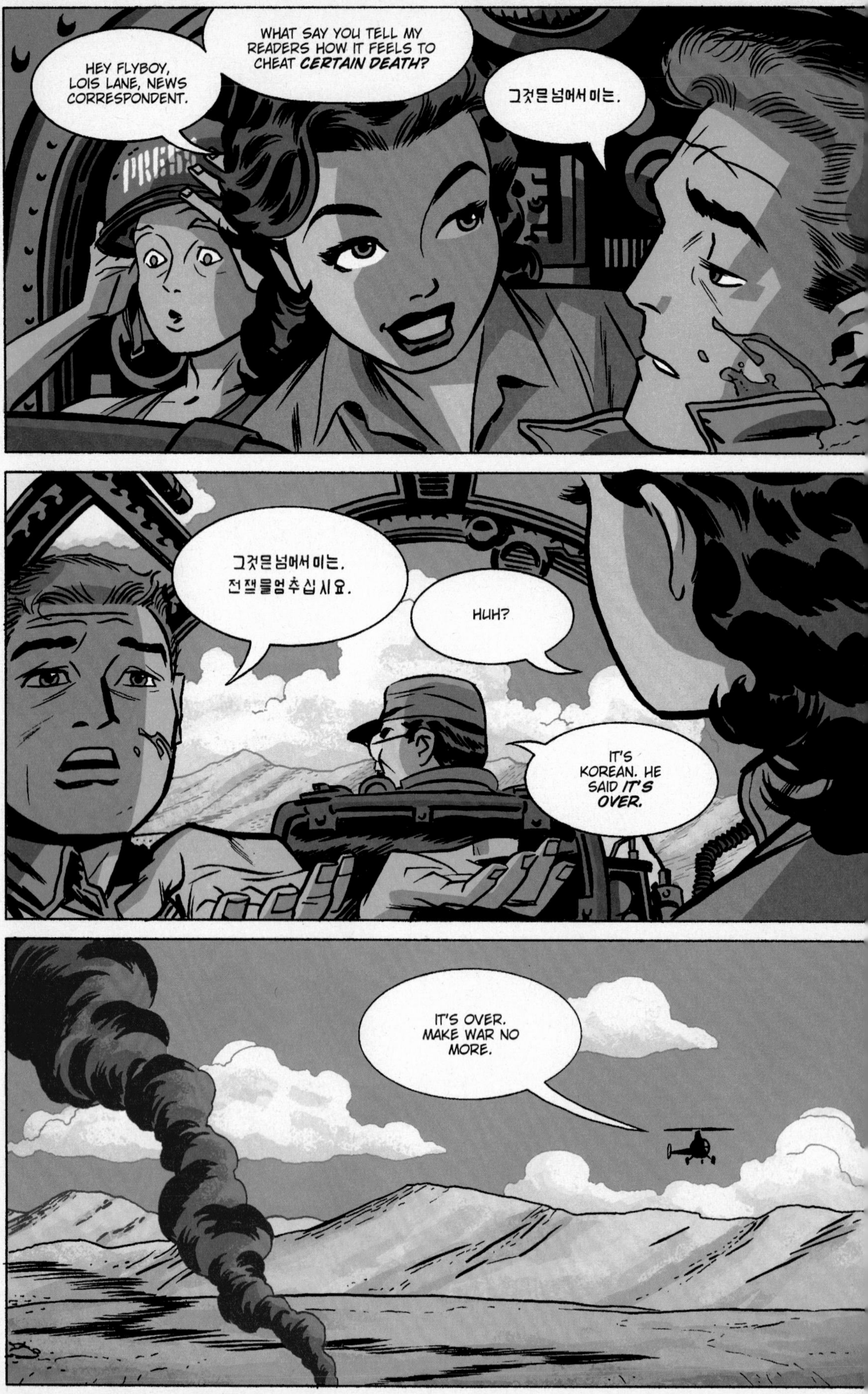
HEY FLYBOY, LOIS LANE, NEWS CORRESPONDENT.
WHAT SAY YOU TELL MY READERS HOW IT FEELS TO CHEAT *CERTAIN DEATH?*
그것은넘어서미는.
그것은넘어서미는. 전잴믈멍추십시요.
HUH?
IT'S KOREAN. HE SAID *IT'S OVER.*
IT'S OVER. MAKE WAR NO MORE.

CHAPTER FOUR
GODS AND MONSTERS

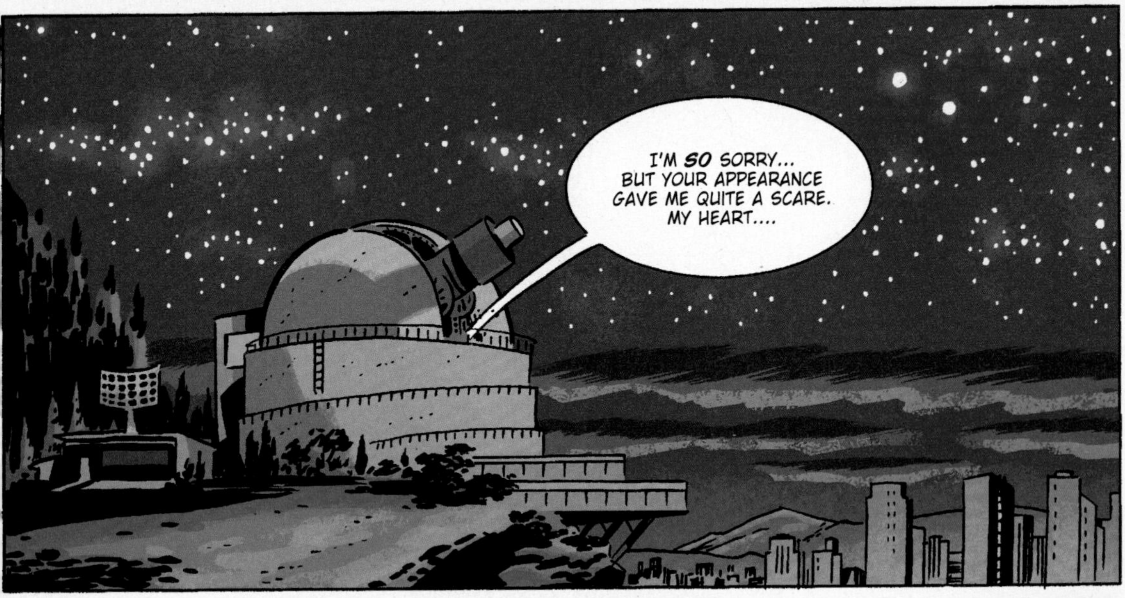
I'M SO SORRY... BUT YOUR APPEARANCE GAVE ME QUITE A SCARE. MY HEART....

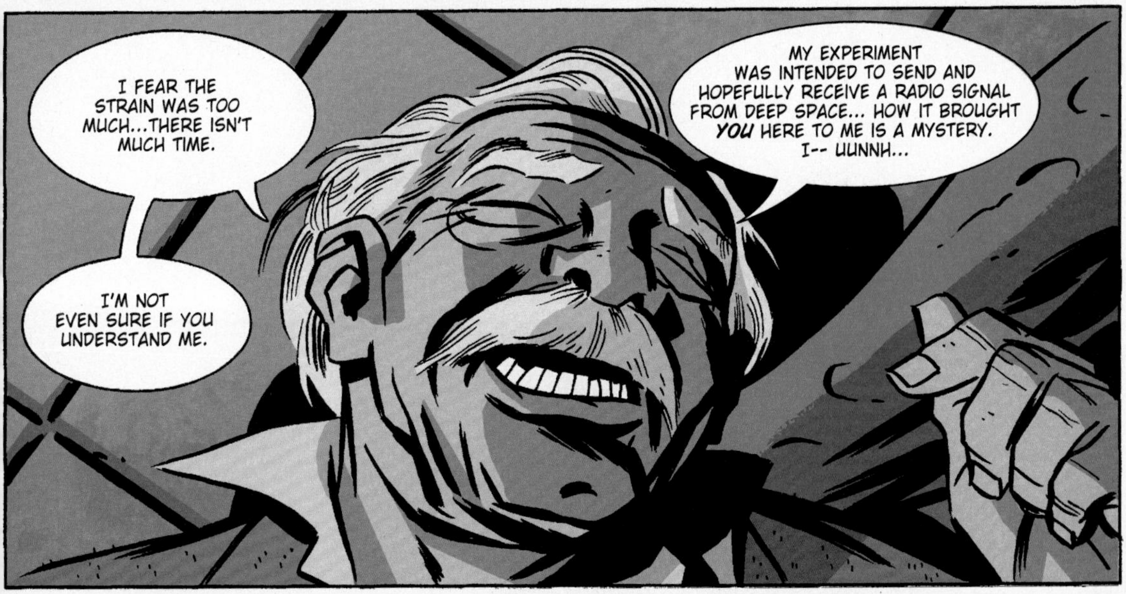
I FEAR THE STRAIN WAS TOO MUCH...THERE ISN'T MUCH TIME.
I'M NOT EVEN SURE IF YOU UNDERSTAND ME.
MY EXPERIMENT WAS INTENDED TO SEND AND HOPEFULLY RECEIVE A RADIO SIGNAL FROM DEEP SPACE... HOW IT BROUGHT YOU HERE TO ME IS A MYSTERY. I-- UUNNH...

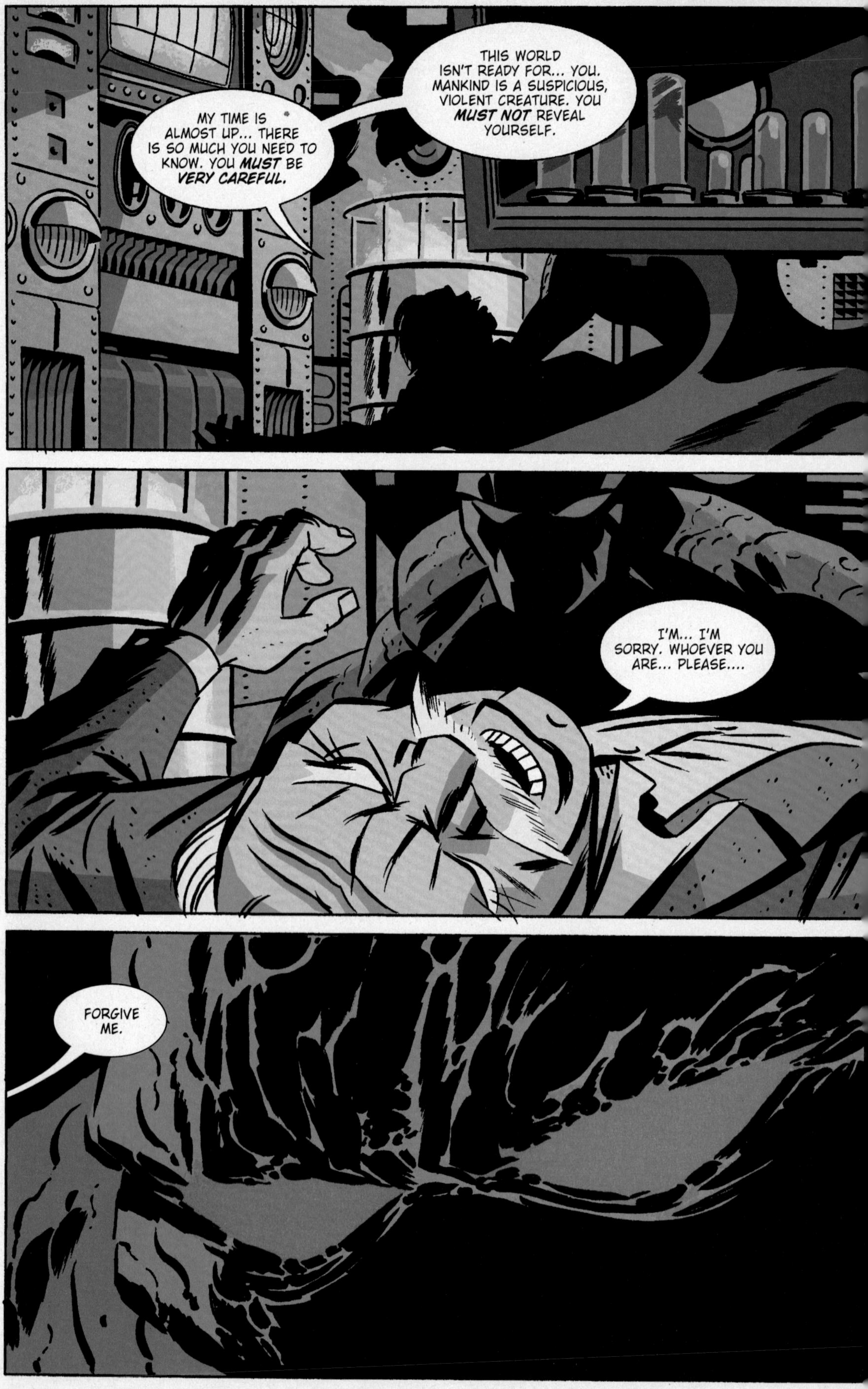
MY TIME IS ALMOST UP... THERE IS SO MUCH YOU NEED TO KNOW. YOU MUST BE VERY CAREFUL.
THIS WORLD ISN'T READY FOR... YOU. MANKIND IS A SUSPICIOUS, VIOLENT CREATURE. YOU MUST NOT REVEAL YOURSELF.
I'M... I'M SORRY. WHOEVER YOU ARE... PLEASE....
FORGIVE ME.

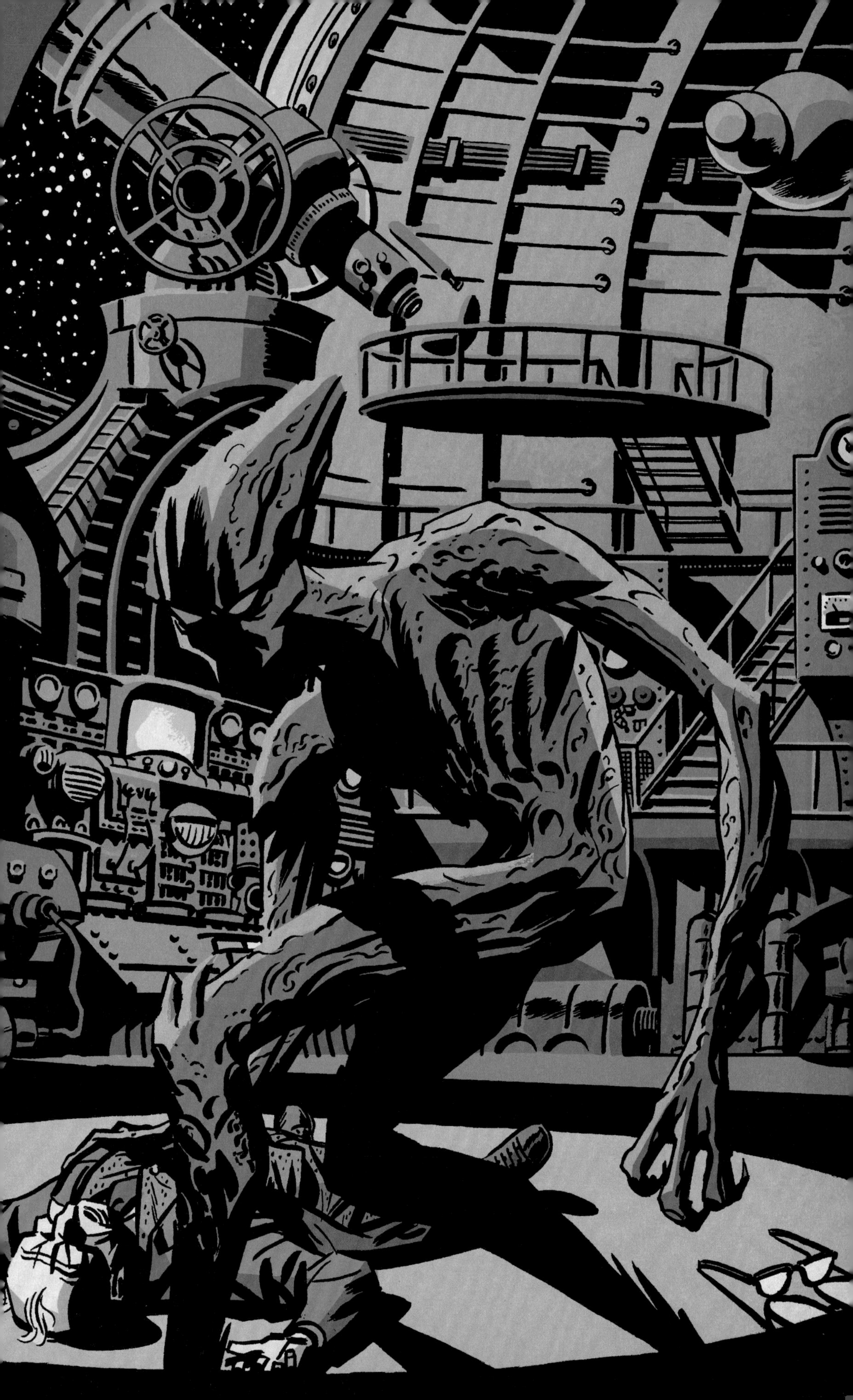

SUPERMAN AND WONDER WOMAN EASE SUFFERING FOR INDO-CHINA

AMERICA OFFERS RELIEF TO WAR-TORN REGION

By Clark Kent

Fighting continues in the nation known as Indo-China. The French forces that govern the region have sustained heavy losses from rebel forces in the North, led by the charismatic Ho Chi Minh. It is believed that the Communist Russians and Chinese have been funding and arming the rebels, in an attempt to gain control over Indo-China and strengthen the Communist foothold in the Far East. UN condemnation has done nothing to ease the tensions between these two factions and the ___ government has requested

"although we have no interest in becoming involved with the conflict in the East, we do feel a humanitarian responsibility to help those people whose lives are being destroyed by this conflict. To that end, both Superman and Wonder Woman are involved in relief efforts in Indo-China. This administration would like to stress that their mission is humanitarian, not military, in nature."

As the fighting escalates and the French position becomes more desperate, the question remains whether America ___ in another

PHOTO: James Olsen

WONDER WOMAN: Winning the hearts and minds of the disenfranchised.

MY GOD... WHAT KIND OF *PEOPLE* ARE THESE?

THIS ISN'T WAR. IT'S... BUTCHERY.

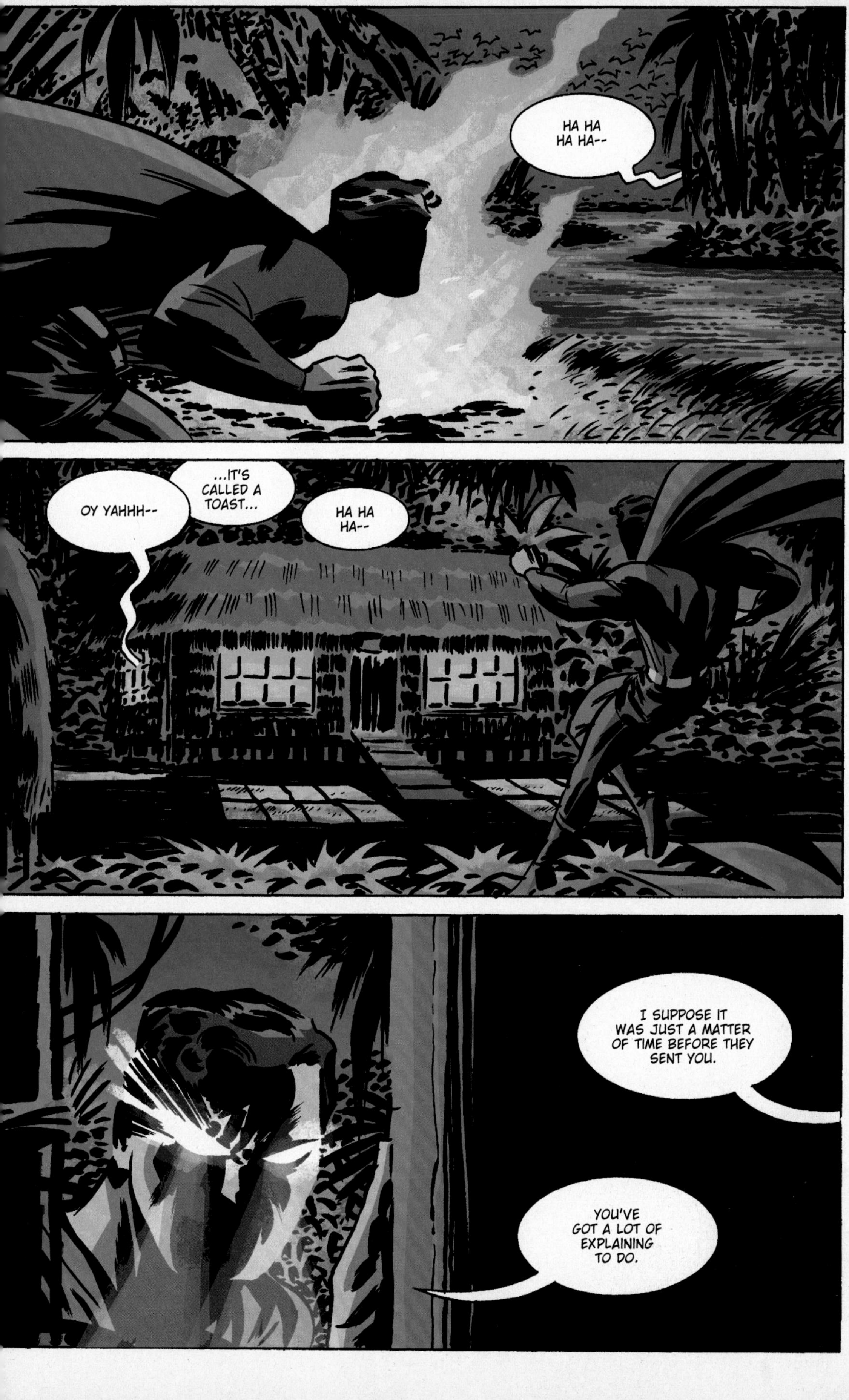
HA HA HA HA--
OY YAHHH--
...IT'S CALLED A TOAST...
HA HA HA--
I SUPPOSE IT WAS JUST A MATTER OF TIME BEFORE THEY SENT YOU.
YOU'VE GOT A LOT OF EXPLAINING TO DO.

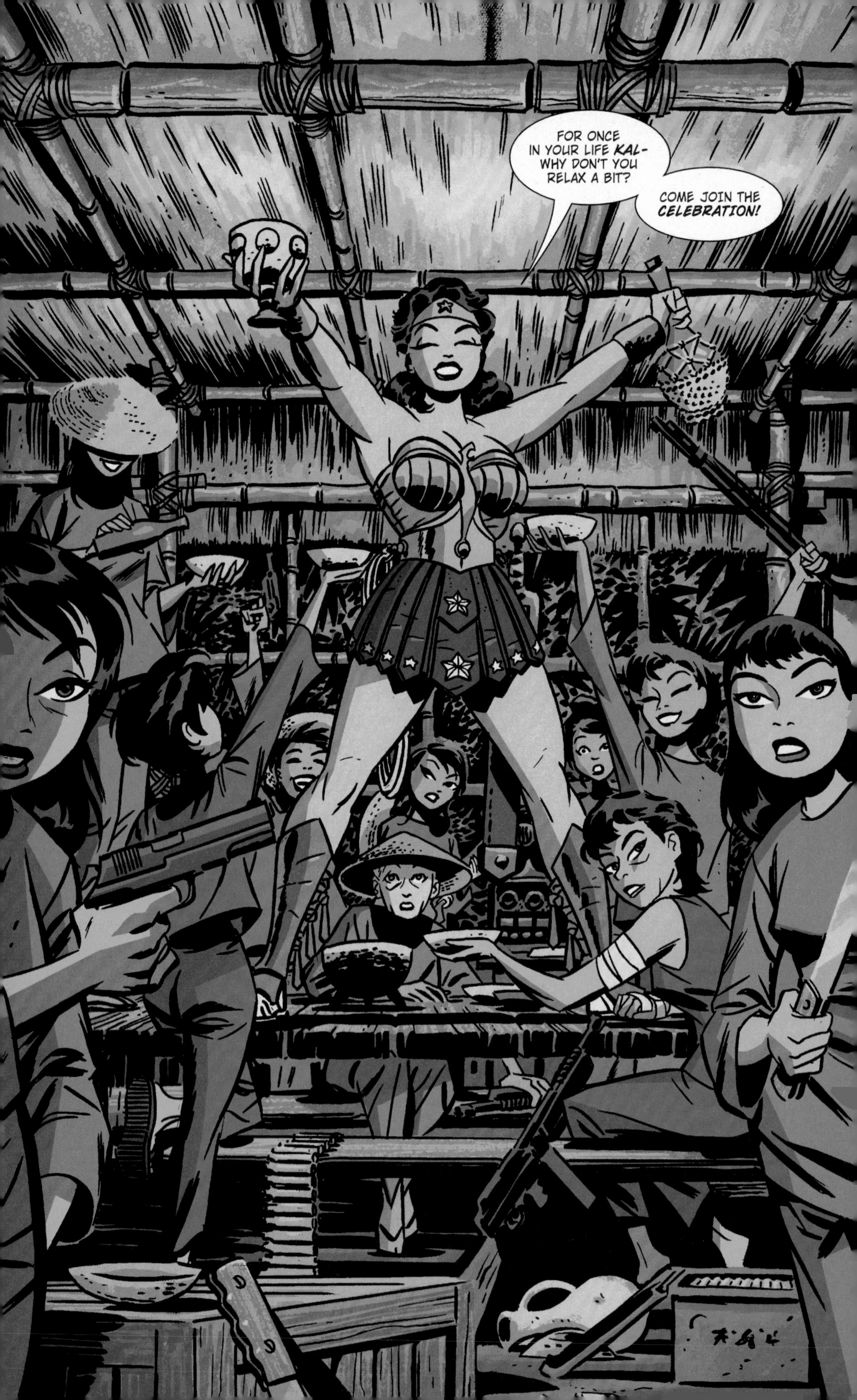
FOR ONCE IN YOUR LIFE KAL- WHY DON'T YOU RELAX A BIT?
COME JOIN THE CELEBRATION!

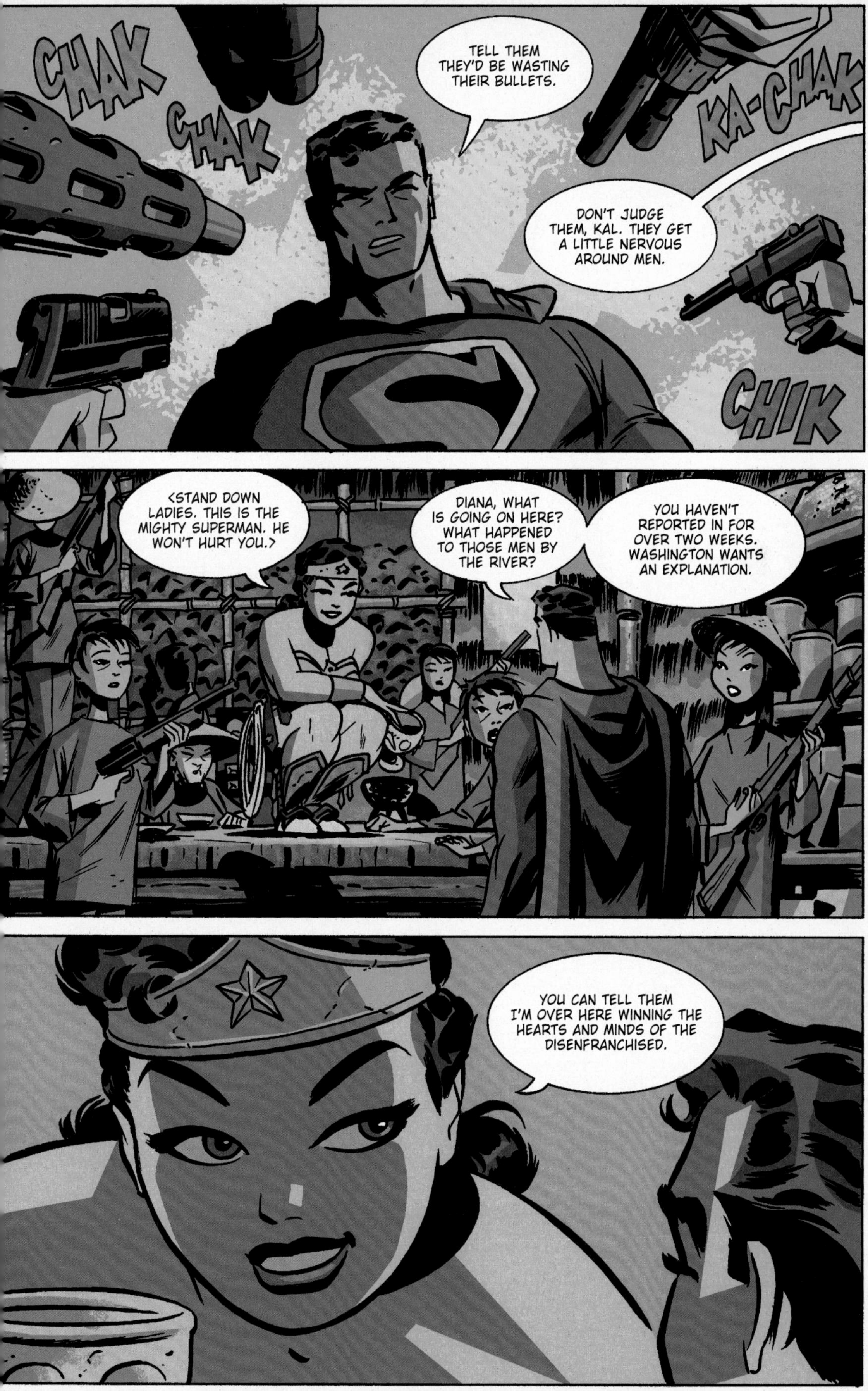
CHAK
CHAK
TELL THEM THEY'D BE WASTING THEIR BULLETS.
KA-CHAK
DON'T JUDGE THEM, KAL. THEY GET A LITTLE NERVOUS AROUND MEN.
CHIK
<STAND DOWN LADIES. THIS IS THE MIGHTY SUPERMAN. HE WON'T HURT YOU.>
DIANA, WHAT IS GOING ON HERE? WHAT HAPPENED TO THOSE MEN BY THE RIVER?
YOU HAVEN'T REPORTED IN FOR OVER TWO WEEKS. WASHINGTON WANTS AN EXPLANATION.
YOU CAN TELL THEM I'M OVER HERE WINNING THE HEARTS AND MINDS OF THE DISENFRANCHISED.

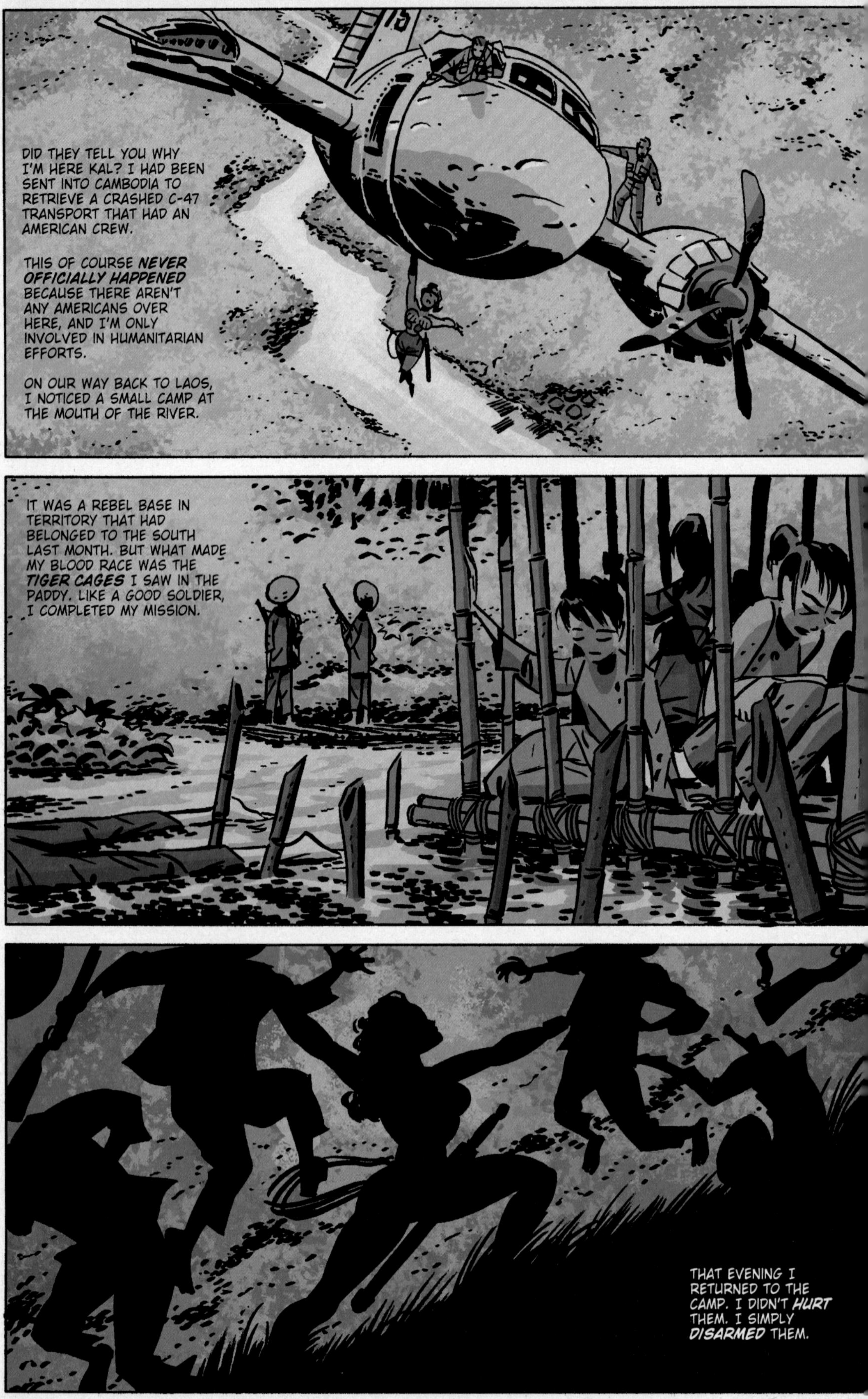
DID THEY TELL YOU WHY I'M HERE KAL? I HAD BEEN SENT INTO CAMBODIA TO RETRIEVE A CRASHED C-47 TRANSPORT THAT HAD AN AMERICAN CREW.
THIS OF COURSE NEVER OFFICIALLY HAPPENED BECAUSE THERE AREN'T ANY AMERICANS OVER HERE, AND I'M ONLY INVOLVED IN HUMANITARIAN EFFORTS.
ON OUR WAY BACK TO LAOS, I NOTICED A SMALL CAMP AT THE MOUTH OF THE RIVER.
IT WAS A REBEL BASE IN TERRITORY THAT HAD BELONGED TO THE SOUTH LAST MONTH. BUT WHAT MADE MY BLOOD RACE WAS THE TIGER CAGES I SAW IN THE PADDY. LIKE A GOOD SOLDIER, I COMPLETED MY MISSION.
THAT EVENING I RETURNED TO THE CAMP. I DIDN'T HURT THEM. I SIMPLY DISARMED THEM.

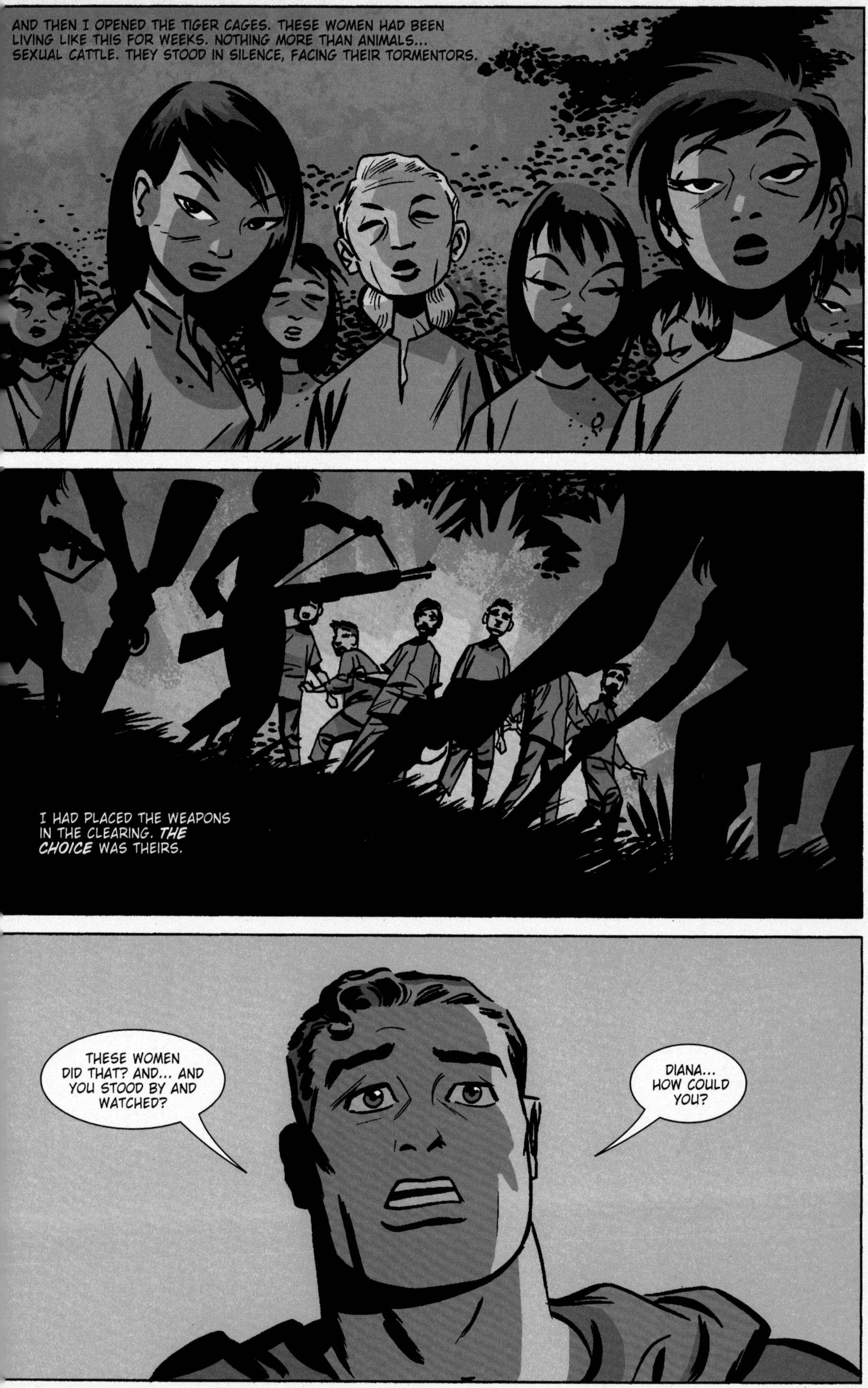
AND THEN I OPENED THE TIGER CAGES. THESE WOMEN HAD BEEN LIVING LIKE THIS FOR WEEKS. NOTHING MORE THAN ANIMALS... SEXUAL CATTLE. THEY STOOD IN SILENCE, FACING THEIR TORMENTORS.
I HAD PLACED THE WEAPONS IN THE CLEARING. *THE CHOICE* WAS THEIRS.
THESE WOMEN DID THAT? AND... AND YOU STOOD BY AND WATCHED?
DIANA... HOW COULD YOU?

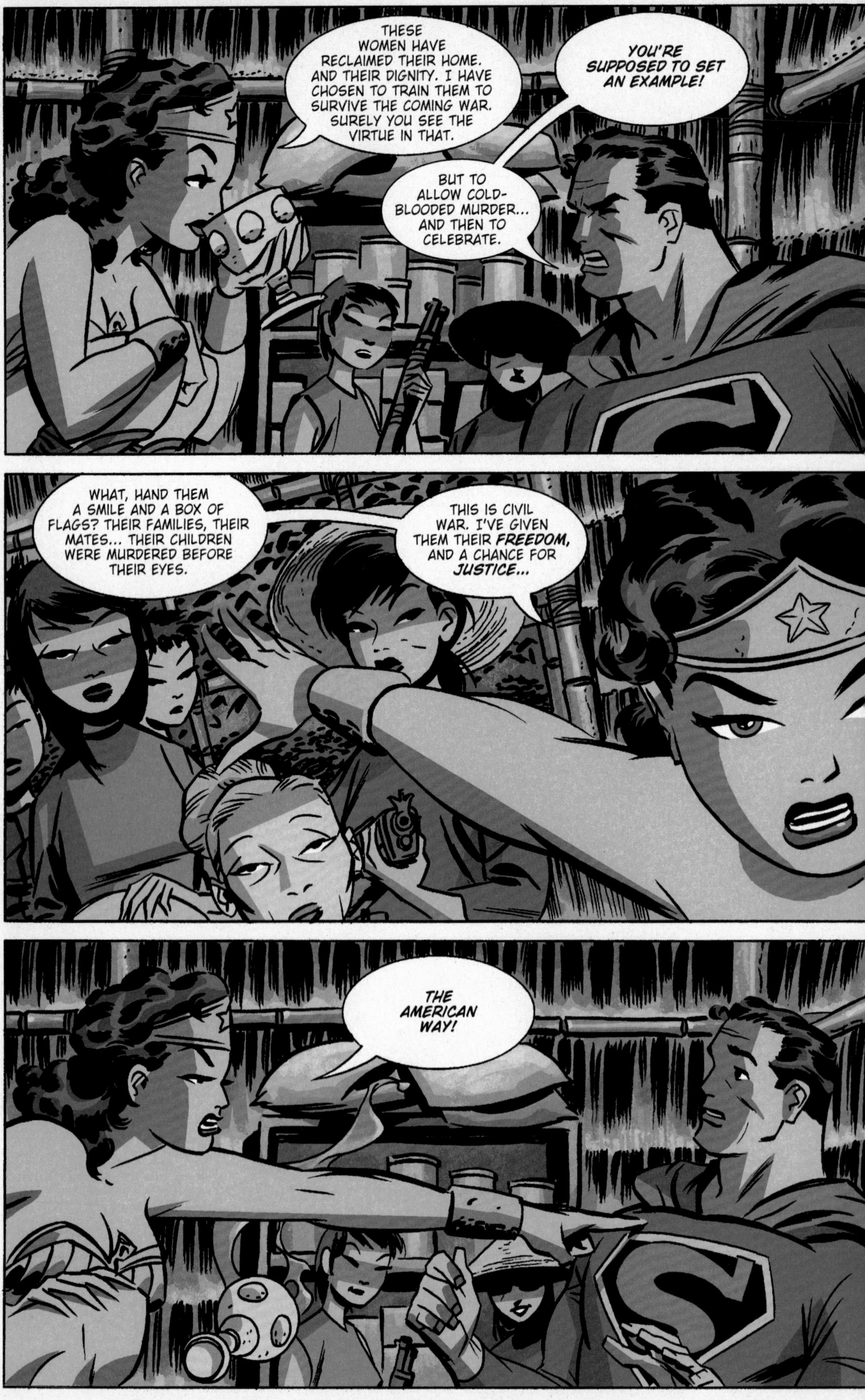
THESE WOMEN HAVE RECLAIMED THEIR HOME. AND THEIR DIGNITY. I HAVE CHOSEN TO TRAIN THEM TO SURVIVE THE COMING WAR. SURELY YOU SEE THE VIRTUE IN THAT.
YOU'RE SUPPOSED TO SET AN EXAMPLE!
BUT TO ALLOW COLD-BLOODED MURDER... AND THEN TO CELEBRATE.
WHAT, HAND THEM A SMILE AND A BOX OF FLAGS? THEIR FAMILIES, THEIR MATES... THEIR CHILDREN WERE MURDERED BEFORE THEIR EYES.
THIS IS CIVIL WAR. I'VE GIVEN THEM THEIR FREEDOM, AND A CHANCE FOR JUSTICE...
THE AMERICAN WAY!

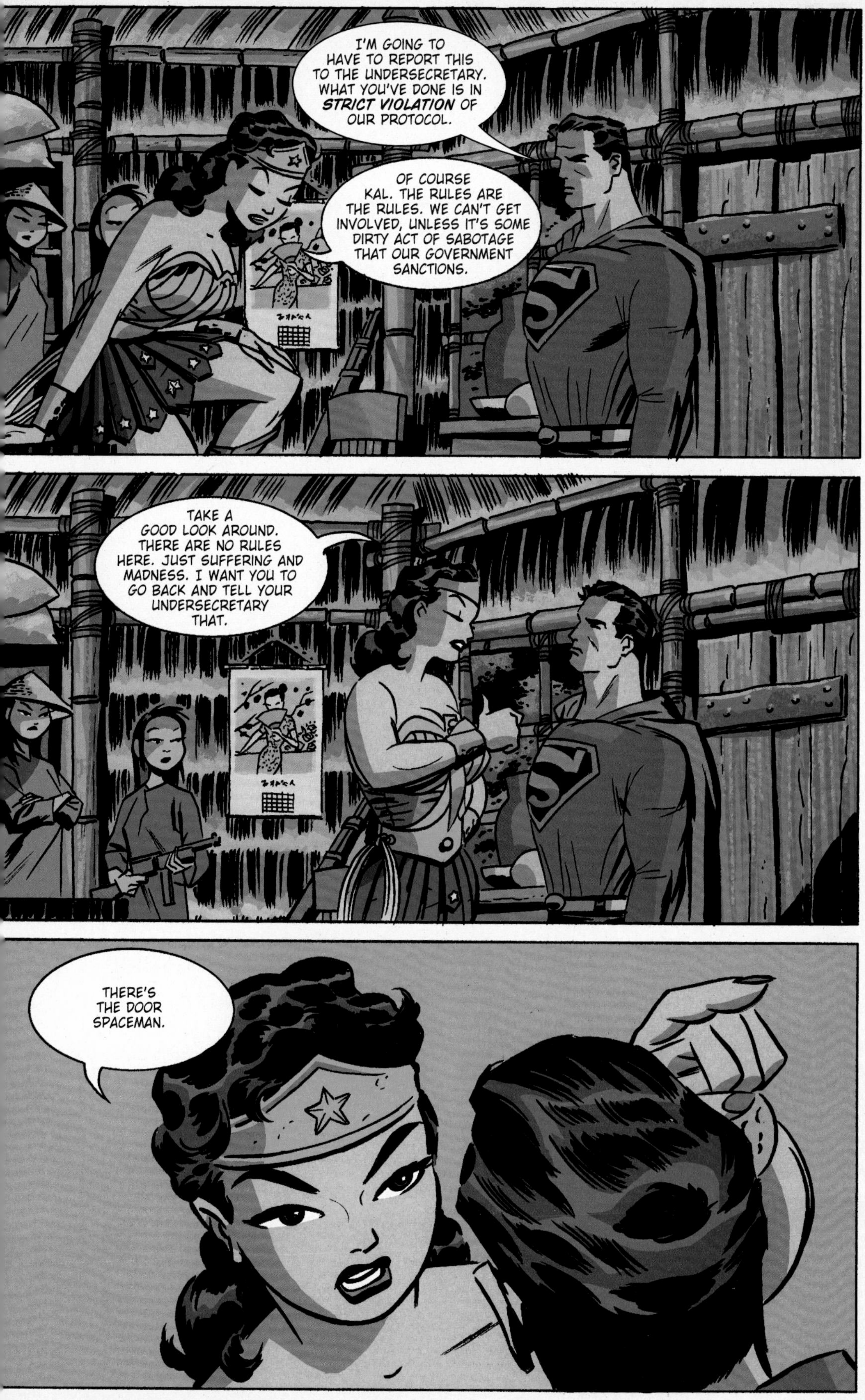
I'M GOING TO HAVE TO REPORT THIS TO THE UNDERSECRETARY. WHAT YOU'VE DONE IS IN **STRICT VIOLATION** OF OUR PROTOCOL.
OF COURSE KAL. THE RULES ARE THE RULES. WE CAN'T GET INVOLVED, UNLESS IT'S SOME DIRTY ACT OF SABOTAGE THAT OUR GOVERNMENT SANCTIONS.
TAKE A GOOD LOOK AROUND. THERE ARE NO RULES HERE. JUST SUFFERING AND MADNESS. I WANT YOU TO GO BACK AND TELL YOUR UNDERSECRETARY THAT.
THERE'S THE DOOR SPACEMAN.

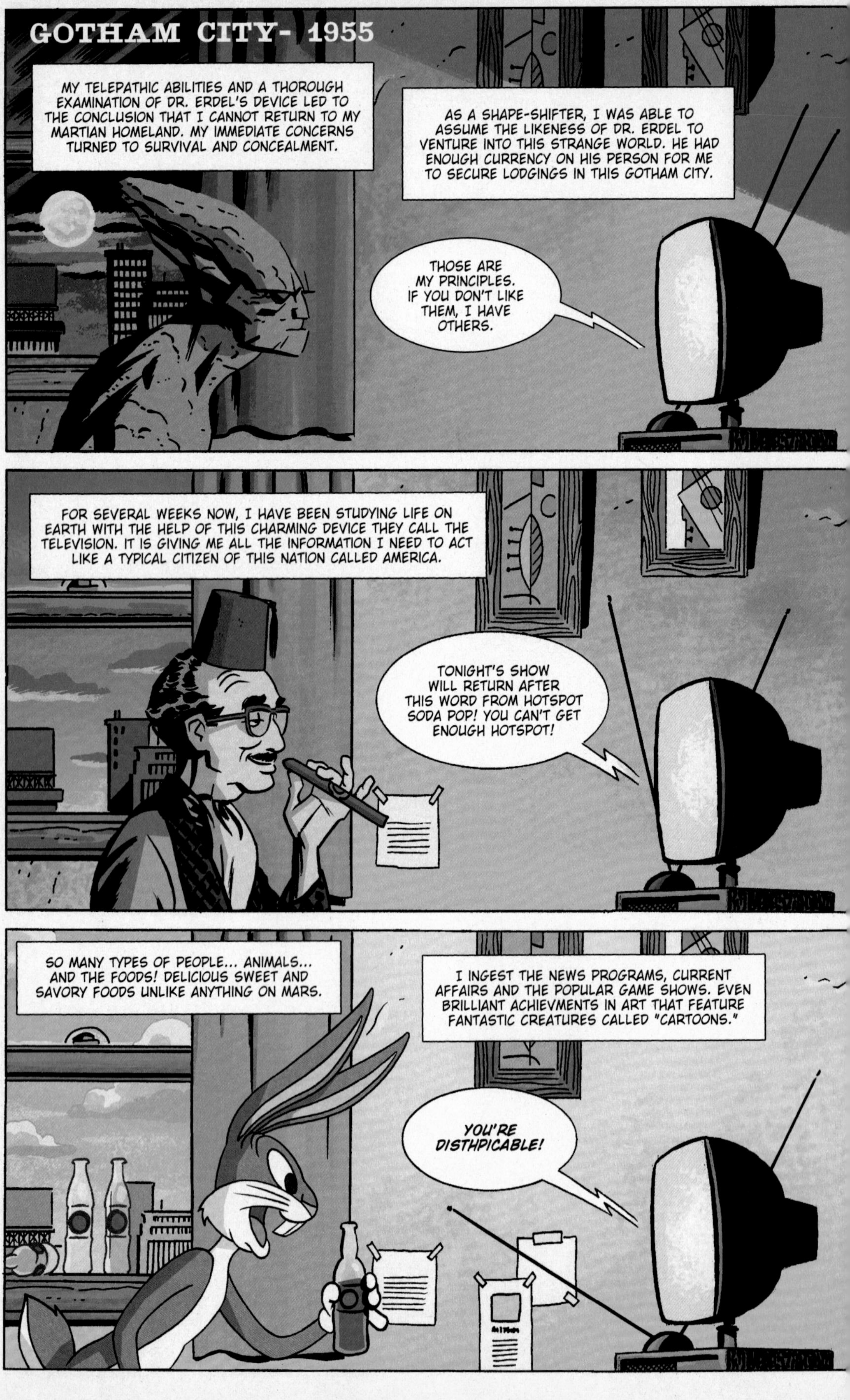
GOTHAM CITY- 1955
MY TELEPATHIC ABILITIES AND A THOROUGH EXAMINATION OF DR. ERDEL'S DEVICE LED TO THE CONCLUSION THAT I CANNOT RETURN TO MY MARTIAN HOMELAND. MY IMMEDIATE CONCERNS TURNED TO SURVIVAL AND CONCEALMENT.
AS A SHAPE-SHIFTER, I WAS ABLE TO ASSUME THE LIKENESS OF DR. ERDEL TO VENTURE INTO THIS STRANGE WORLD. HE HAD ENOUGH CURRENCY ON HIS PERSON FOR ME TO SECURE LODGINGS IN THIS GOTHAM CITY.
THOSE ARE MY PRINCIPLES. IF YOU DON'T LIKE THEM, I HAVE OTHERS.
FOR SEVERAL WEEKS NOW, I HAVE BEEN STUDYING LIFE ON EARTH WITH THE HELP OF THIS CHARMING DEVICE THEY CALL THE TELEVISION. IT IS GIVING ME ALL THE INFORMATION I NEED TO ACT LIKE A TYPICAL CITIZEN OF THIS NATION CALLED AMERICA.
TONIGHT'S SHOW WILL RETURN AFTER THIS WORD FROM HOTSPOT SODA POP! YOU CAN'T GET ENOUGH HOTSPOT!
SO MANY TYPES OF PEOPLE... ANIMALS... AND THE FOODS! DELICIOUS SWEET AND SAVORY FOODS UNLIKE ANYTHING ON MARS.
I INGEST THE NEWS PROGRAMS, CURRENT AFFAIRS AND THE POPULAR GAME SHOWS. EVEN BRILLIANT ACHIEVMENTS IN ART THAT FEATURE FANTASTIC CREATURES CALLED "CARTOONS."
YOU'RE DISTHPICABLE!

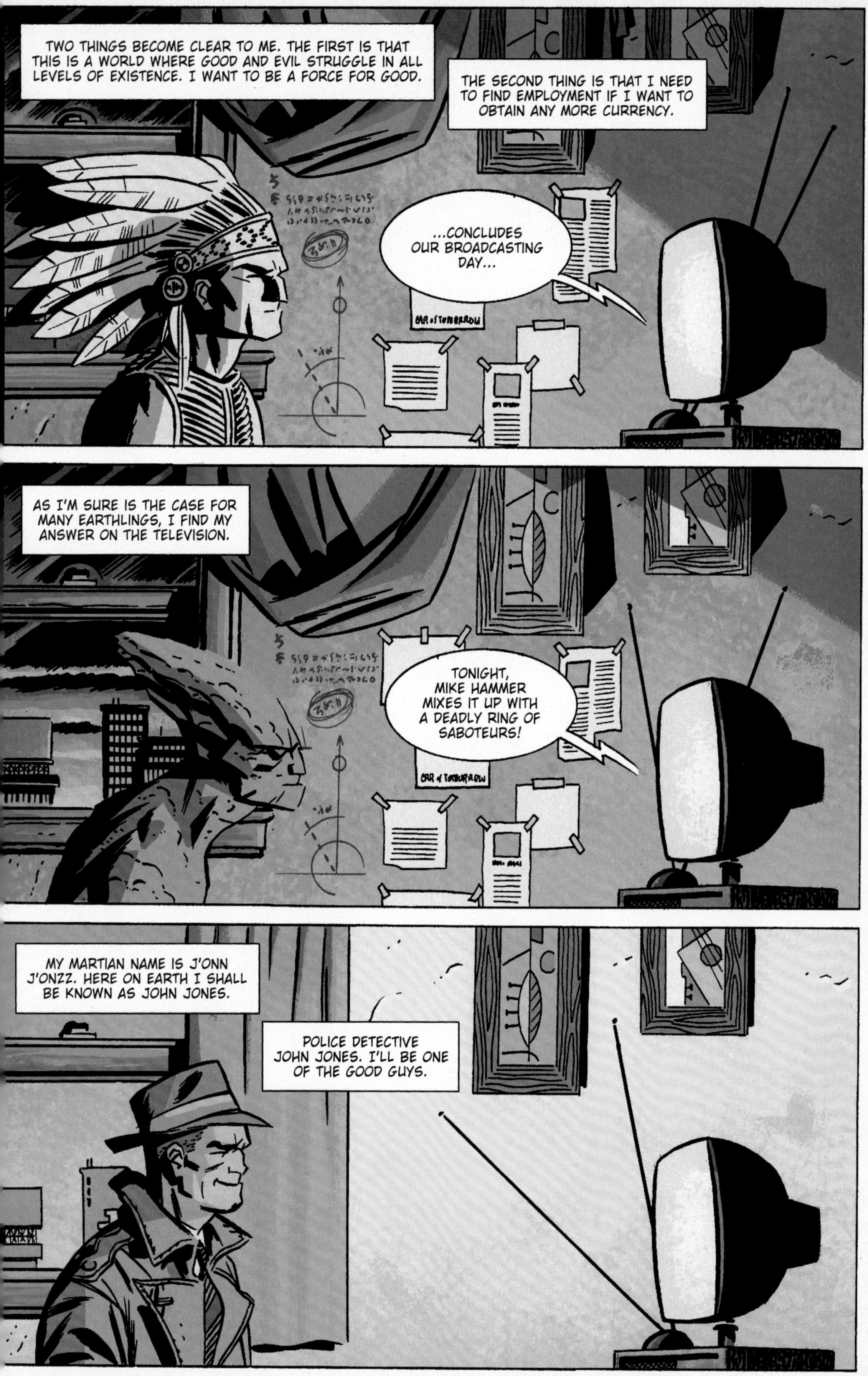
TWO THINGS BECOME CLEAR TO ME. THE FIRST IS THAT THIS IS A WORLD WHERE GOOD AND EVIL STRUGGLE IN ALL LEVELS OF EXISTENCE. I WANT TO BE A FORCE FOR GOOD.
THE SECOND THING IS THAT I NEED TO FIND EMPLOYMENT IF I WANT TO OBTAIN ANY MORE CURRENCY.
...CONCLUDES OUR BROADCASTING DAY...
AS I'M SURE IS THE CASE FOR MANY EARTHLINGS, I FIND MY ANSWER ON THE TELEVISION.
TONIGHT, MIKE HAMMER MIXES IT UP WITH A DEADLY RING OF SABOTEURS!
MY MARTIAN NAME IS J'ONN J'ONZZ. HERE ON EARTH I SHALL BE KNOWN AS JOHN JONES.
POLICE DETECTIVE JOHN JONES. I'LL BE ONE OF THE GOOD GUYS.

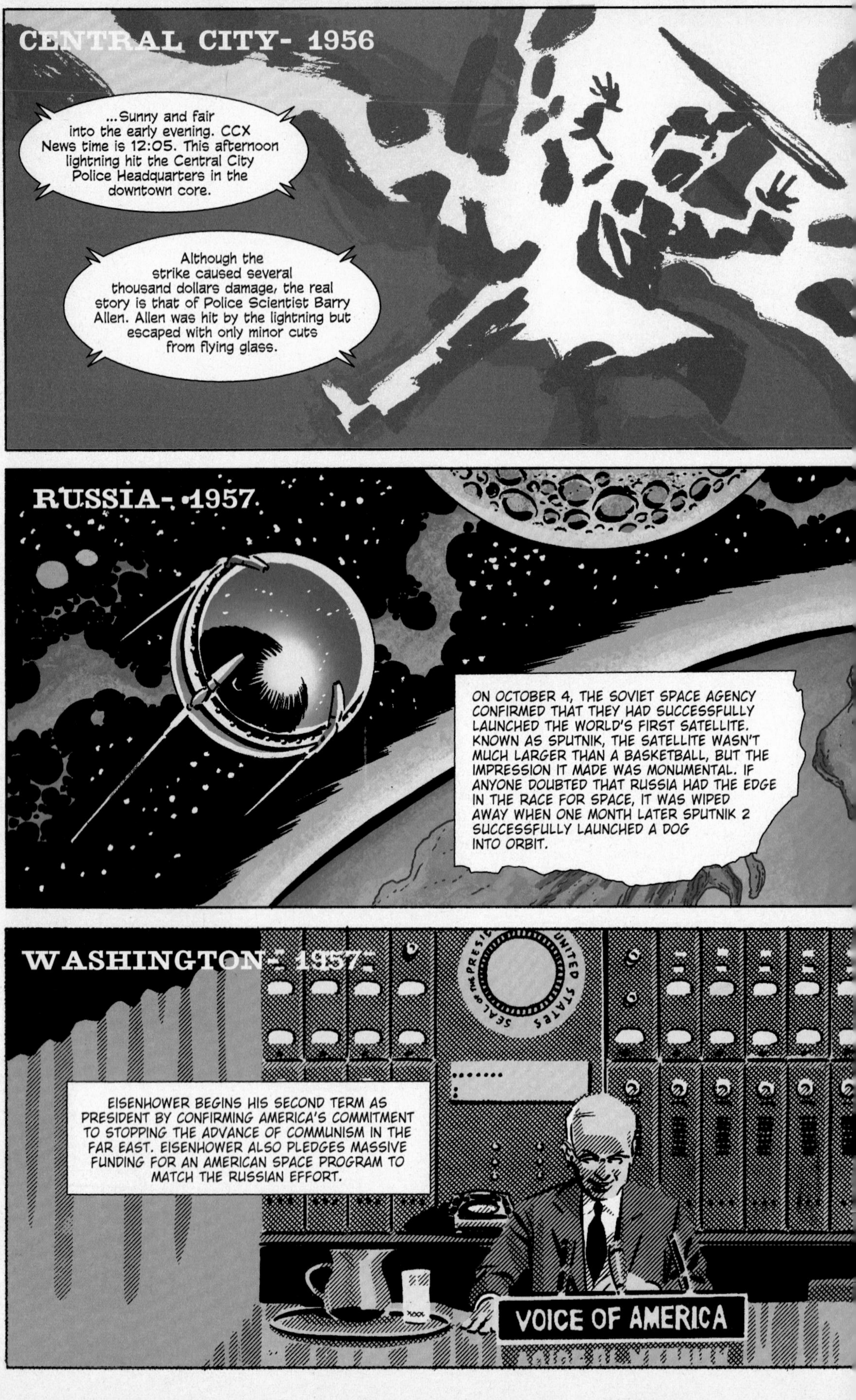
CENTRAL CITY- 1956
...Sunny and fair into the early evening. CCX News time is 12:05. This afternoon lightning hit the Central City Police Headquarters in the downtown core.
Although the strike caused several thousand dollars damage, the real story is that of Police Scientist Barry Allen. Allen was hit by the lightning but escaped with only minor cuts from flying glass.
RUSSIA- 1957
ON OCTOBER 4, THE SOVIET SPACE AGENCY CONFIRMED THAT THEY HAD SUCCESSFULLY LAUNCHED THE WORLD'S FIRST SATELLITE. KNOWN AS SPUTNIK, THE SATELLITE WASN'T MUCH LARGER THAN A BASKETBALL, BUT THE IMPRESSION IT MADE WAS MONUMENTAL. IF ANYONE DOUBTED THAT RUSSIA HAD THE EDGE IN THE RACE FOR SPACE, IT WAS WIPED AWAY WHEN ONE MONTH LATER SPUTNIK 2 SUCCESSFULLY LAUNCHED A DOG INTO ORBIT.
WASHINGTON- 1957
SEAL OF THE PRESIDENT OF THE UNITED STATES
EISENHOWER BEGINS HIS SECOND TERM AS PRESIDENT BY CONFIRMING AMERICA'S COMMITMENT TO STOPPING THE ADVANCE OF COMMUNISM IN THE FAR EAST. EISENHOWER ALSO PLEDGES MASSIVE FUNDING FOR AN AMERICAN SPACE PROGRAM TO MATCH THE RUSSIAN EFFORT.
VOICE OF AMERICA

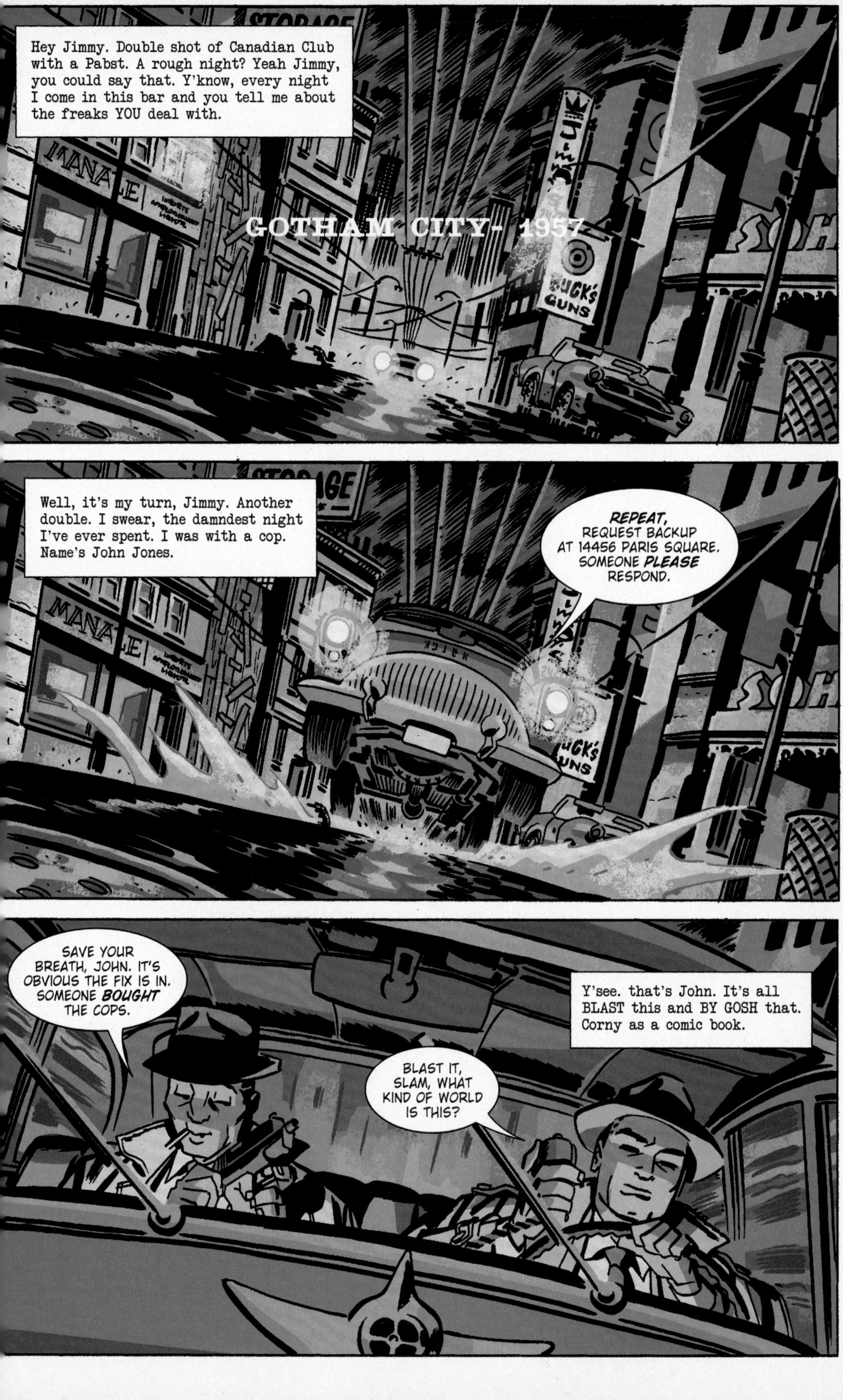

Hey Jimmy. Double shot of Canadian Club with a Pabst. A rough night? Yeah Jimmy, you could say that. Y'know, every night I come in this bar and you tell me about the freaks YOU deal with.
GOTHAM CITY- 1957
BUCK'S GUNS
Well, it's my turn, Jimmy. Another double. I swear, the damndest night I've ever spent. I was with a cop. Name's John Jones.
REPEAT, REQUEST BACKUP AT 14456 PARIS SQUARE. SOMEONE PLEASE RESPOND.
SAVE YOUR BREATH, JOHN. IT'S OBVIOUS THE FIX IS IN. SOMEONE BOUGHT THE COPS.
Y'see. that's John. It's all BLAST this and BY GOSH that. Corny as a comic book.
BLAST IT, SLAM, WHAT KIND OF WORLD IS THIS?

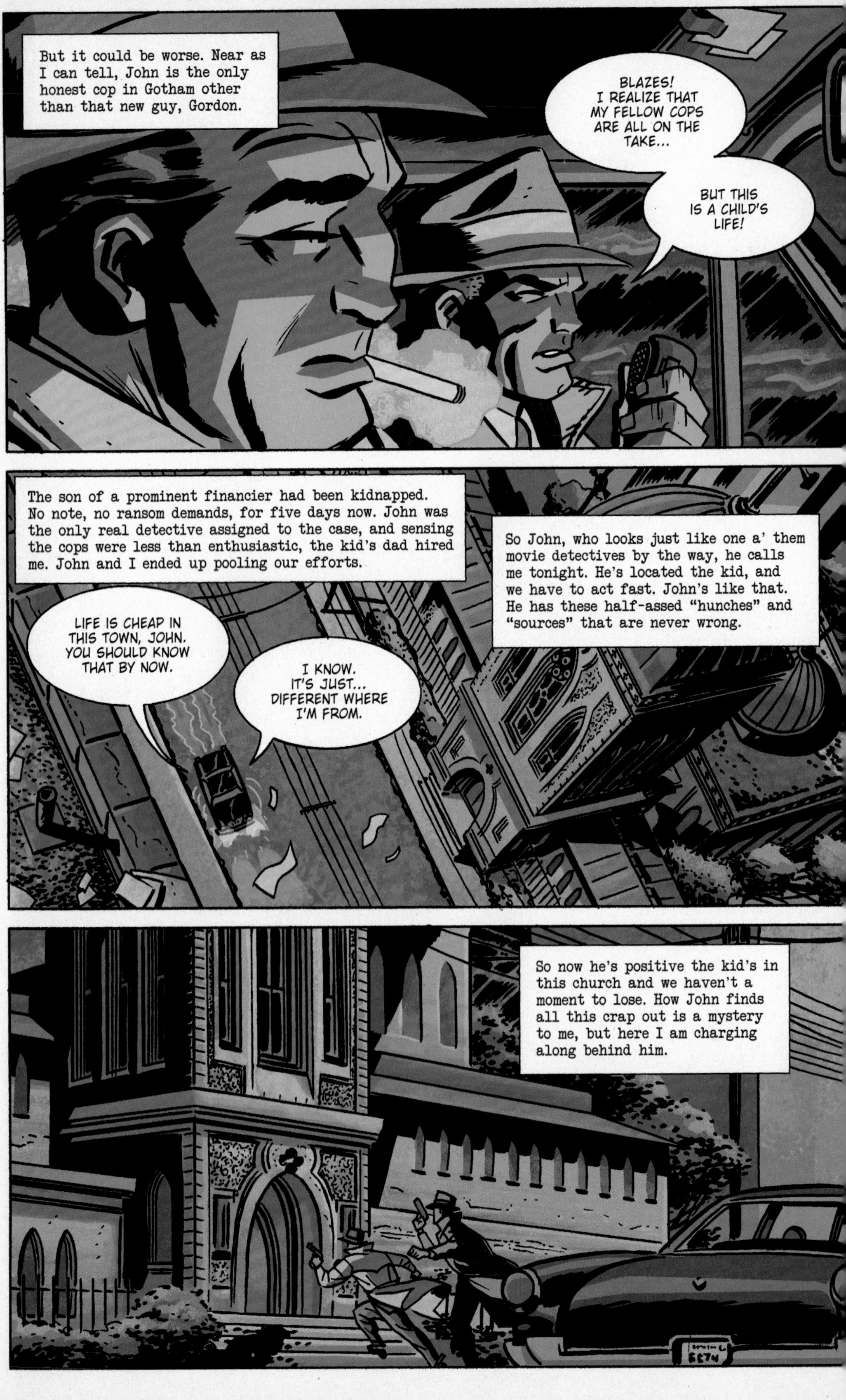
But it could be worse. Near as I can tell, John is the only honest cop in Gotham other than that new guy, Gordon.
BLAZES! I REALIZE THAT MY FELLOW COPS ARE ALL ON THE TAKE...
BUT THIS IS A CHILD'S LIFE!
The son of a prominent financier had been kidnapped. No note, no ransom demands, for five days now. John was the only real detective assigned to the case, and sensing the cops were less than enthusiastic, the kid's dad hired me. John and I ended up pooling our efforts.
So John, who looks just like one a' them movie detectives by the way, he calls me tonight. He's located the kid, and we have to act fast. John's like that. He has these half-assed "hunches" and "sources" that are never wrong.
LIFE IS CHEAP IN THIS TOWN, JOHN. YOU SHOULD KNOW THAT BY NOW.
I KNOW. IT'S JUST... DIFFERENT WHERE I'M FROM.
So now he's positive the kid's in this church and we haven't a moment to lose. How John finds all this crap out is a mystery to me, but here I am charging along behind him.

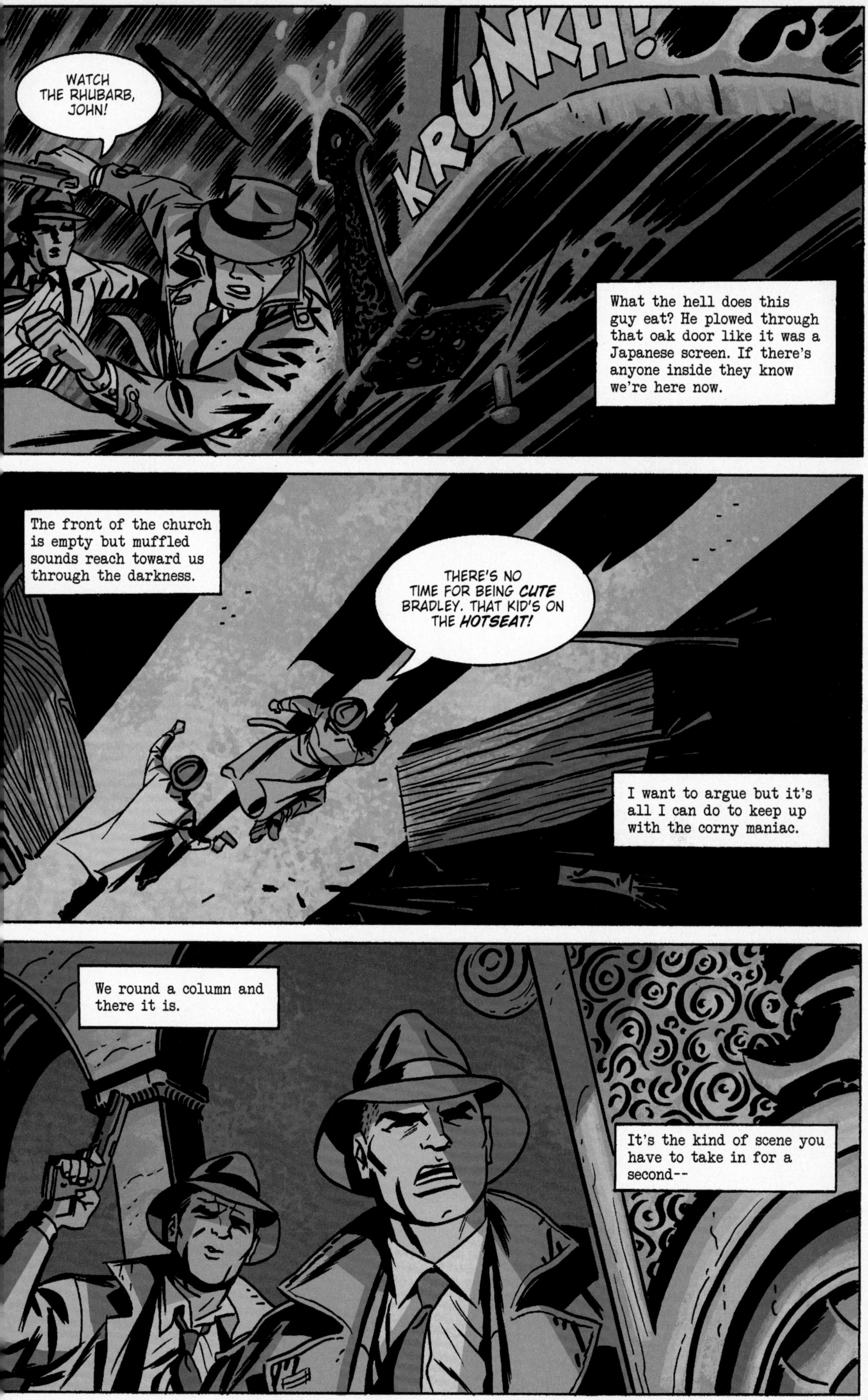
WATCH THE RHUBARB, JOHN!
KRUNKH!
What the hell does this guy eat? He plowed through that oak door like it was a Japanese screen. If there's anyone inside they know we're here now.
The front of the church is empty but muffled sounds reach toward us through the darkness.
THERE'S NO TIME FOR BEING CUTE BRADLEY. THAT KID'S ON THE HOTSEAT!
I want to argue but it's all I can do to keep up with the corny maniac.
We round a column and there it is.
It's the kind of scene you have to take in for a second--

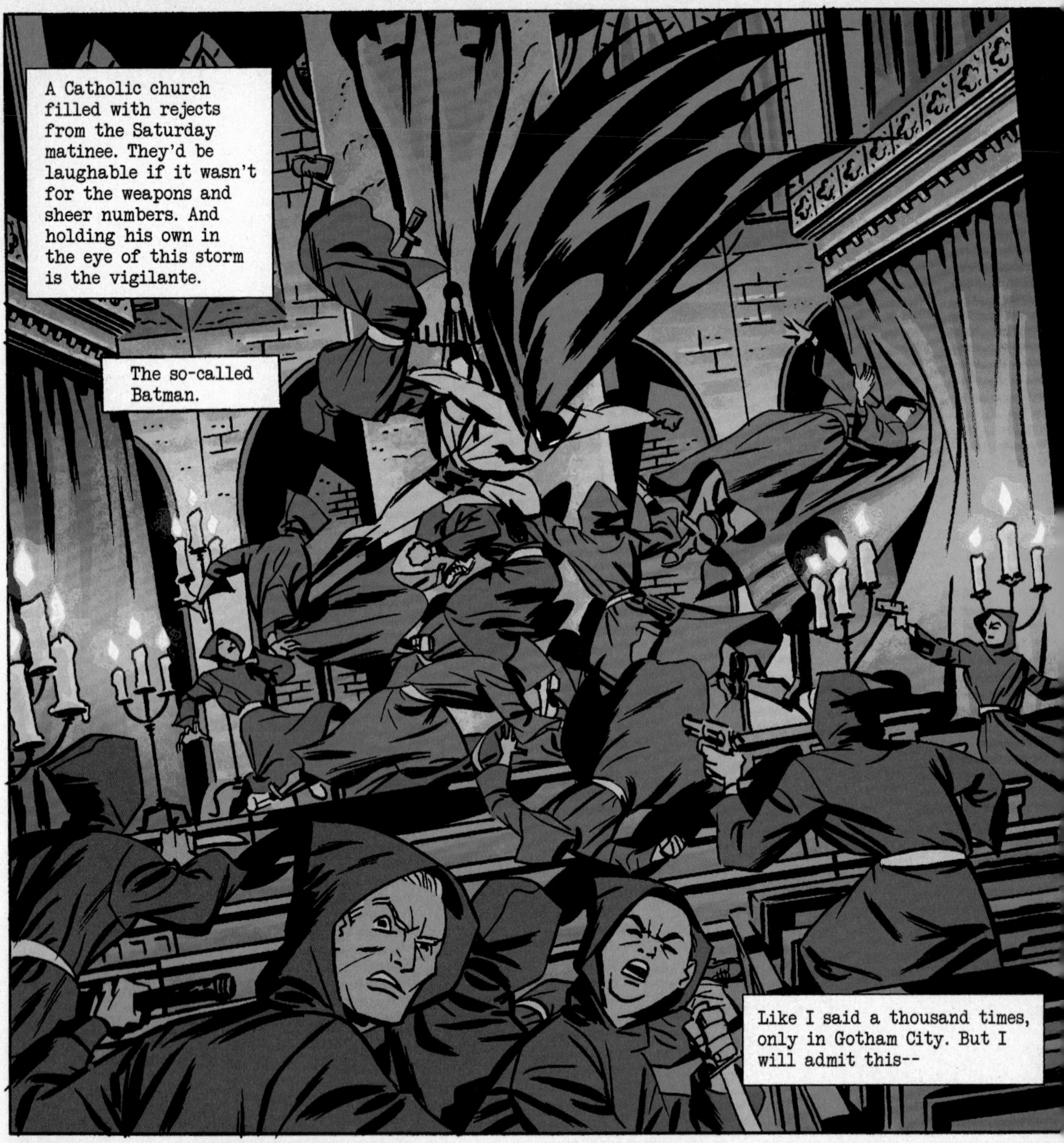
A Catholic church filled with rejects from the Saturday matinee. They'd be laughable if it wasn't for the weapons and sheer numbers. And holding his own in the eye of this storm is the vigilante.
The so-called Batman.
Like I said a thousand times, only in Gotham City. But I will admit this--

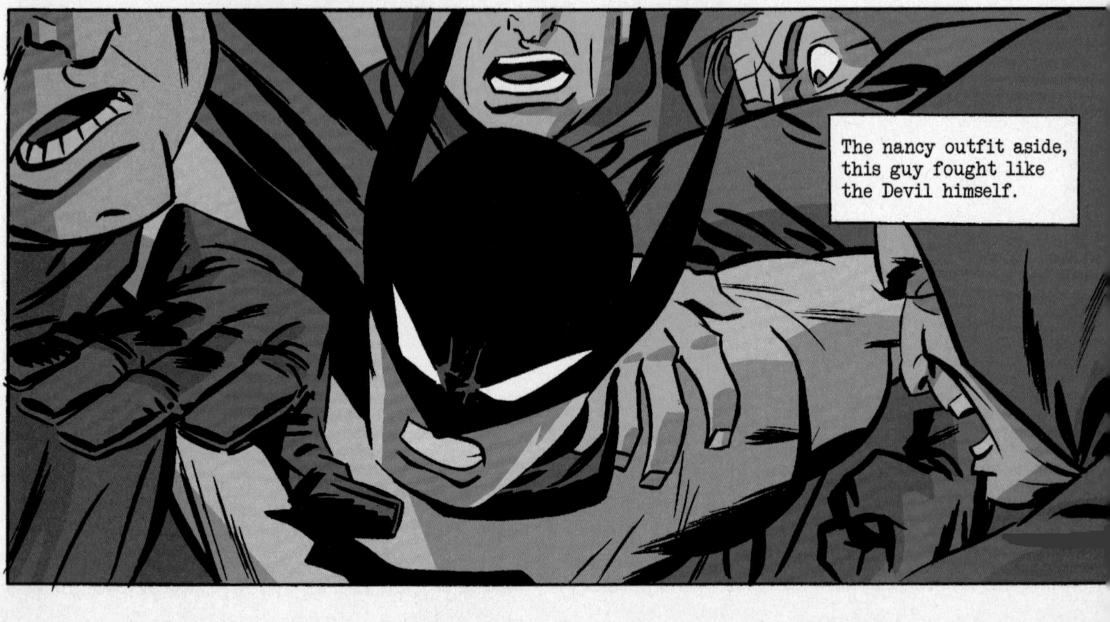
The nancy outfit aside, this guy fought like the Devil himself.

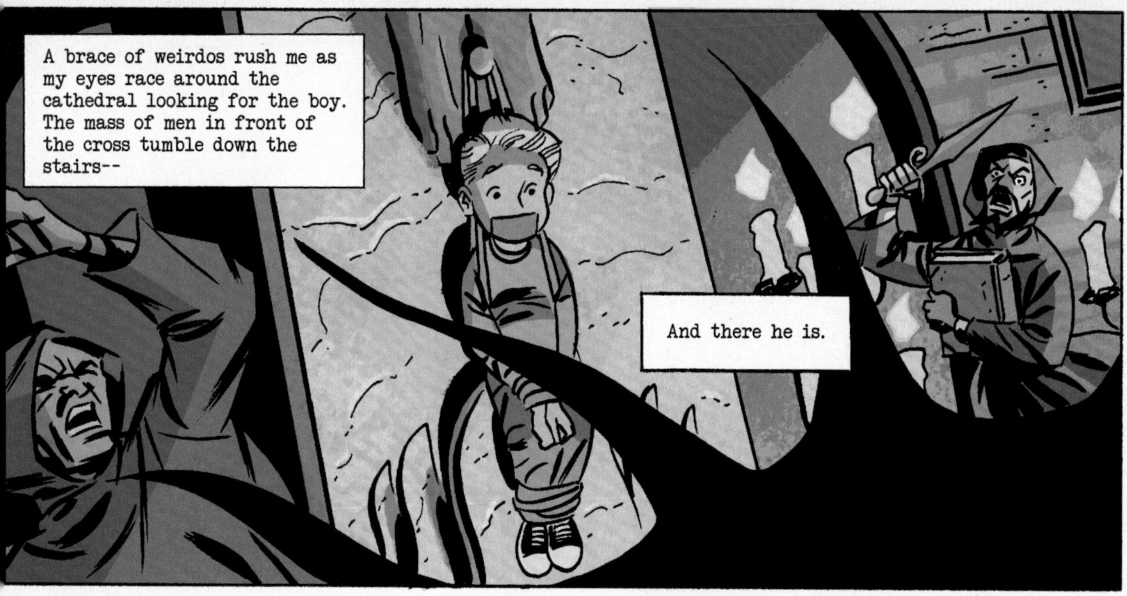
A brace of weirdos rush me as my eyes race around the cathedral looking for the boy. The mass of men in front of the cross tumble down the stairs--
And there he is.

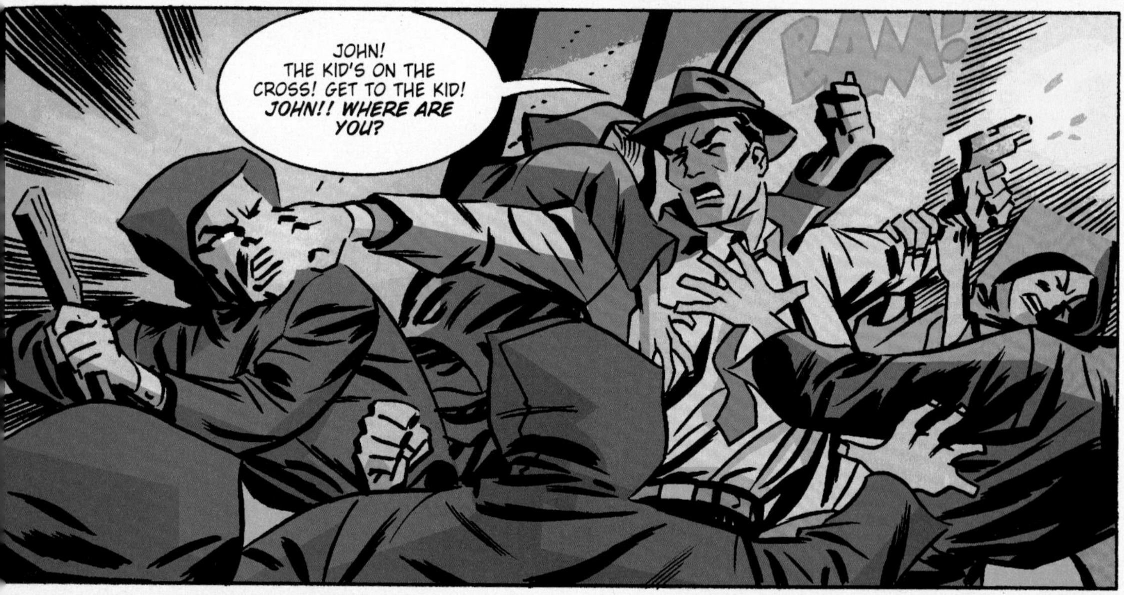
JOHN! THE KID'S ON THE CROSS! GET TO THE KID! JOHN!! WHERE ARE YOU?
BAM!

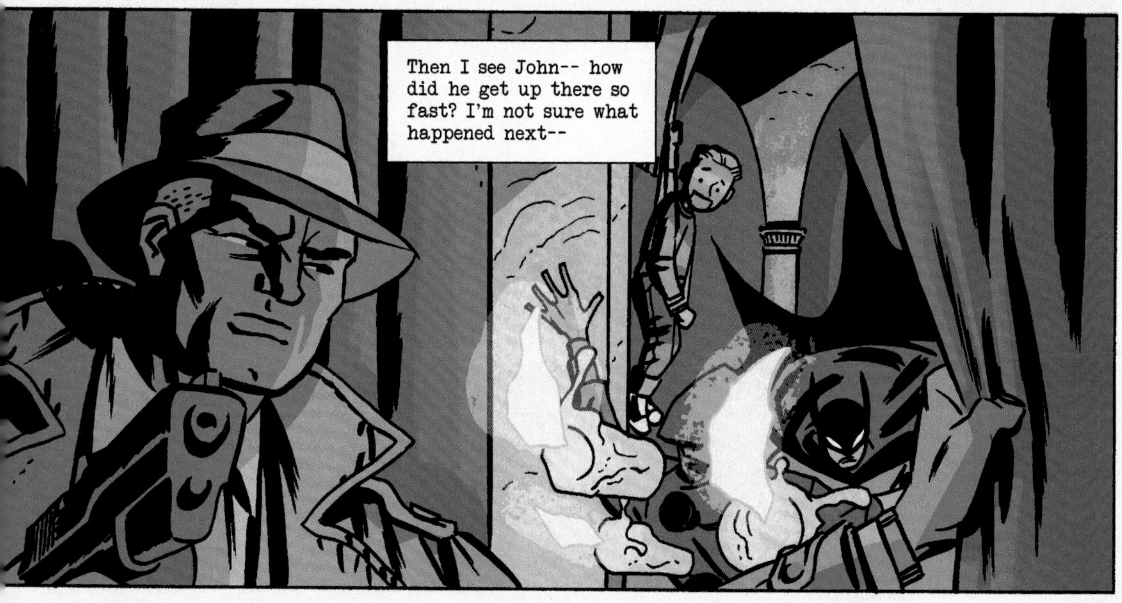
Then I see John-- how did he get up there so fast? I'm not sure what happened next--

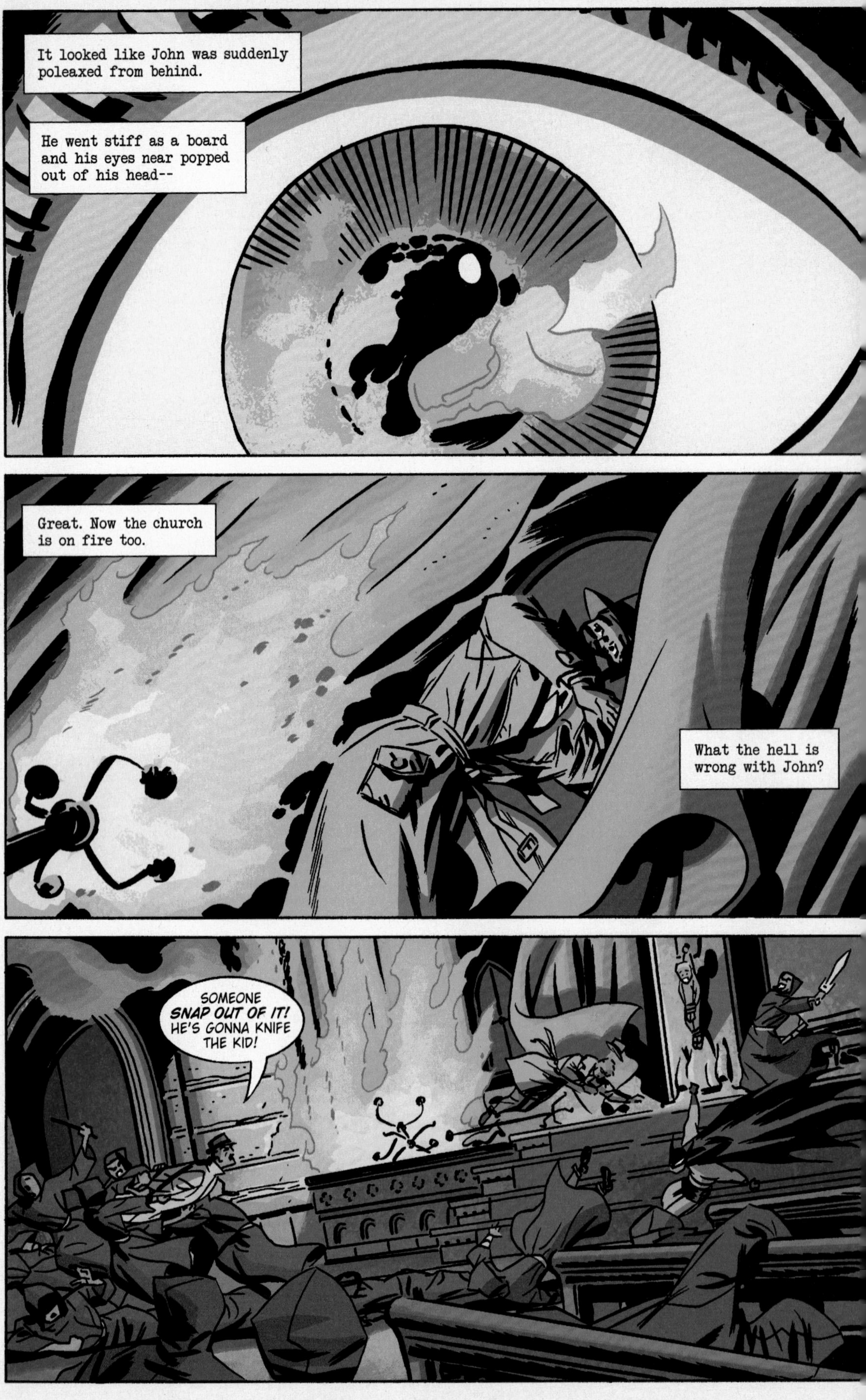
It looked like John was suddenly poleaxed from behind.
He went stiff as a board and his eyes near popped out of his head--
Great. Now the church is on fire too.
What the hell is wrong with John?
SOMEONE *SNAP OUT OF IT!* HE'S GONNA KNIFE THE KID!

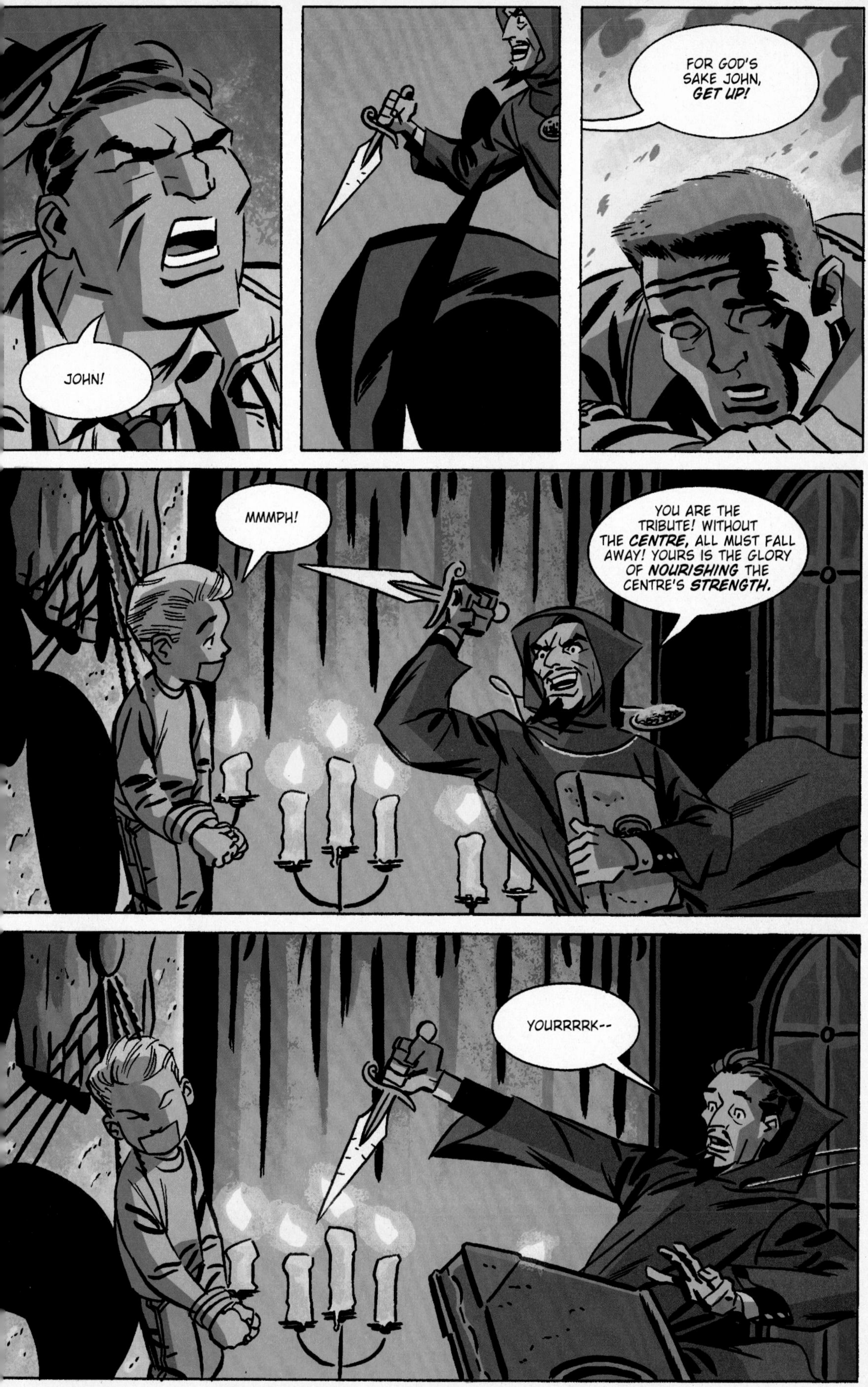
JOHN!
FOR GOD'S SAKE JOHN, GET UP!
MMMPH!
YOU ARE THE TRIBUTE! WITHOUT THE CENTRE, ALL MUST FALL AWAY! YOURS IS THE GLORY OF NOURISHING THE CENTRE'S STRENGTH.
YOURRRRK--

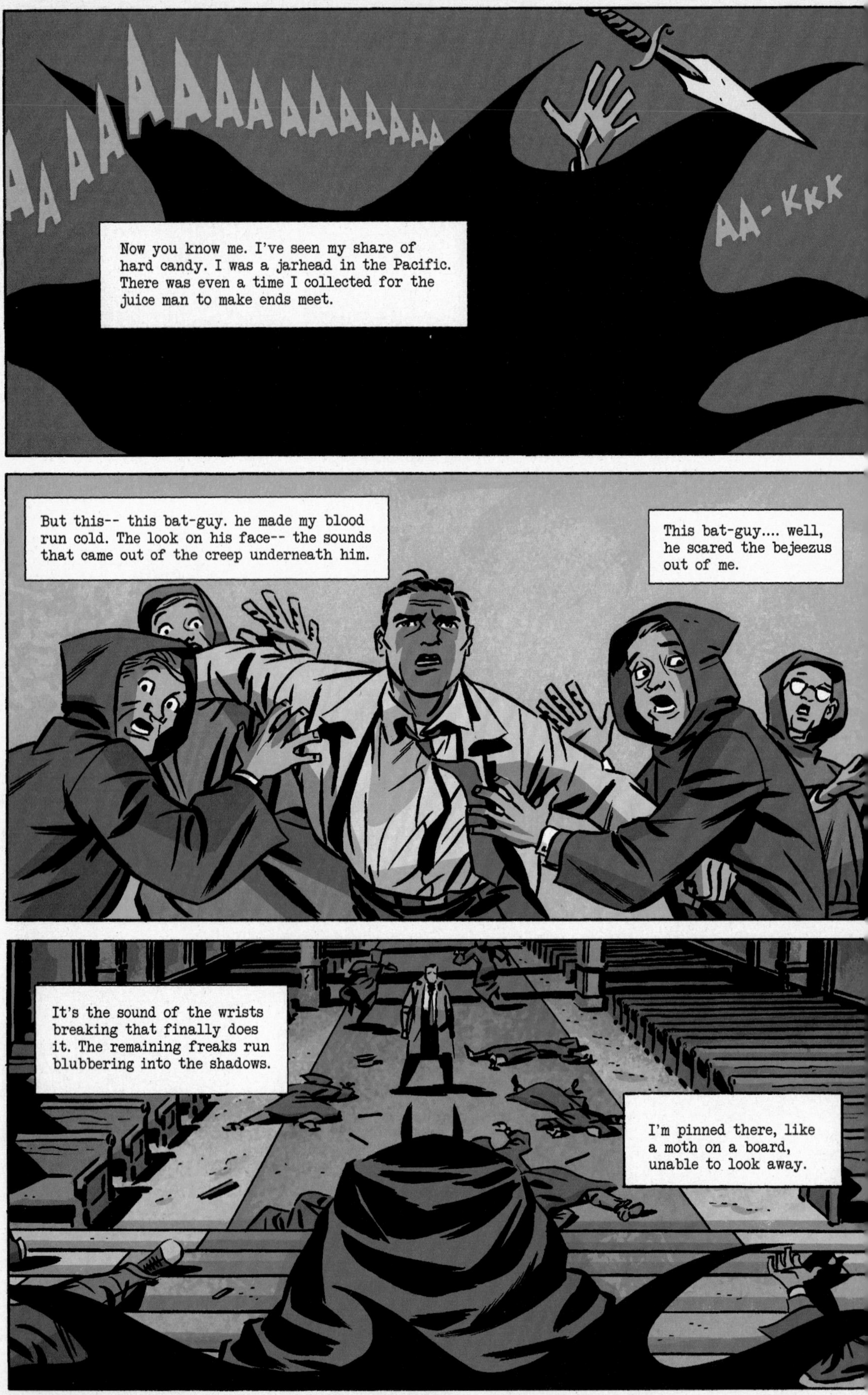
AAAAAAAAAAAAAAAA
Now you know me. I've seen my share of hard candy. I was a jarhead in the Pacific. There was even a time I collected for the juice man to make ends meet.
AA-KKK
But this-- this bat-guy. he made my blood run cold. The look on his face-- the sounds that came out of the creep underneath him.
This bat-guy.... well, he scared the bejeezus out of me.
It's the sound of the wrists breaking that finally does it. The remaining freaks run blubbering into the shadows.
I'm pinned there, like a moth on a board, unable to look away.

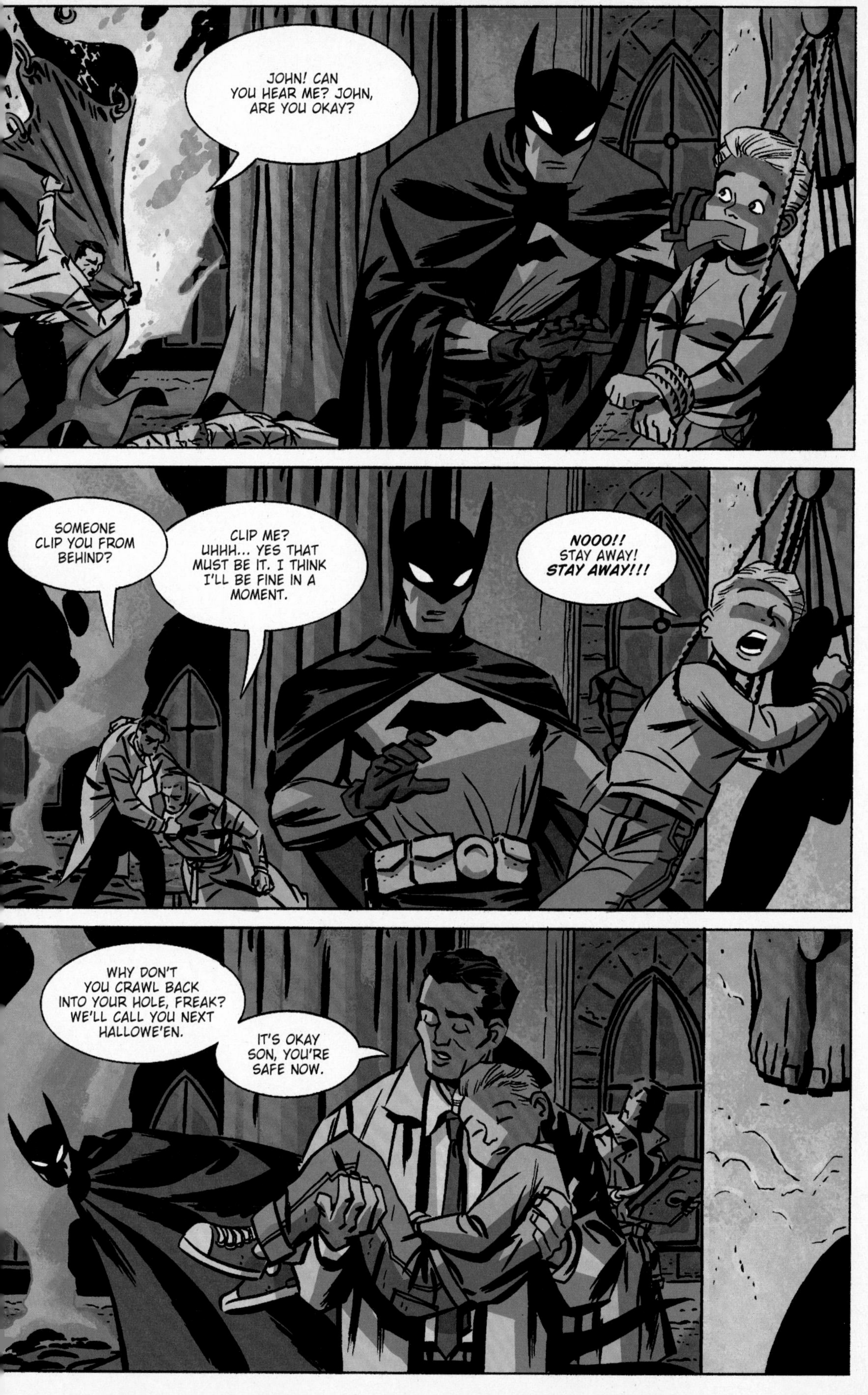
JOHN! CAN YOU HEAR ME? JOHN, ARE YOU OKAY?
SOMEONE CLIP YOU FROM BEHIND?
CLIP ME? UHHH... YES THAT MUST BE IT. I THINK I'LL BE FINE IN A MOMENT.
NOOO!! STAY AWAY! STAY AWAY!!!
WHY DON'T YOU CRAWL BACK INTO YOUR HOLE, FREAK? WE'LL CALL YOU NEXT HALLOWE'EN.
IT'S OKAY SON, YOU'RE SAFE NOW.

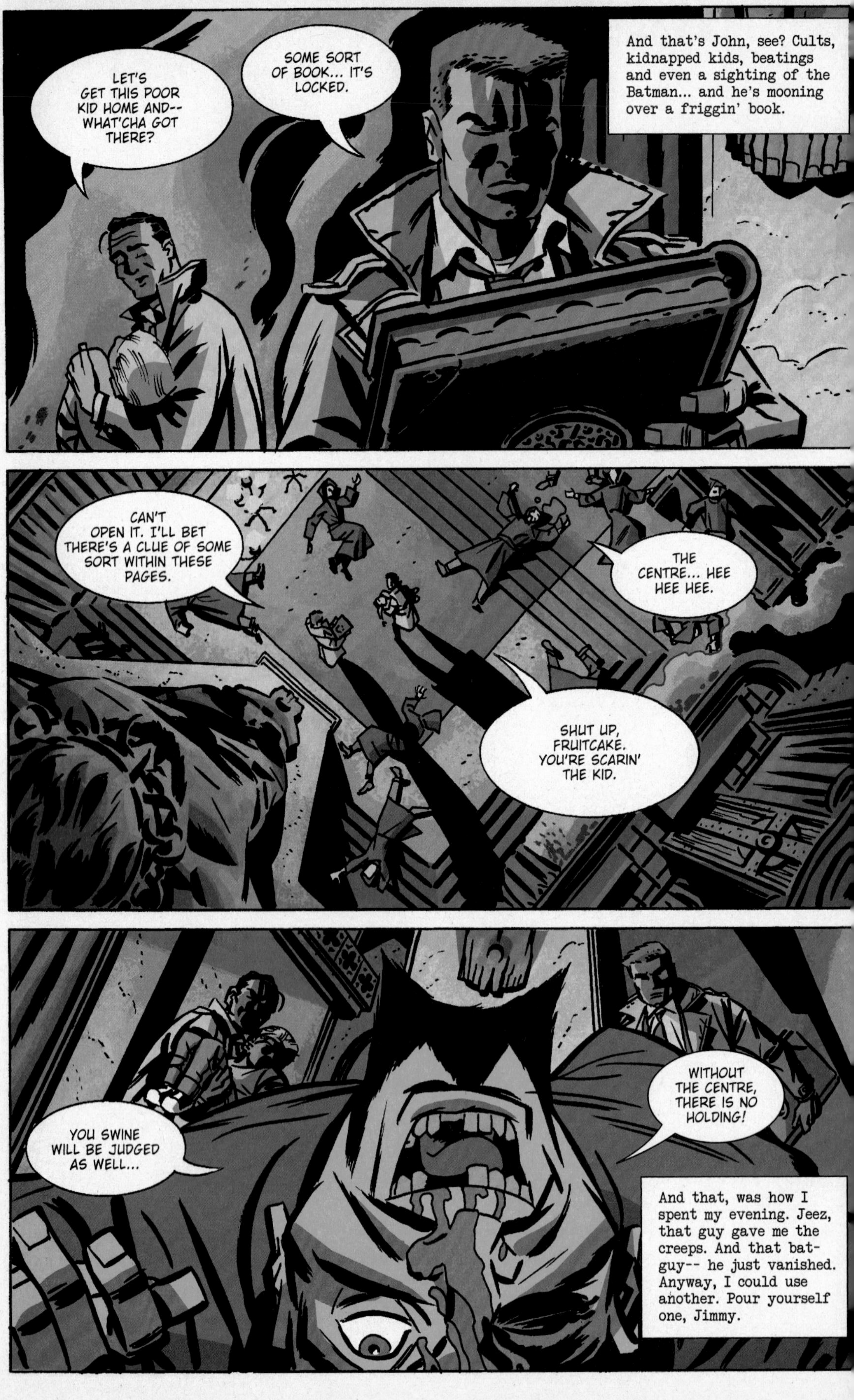
LET'S GET THIS POOR KID HOME AND-- WHAT'CHA GOT THERE?
SOME SORT OF BOOK... IT'S LOCKED.
And that's John, see? Cults, kidnapped kids, beatings and even a sighting of the Batman... and he's mooning over a friggin' book.
CAN'T OPEN IT. I'LL BET THERE'S A CLUE OF SOME SORT WITHIN THESE PAGES.
THE CENTRE... HEE HEE HEE.
SHUT UP, FRUITCAKE. YOU'RE SCARIN' THE KID.
YOU SWINE WILL BE JUDGED AS WELL...
WITHOUT THE CENTRE, THERE IS NO HOLDING!
And that, was how I spent my evening. Jeez, that guy gave me the creeps. And that bat-guy-- he just vanished. Anyway, I could use another. Pour yourself one, Jimmy.

CHAPTER FIVE
FUN CITY

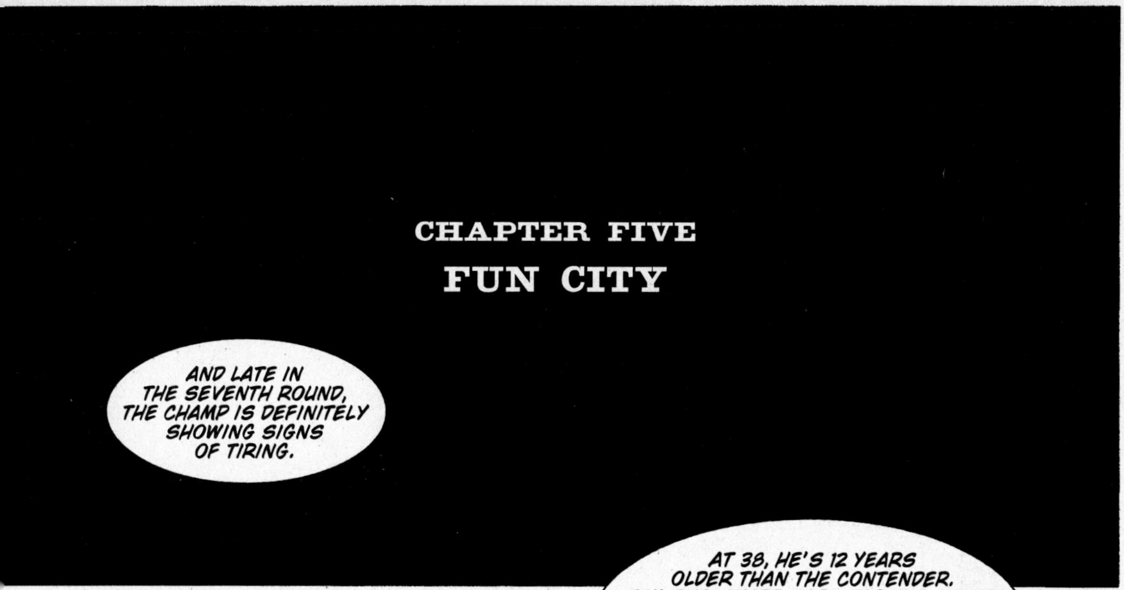
AND LATE IN THE SEVENTH ROUND, THE CHAMP IS DEFINITELY SHOWING SIGNS OF TIRING.

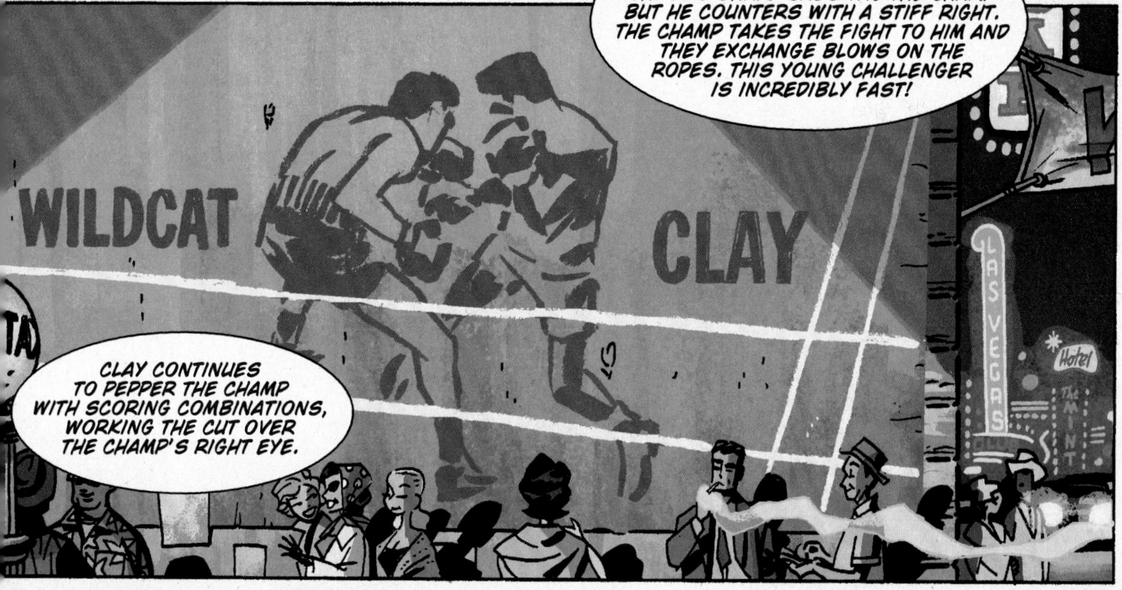
AT 38, HE'S 12 YEARS OLDER THAN THE CONTENDER. OH! TWO SHARP JABS TAG THE CHAMP BUT HE COUNTERS WITH A STIFF RIGHT. THE CHAMP TAKES THE FIGHT TO HIM AND THEY EXCHANGE BLOWS ON THE ROPES. THIS YOUNG CHALLENGER IS INCREDIBLY FAST!
WILDCAT
CLAY
LAS VEGAS
Hotel
CLAY CONTINUES TO PEPPER THE CHAMP WITH SCORING COMBINATIONS, WORKING THE CUT OVER THE CHAMP'S RIGHT EYE.

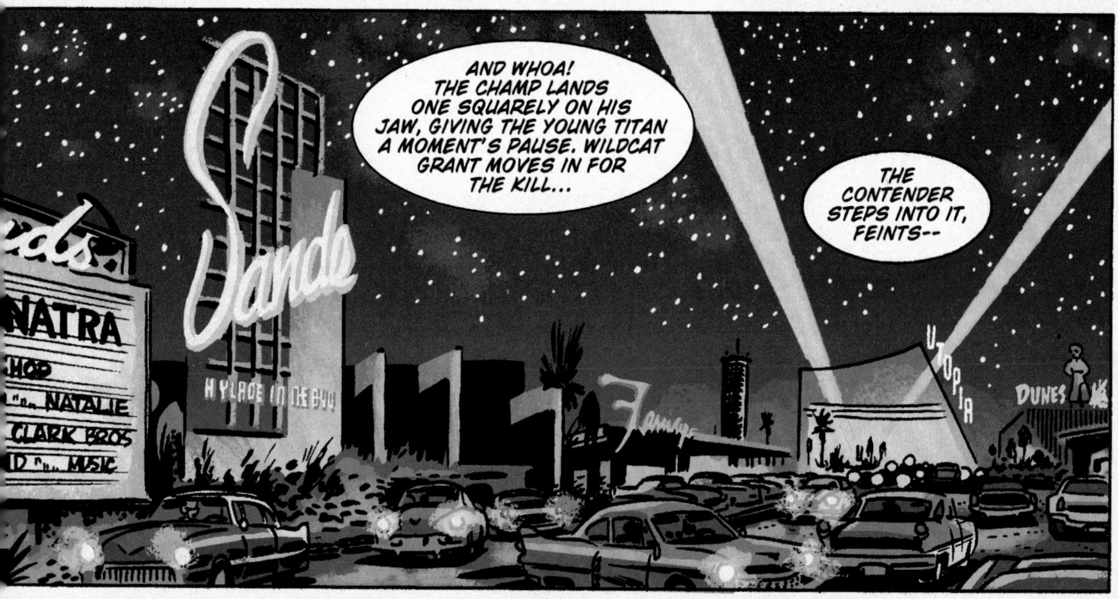
AND WHOA! THE CHAMP LANDS ONE SQUARELY ON HIS JAW, GIVING THE YOUNG TITAN A MOMENT'S PAUSE. WILDCAT GRANT MOVES IN FOR THE KILL...
THE CONTENDER STEPS INTO IT, FEINTS--
Sands
NATRA
NATALIE
CLARK BROS
MUSIC
UTOPIA
DUNES

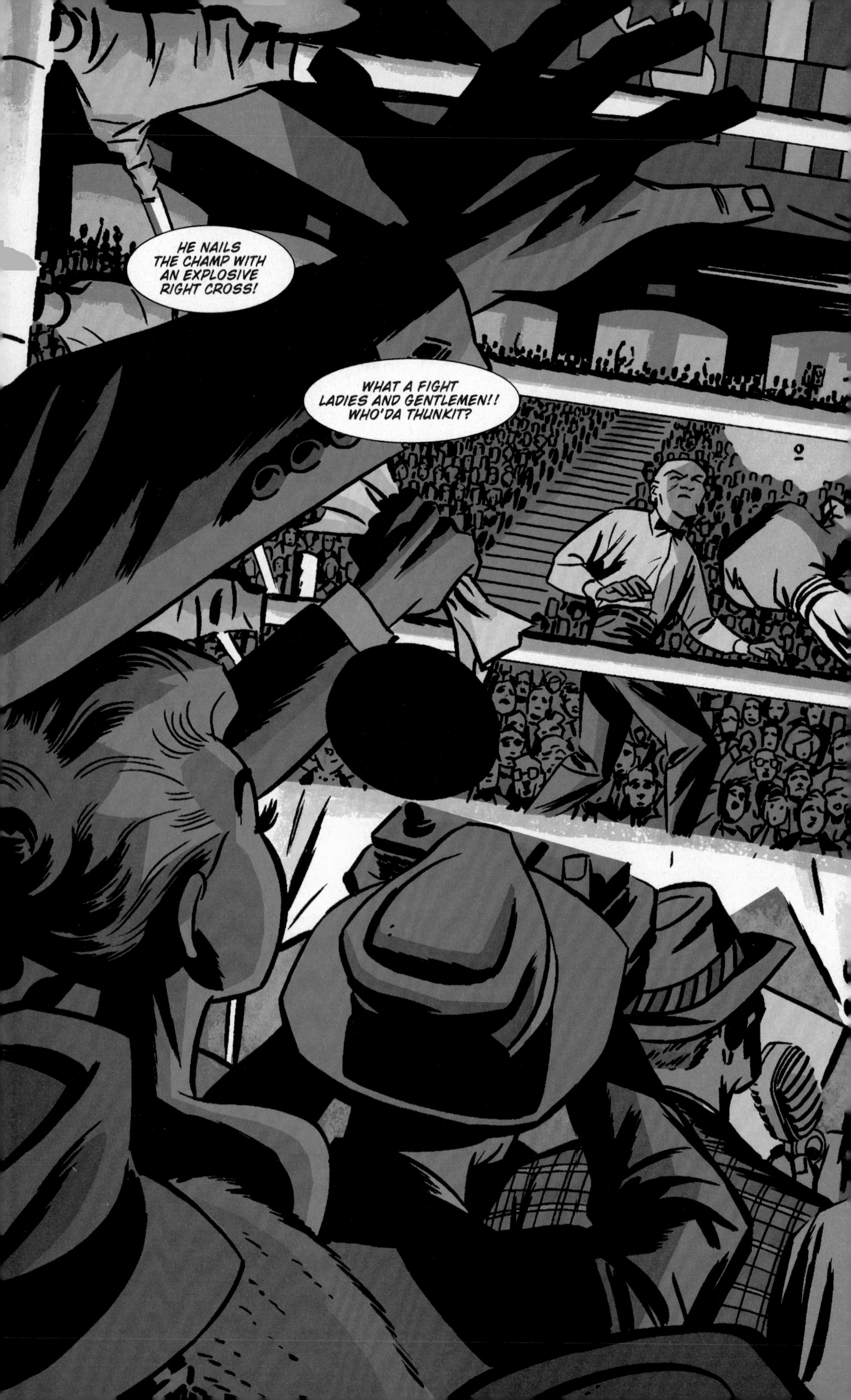
HE NAILS THE CHAMP WITH AN EXPLOSIVE RIGHT CROSS!
WHAT A FIGHT LADIES AND GENTLEMEN!! WHO'DA THUNKIT?

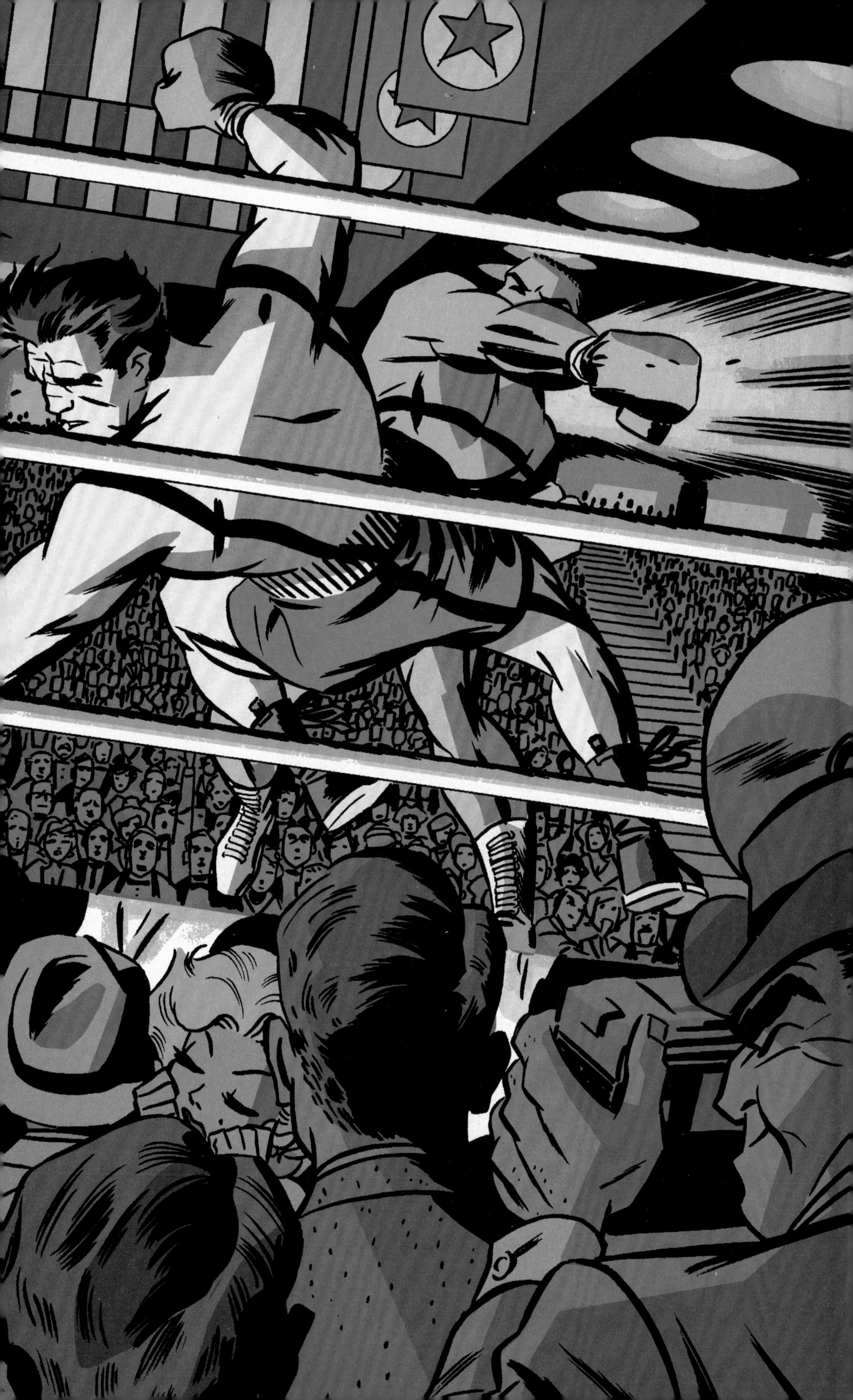

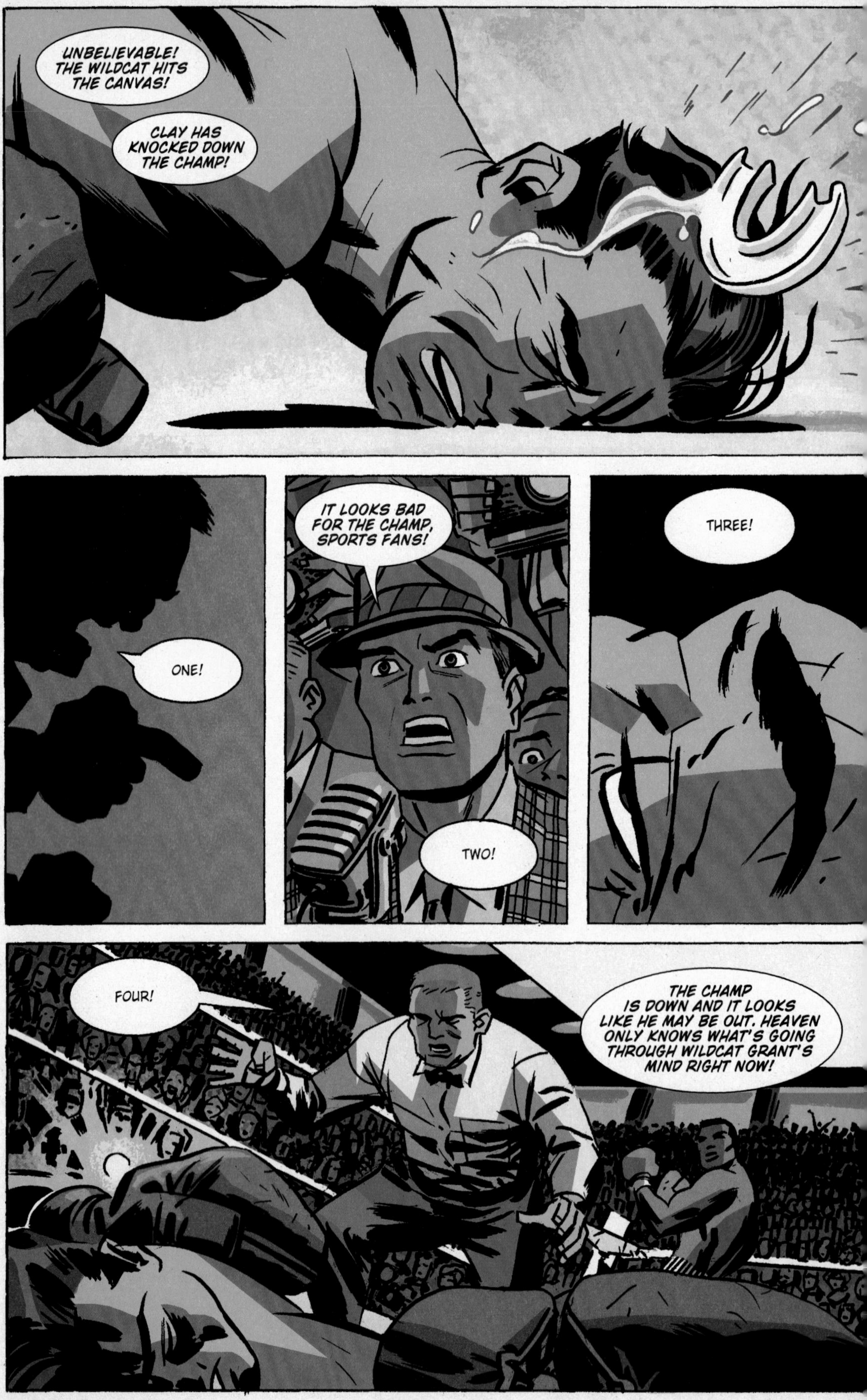
UNBELIEVABLE! THE WILDCAT HITS THE CANVAS!
CLAY HAS KNOCKED DOWN THE CHAMP!
ONE!
IT LOOKS BAD FOR THE CHAMP, SPORTS FANS!
TWO!
THREE!
FOUR!
THE CHAMP IS DOWN AND IT LOOKS LIKE HE MAY BE OUT. HEAVEN ONLY KNOWS WHAT'S GOING THROUGH WILDCAT GRANT'S MIND RIGHT NOW!

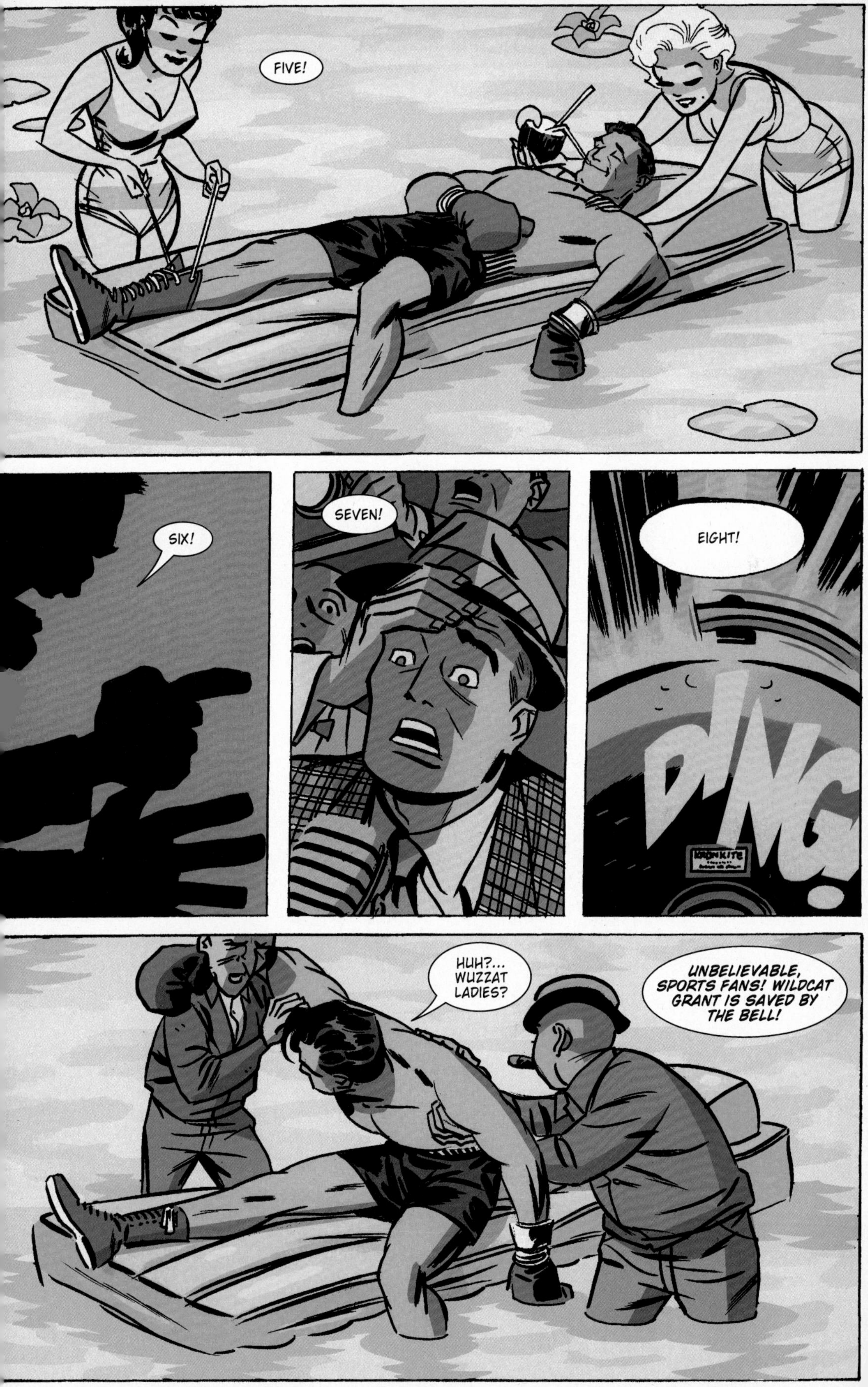
FIVE!
SIX!
SEVEN!
EIGHT!
DING!
HUH?... WUZZAT LADIES?
UNBELIEVABLE, SPORTS FANS! WILDCAT GRANT IS SAVED BY THE BELL!

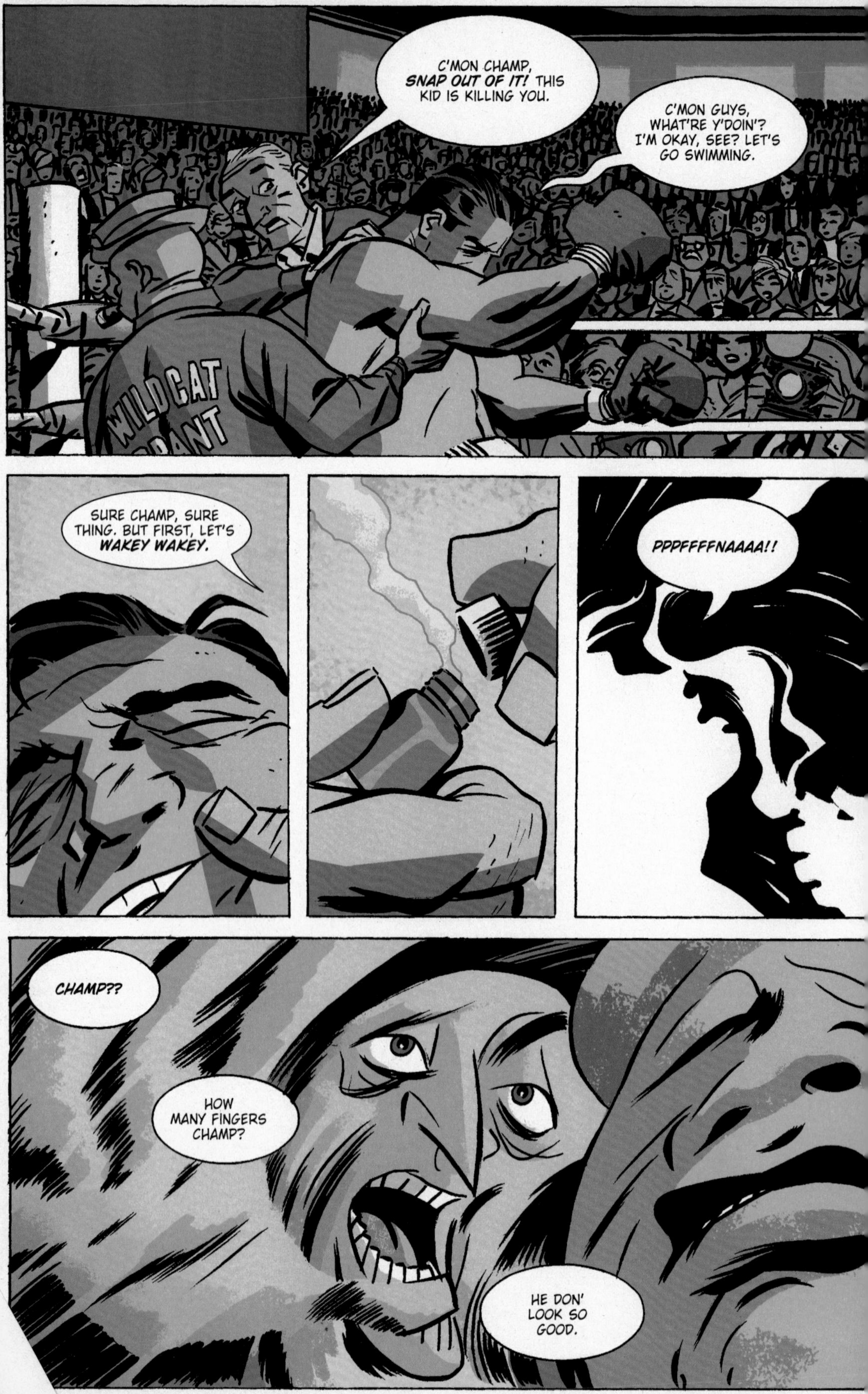
C'MON CHAMP, SNAP OUT OF IT! THIS KID IS KILLING YOU.
C'MON GUYS, WHAT'RE Y'DOIN'? I'M OKAY, SEE? LET'S GO SWIMMING.
WILDCAT GRANT
SURE CHAMP, SURE THING. BUT FIRST, LET'S WAKEY WAKEY.
PPPFFFFNAAAA!!
CHAMP??
HOW MANY FINGERS CHAMP?
HE DON' LOOK SO GOOD.

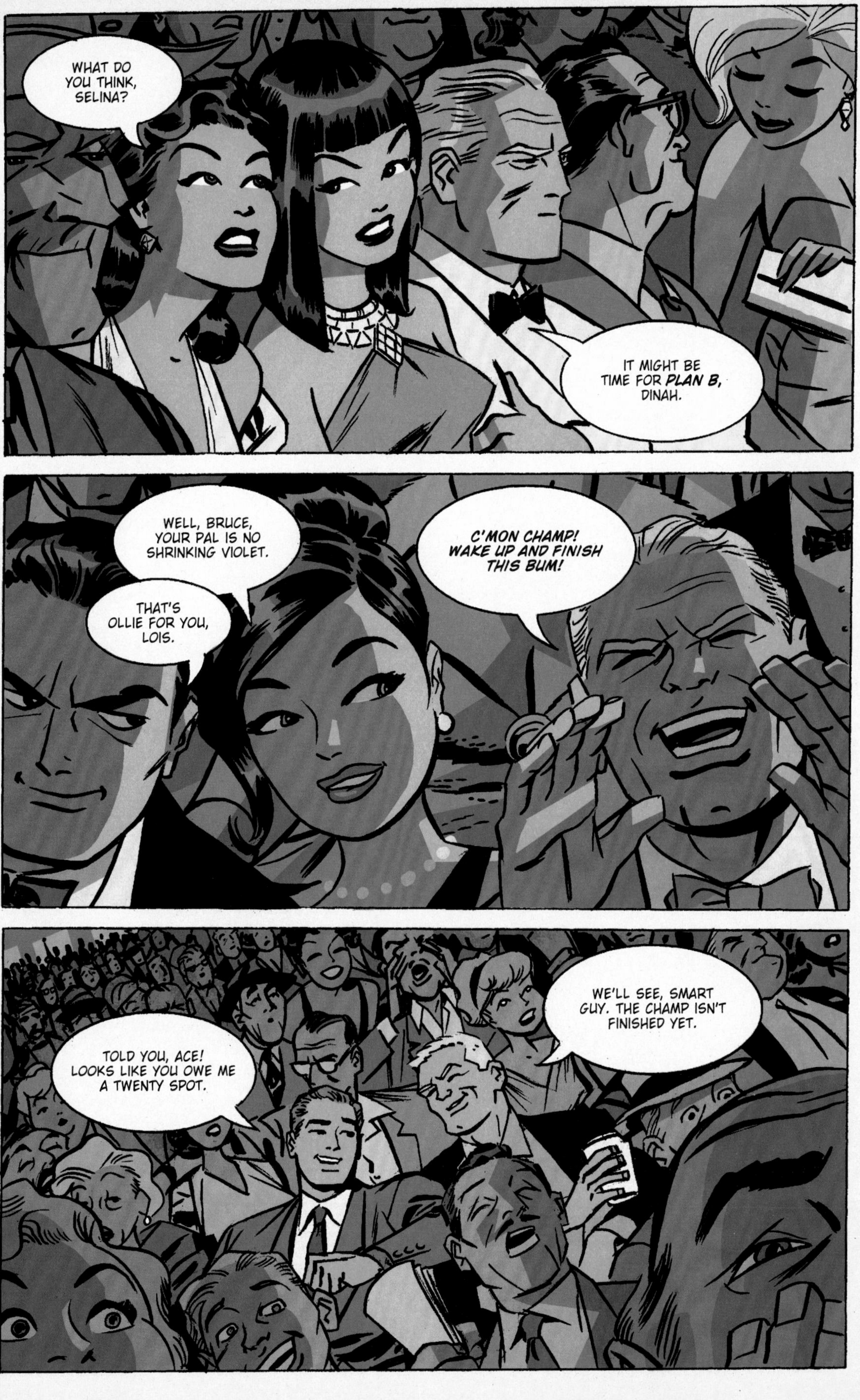
WHAT DO YOU THINK, SELINA?
IT MIGHT BE TIME FOR PLAN B, DINAH.
WELL, BRUCE, YOUR PAL IS NO SHRINKING VIOLET.
THAT'S OLLIE FOR YOU, LOIS.
C'MON CHAMP! WAKE UP AND FINISH THIS BUM!
TOLD YOU, ACE! LOOKS LIKE YOU OWE ME A TWENTY SPOT.
WE'LL SEE, SMART GUY. THE CHAMP ISN'T FINISHED YET.

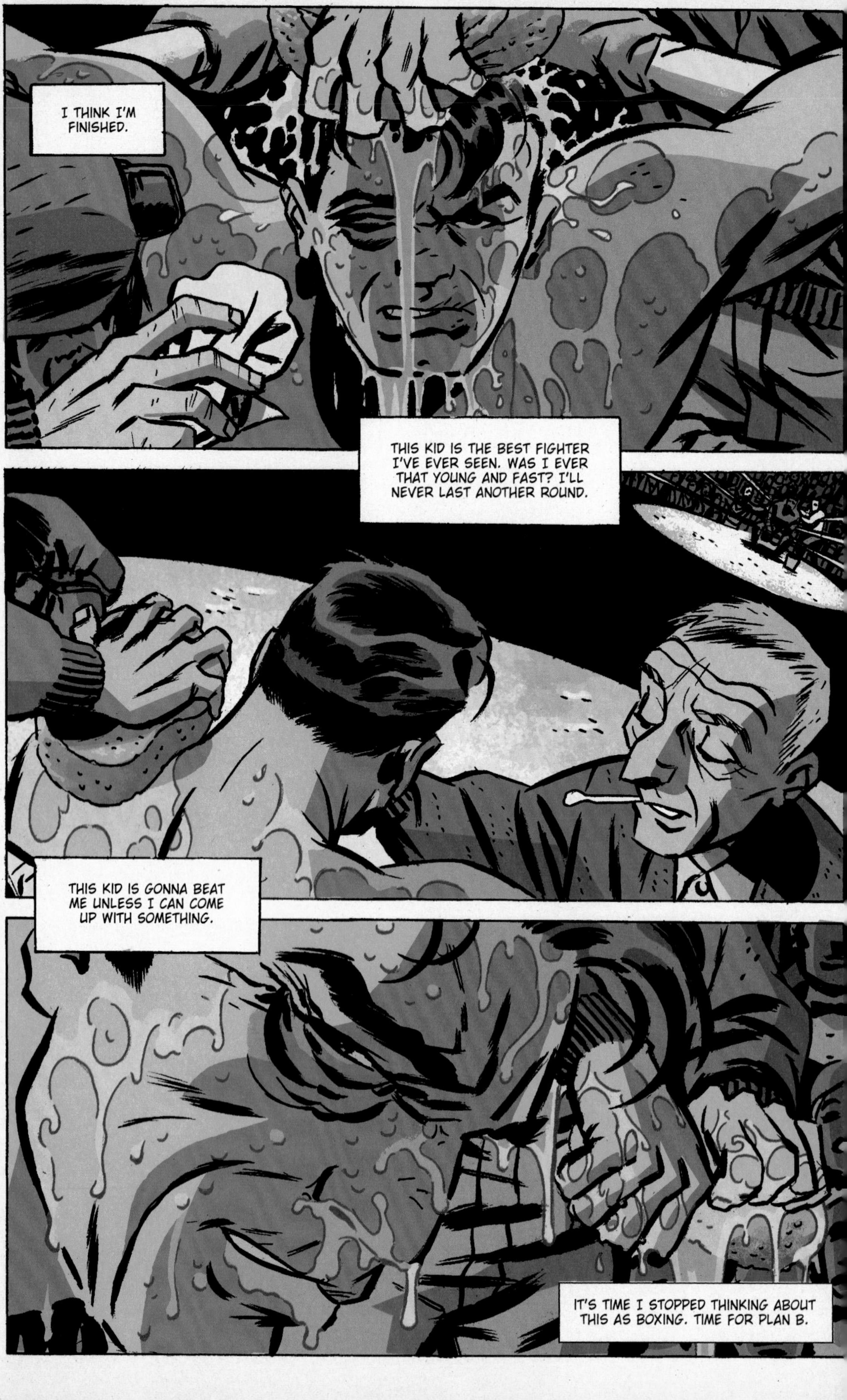

I THINK I'M FINISHED.
THIS KID IS THE BEST FIGHTER I'VE EVER SEEN. WAS I EVER THAT YOUNG AND FAST? I'LL NEVER LAST ANOTHER ROUND.
THIS KID IS GONNA BEAT ME UNLESS I CAN COME UP WITH SOMETHING.
IT'S TIME I STOPPED THINKING ABOUT THIS AS BOXING. TIME FOR PLAN B.

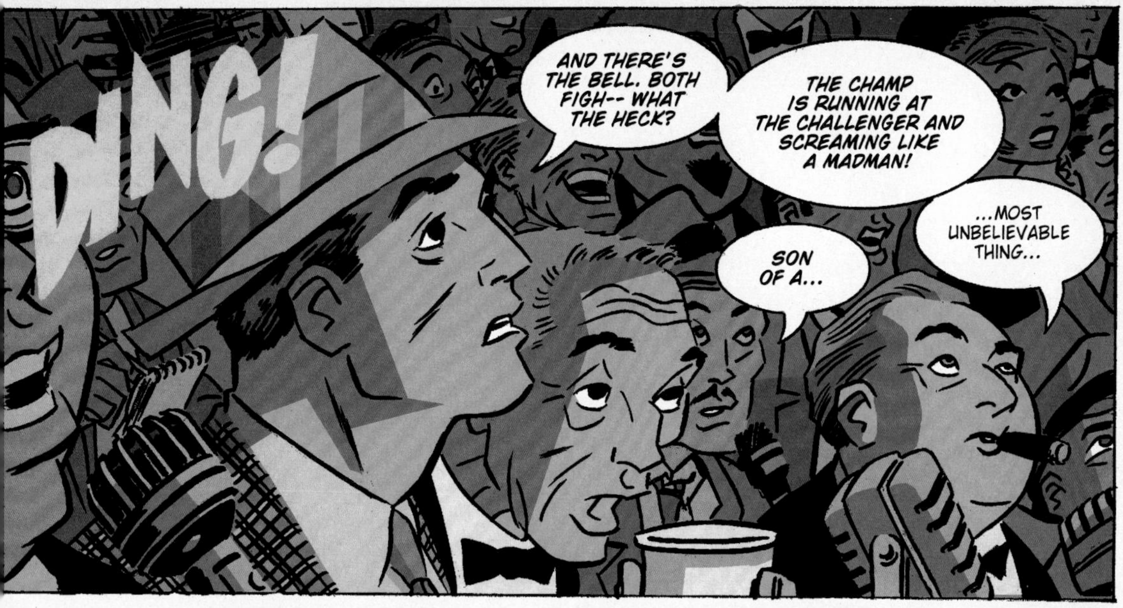
DING!
AND THERE'S THE BELL. BOTH FIGH-- WHAT THE HECK?
THE CHAMP IS RUNNING AT THE CHALLENGER AND SCREAMING LIKE A MADMAN!
SON OF A...
...MOST UNBELIEVABLE THING...

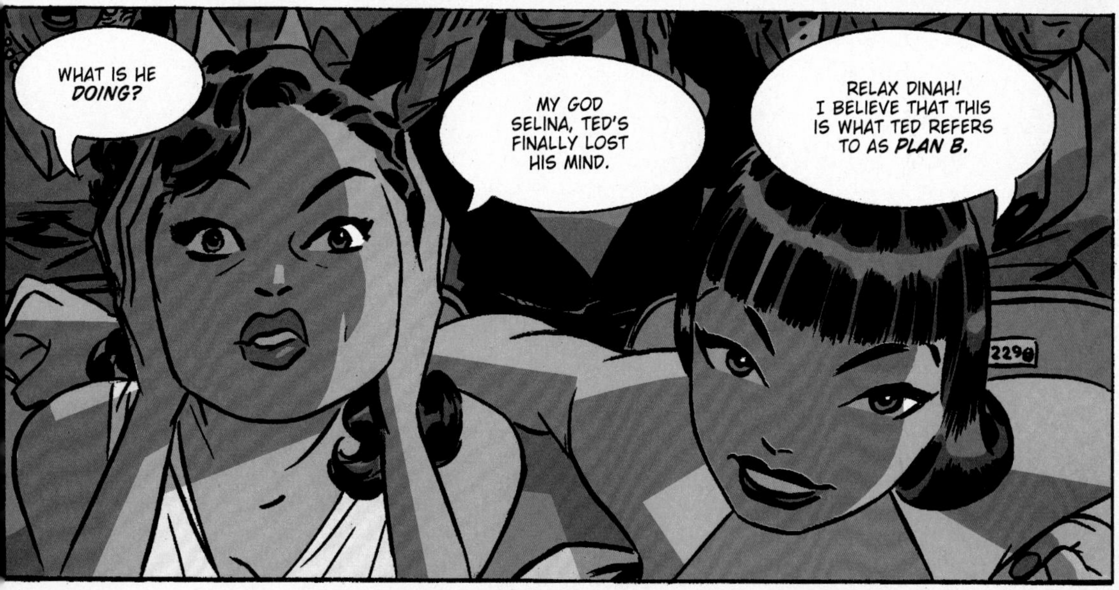
WHAT IS HE DOING?
MY GOD SELINA, TED'S FINALLY LOST HIS MIND.
RELAX DINAH! I BELIEVE THAT THIS IS WHAT TED REFERS TO AS PLAN B.

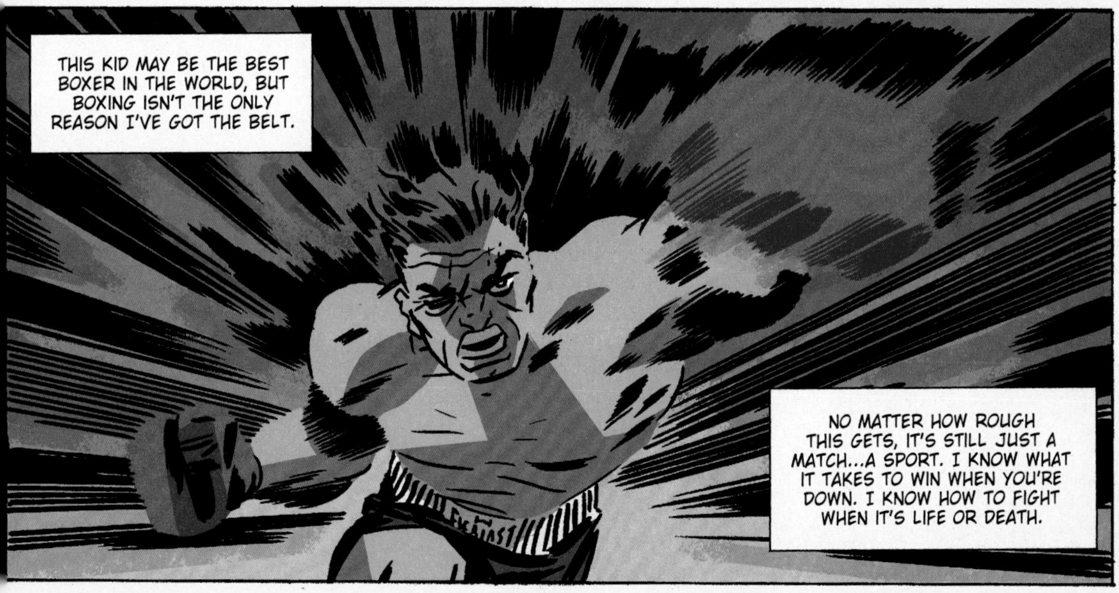
THIS KID MAY BE THE BEST BOXER IN THE WORLD, BUT BOXING ISN'T THE ONLY REASON I'VE GOT THE BELT.
NO MATTER HOW ROUGH THIS GETS, IT'S STILL JUST A MATCH...A SPORT. I KNOW WHAT IT TAKES TO WIN WHEN YOU'RE DOWN. I KNOW HOW TO FIGHT WHEN IT'S LIFE OR DEATH.

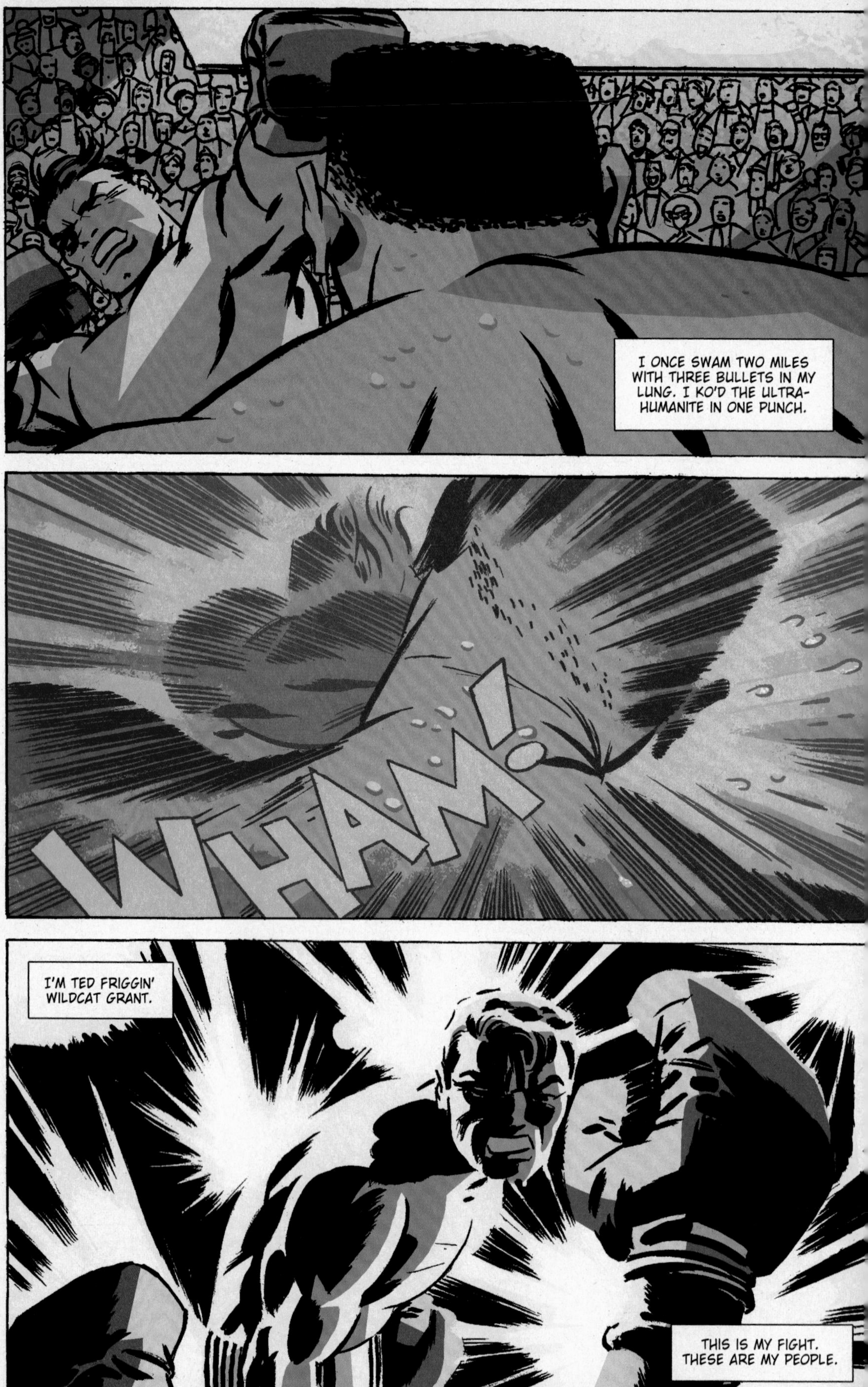
I ONCE SWAM TWO MILES WITH THREE BULLETS IN MY LUNG. I KO'D THE ULTRA-HUMANITE IN ONE PUNCH.
WHAM!
I'M TED FRIGGIN' WILDCAT GRANT.
THIS IS MY FIGHT. THESE ARE MY PEOPLE.

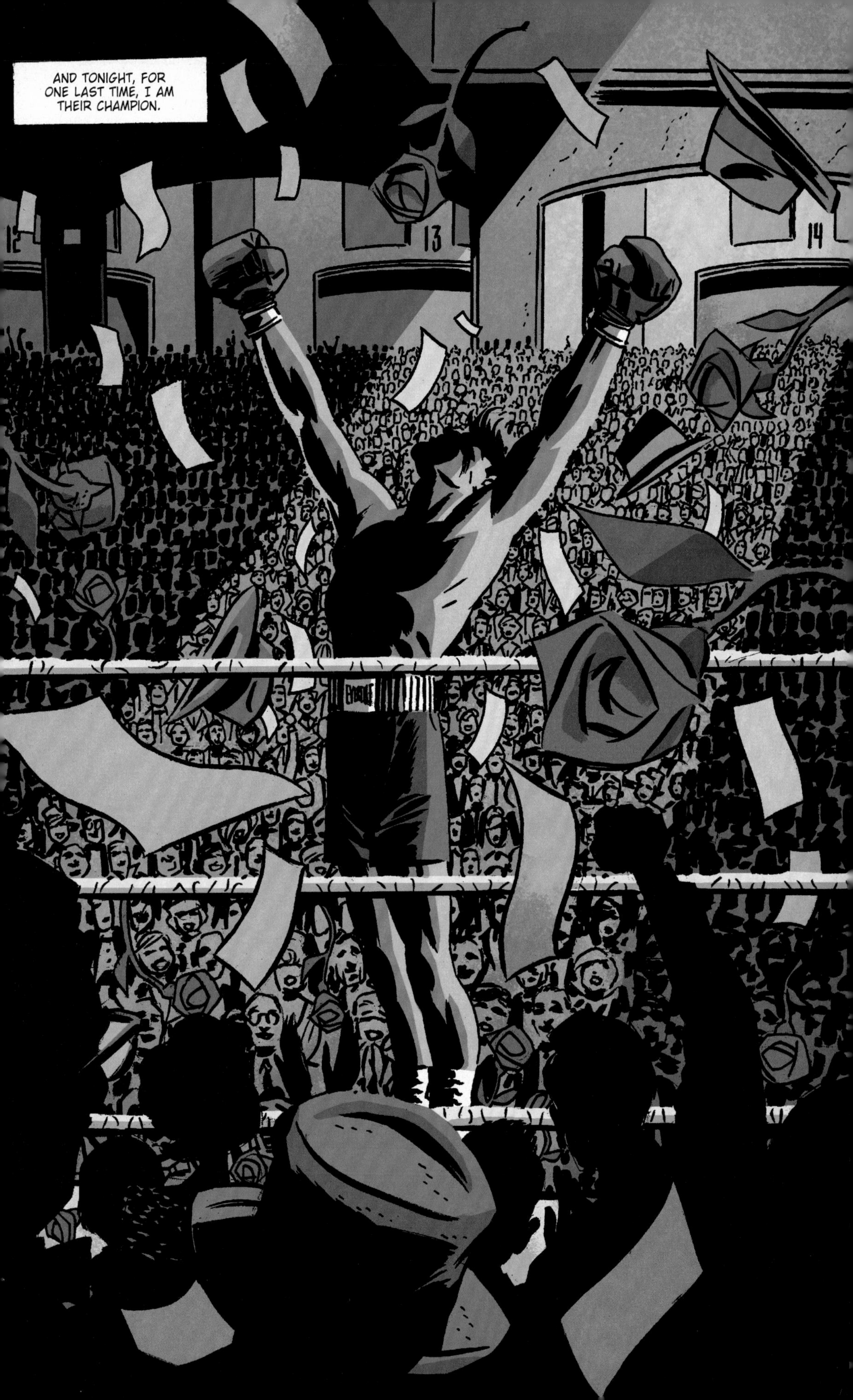
AND TONIGHT, FOR ONE LAST TIME, I AM THEIR CHAMPION.
12
13
14

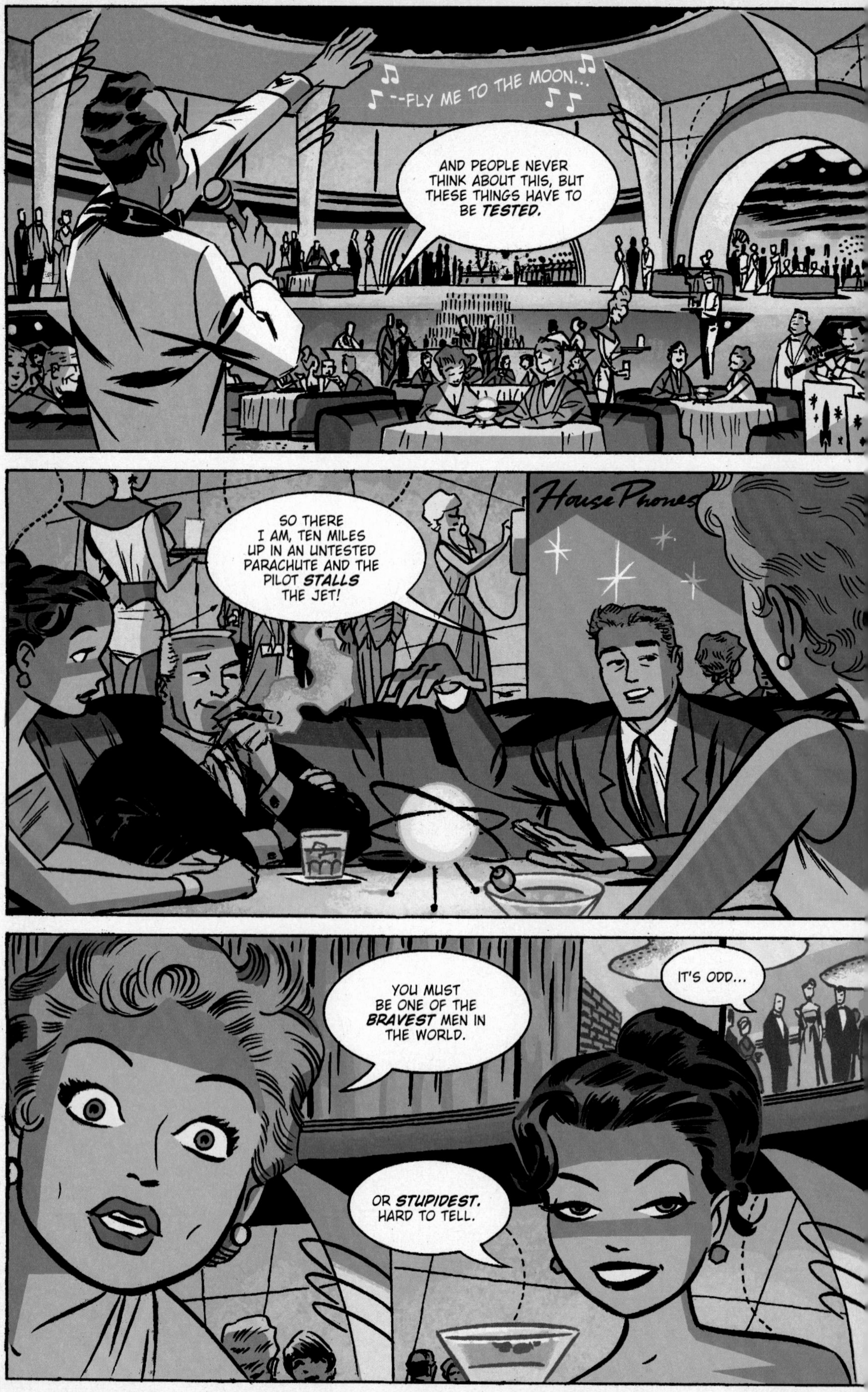
--FLY ME TO THE MOON...
AND PEOPLE NEVER THINK ABOUT THIS, BUT THESE THINGS HAVE TO BE TESTED.
SO THERE I AM, TEN MILES UP IN AN UNTESTED PARACHUTE AND THE PILOT STALLS THE JET!
House Phones
YOU MUST BE ONE OF THE BRAVEST MEN IN THE WORLD.
IT'S ODD...
OR STUPIDEST. HARD TO TELL.

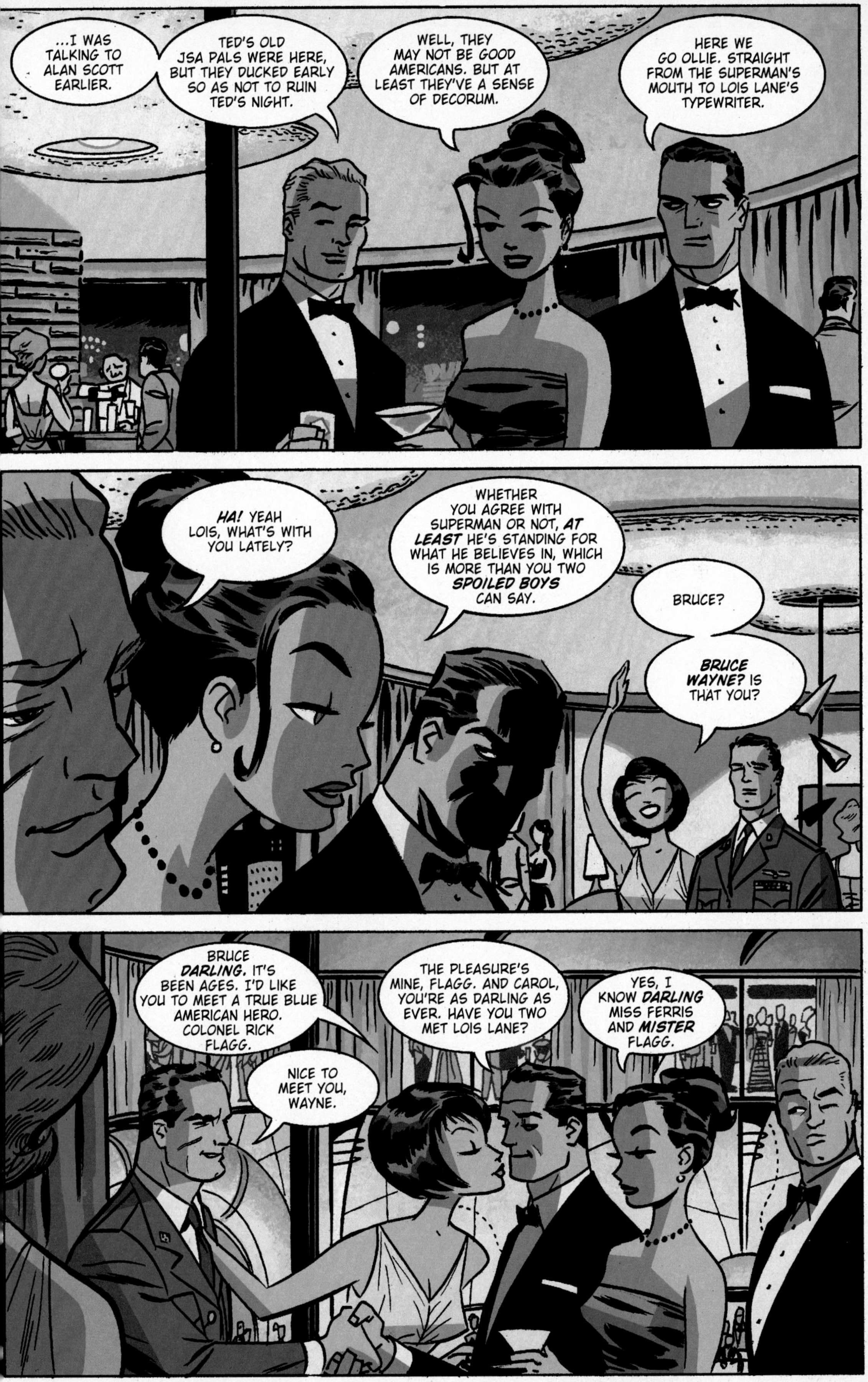
...I WAS TALKING TO ALAN SCOTT EARLIER.
TED'S OLD JSA PALS WERE HERE, BUT THEY DUCKED EARLY SO AS NOT TO RUIN TED'S NIGHT.
WELL, THEY MAY NOT BE GOOD AMERICANS. BUT AT LEAST THEY'VE A SENSE OF DECORUM.
HERE WE GO OLLIE. STRAIGHT FROM THE SUPERMAN'S MOUTH TO LOIS LANE'S TYPEWRITER.
HA! YEAH LOIS, WHAT'S WITH YOU LATELY?
WHETHER YOU AGREE WITH SUPERMAN OR NOT, AT LEAST HE'S STANDING FOR WHAT HE BELIEVES IN, WHICH IS MORE THAN YOU TWO SPOILED BOYS CAN SAY.
BRUCE?
BRUCE WAYNE? IS THAT YOU?
BRUCE DARLING. IT'S BEEN AGES. I'D LIKE YOU TO MEET A TRUE BLUE AMERICAN HERO. COLONEL RICK FLAGG.
NICE TO MEET YOU, WAYNE.
THE PLEASURE'S MINE, FLAGG. AND CAROL, YOU'RE AS DARLING AS EVER. HAVE YOU TWO MET LOIS LANE?
YES, I KNOW DARLING MISS FERRIS AND MISTER FLAGG.

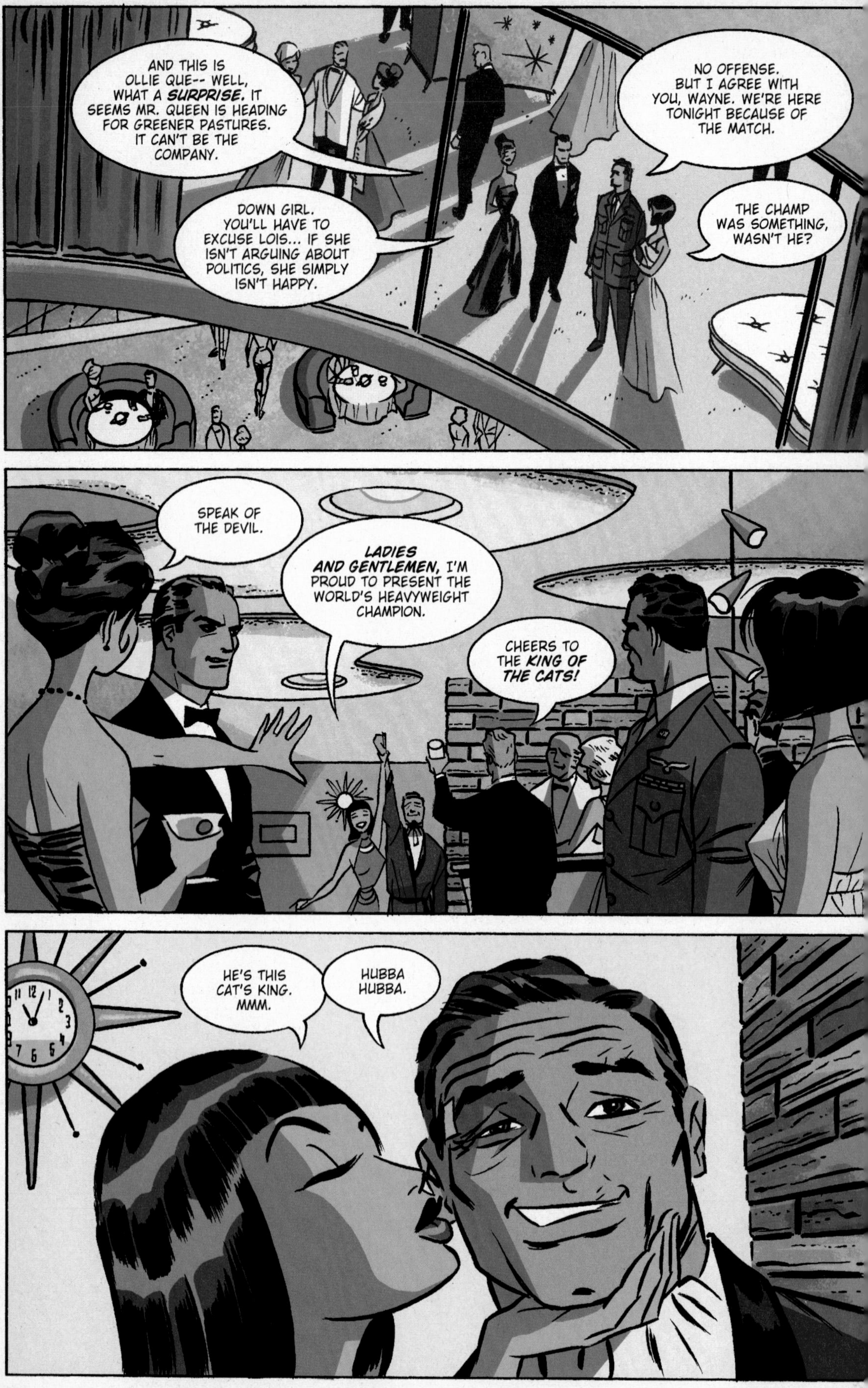
AND THIS IS OLLIE QUE-- WELL, WHAT A SURPRISE. IT SEEMS MR. QUEEN IS HEADING FOR GREENER PASTURES. IT CAN'T BE THE COMPANY.
DOWN GIRL. YOU'LL HAVE TO EXCUSE LOIS... IF SHE ISN'T ARGUING ABOUT POLITICS, SHE SIMPLY ISN'T HAPPY.
NO OFFENSE. BUT I AGREE WITH YOU, WAYNE. WE'RE HERE TONIGHT BECAUSE OF THE MATCH.
THE CHAMP WAS SOMETHING, WASN'T HE?
SPEAK OF THE DEVIL.
LADIES AND GENTLEMEN, I'M PROUD TO PRESENT THE WORLD'S HEAVYWEIGHT CHAMPION.
CHEERS TO THE KING OF THE CATS!
HE'S THIS CAT'S KING. MMM.
HUBBA HUBBA.

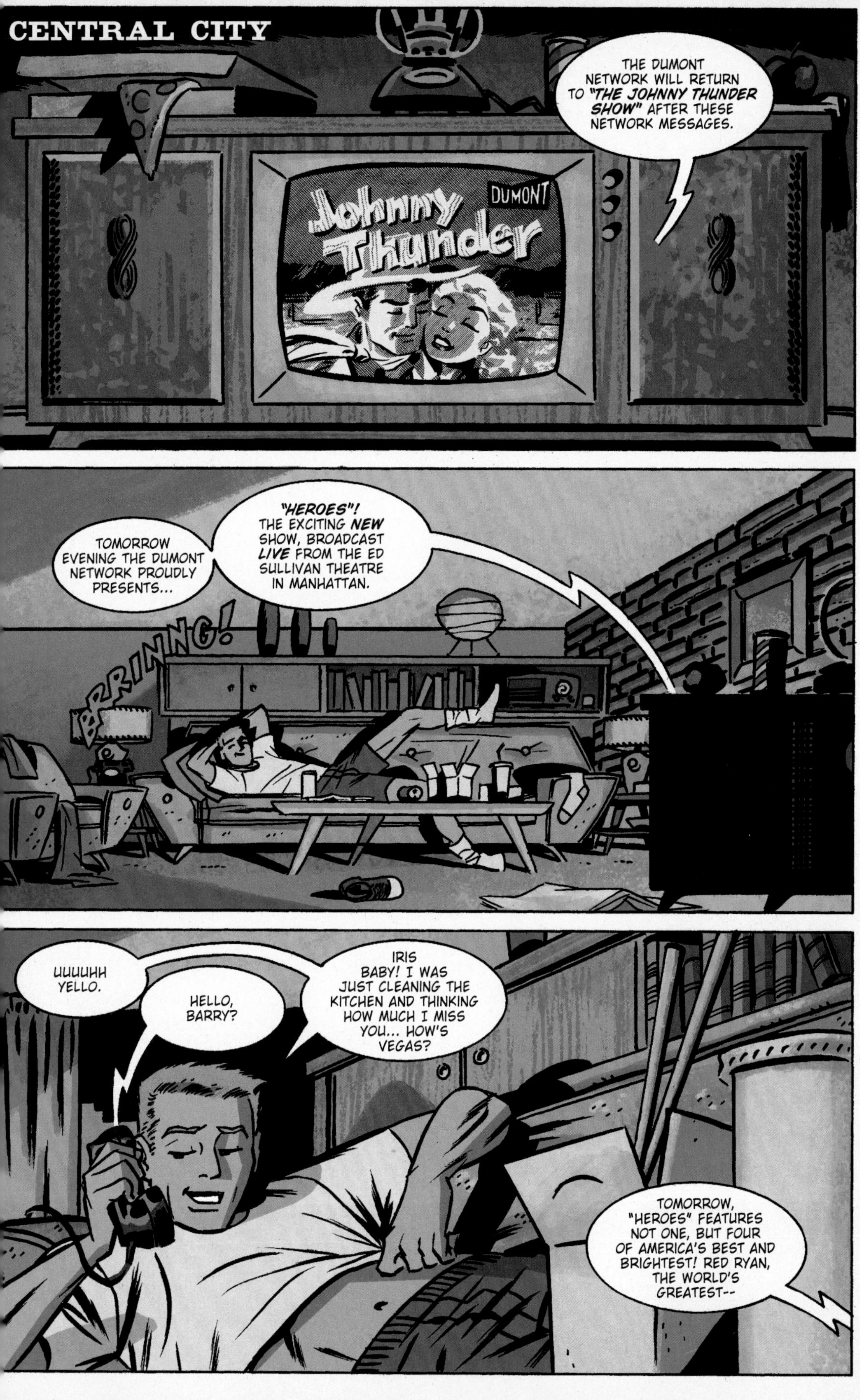
CENTRAL CITY
THE DUMONT NETWORK WILL RETURN TO "THE JOHNNY THUNDER SHOW" AFTER THESE NETWORK MESSAGES.
Johnny Thunder
DUMONT
TOMORROW EVENING THE DUMONT NETWORK PROUDLY PRESENTS...
"HEROES"! THE EXCITING NEW SHOW, BROADCAST LIVE FROM THE ED SULLIVAN THEATRE IN MANHATTAN.
BRRINNNG!
UUUUHH YELLO.
HELLO, BARRY?
IRIS BABY! I WAS JUST CLEANING THE KITCHEN AND THINKING HOW MUCH I MISS YOU... HOW'S VEGAS?
TOMORROW, "HEROES" FEATURES NOT ONE, BUT FOUR OF AMERICA'S BEST AND BRIGHTEST! RED RYAN, THE WORLD'S GREATEST--

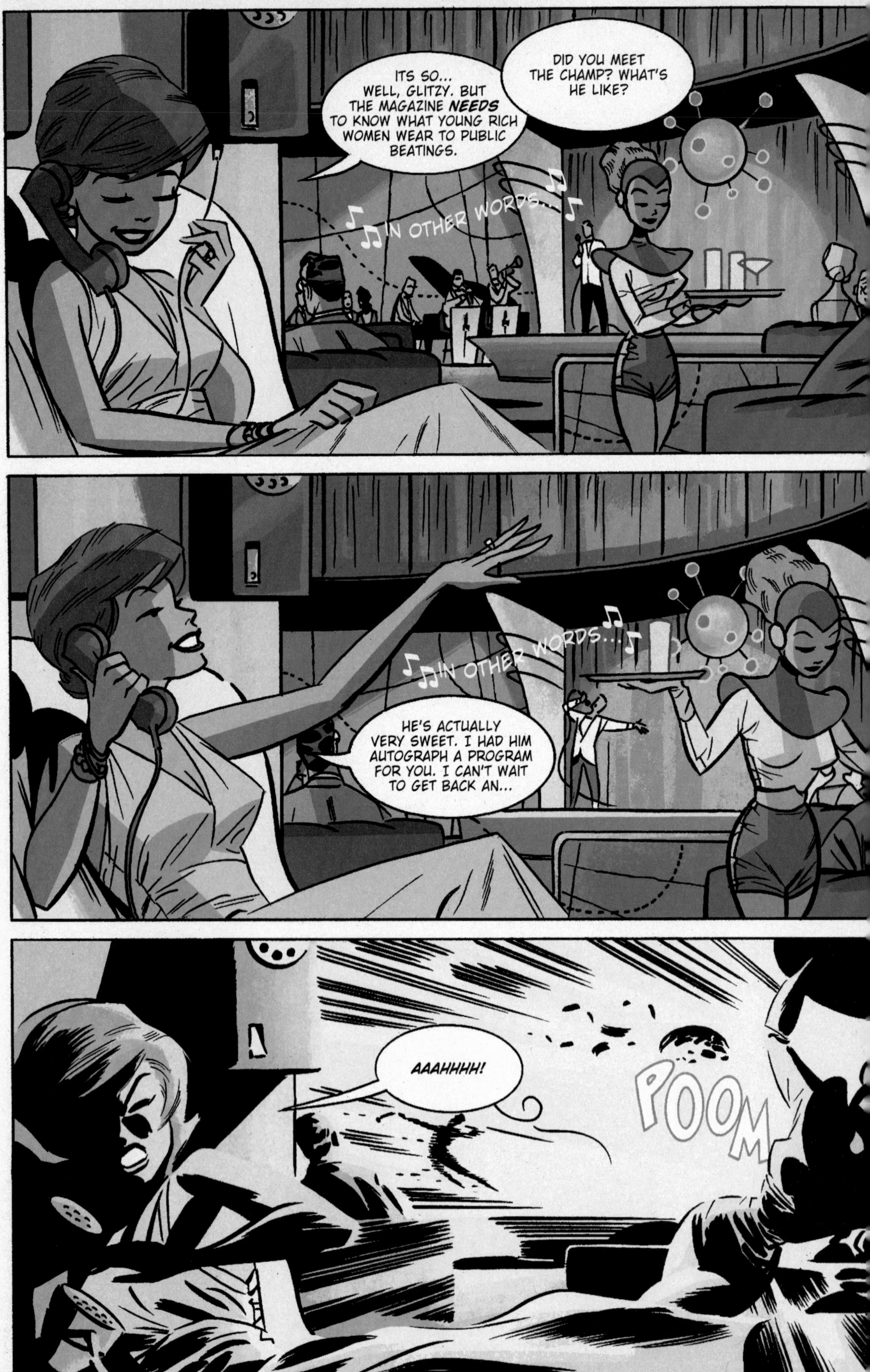

ITS SO... WELL, GLITZY. BUT THE MAGAZINE NEEDS TO KNOW WHAT YOUNG RICH WOMEN WEAR TO PUBLIC BEATINGS.
DID YOU MEET THE CHAMP? WHAT'S HE LIKE?
IN OTHER WORDS...
IN OTHER WORDS...
HE'S ACTUALLY VERY SWEET. I HAD HIM AUTOGRAPH A PROGRAM FOR YOU. I CAN'T WAIT TO GET BACK AN...
AAAHHHH!
POOM

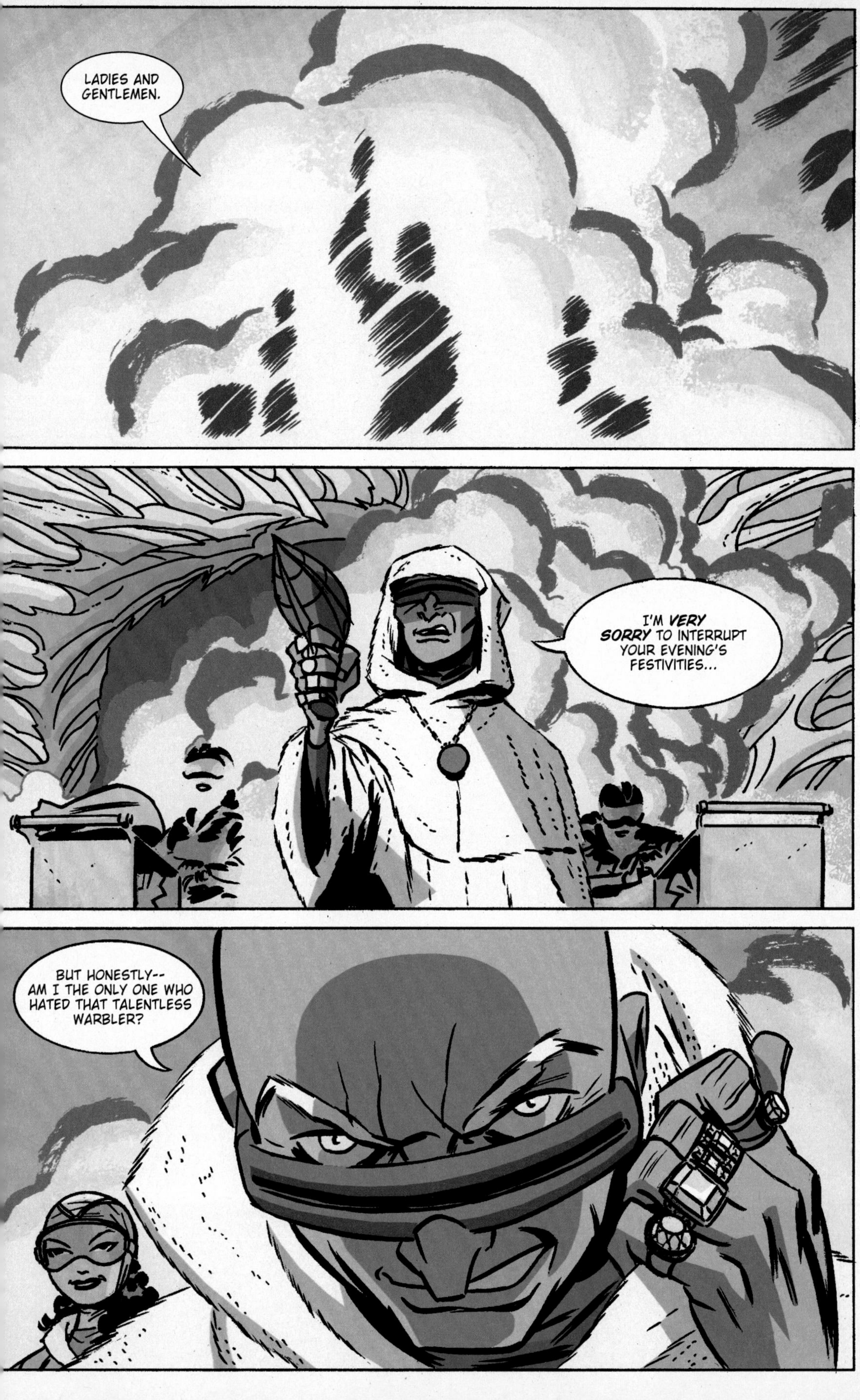
LADIES AND GENTLEMEN.
I'M VERY SORRY TO INTERRUPT YOUR EVENING'S FESTIVITIES...
BUT HONESTLY-- AM I THE ONLY ONE WHO HATED THAT TALENTLESS WARBLER?

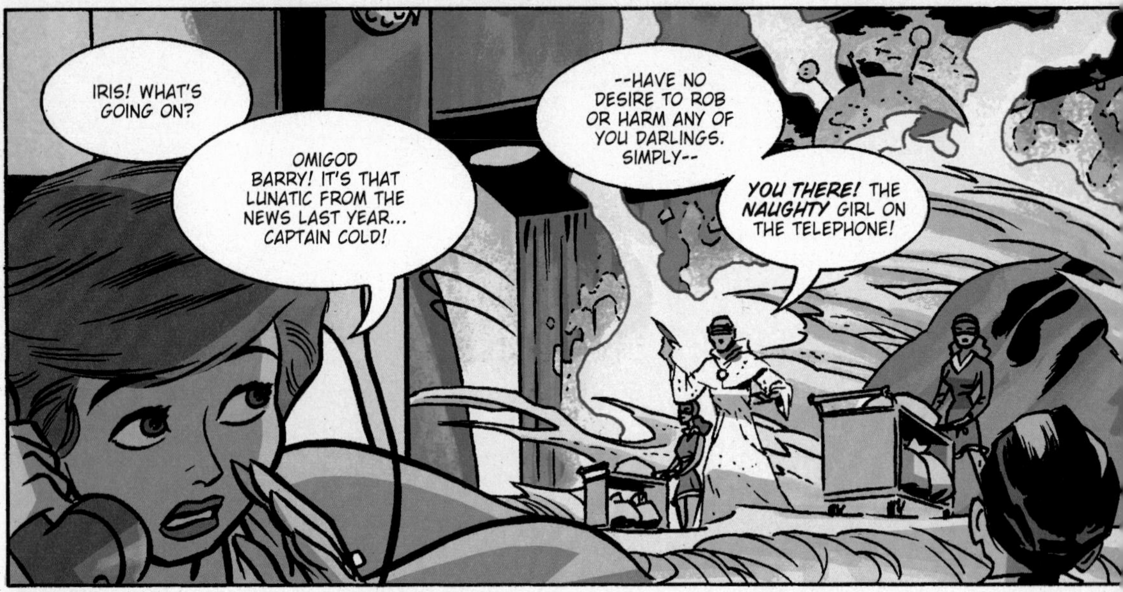
IRIS! WHAT'S GOING ON?
OMIGOD BARRY! IT'S THAT LUNATIC FROM THE NEWS LAST YEAR... CAPTAIN COLD!
--HAVE NO DESIRE TO ROB OR HARM ANY OF YOU DARLINGS. SIMPLY--
YOU THERE! THE NAUGHTY GIRL ON THE TELEPHONE!

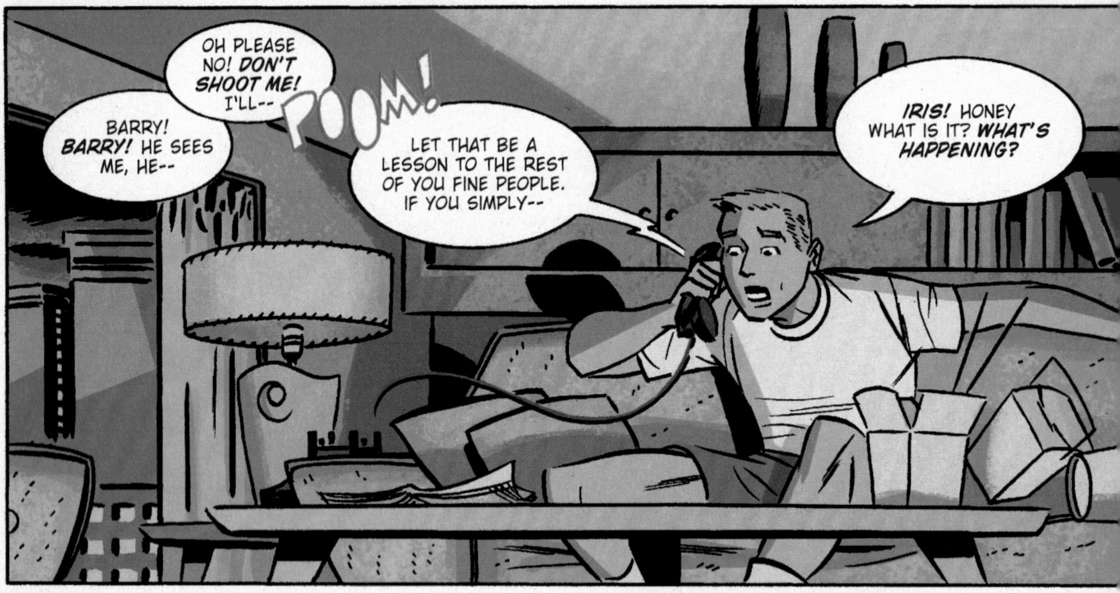
BARRY! BARRY! HE SEES ME, HE--
OH PLEASE NO! DON'T SHOOT ME! I'LL--
POOM!
LET THAT BE A LESSON TO THE REST OF YOU FINE PEOPLE. IF YOU SIMPLY--
IRIS! HONEY WHAT IS IT? WHAT'S HAPPENING?

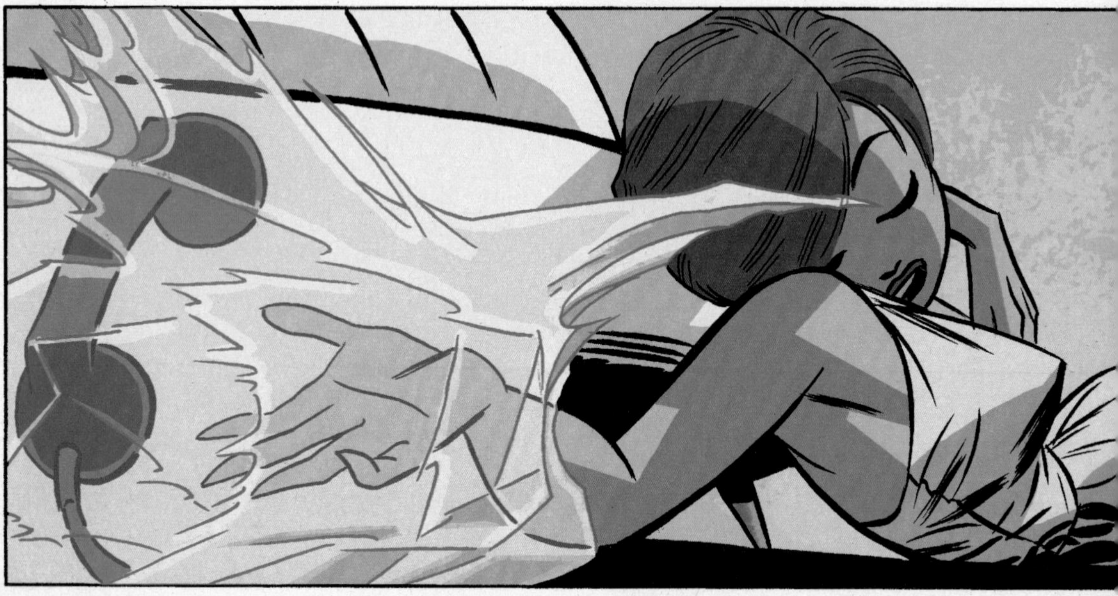

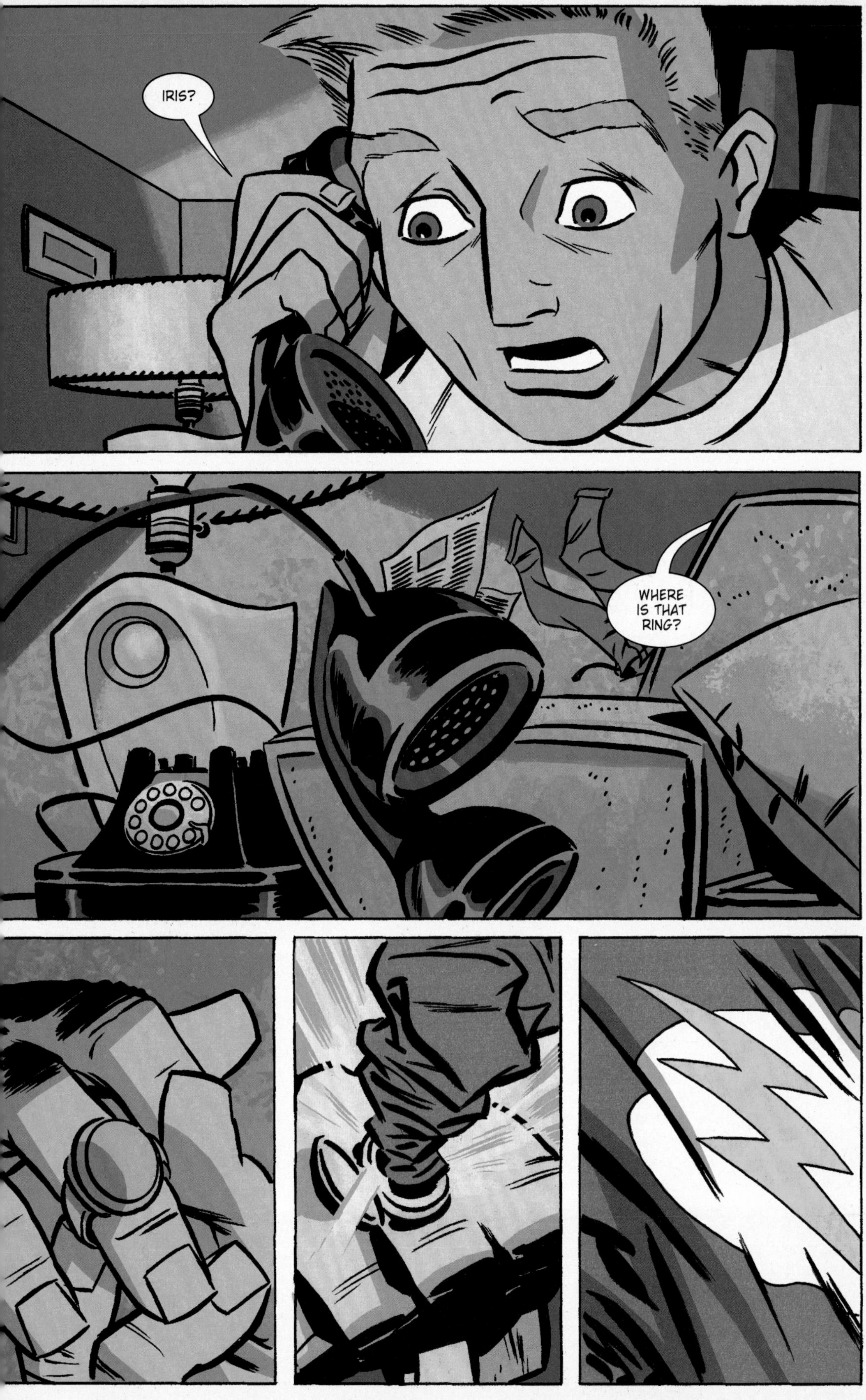
IRIS?
WHERE IS THAT RING?

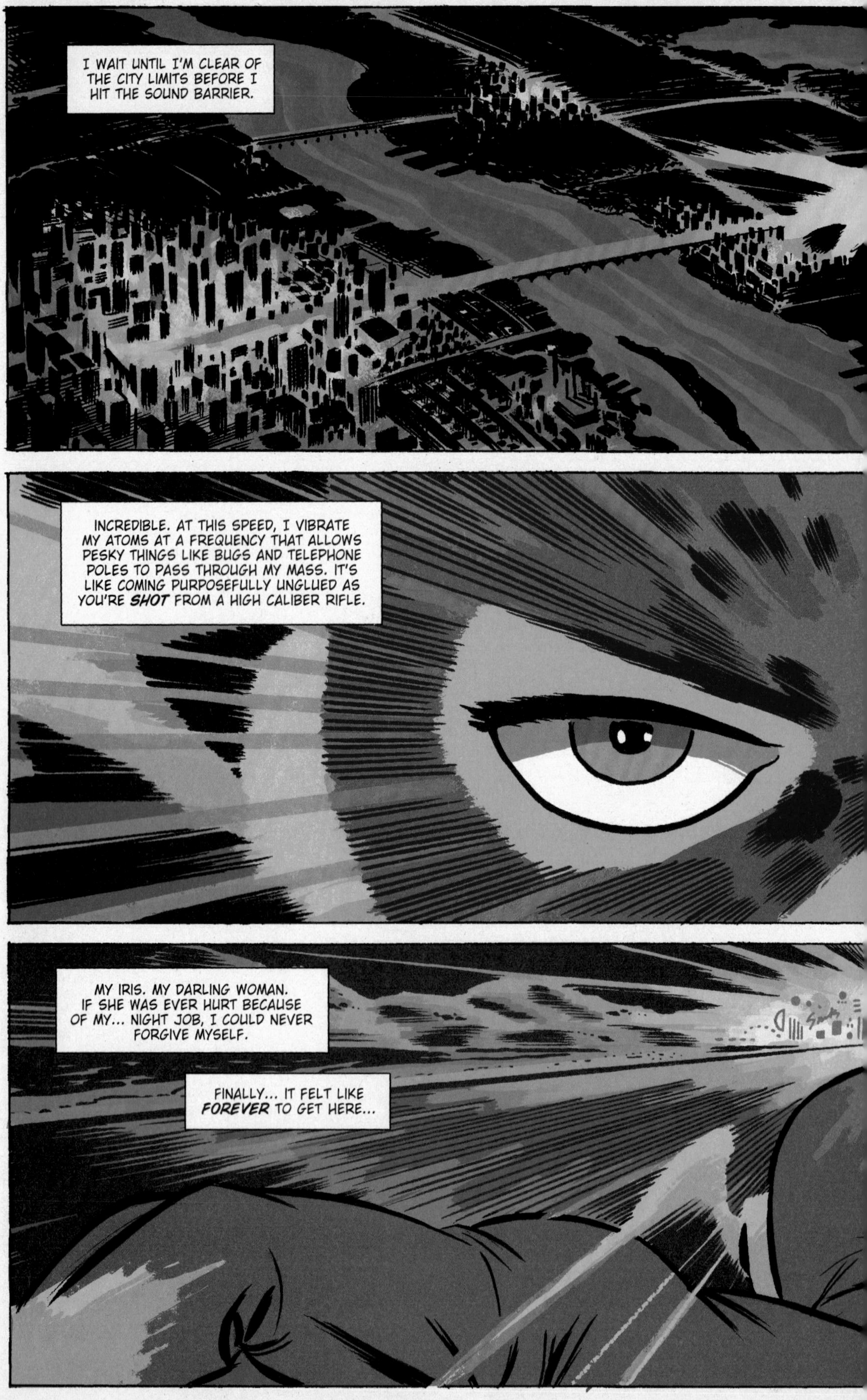
I WAIT UNTIL I'M CLEAR OF THE CITY LIMITS BEFORE I HIT THE SOUND BARRIER.
INCREDIBLE. AT THIS SPEED, I VIBRATE MY ATOMS AT A FREQUENCY THAT ALLOWS PESKY THINGS LIKE BUGS AND TELEPHONE POLES TO PASS THROUGH MY MASS. IT'S LIKE COMING PURPOSEFULLY UNGLUED AS YOU'RE SHOT FROM A HIGH CALIBER RIFLE.
MY IRIS. MY DARLING WOMAN. IF SHE WAS EVER HURT BECAUSE OF MY... NIGHT JOB, I COULD NEVER FORGIVE MYSELF.
FINALLY... IT FELT LIKE FOREVER TO GET HERE...

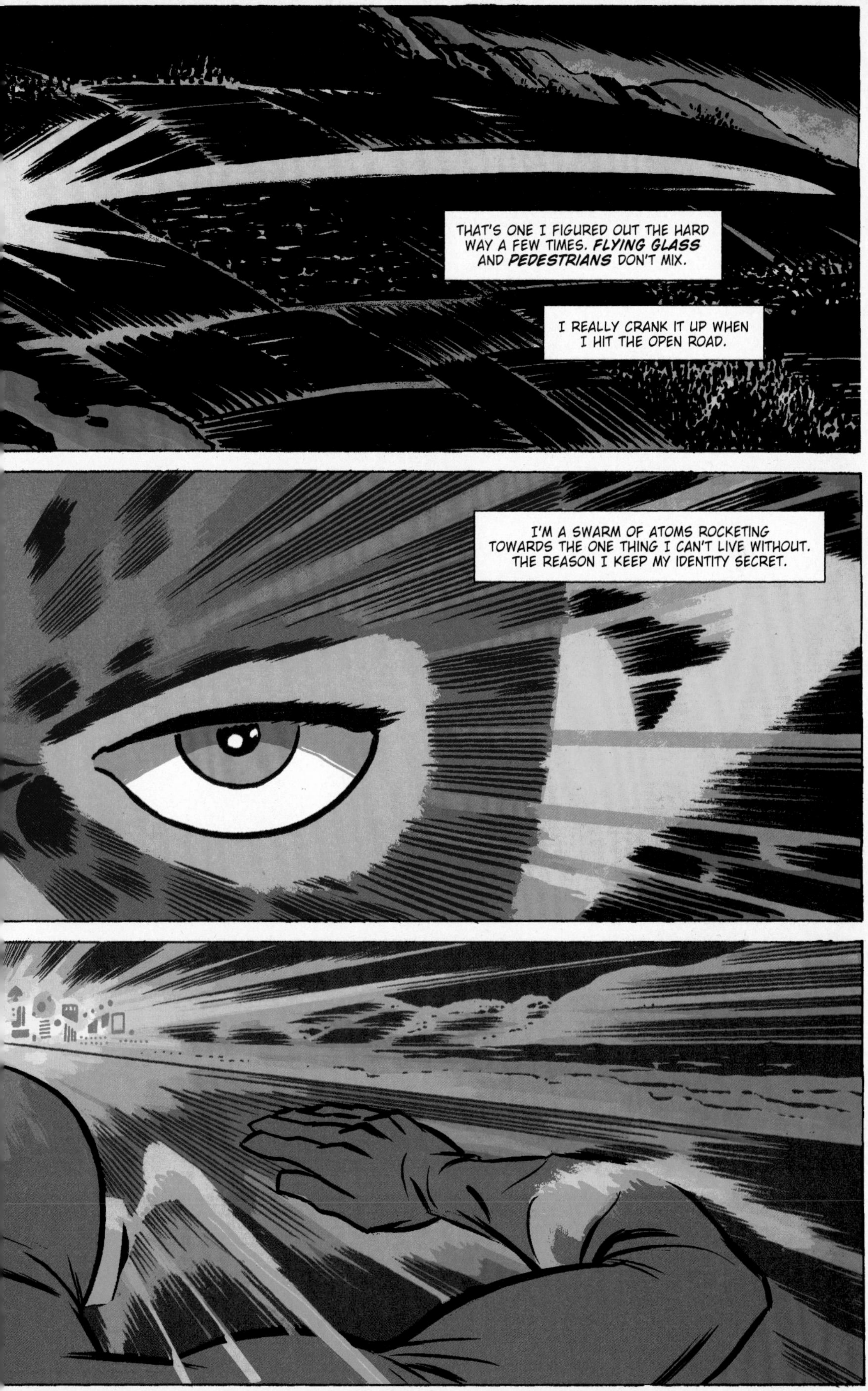
THAT'S ONE I FIGURED OUT THE HARD WAY A FEW TIMES. FLYING GLASS AND PEDESTRIANS DON'T MIX.
I REALLY CRANK IT UP WHEN I HIT THE OPEN ROAD.
I'M A SWARM OF ATOMS ROCKETING TOWARDS THE ONE THING I CAN'T LIVE WITHOUT. THE REASON I KEEP MY IDENTITY SECRET.

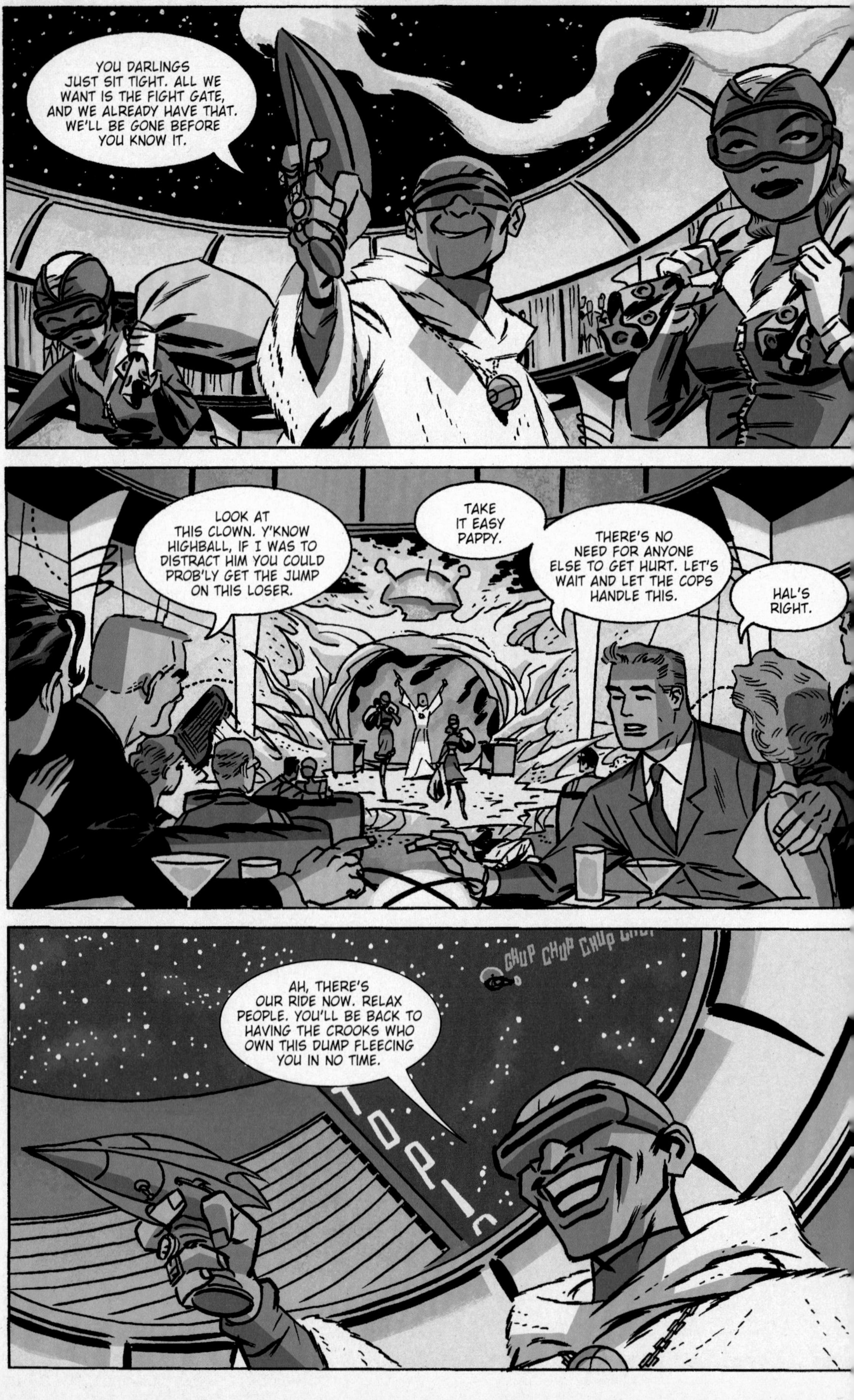
YOU DARLINGS JUST SIT TIGHT. ALL WE WANT IS THE FIGHT GATE, AND WE ALREADY HAVE THAT. WE'LL BE GONE BEFORE YOU KNOW IT.
LOOK AT THIS CLOWN. Y'KNOW HIGHBALL, IF I WAS TO DISTRACT HIM YOU COULD PROB'LY GET THE JUMP ON THIS LOSER.
TAKE IT EASY PAPPY.
THERE'S NO NEED FOR ANYONE ELSE TO GET HURT. LET'S WAIT AND LET THE COPS HANDLE THIS.
HAL'S RIGHT.
CHUP CHUP CHUP
AH, THERE'S OUR RIDE NOW. RELAX PEOPLE. YOU'LL BE BACK TO HAVING THE CROOKS WHO OWN THIS DUMP FLEECING YOU IN NO TIME.

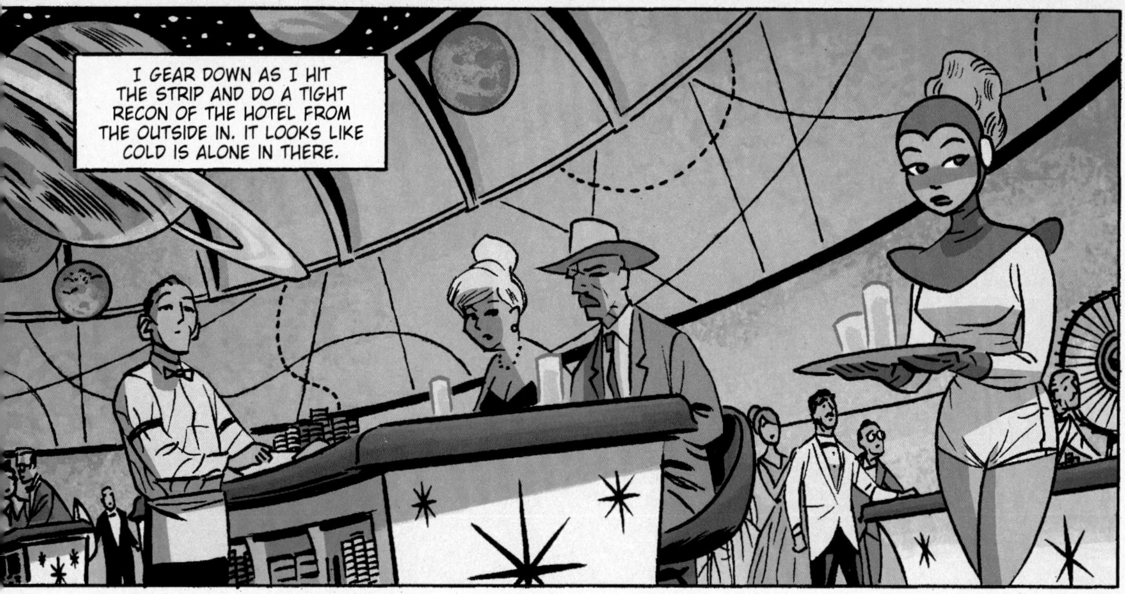
I GEAR DOWN AS I HIT THE STRIP AND DO A TIGHT RECON OF THE HOTEL FROM THE OUTSIDE IN. IT LOOKS LIKE COLD IS ALONE IN THERE.

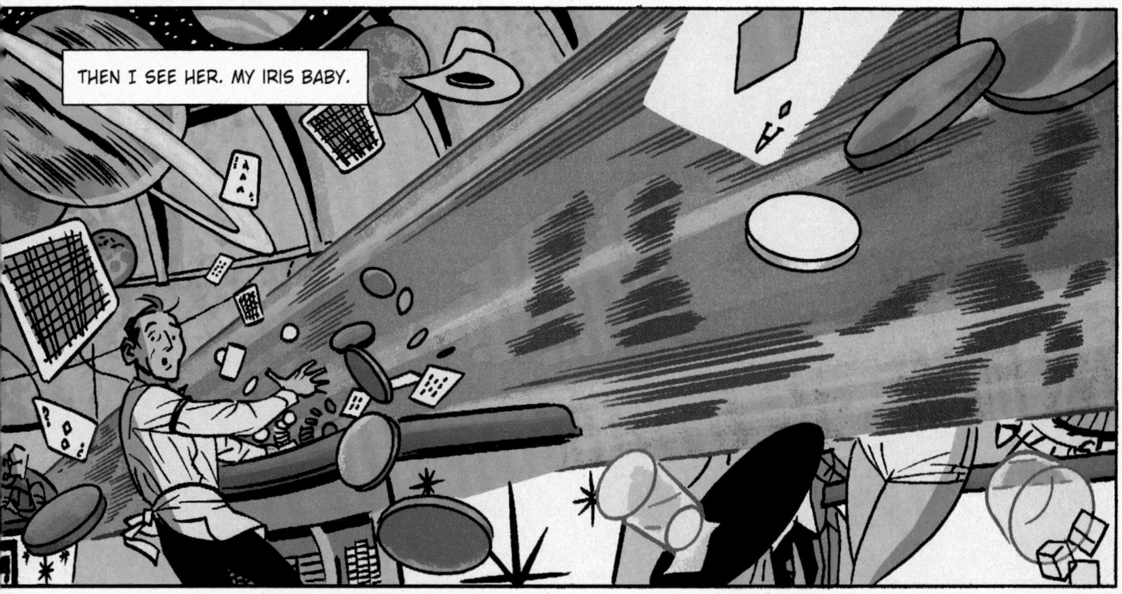
THEN I SEE HER. MY IRIS BABY.

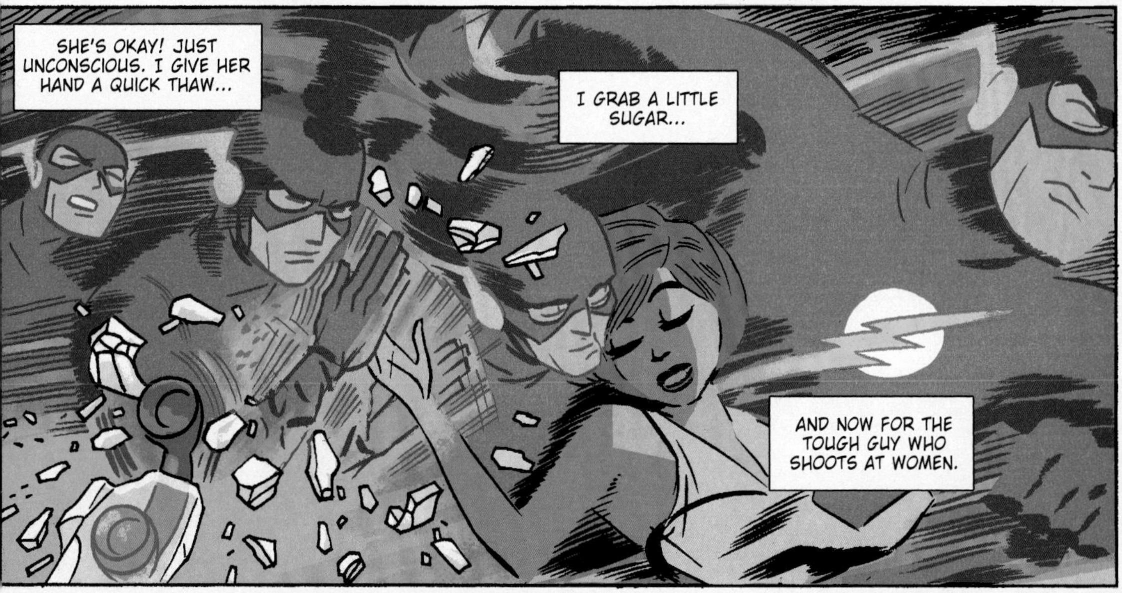
SHE'S OKAY! JUST UNCONSCIOUS. I GIVE HER HAND A QUICK THAW...
I GRAB A LITTLE SUGAR...
AND NOW FOR THE TOUGH GUY WHO SHOOTS AT WOMEN.

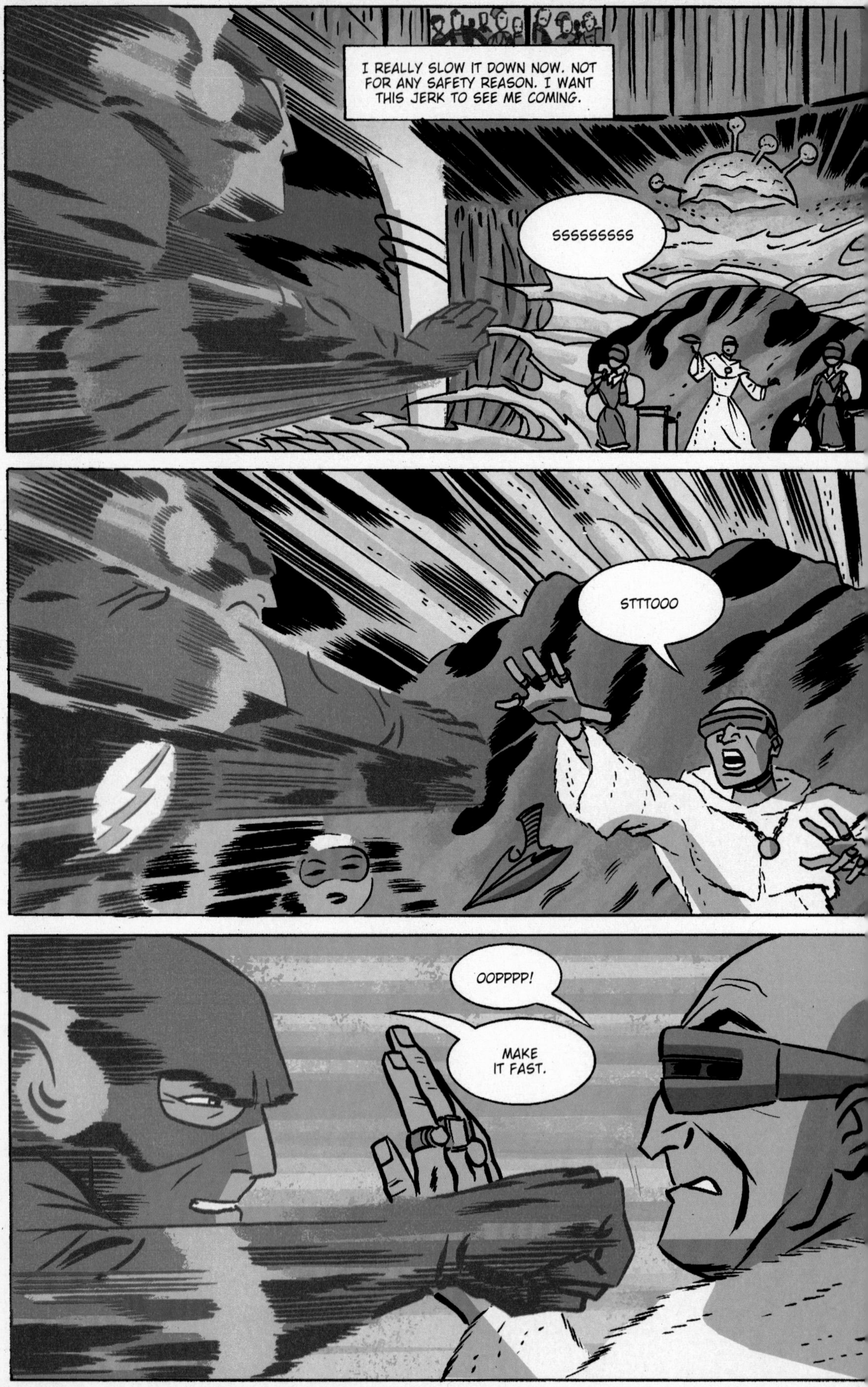
I REALLY SLOW IT DOWN NOW. NOT FOR ANY SAFETY REASON. I WANT THIS JERK TO SEE ME COMING.
SSSSSSSSS
STTTOOO
OOPPPP!
MAKE IT FAST.

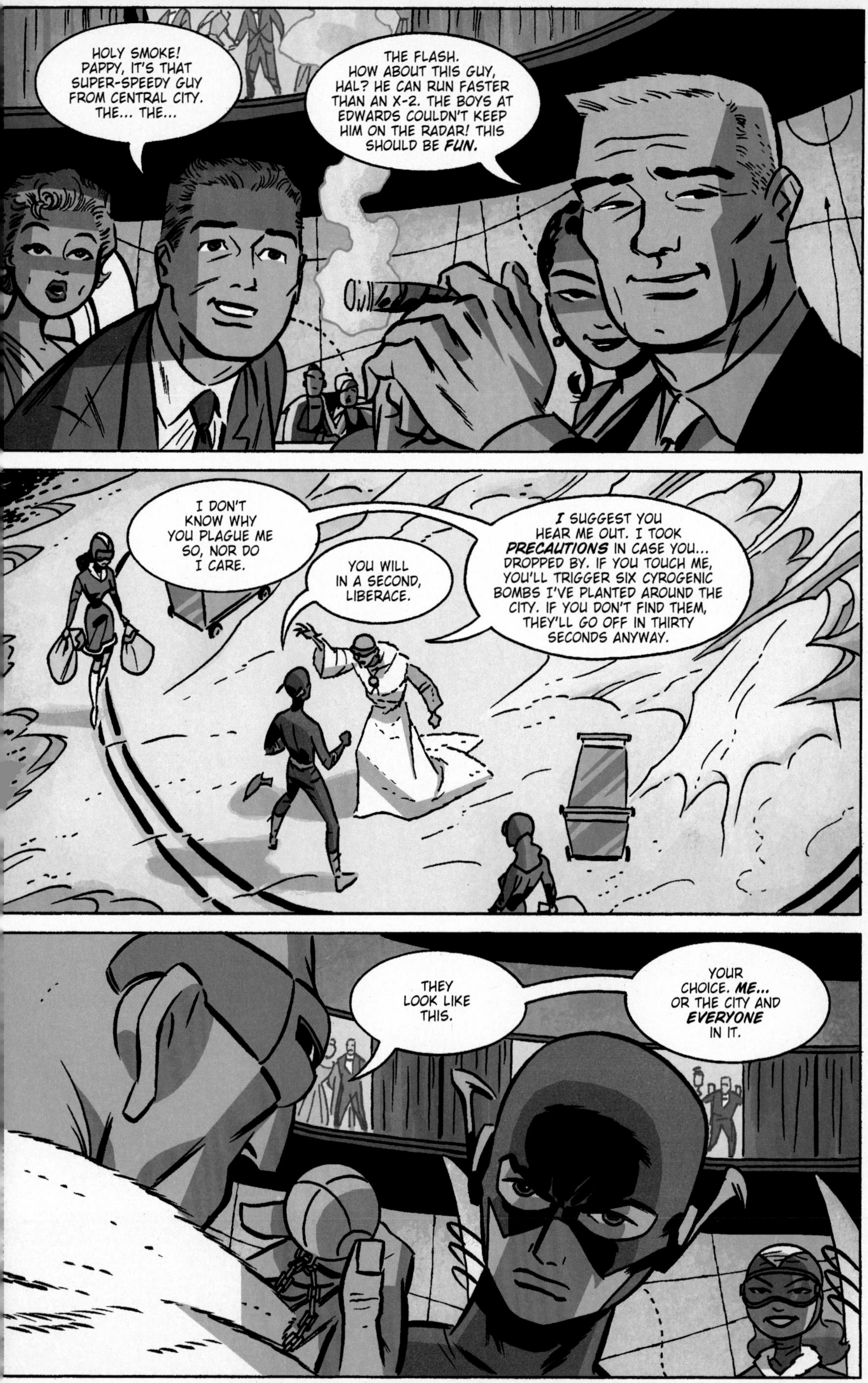
HOLY SMOKE! PAPPY, IT'S THAT SUPER-SPEEDY GUY FROM CENTRAL CITY. THE... THE...
THE FLASH. HOW ABOUT THIS GUY, HAL? HE CAN RUN FASTER THAN AN X-2. THE BOYS AT EDWARDS COULDN'T KEEP HIM ON THE RADAR! THIS SHOULD BE FUN.
I DON'T KNOW WHY YOU PLAGUE ME SO, NOR DO I CARE.
YOU WILL IN A SECOND, LIBERACE.
I SUGGEST YOU HEAR ME OUT. I TOOK PRECAUTIONS IN CASE YOU... DROPPED BY. IF YOU TOUCH ME, YOU'LL TRIGGER SIX CYROGENIC BOMBS I'VE PLANTED AROUND THE CITY. IF YOU DON'T FIND THEM, THEY'LL GO OFF IN THIRTY SECONDS ANYWAY.
THEY LOOK LIKE THIS.
YOUR CHOICE. ME... OR THE CITY AND EVERYONE IN IT.

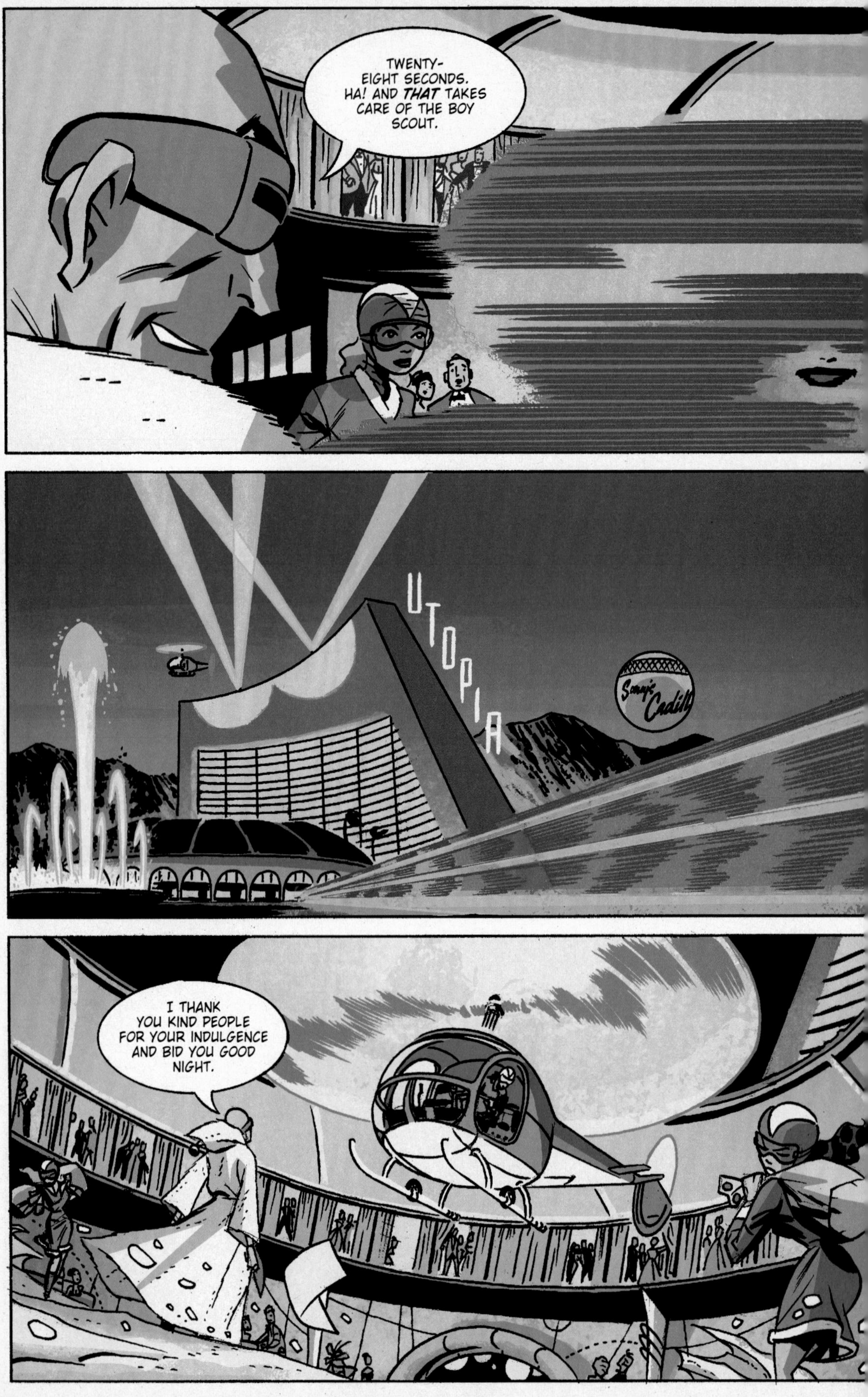
TWENTY-EIGHT SECONDS. HA! AND *THAT* TAKES CARE OF THE BOY SCOUT.
UTOPIA
I THANK YOU KIND PEOPLE FOR YOUR INDULGENCE AND BID YOU GOOD NIGHT.

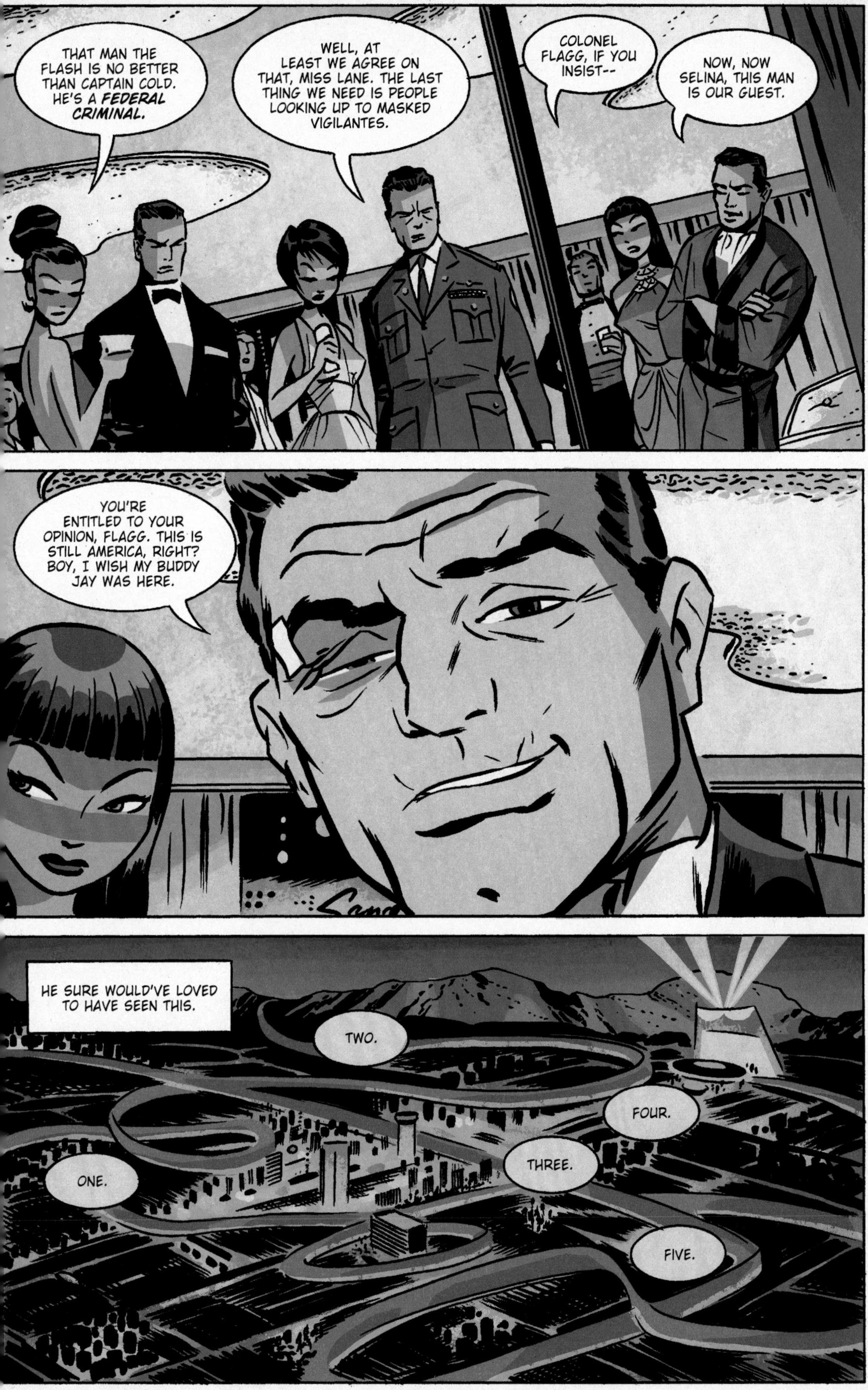
THAT MAN THE FLASH IS NO BETTER THAN CAPTAIN COLD. HE'S A **FEDERAL CRIMINAL.**
WELL, AT LEAST WE AGREE ON THAT, MISS LANE. THE LAST THING WE NEED IS PEOPLE LOOKING UP TO MASKED VIGILANTES.
COLONEL FLAGG, IF YOU INSIST--
NOW, NOW SELINA, THIS MAN IS OUR GUEST.
YOU'RE ENTITLED TO YOUR OPINION, FLAGG. THIS IS STILL AMERICA, RIGHT? BOY, I WISH MY BUDDY JAY WAS HERE.
HE SURE WOULD'VE LOVED TO HAVE SEEN THIS.
ONE.
TWO.
THREE.
FOUR.
FIVE.

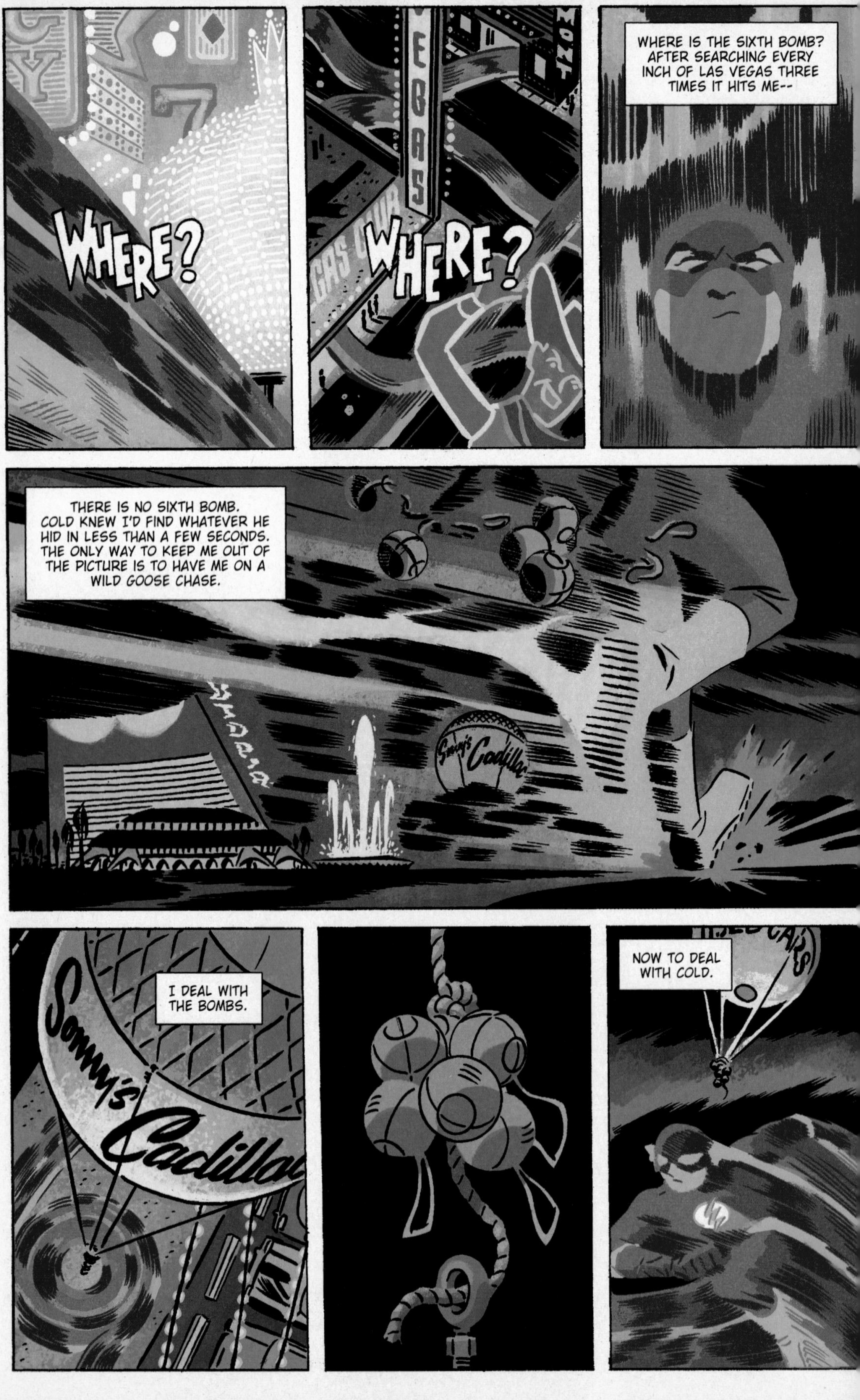

WHERE?
WHERE?
WHERE IS THE SIXTH BOMB? AFTER SEARCHING EVERY INCH OF LAS VEGAS THREE TIMES IT HITS ME--
THERE IS NO SIXTH BOMB. COLD KNEW I'D FIND WHATEVER HE HID IN LESS THAN A FEW SECONDS. THE ONLY WAY TO KEEP ME OUT OF THE PICTURE IS TO HAVE ME ON A WILD GOOSE CHASE.
I DEAL WITH THE BOMBS.
NOW TO DEAL WITH COLD.

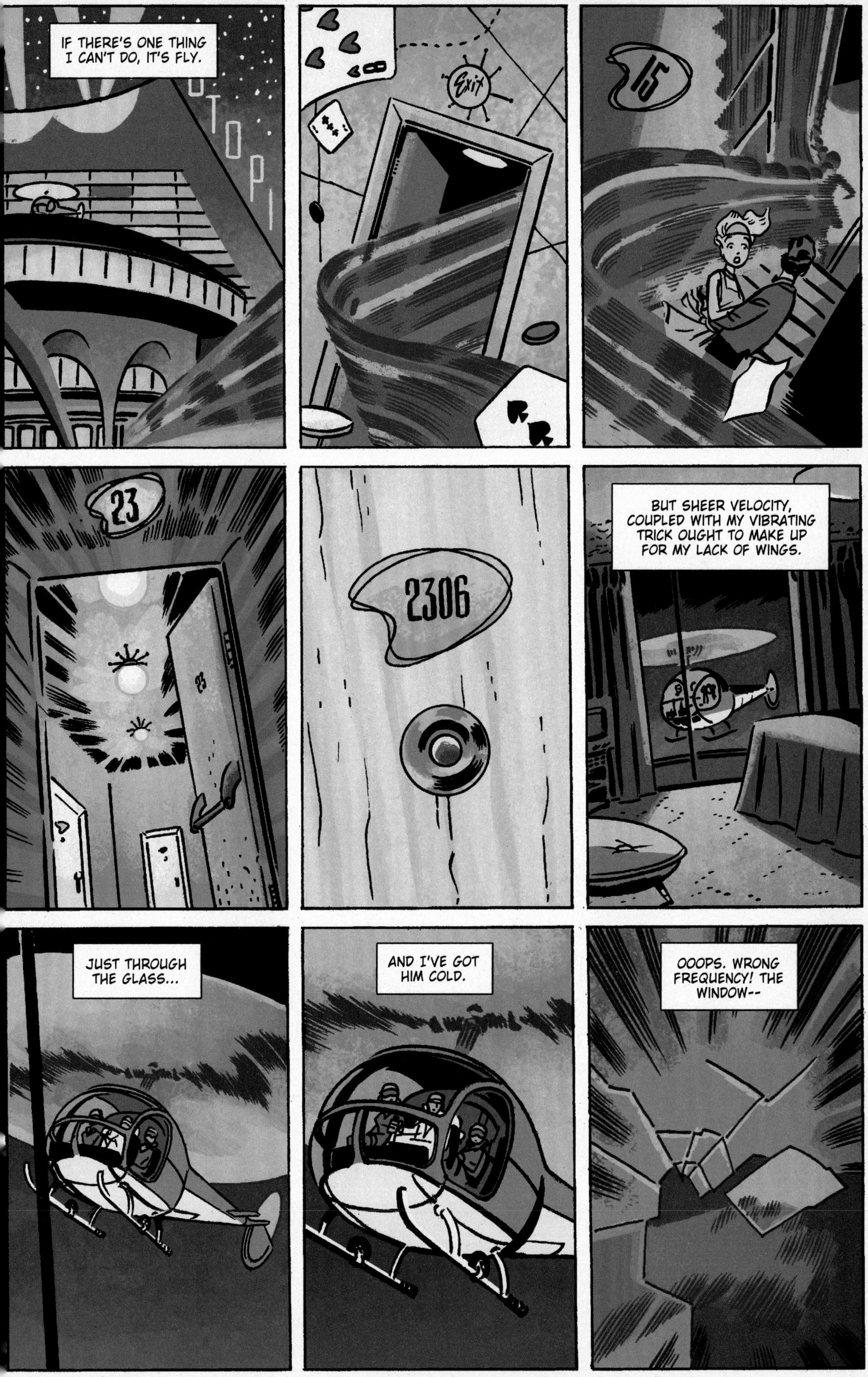
IF THERE'S ONE THING I CAN'T DO, IT'S FLY.
Exit
15
23
2306
BUT SHEER VELOCITY, COUPLED WITH MY VIBRATING TRICK OUGHT TO MAKE UP FOR MY LACK OF WINGS.
JUST THROUGH THE GLASS...
AND I'VE GOT HIM COLD.
OOOPS. WRONG FREQUENCY! THE WINDOW--

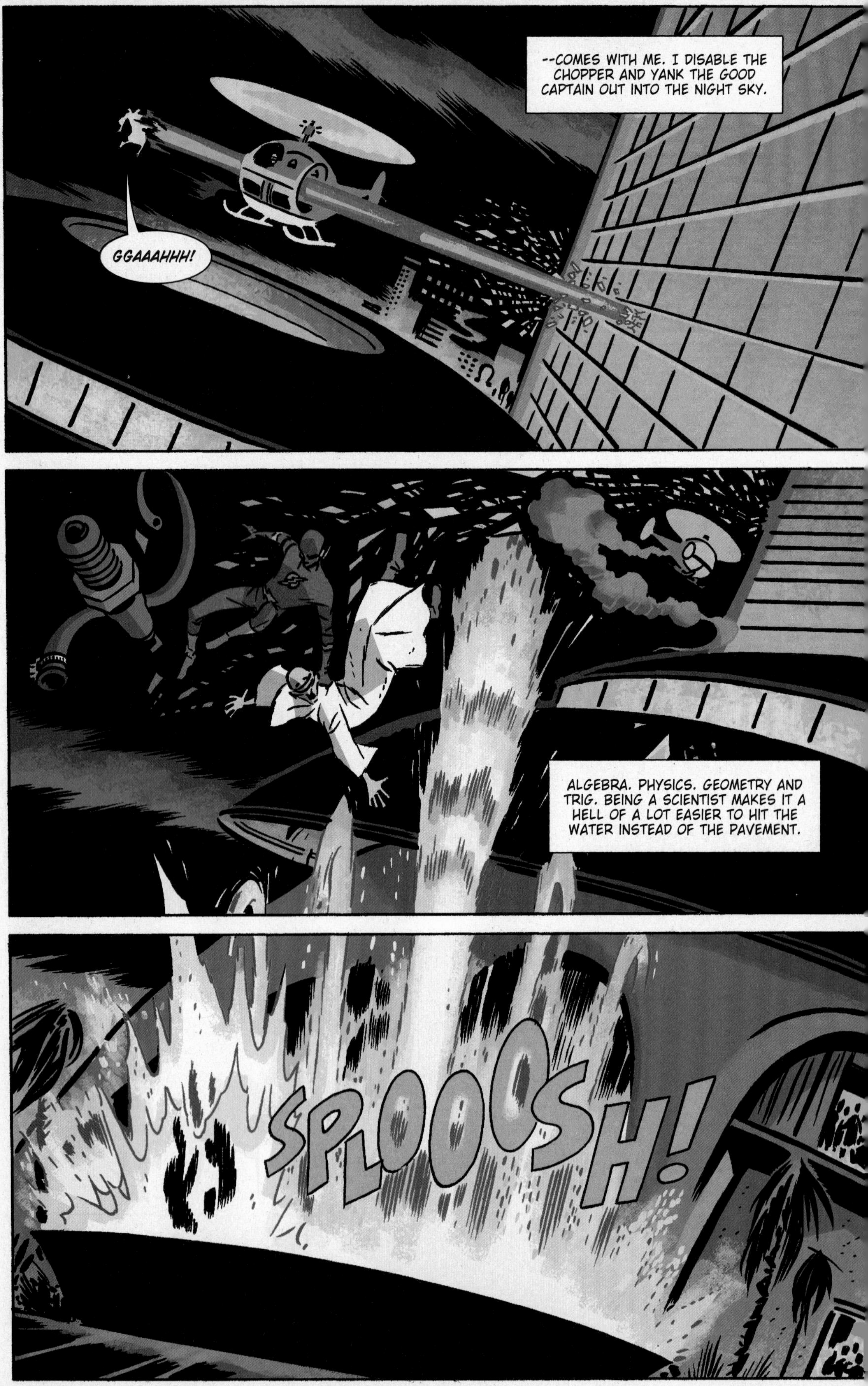
--COMES WITH ME. I DISABLE THE CHOPPER AND YANK THE GOOD CAPTAIN OUT INTO THE NIGHT SKY.
GGAAAAHHH!
ALGEBRA. PHYSICS. GEOMETRY AND TRIG. BEING A SCIENTIST MAKES IT A HELL OF A LOT EASIER TO HIT THE WATER INSTEAD OF THE PAVEMENT.
SPLOOOSH!

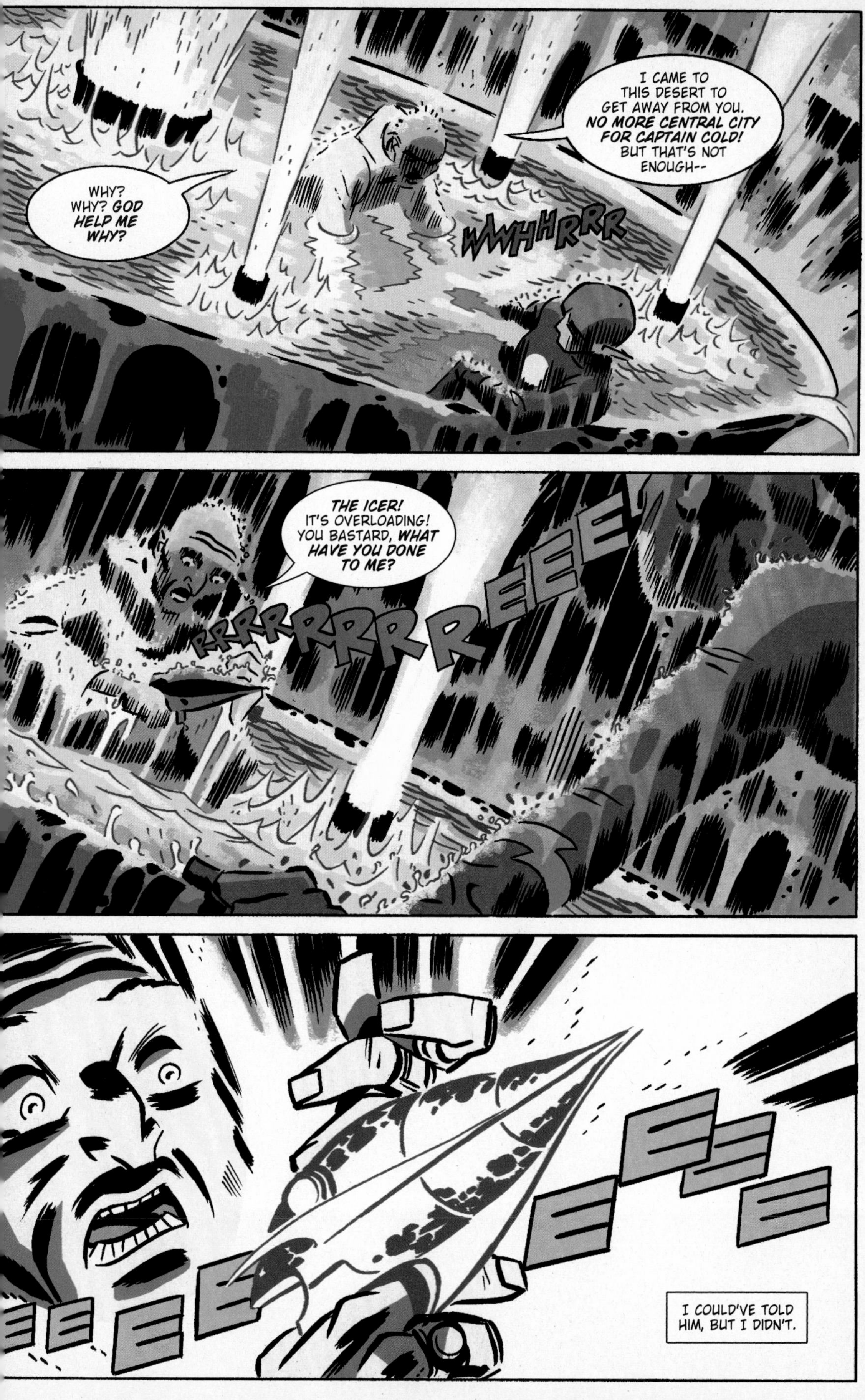
I CAME TO THIS DESERT TO GET AWAY FROM YOU. NO MORE CENTRAL CITY FOR CAPTAIN COLD! BUT THAT'S NOT ENOUGH--
WHY? WHY? GOD HELP ME WHY?
WWHHRRR
THE ICER! IT'S OVERLOADING! YOU BASTARD, WHAT HAVE YOU DONE TO ME?
RRRRRRRREEEE
EEEEEEEEEEE
I COULD'VE TOLD HIM, BUT I DIDN'T.

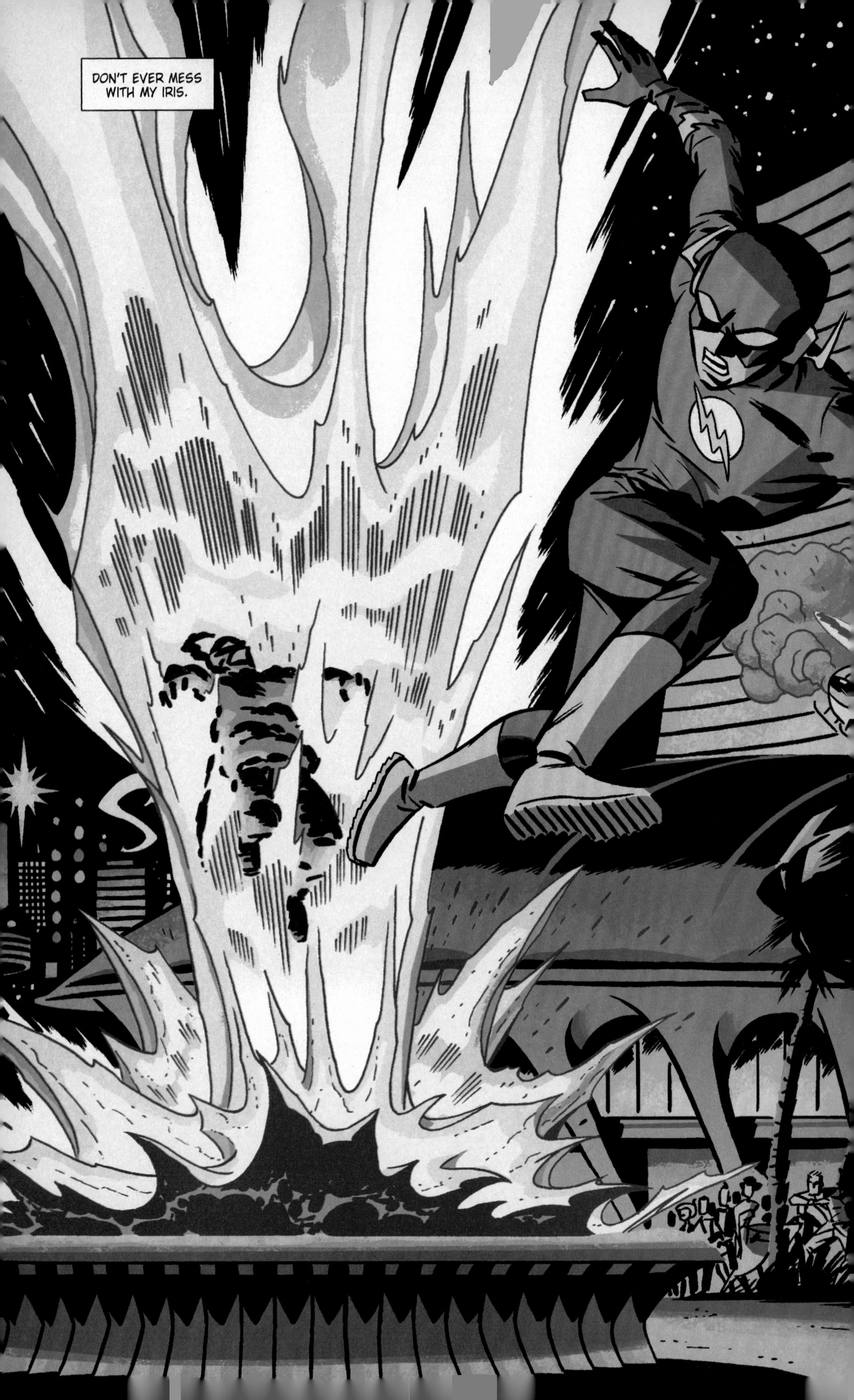
DON'T EVER MESS WITH MY IRIS.

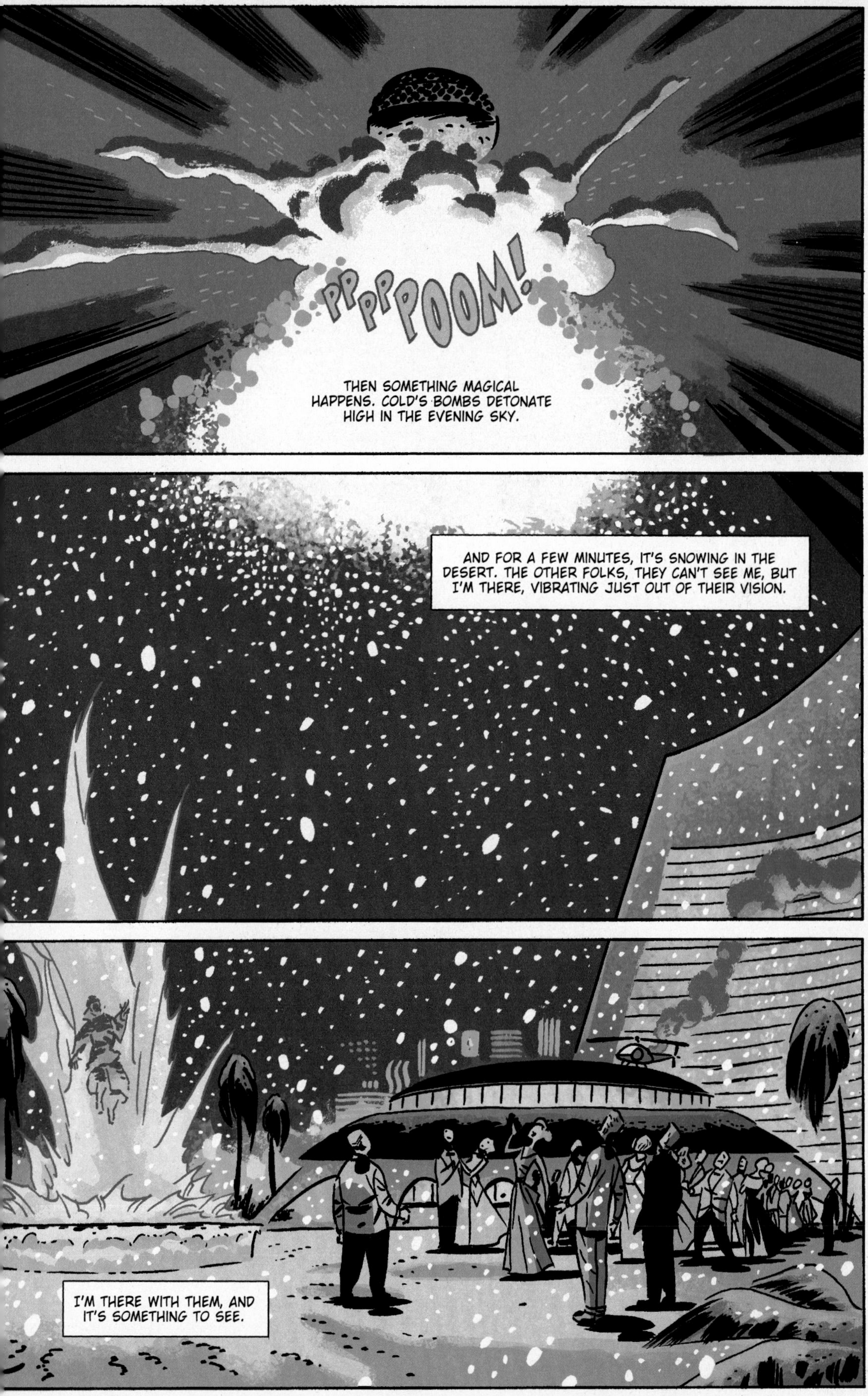
PPPPOOM!
THEN SOMETHING MAGICAL HAPPENS. COLD'S BOMBS DETONATE HIGH IN THE EVENING SKY.
AND FOR A FEW MINUTES, IT'S SNOWING IN THE DESERT. THE OTHER FOLKS, THEY CAN'T SEE ME, BUT I'M THERE, VIBRATING JUST OUT OF THEIR VISION.
I'M THERE WITH THEM, AND IT'S SOMETHING TO SEE.

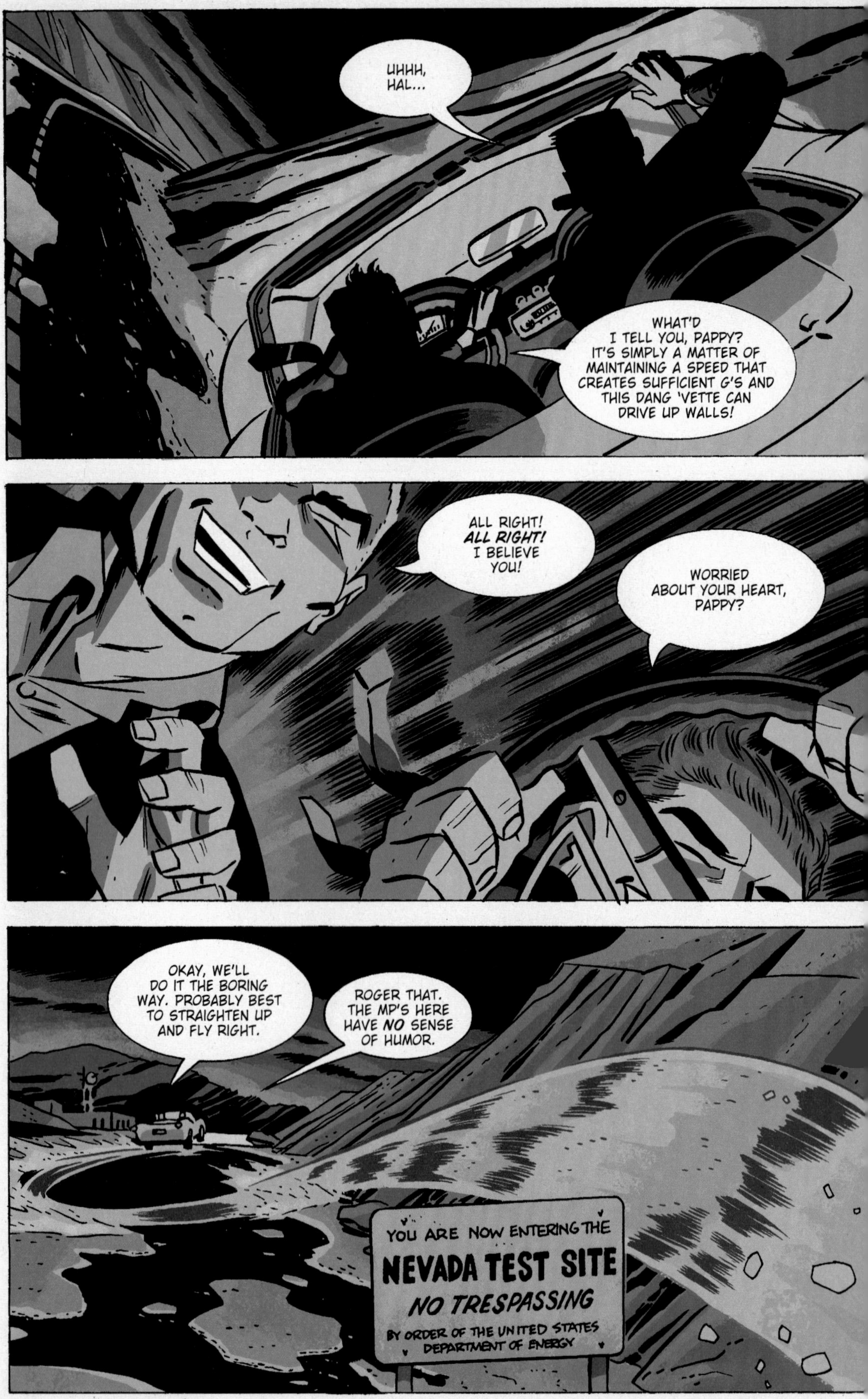
UHHH, HAL...
WHAT'D I TELL YOU, PAPPY? IT'S SIMPLY A MATTER OF MAINTAINING A SPEED THAT CREATES SUFFICIENT G'S AND THIS DANG 'VETTE CAN DRIVE UP WALLS!
ALL RIGHT! ***ALL RIGHT!*** I BELIEVE YOU!
WORRIED ABOUT YOUR HEART, PAPPY?
OKAY, WE'LL DO IT THE BORING WAY. PROBABLY BEST TO STRAIGHTEN UP AND FLY RIGHT.
ROGER THAT. THE MP'S HERE HAVE ***NO*** SENSE OF HUMOR.
YOU ARE NOW ENTERING THE
NEVADA TEST SITE
NO TRESPASSING
BY ORDER OF THE UNITED STATES DEPARTMENT OF ENERGY

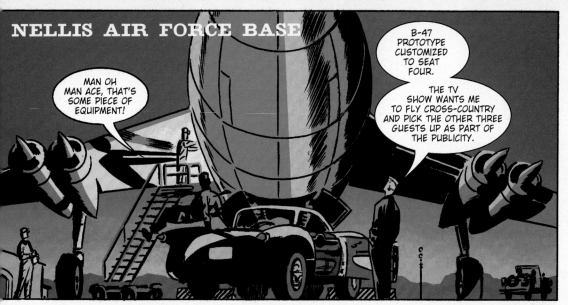

MAN OH MAN ACE, THAT'S SOME PIECE OF EQUIPMENT!

B-47 PROTOTYPE CUSTOMIZED TO SEAT FOUR.

THE TV SHOW WANTS ME TO FLY CROSS-COUNTRY AND PICK THE OTHER THREE GUESTS UP AS PART OF THE PUBLICITY.

CAN YOU IMAGINE ME ON TV?

SURE CAN PAPPY. YOU'LL BE FAMOUS AS UNCLE MILTY.

SPEAKING OF FAMOUS, I CAN'T GET OVER THAT FLASH GUY.

THAT WAS SOMETHING, EH? DID YOU *SEE* THAT GUY MANEUVER? WHAT I WOULDN'T GIVE TO FEEL THAT SPEED.

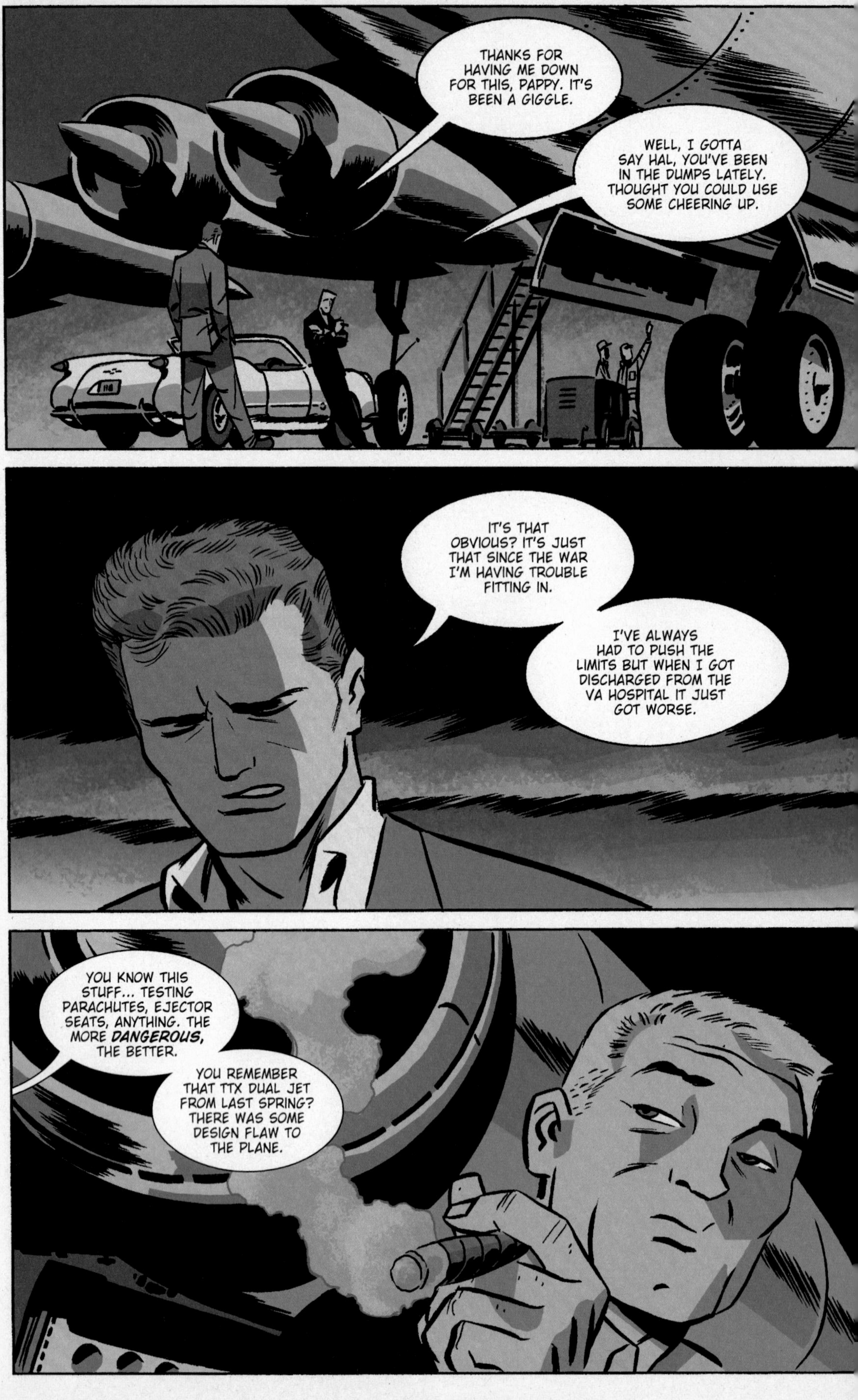
THANKS FOR HAVING ME DOWN FOR THIS, PAPPY. IT'S BEEN A GIGGLE.
WELL, I GOTTA SAY HAL, YOU'VE BEEN IN THE DUMPS LATELY. THOUGHT YOU COULD USE SOME CHEERING UP.
IT'S THAT OBVIOUS? IT'S JUST THAT SINCE THE WAR I'M HAVING TROUBLE FITTING IN.
I'VE ALWAYS HAD TO PUSH THE LIMITS BUT WHEN I GOT DISCHARGED FROM THE VA HOSPITAL IT JUST GOT WORSE.
YOU KNOW THIS STUFF... TESTING PARACHUTES, EJECTOR SEATS, ANYTHING. THE MORE DANGEROUS, THE BETTER.
YOU REMEMBER THAT TTX DUAL JET FROM LAST SPRING? THERE WAS SOME DESIGN FLAW TO THE PLANE.

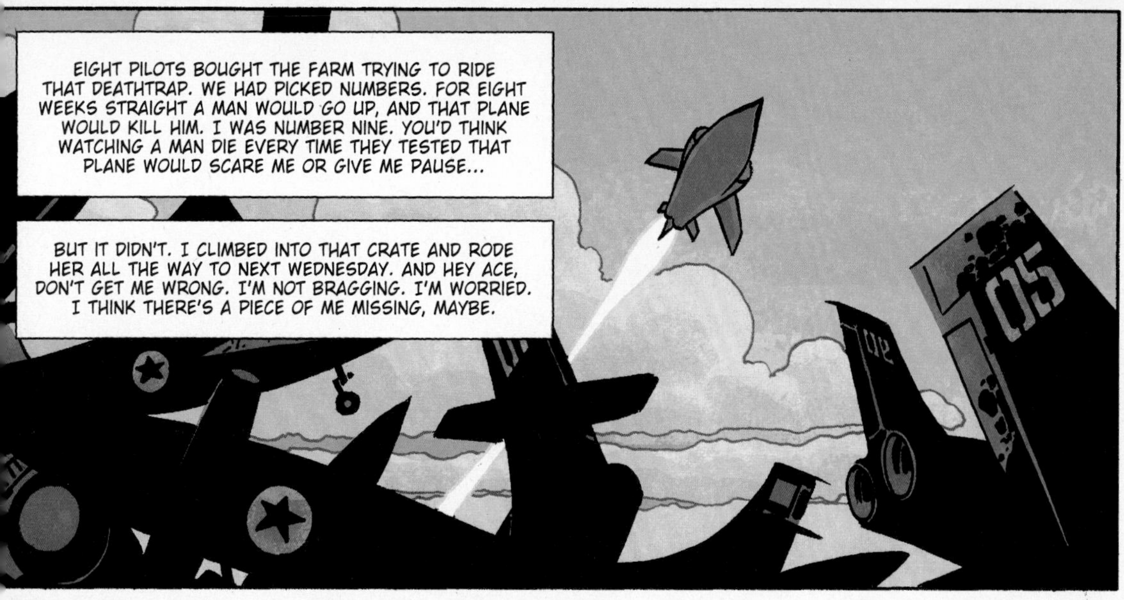
EIGHT PILOTS BOUGHT THE FARM TRYING TO RIDE THAT DEATHTRAP. WE HAD PICKED NUMBERS. FOR EIGHT WEEKS STRAIGHT A MAN WOULD GO UP, AND THAT PLANE WOULD KILL HIM. I WAS NUMBER NINE. YOU'D THINK WATCHING A MAN DIE EVERY TIME THEY TESTED THAT PLANE WOULD SCARE ME OR GIVE ME PAUSE...
BUT IT DIDN'T. I CLIMBED INTO THAT CRATE AND RODE HER ALL THE WAY TO NEXT WEDNESDAY. AND HEY ACE, DON'T GET ME WRONG. I'M NOT BRAGGING. I'M WORRIED. I THINK THERE'S A PIECE OF ME MISSING, MAYBE.
05

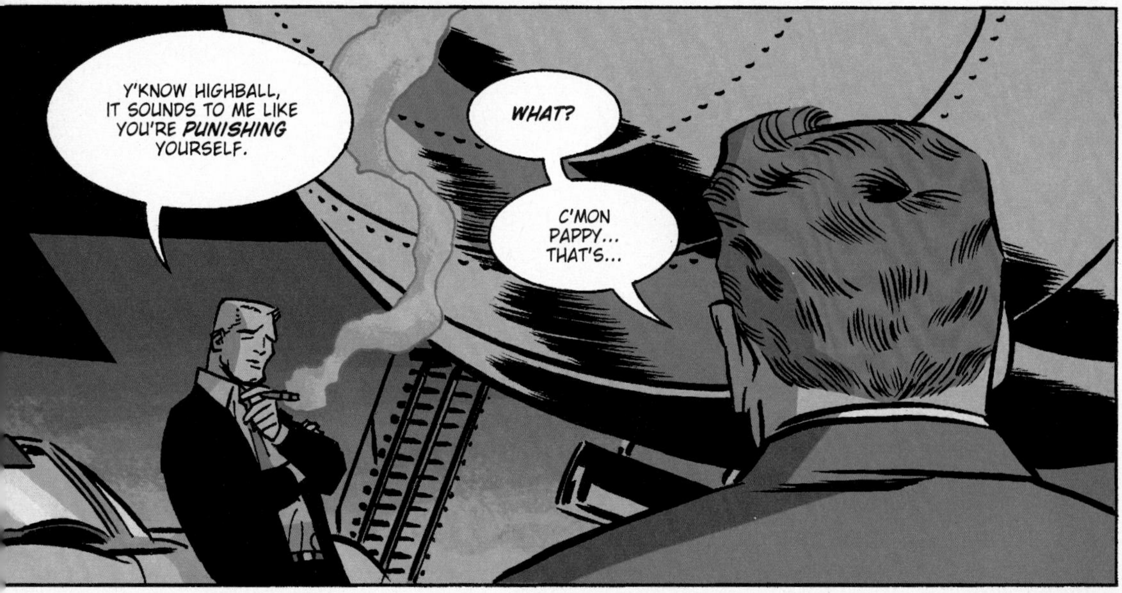
Y'KNOW HIGHBALL, IT SOUNDS TO ME LIKE YOU'RE *PUNISHING* YOURSELF.
WHAT?
C'MON PAPPY... THAT'S...

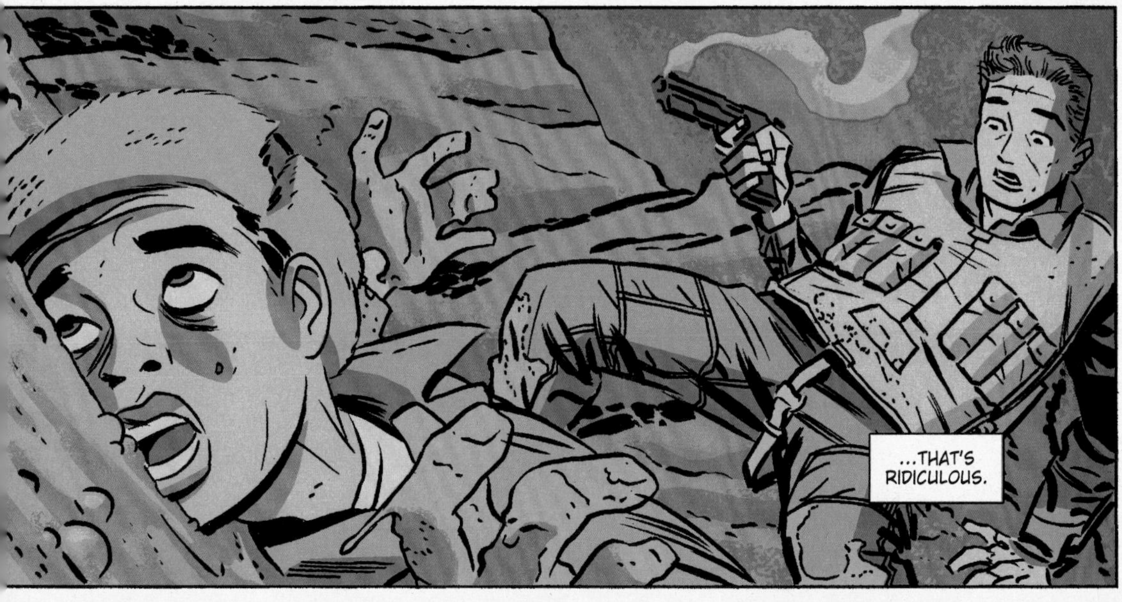
...THAT'S RIDICULOUS.

Y'KNOW PAPPY, MY WHOLE LIFE, MY DREAM HAS BEEN SIMPLE. SINCE I CAN REMEMBER, I'VE KNOWN I WAS GOING TO FLY. I WAS GOING TO SEE THE STARS.

SOMETIMES IT FEELS LIKE I WAS CLOSER THEN THAN I AM NOW. AFTER KOREA I... WELL, I GUESS I'M *DAMAGED GOODS.* I'LL NEVER BE AT THE TOP OF THE PYRAMID.

ALL I'M GOOD FOR IS TESTING FLYING BARBECUES AND PARACHUTES.

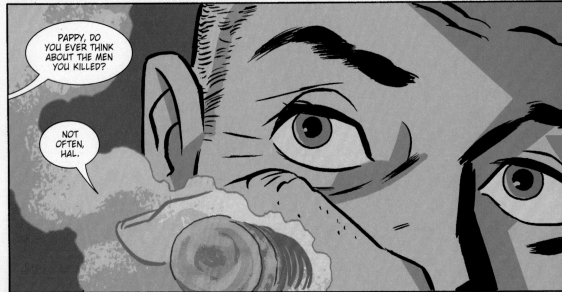

PAPPY, DO YOU EVER THINK ABOUT THE MEN YOU KILLED?

NOT OFTEN, HAL.

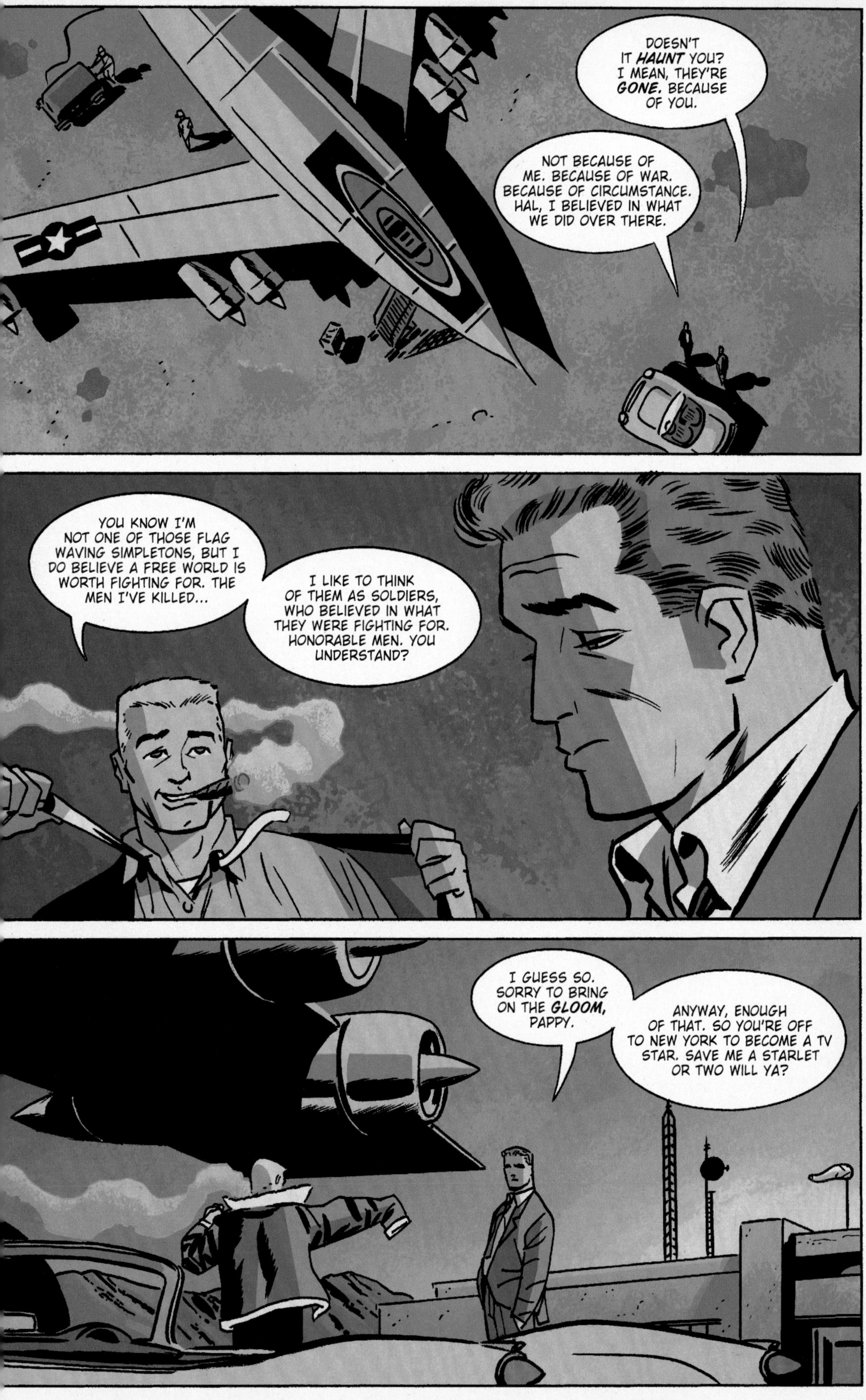
DOESN'T IT HAUNT YOU? I MEAN, THEY'RE GONE. BECAUSE OF YOU.
NOT BECAUSE OF ME. BECAUSE OF WAR. BECAUSE OF CIRCUMSTANCE. HAL, I BELIEVED IN WHAT WE DID OVER THERE.
YOU KNOW I'M NOT ONE OF THOSE FLAG WAVING SIMPLETONS, BUT I DO BELIEVE A FREE WORLD IS WORTH FIGHTING FOR. THE MEN I'VE KILLED...
I LIKE TO THINK OF THEM AS SOLDIERS, WHO BELIEVED IN WHAT THEY WERE FIGHTING FOR. HONORABLE MEN. YOU UNDERSTAND?
I GUESS SO. SORRY TO BRING ON THE GLOOM, PAPPY.
ANYWAY, ENOUGH OF THAT. SO YOU'RE OFF TO NEW YORK TO BECOME A TV STAR. SAVE ME A STARLET OR TWO WILL YA?

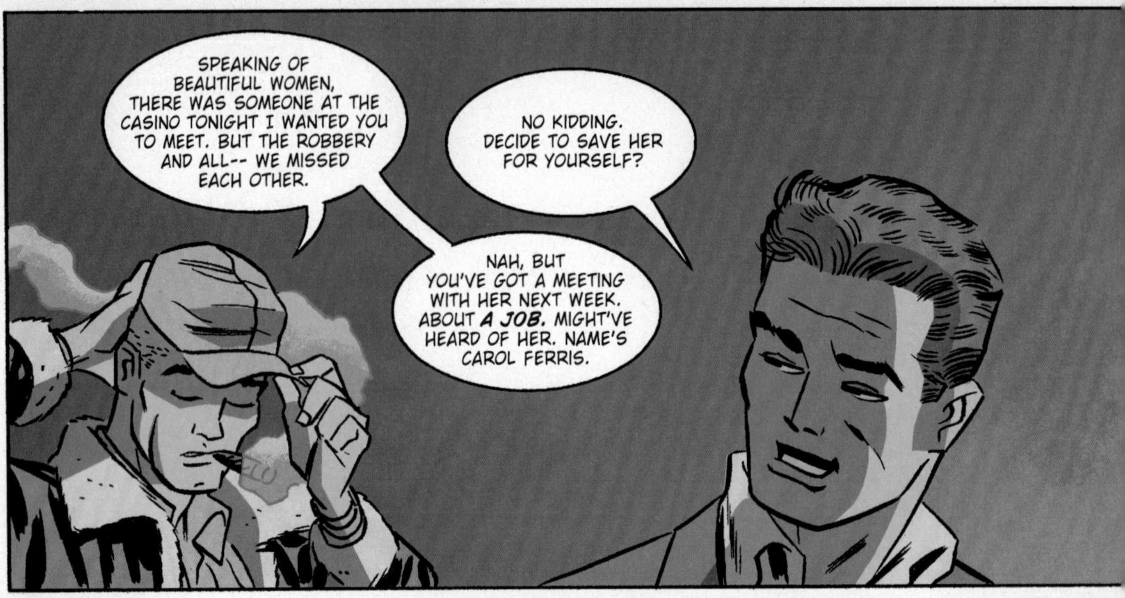
SPEAKING OF BEAUTIFUL WOMEN, THERE WAS SOMEONE AT THE CASINO TONIGHT I WANTED YOU TO MEET. BUT THE ROBBERY AND ALL-- WE MISSED EACH OTHER.
NO KIDDING. DECIDE TO SAVE HER FOR YOURSELF?
NAH, BUT YOU'VE GOT A MEETING WITH HER NEXT WEEK. ABOUT ***A JOB.*** MIGHT'VE HEARD OF HER. NAME'S CAROL FERRIS.

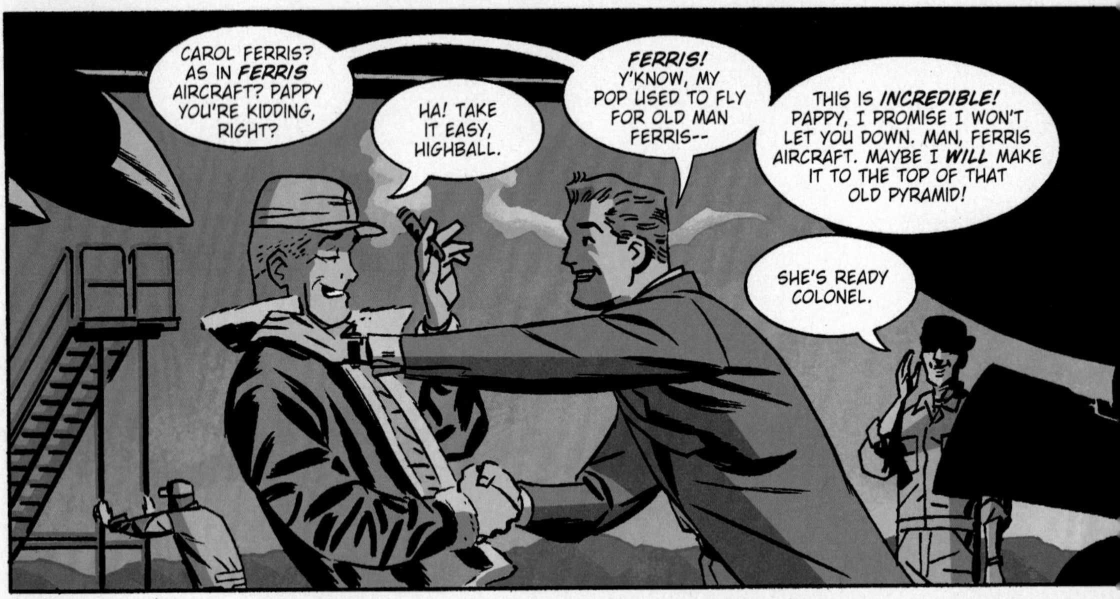
CAROL FERRIS? AS IN ***FERRIS*** AIRCRAFT? PAPPY YOU'RE KIDDING, RIGHT?
HA! TAKE IT EASY, HIGHBALL.
FERRIS! Y'KNOW, MY POP USED TO FLY FOR OLD MAN FERRIS--
THIS IS ***INCREDIBLE!*** PAPPY, I PROMISE I WON'T LET YOU DOWN. MAN, FERRIS AIRCRAFT. MAYBE I ***WILL*** MAKE IT TO THE TOP OF THAT OLD PYRAMID!
SHE'S READY COLONEL.

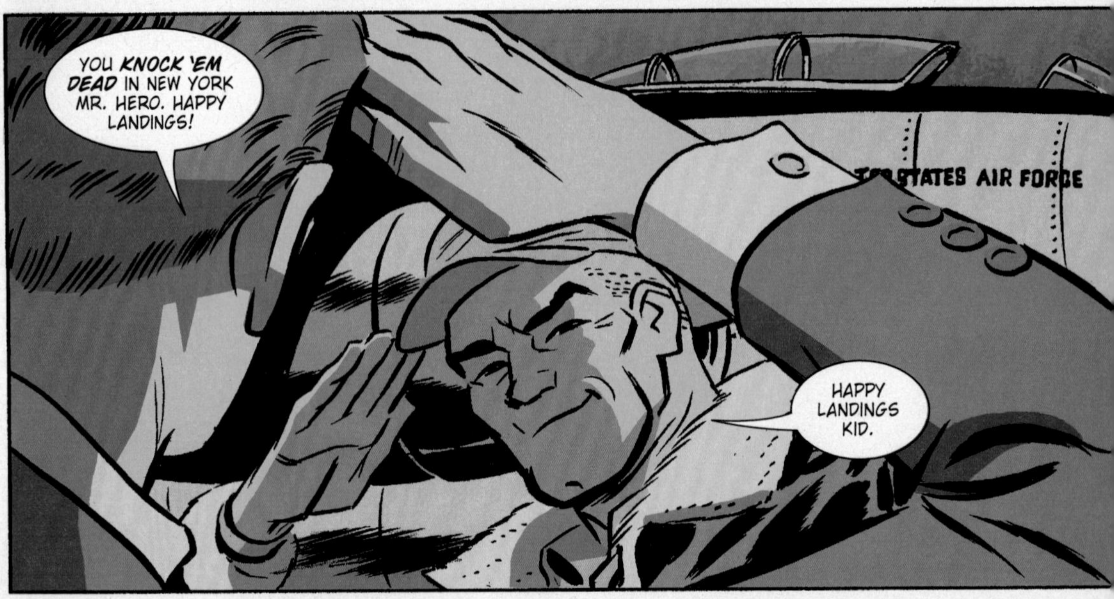
YOU ***KNOCK 'EM DEAD*** IN NEW YORK MR. HERO. HAPPY LANDINGS!
STATES AIR FORCE
HAPPY LANDINGS KID.

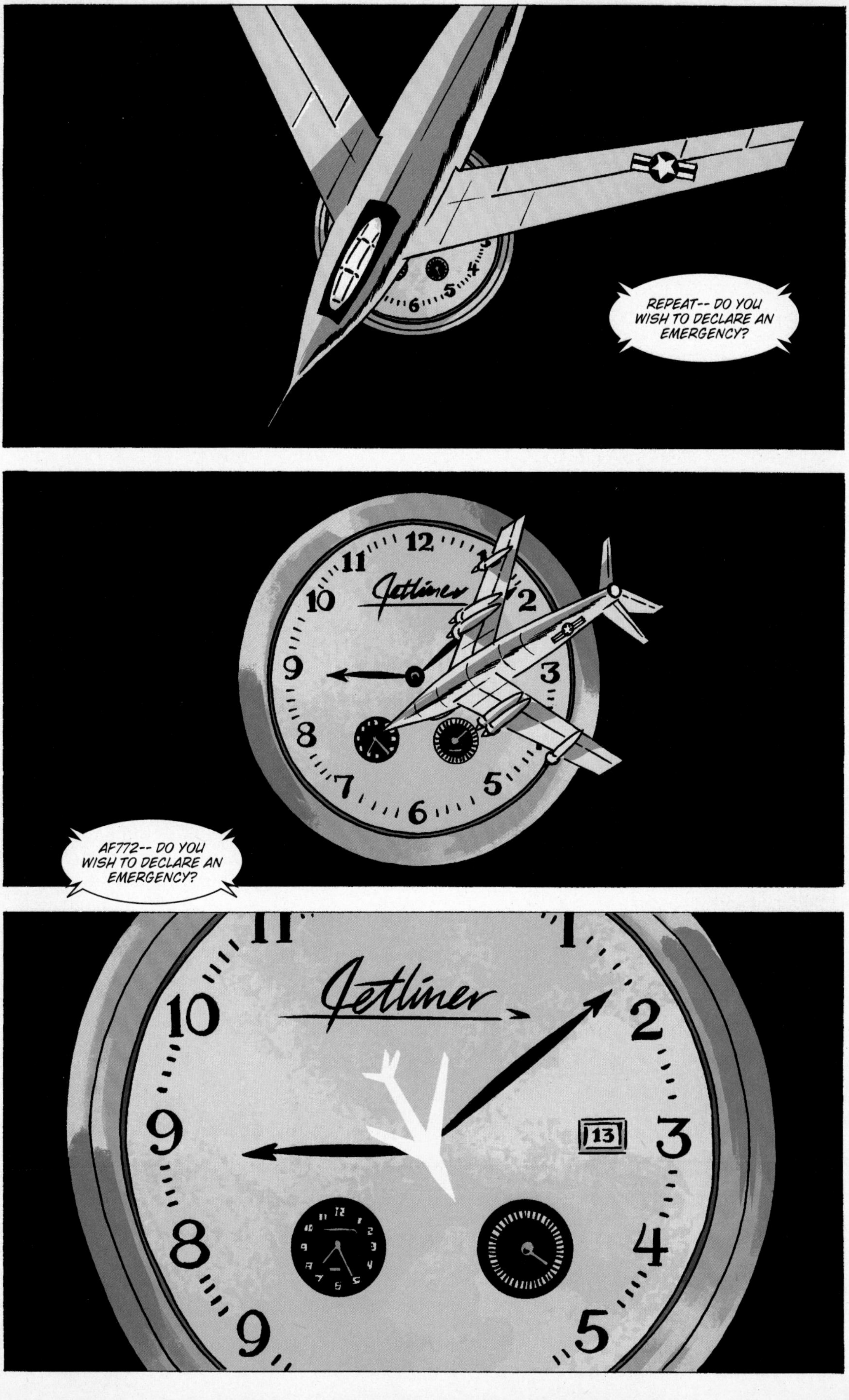
REPEAT-- DO YOU WISH TO DECLARE AN EMERGENCY?
Jetliner
AF772-- DO YOU WISH TO DECLARE AN EMERGENCY?
Jetliner

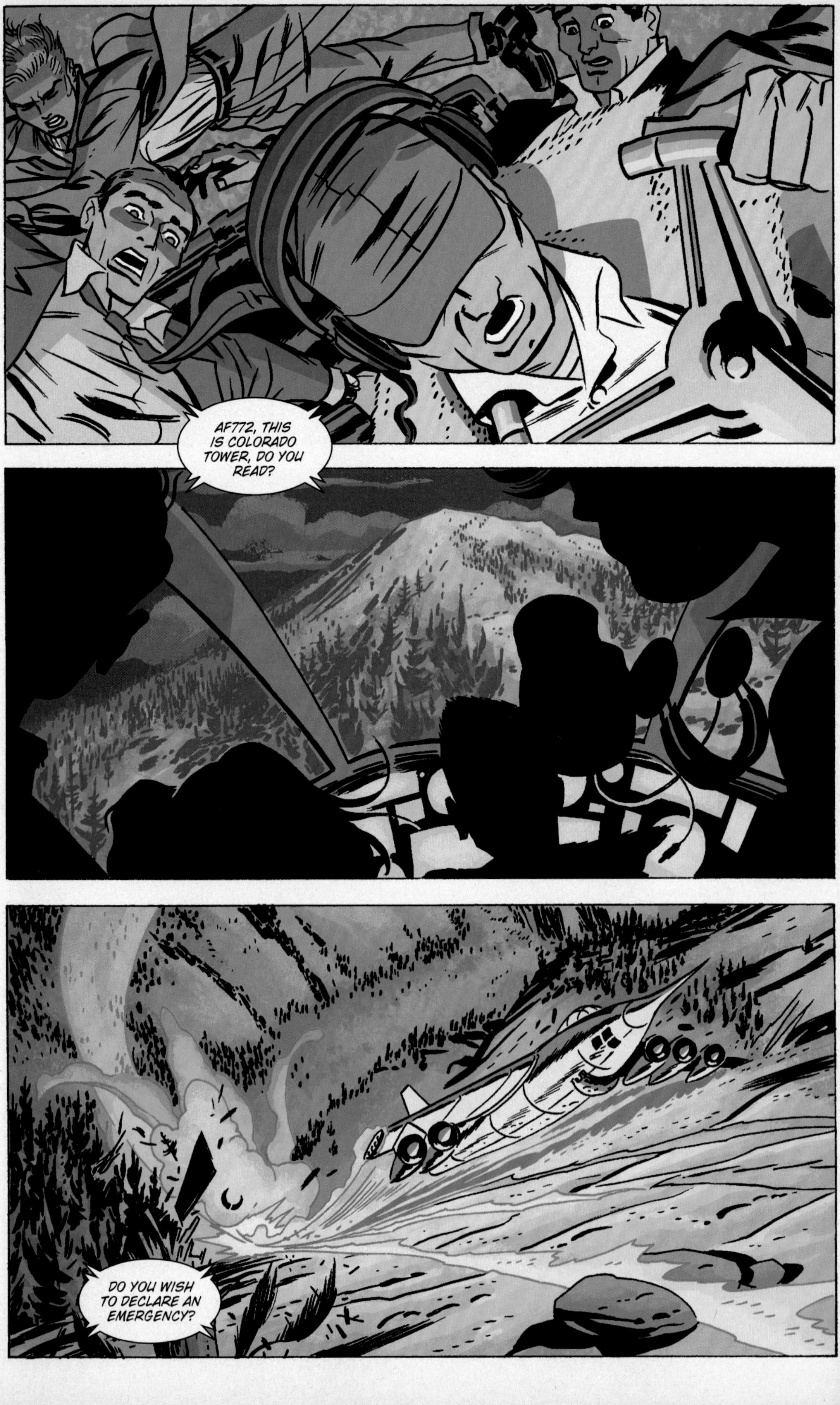
AF772, THIS IS COLORADO TOWER, DO YOU READ?
DO YOU WISH TO DECLARE AN EMERGENCY?

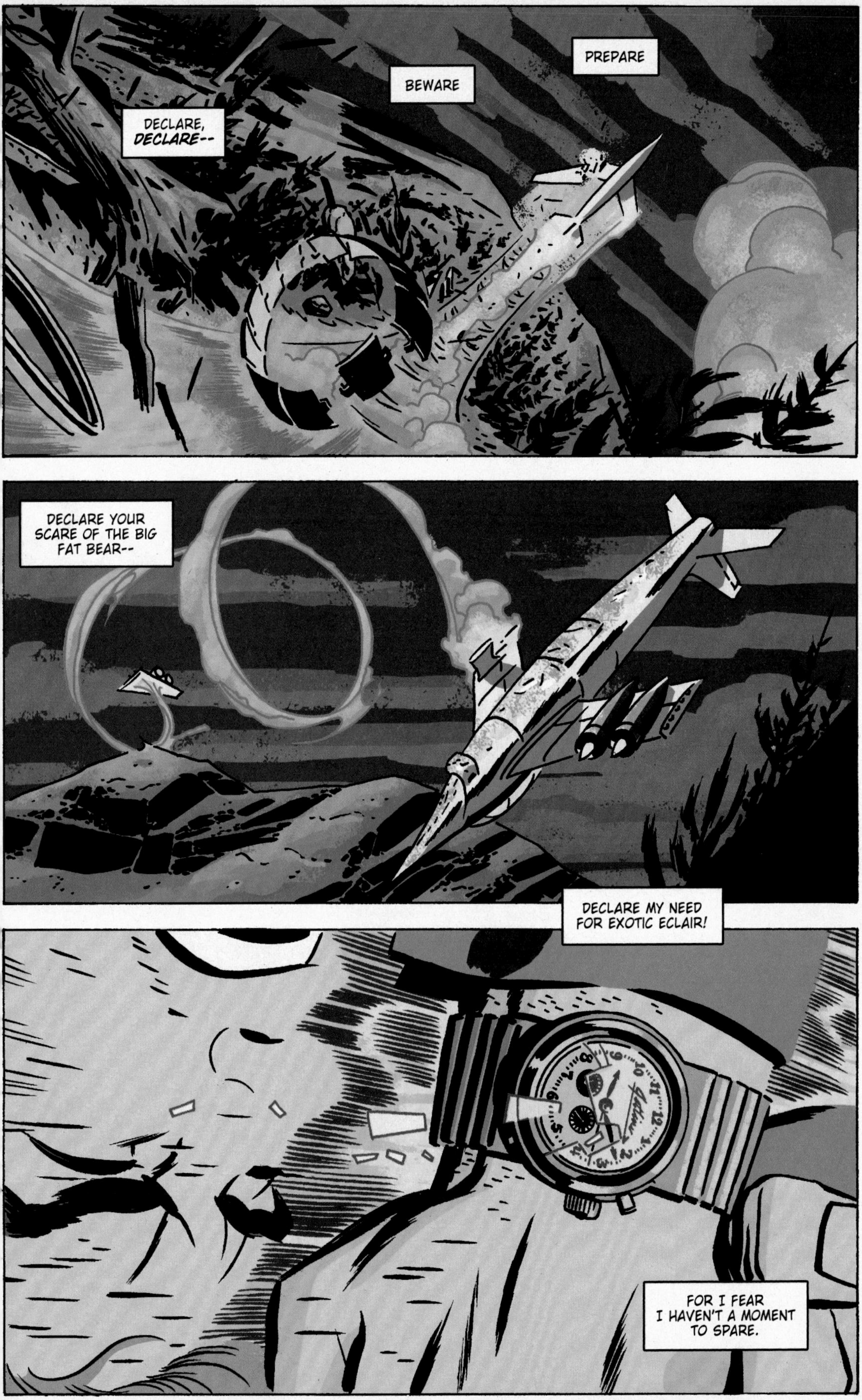
DECLARE, *DECLARE*--
BEWARE
PREPARE
DECLARE YOUR SCARE OF THE BIG FAT BEAR--
DECLARE MY NEED FOR EXOTIC ECLAIR!
FOR I FEAR I HAVEN'T A MOMENT TO SPARE.

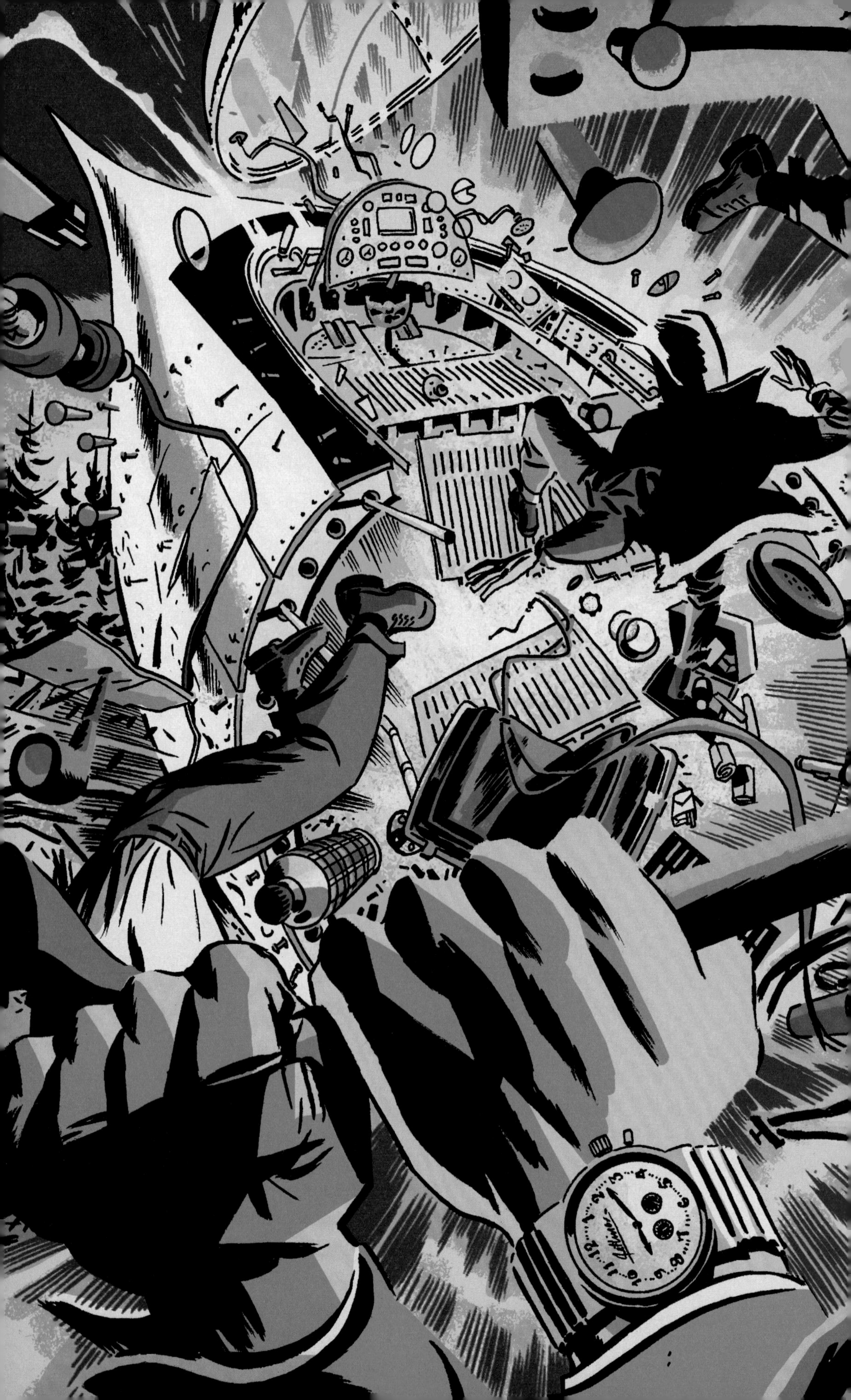

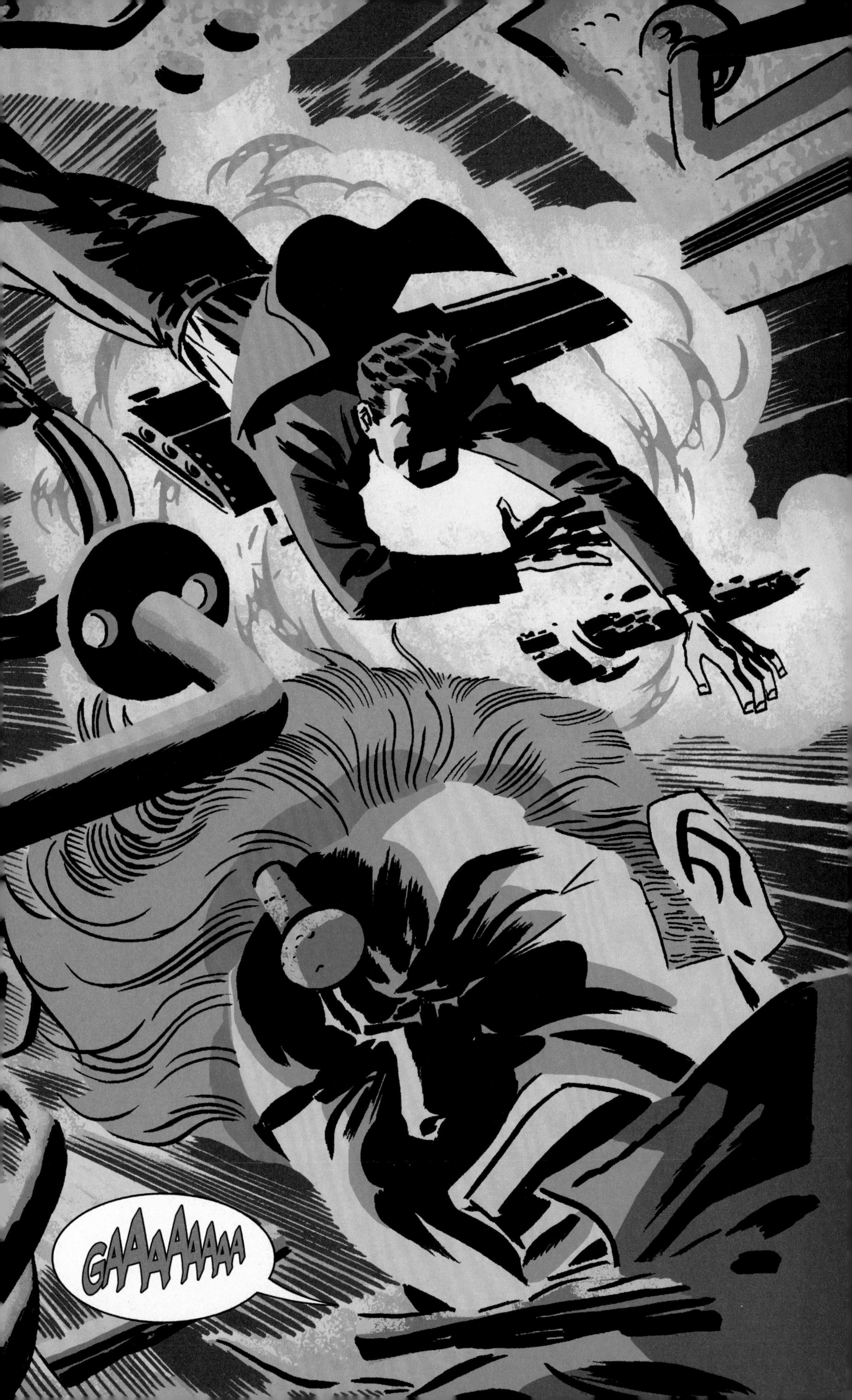
GAAAAAAA

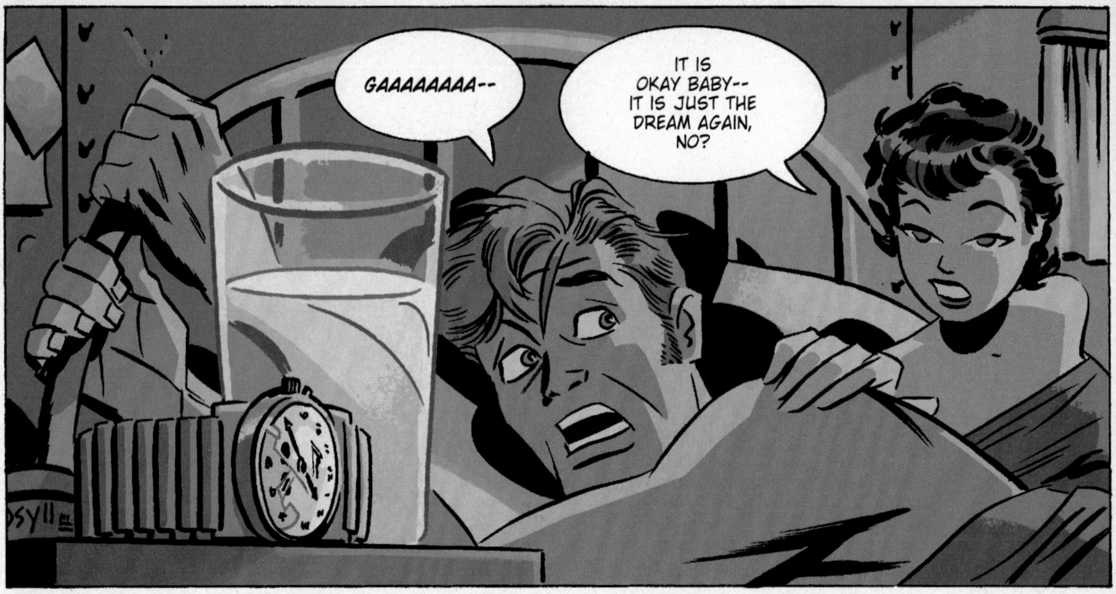
GAAAAAAAA--
IT IS OKAY BABY-- IT IS JUST THE DREAM AGAIN, NO?

CHAPTER SIX
THE MEN WHO FELL TO EARTH

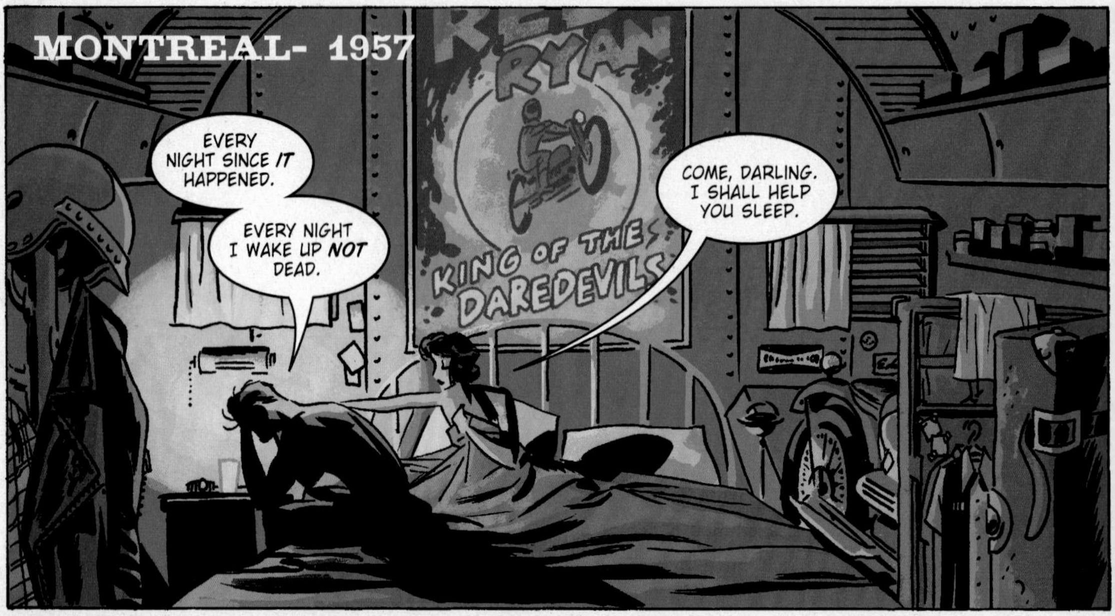
MONTREAL- 1957
RYAN
KING OF THE DAREDEVILS
EVERY NIGHT SINCE *IT* HAPPENED.
EVERY NIGHT I WAKE UP ***NOT*** DEAD.
COME, DARLING. I SHALL HELP YOU SLEEP.

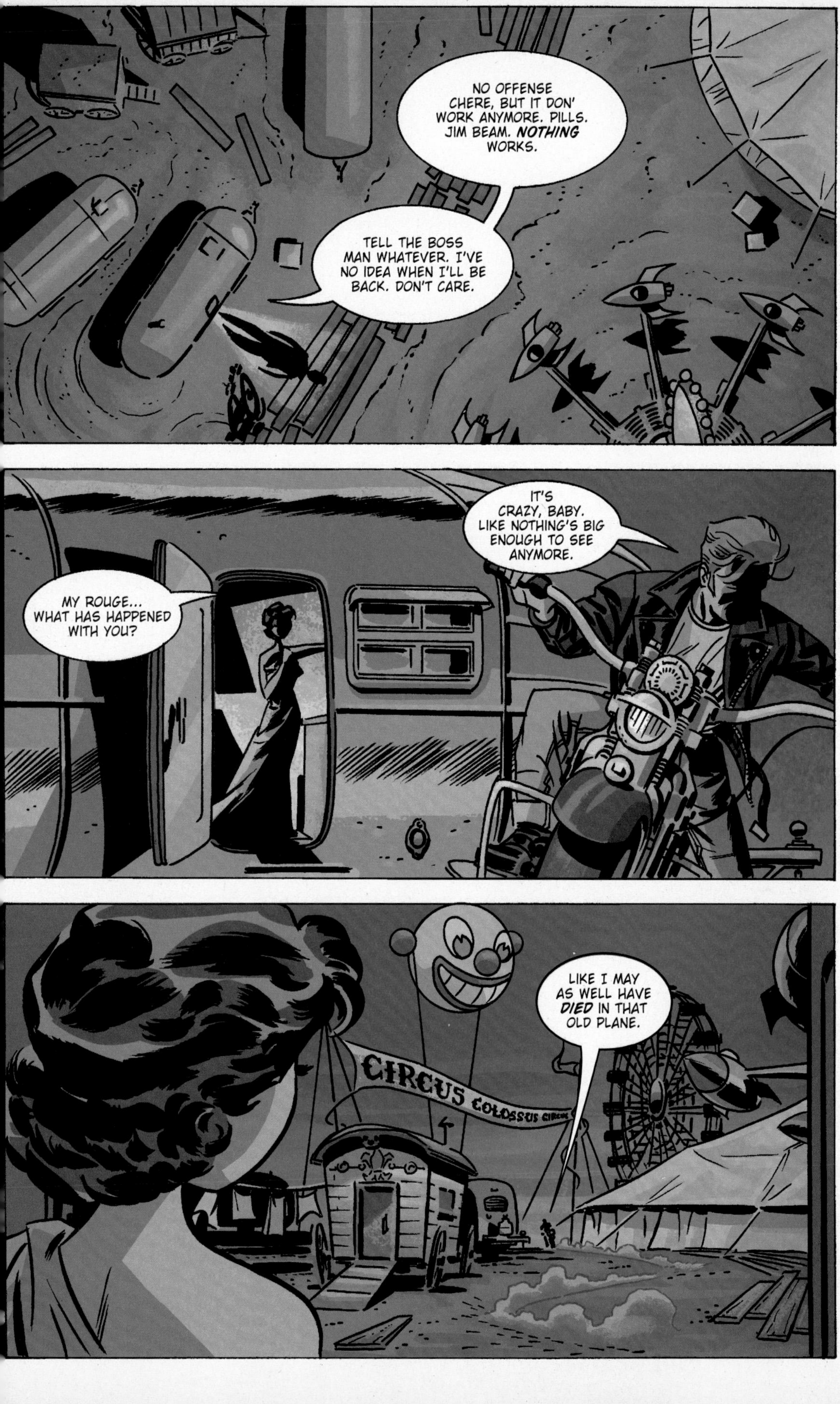
NO OFFENSE CHERE, BUT IT DON' WORK ANYMORE. PILLS. JIM BEAM. *NOTHING* WORKS.
TELL THE BOSS MAN WHATEVER. I'VE NO IDEA WHEN I'LL BE BACK. DON'T CARE.
MY ROUGE... WHAT HAS HAPPENED WITH YOU?
IT'S CRAZY, BABY. LIKE NOTHING'S BIG ENOUGH TO SEE ANYMORE.
CIRCUS
COLOSSUS CIRCUS
LIKE I MAY AS WELL HAVE *DIED* IN THAT OLD PLANE.

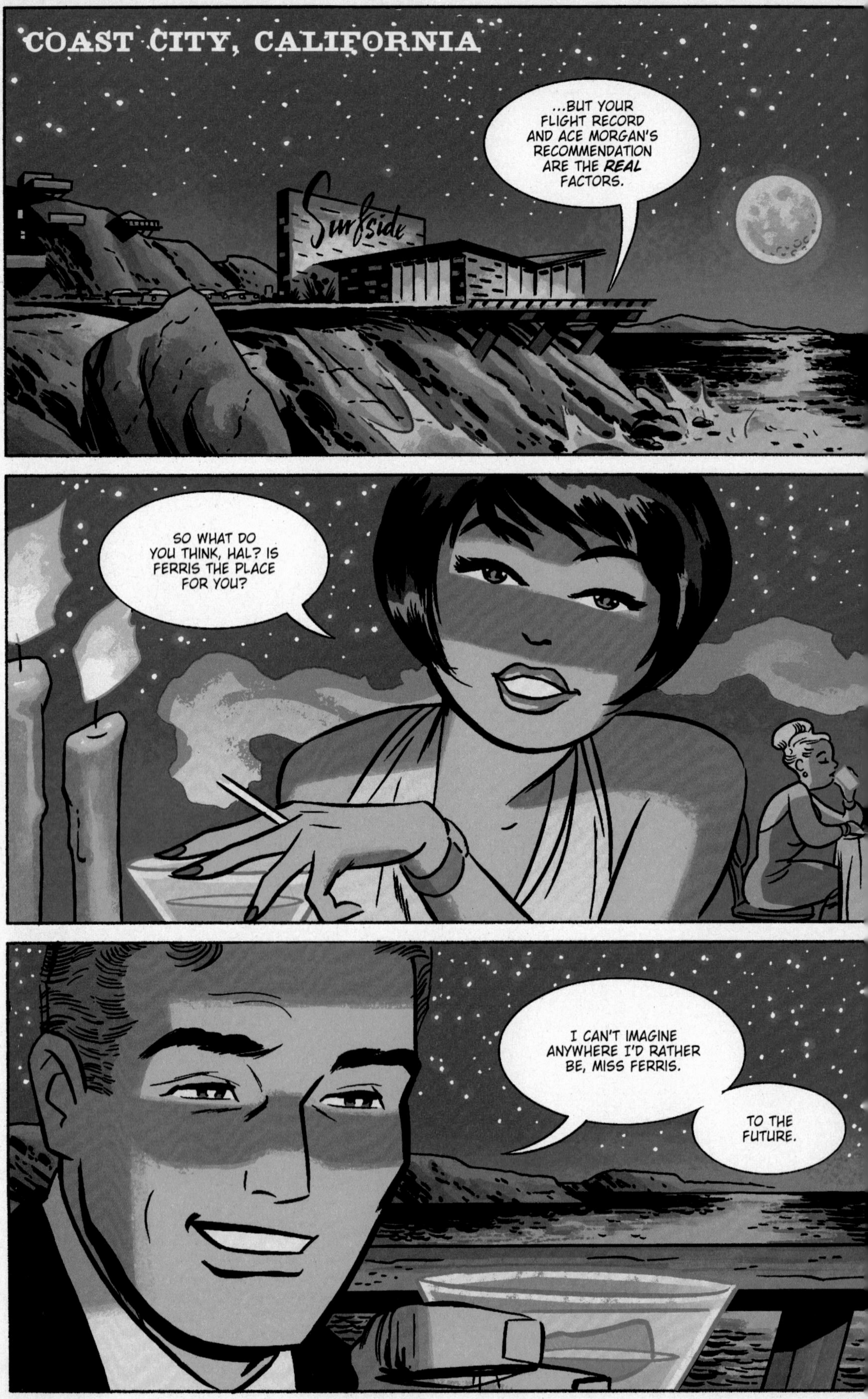
COAST CITY, CALIFORNIA
...BUT YOUR FLIGHT RECORD AND ACE MORGAN'S RECOMMENDATION ARE THE REAL FACTORS.
Surfside
SO WHAT DO YOU THINK, HAL? IS FERRIS THE PLACE FOR YOU?
I CAN'T IMAGINE ANYWHERE I'D RATHER BE, MISS FERRIS.
TO THE FUTURE.

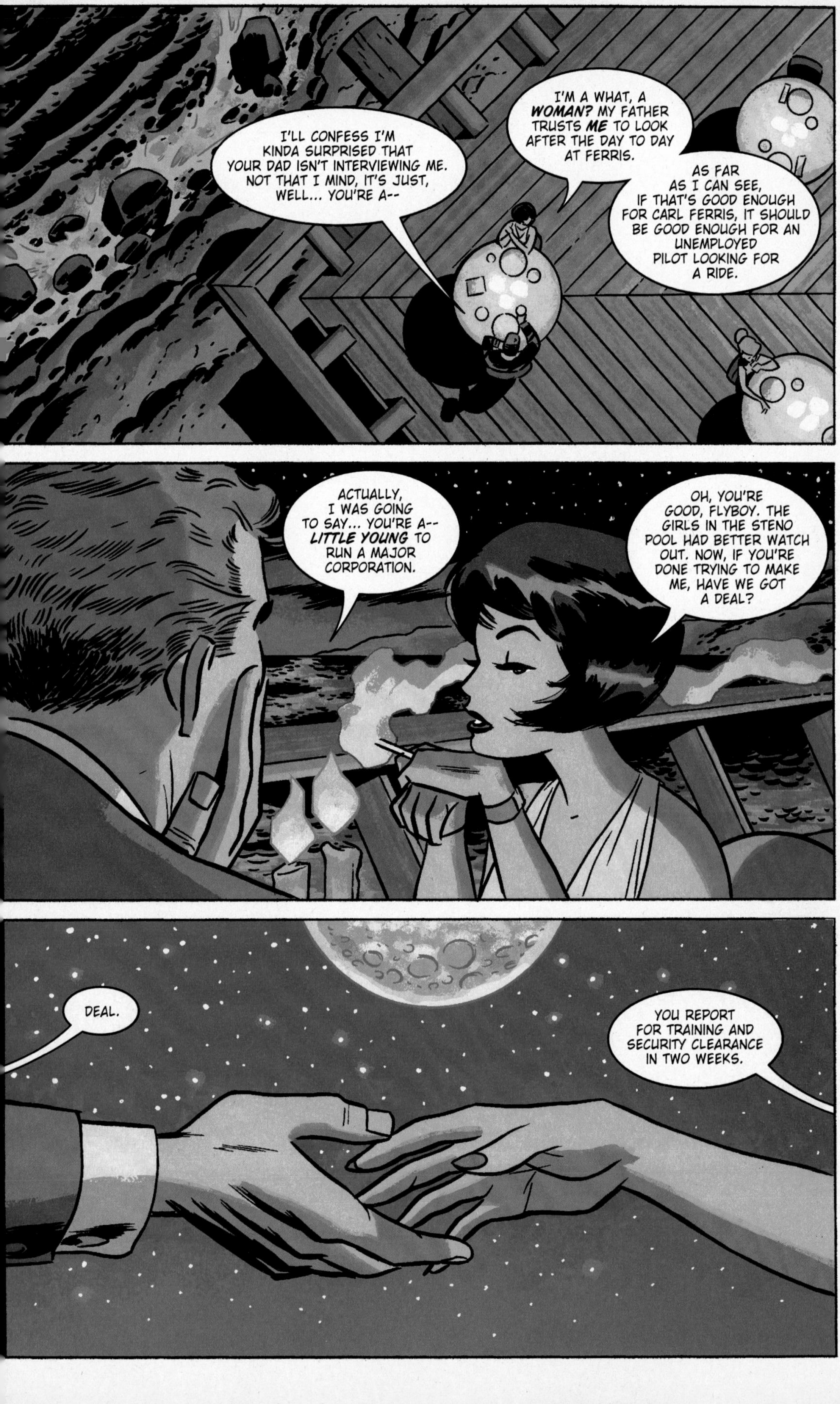
I'LL CONFESS I'M KINDA SURPRISED THAT YOUR DAD ISN'T INTERVIEWING ME. NOT THAT I MIND, IT'S JUST, WELL... YOU'RE A--
I'M A WHAT, A WOMAN? MY FATHER TRUSTS ME TO LOOK AFTER THE DAY TO DAY AT FERRIS.
AS FAR AS I CAN SEE, IF THAT'S GOOD ENOUGH FOR CARL FERRIS, IT SHOULD BE GOOD ENOUGH FOR AN UNEMPLOYED PILOT LOOKING FOR A RIDE.
ACTUALLY, I WAS GOING TO SAY... YOU'RE A-- LITTLE YOUNG TO RUN A MAJOR CORPORATION.
OH, YOU'RE GOOD, FLYBOY. THE GIRLS IN THE STENO POOL HAD BETTER WATCH OUT. NOW, IF YOU'RE DONE TRYING TO MAKE ME, HAVE WE GOT A DEAL?
DEAL.
YOU REPORT FOR TRAINING AND SECURITY CLEARANCE IN TWO WEEKS.

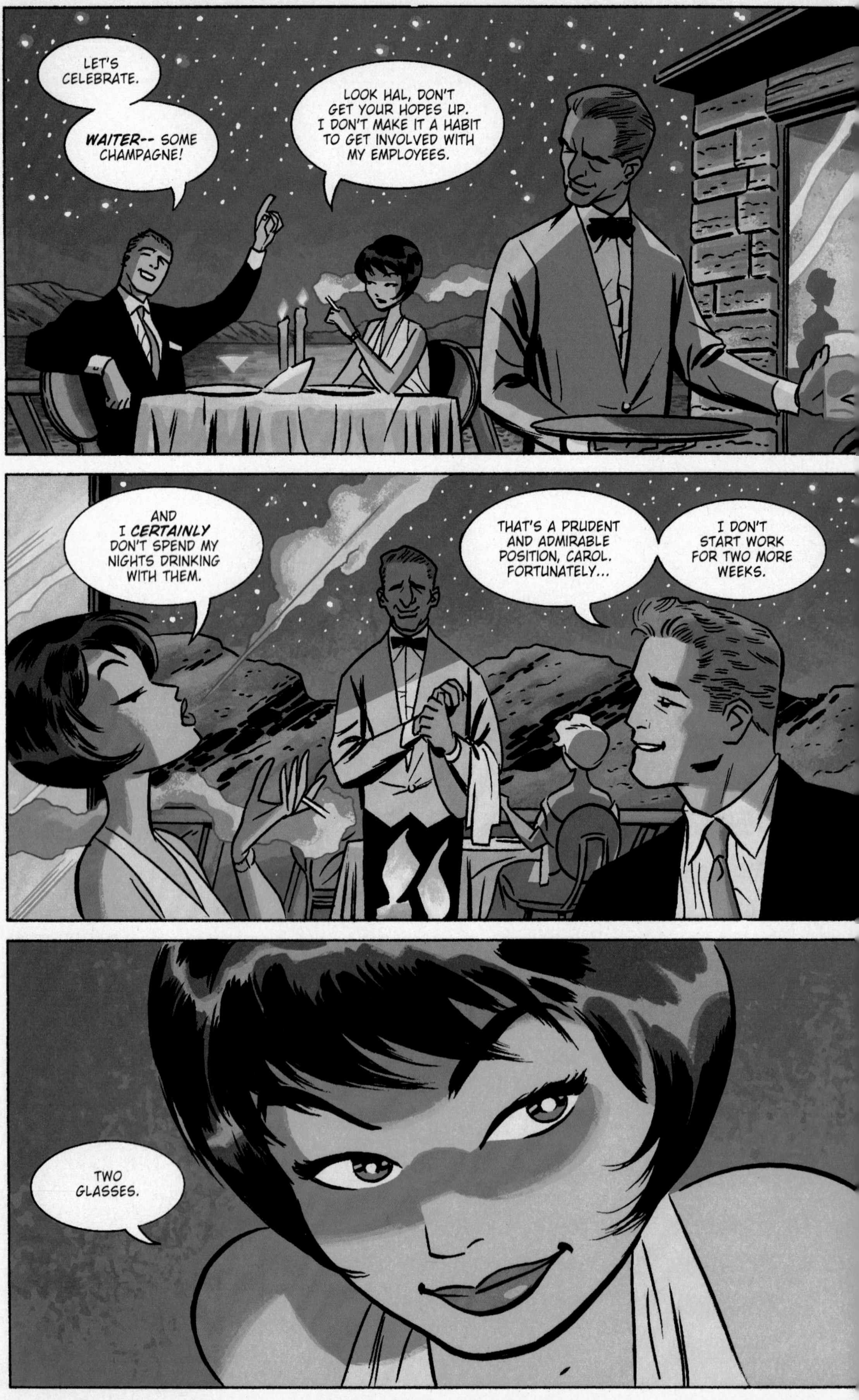
LET'S CELEBRATE.
WAITER-- SOME CHAMPAGNE!
LOOK HAL, DON'T GET YOUR HOPES UP. I DON'T MAKE IT A HABIT TO GET INVOLVED WITH MY EMPLOYEES.
AND I *CERTAINLY* DON'T SPEND MY NIGHTS DRINKING WITH THEM.
THAT'S A PRUDENT AND ADMIRABLE POSITION, CAROL. FORTUNATELY...
I DON'T START WORK FOR TWO MORE WEEKS.
TWO GLASSES.

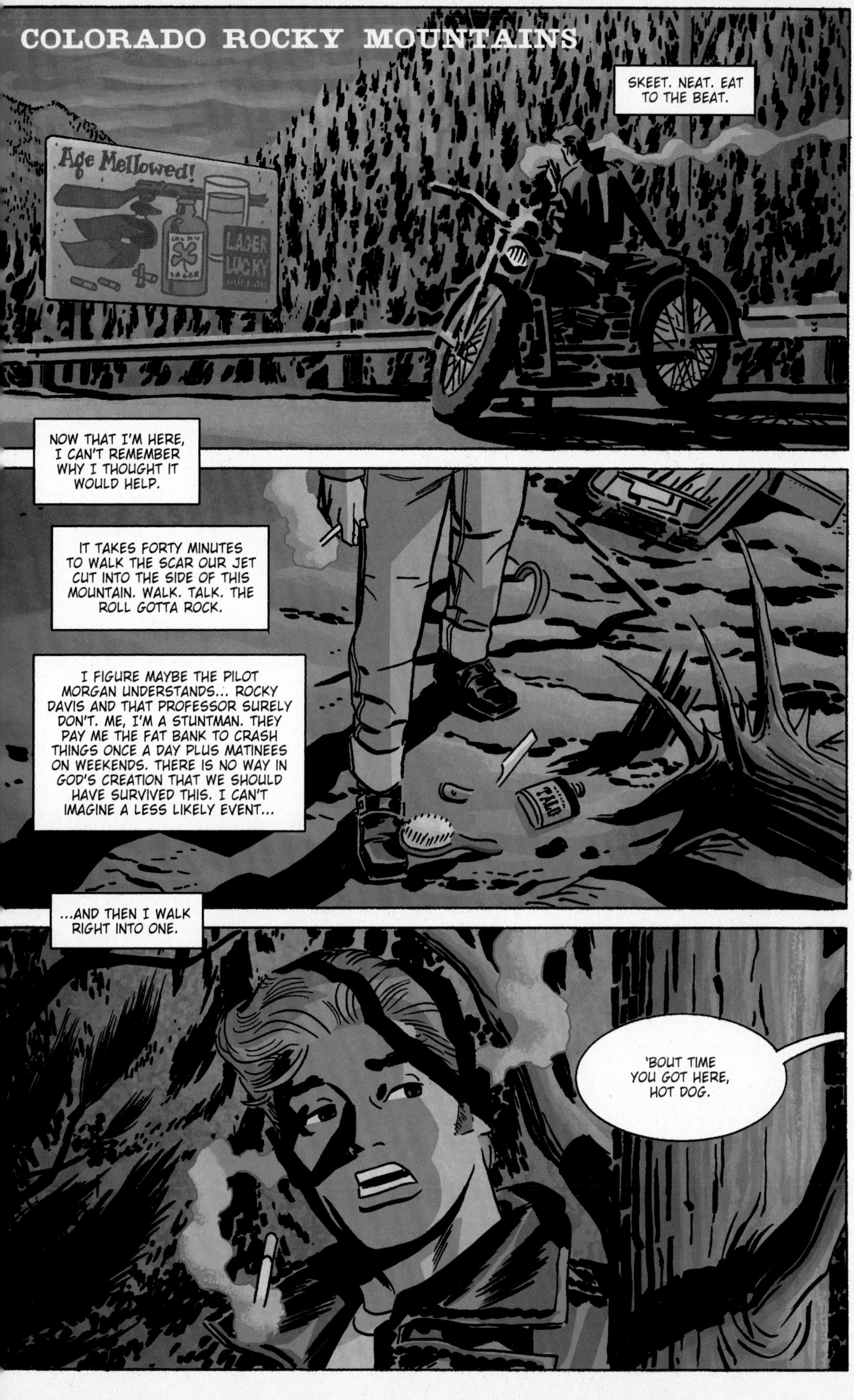
COLORADO ROCKY MOUNTAINS
Age Mellowed!
LADER LUCKY
SKEET. NEAT. EAT TO THE BEAT.
NOW THAT I'M HERE, I CAN'T REMEMBER WHY I THOUGHT IT WOULD HELP.
IT TAKES FORTY MINUTES TO WALK THE SCAR OUR JET CUT INTO THE SIDE OF THIS MOUNTAIN. WALK. TALK. THE ROLL GOTTA ROCK.
I FIGURE MAYBE THE PILOT MORGAN UNDERSTANDS... ROCKY DAVIS AND THAT PROFESSOR SURELY DON'T. ME, I'M A STUNTMAN. THEY PAY ME THE FAT BANK TO CRASH THINGS ONCE A DAY PLUS MATINEES ON WEEKENDS. THERE IS NO WAY IN GOD'S CREATION THAT WE SHOULD HAVE SURVIVED THIS. I CAN'T IMAGINE A LESS LIKELY EVENT...
...AND THEN I WALK RIGHT INTO ONE.
'BOUT TIME YOU GOT HERE, HOT DOG.

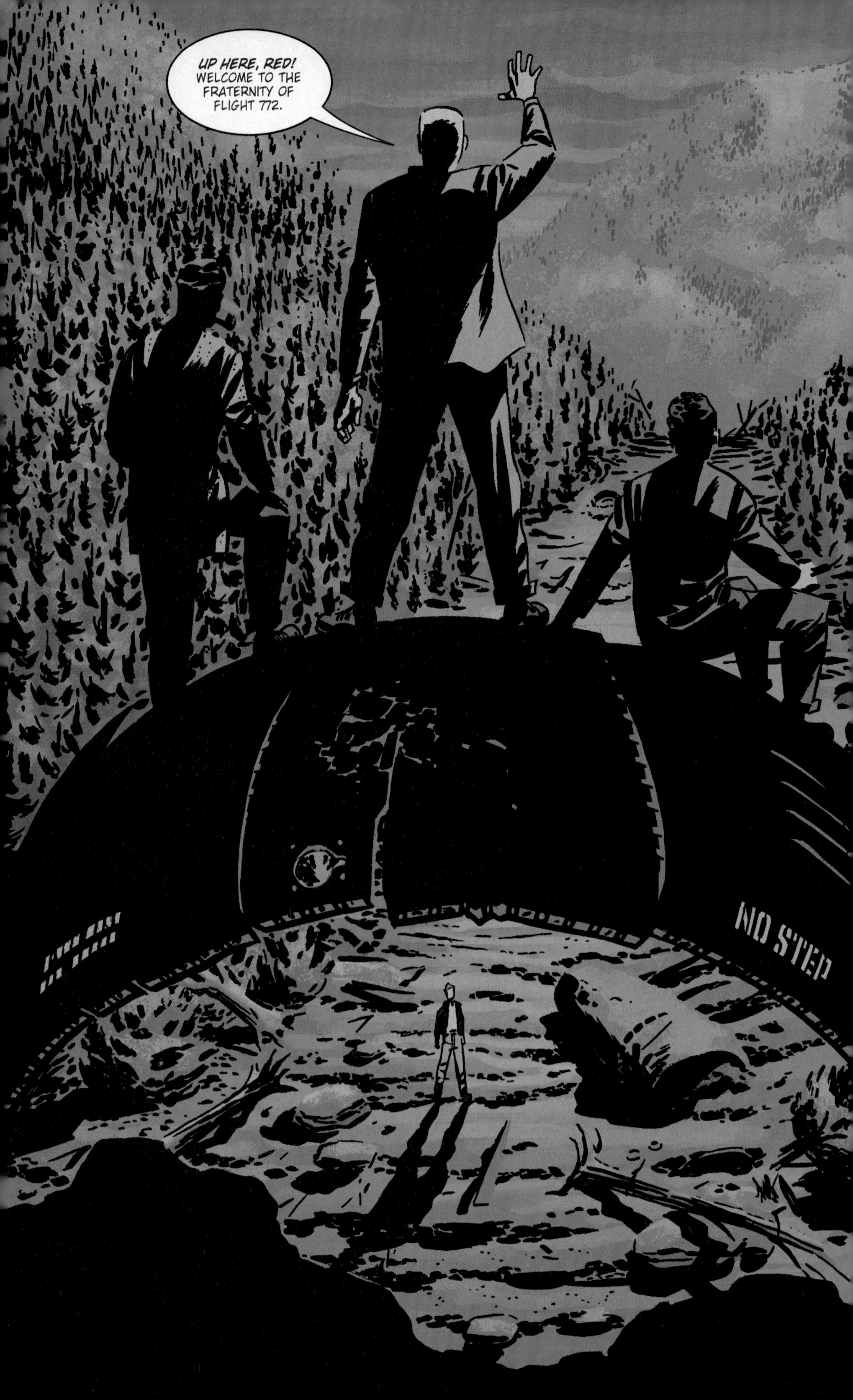
UP HERE, RED! WELCOME TO THE FRATERNITY OF FLIGHT 772.
NO STEP

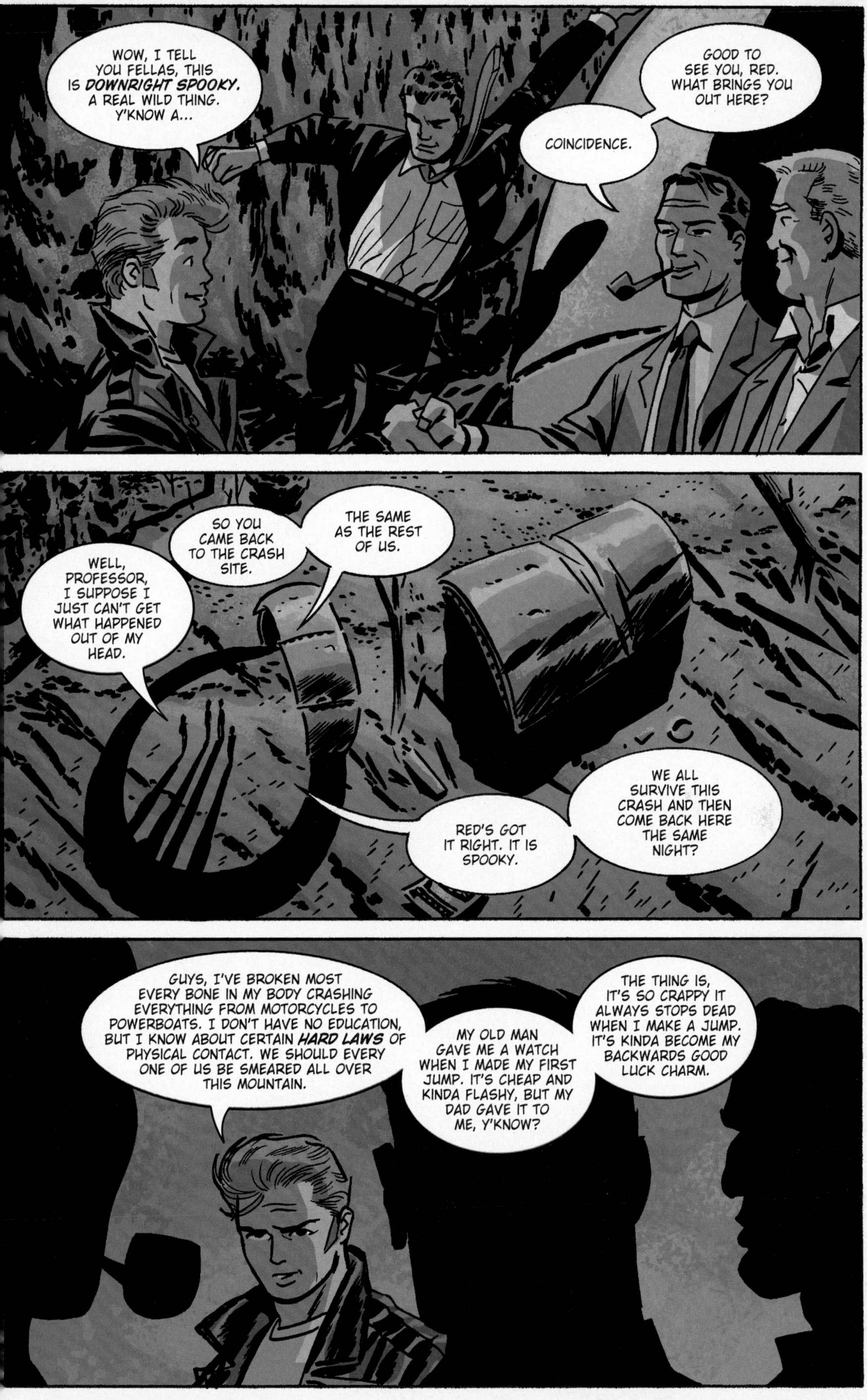
WOW, I TELL YOU FELLAS, THIS IS DOWNRIGHT SPOOKY. A REAL WILD THING. Y'KNOW A...
GOOD TO SEE YOU, RED. WHAT BRINGS YOU OUT HERE?
COINCIDENCE.
WELL, PROFESSOR, I SUPPOSE I JUST CAN'T GET WHAT HAPPENED OUT OF MY HEAD.
SO YOU CAME BACK TO THE CRASH SITE.
THE SAME AS THE REST OF US.
RED'S GOT IT RIGHT. IT IS SPOOKY.
WE ALL SURVIVE THIS CRASH AND THEN COME BACK HERE THE SAME NIGHT?
GUYS, I'VE BROKEN MOST EVERY BONE IN MY BODY CRASHING EVERYTHING FROM MOTORCYCLES TO POWERBOATS. I DON'T HAVE NO EDUCATION, BUT I KNOW ABOUT CERTAIN HARD LAWS OF PHYSICAL CONTACT. WE SHOULD EVERY ONE OF US BE SMEARED ALL OVER THIS MOUNTAIN.
MY OLD MAN GAVE ME A WATCH WHEN I MADE MY FIRST JUMP. IT'S CHEAP AND KINDA FLASHY, BUT MY DAD GAVE IT TO ME, Y'KNOW?
THE THING IS, IT'S SO CRAPPY IT ALWAYS STOPS DEAD WHEN I MAKE A JUMP. IT'S KINDA BECOME MY BACKWARDS GOOD LUCK CHARM.

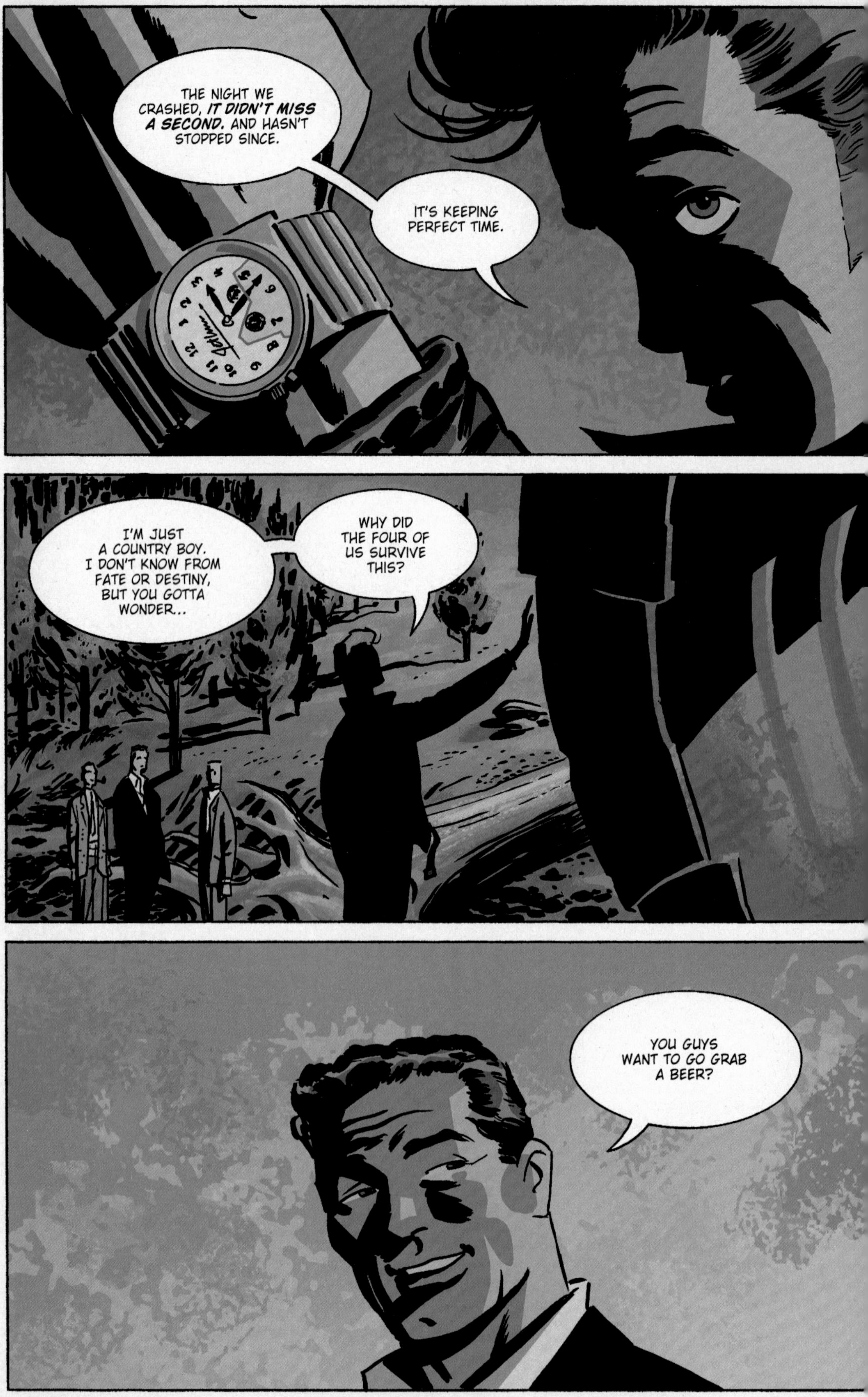
THE NIGHT WE CRASHED, ***IT DIDN'T MISS A SECOND.*** AND HASN'T STOPPED SINCE.
IT'S KEEPING PERFECT TIME.
I'M JUST A COUNTRY BOY. I DON'T KNOW FROM FATE OR DESTINY, BUT YOU GOTTA WONDER...
WHY DID THE FOUR OF US SURVIVE THIS?
YOU GUYS WANT TO GO GRAB A BEER?

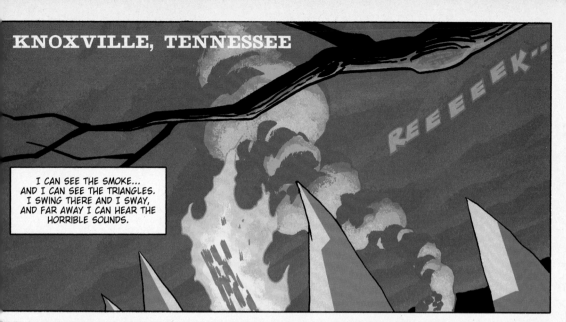

I CAN SEE THE SMOKE... AND I CAN SEE THE TRIANGLES. I SWING THERE AND I SWAY, AND FAR AWAY I CAN HEAR THE HORRIBLE SOUNDS.

REEEEEK--

AFTER A TIME, THE TRIANGLES GROW BORED, AND I WATCH THEIR GHOSTLY WHITE SHAPES RECEDE PAST THE EDGES OF MY CONSCIOUSNESS. I AM ANXIOUS NOW... FOR DEATH TO TAKE ME AWAY FROM HERE.

RRR......KKKKRRRAA

BUT FATE HAS OTHER PLANS FOR ME.

THUMP!!

I LAND HARD ON THE GROUND, AND FOR A WHILE I'M UNABLE TO MOVE.

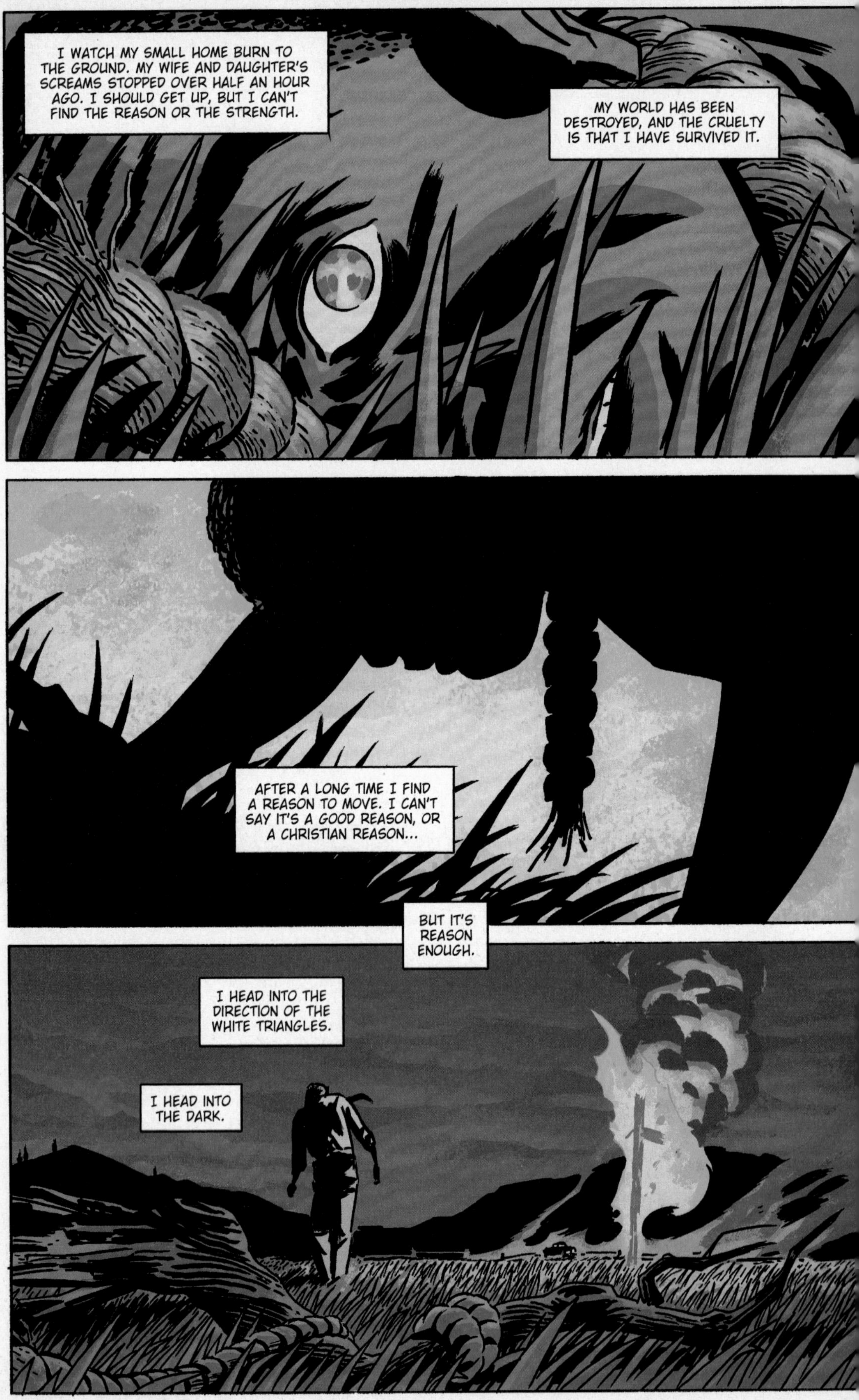
I WATCH MY SMALL HOME BURN TO THE GROUND. MY WIFE AND DAUGHTER'S SCREAMS STOPPED OVER HALF AN HOUR AGO. I SHOULD GET UP, BUT I CAN'T FIND THE REASON OR THE STRENGTH.
MY WORLD HAS BEEN DESTROYED, AND THE CRUELTY IS THAT I HAVE SURVIVED IT.
AFTER A LONG TIME I FIND A REASON TO MOVE. I CAN'T SAY IT'S A GOOD REASON, OR A CHRISTIAN REASON...
BUT IT'S REASON ENOUGH.
I HEAD INTO THE DIRECTION OF THE WHITE TRIANGLES.
I HEAD INTO THE DARK.

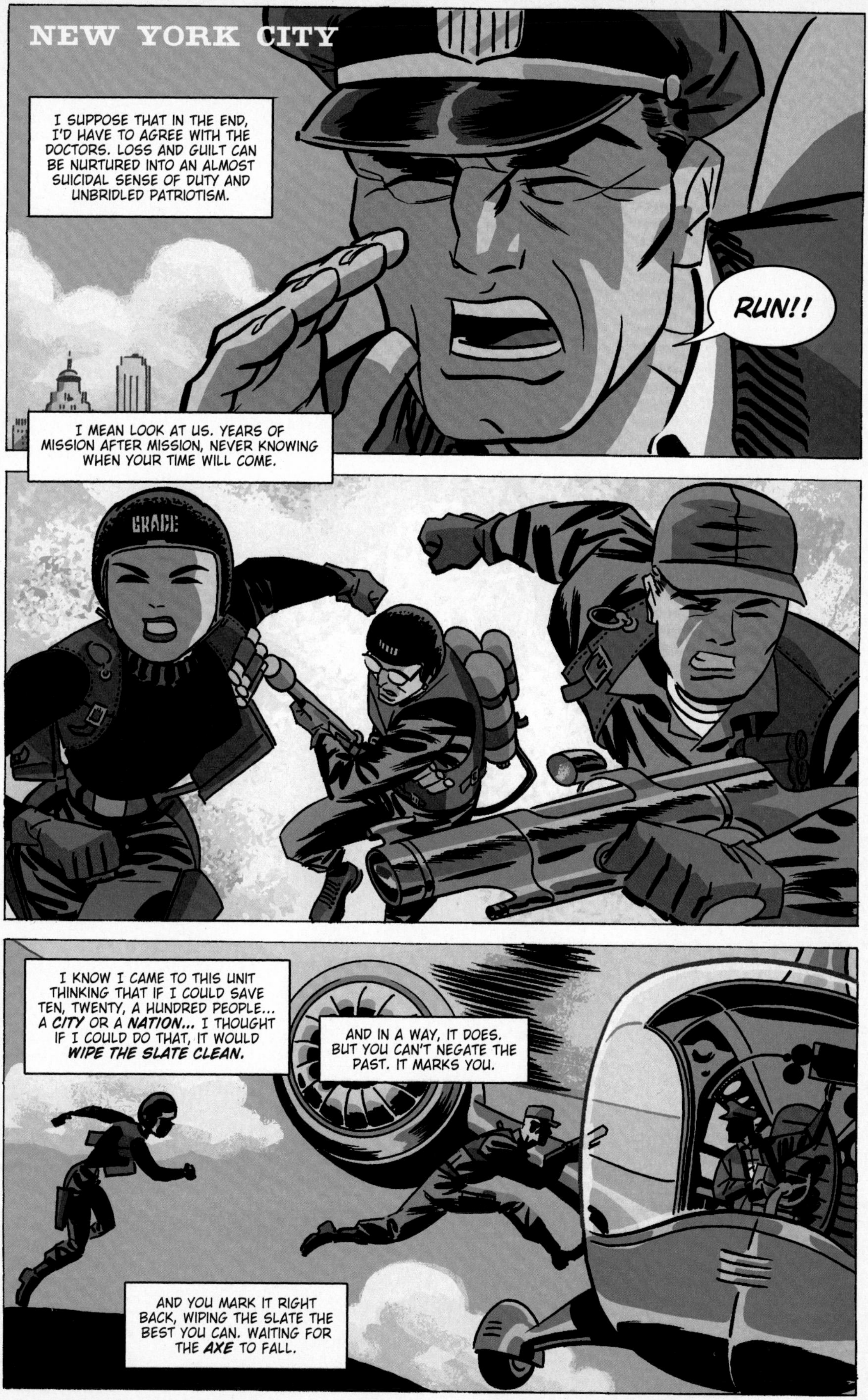
NEW YORK CITY
I SUPPOSE THAT IN THE END, I'D HAVE TO AGREE WITH THE DOCTORS. LOSS AND GUILT CAN BE NURTURED INTO AN ALMOST SUICIDAL SENSE OF DUTY AND UNBRIDLED PATRIOTISM.
RUN!!
I MEAN LOOK AT US. YEARS OF MISSION AFTER MISSION, NEVER KNOWING WHEN YOUR TIME WILL COME.
GRACE
I KNOW I CAME TO THIS UNIT THINKING THAT IF I COULD SAVE TEN, TWENTY, A HUNDRED PEOPLE... A *CITY* OR A *NATION...* I THOUGHT IF I COULD DO THAT, IT WOULD ***WIPE THE SLATE CLEAN.***
AND IN A WAY, IT DOES. BUT YOU CAN'T NEGATE THE PAST. IT MARKS YOU.
AND YOU MARK IT RIGHT BACK, WIPING THE SLATE THE BEST YOU CAN. WAITING FOR THE ***AXE*** TO FALL.

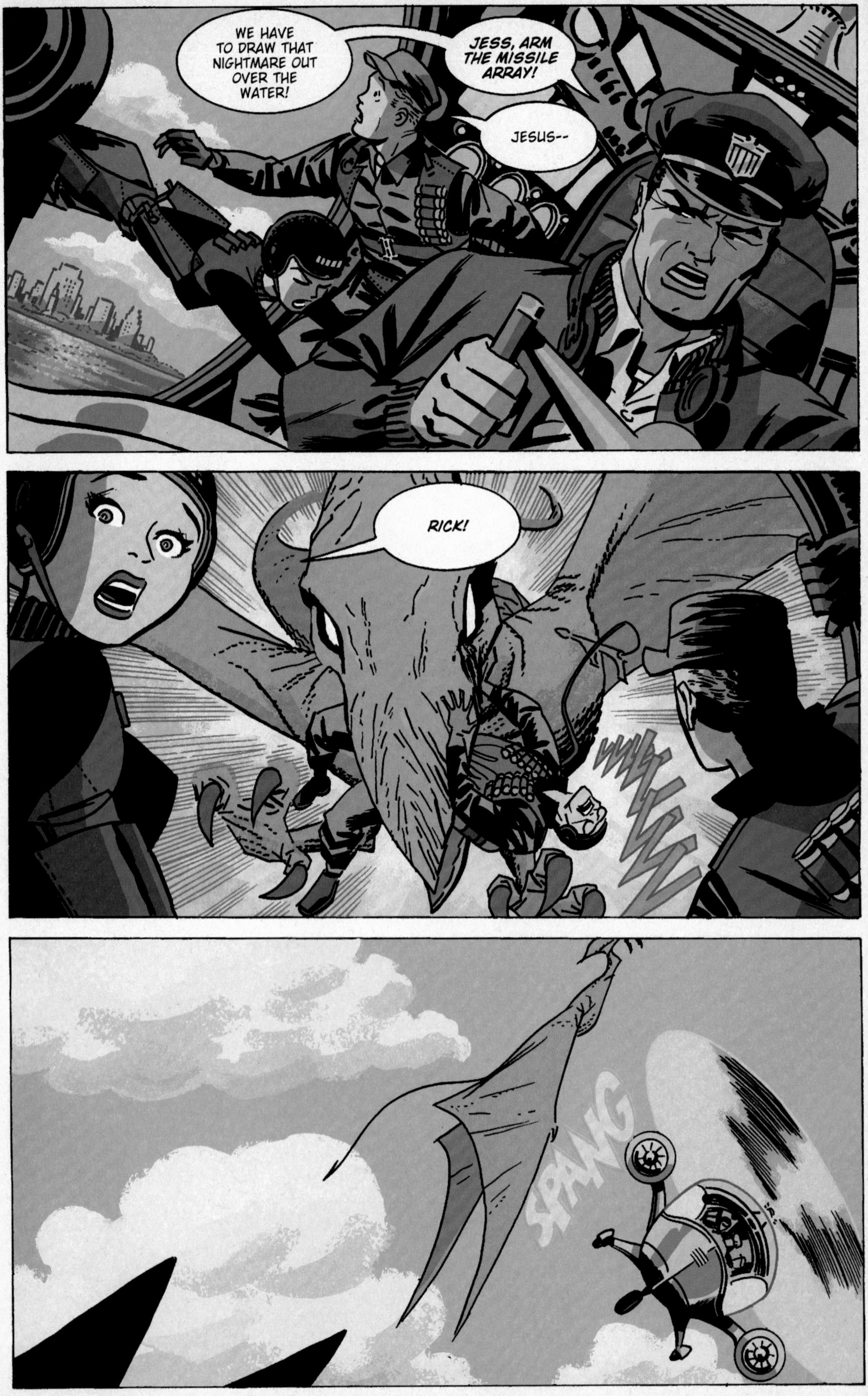
WE HAVE TO DRAW THAT NIGHTMARE OUT OVER THE WATER!
JESS, ARM THE MISSILE ARRAY!
JESUS--
RICK!
SPANG

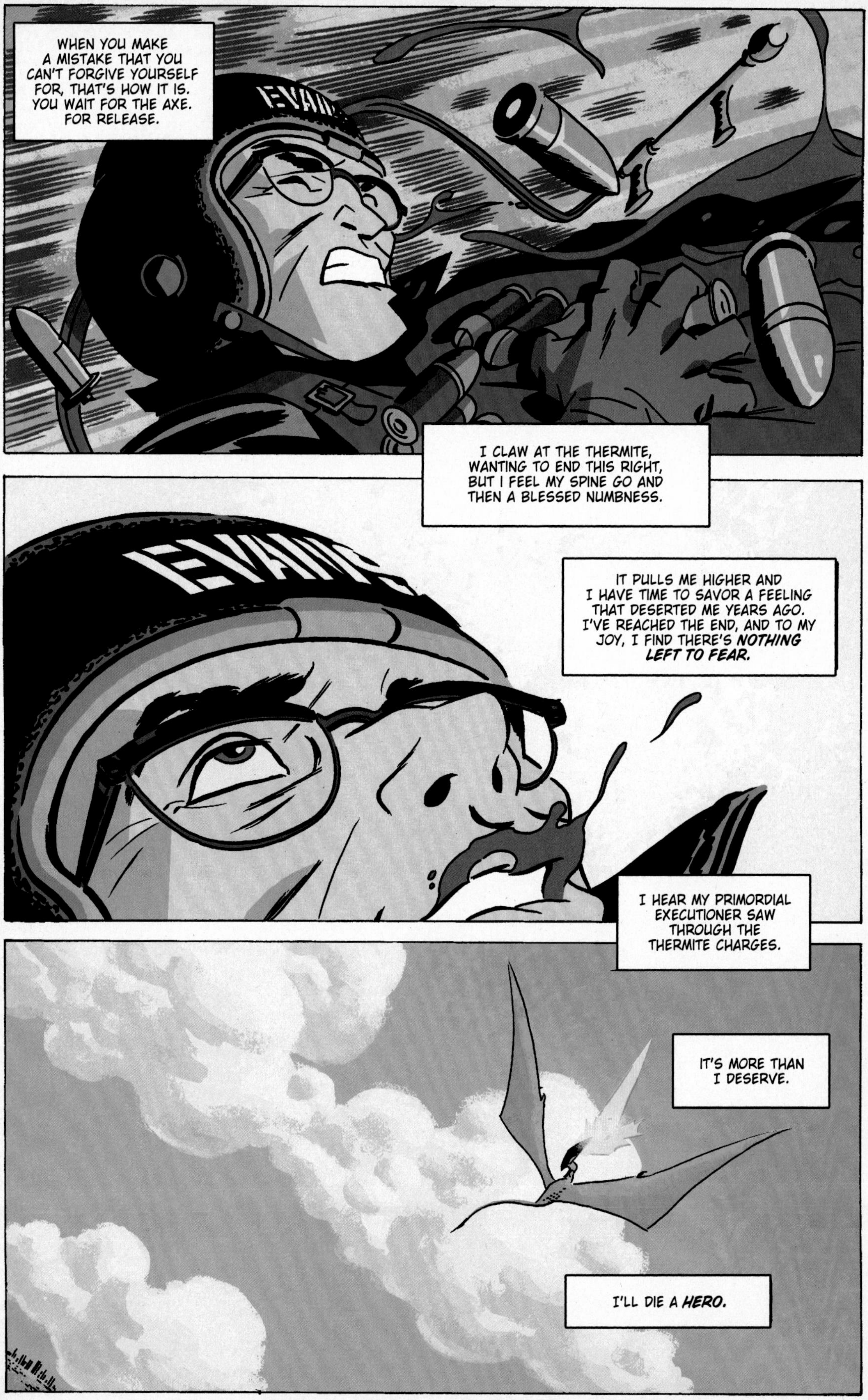
WHEN YOU MAKE A MISTAKE THAT YOU CAN'T FORGIVE YOURSELF FOR, THAT'S HOW IT IS. YOU WAIT FOR THE AXE. FOR RELEASE.
EVANS
I CLAW AT THE THERMITE, WANTING TO END THIS RIGHT, BUT I FEEL MY SPINE GO AND THEN A BLESSED NUMBNESS.
IT PULLS ME HIGHER AND I HAVE TIME TO SAVOR A FEELING THAT DESERTED ME YEARS AGO. I'VE REACHED THE END, AND TO MY JOY, I FIND THERE'S *NOTHING LEFT TO FEAR.*
I HEAR MY PRIMORDIAL EXECUTIONER SAW THROUGH THE THERMITE CHARGES.
IT'S MORE THAN I DESERVE.
I'LL DIE A *HERO.*

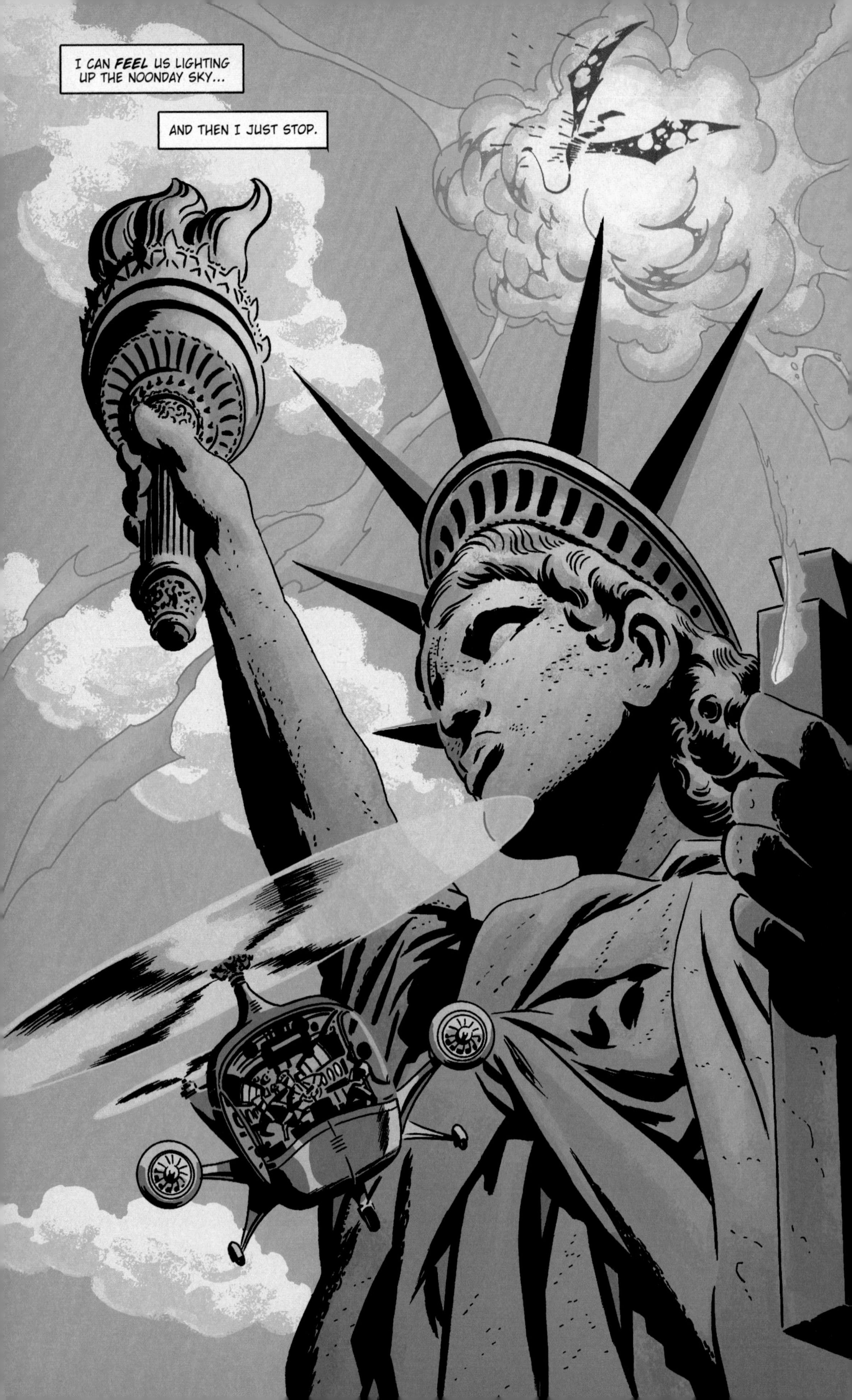
I CAN FEEL US LIGHTING UP THE NOONDAY SKY...
AND THEN I JUST STOP.

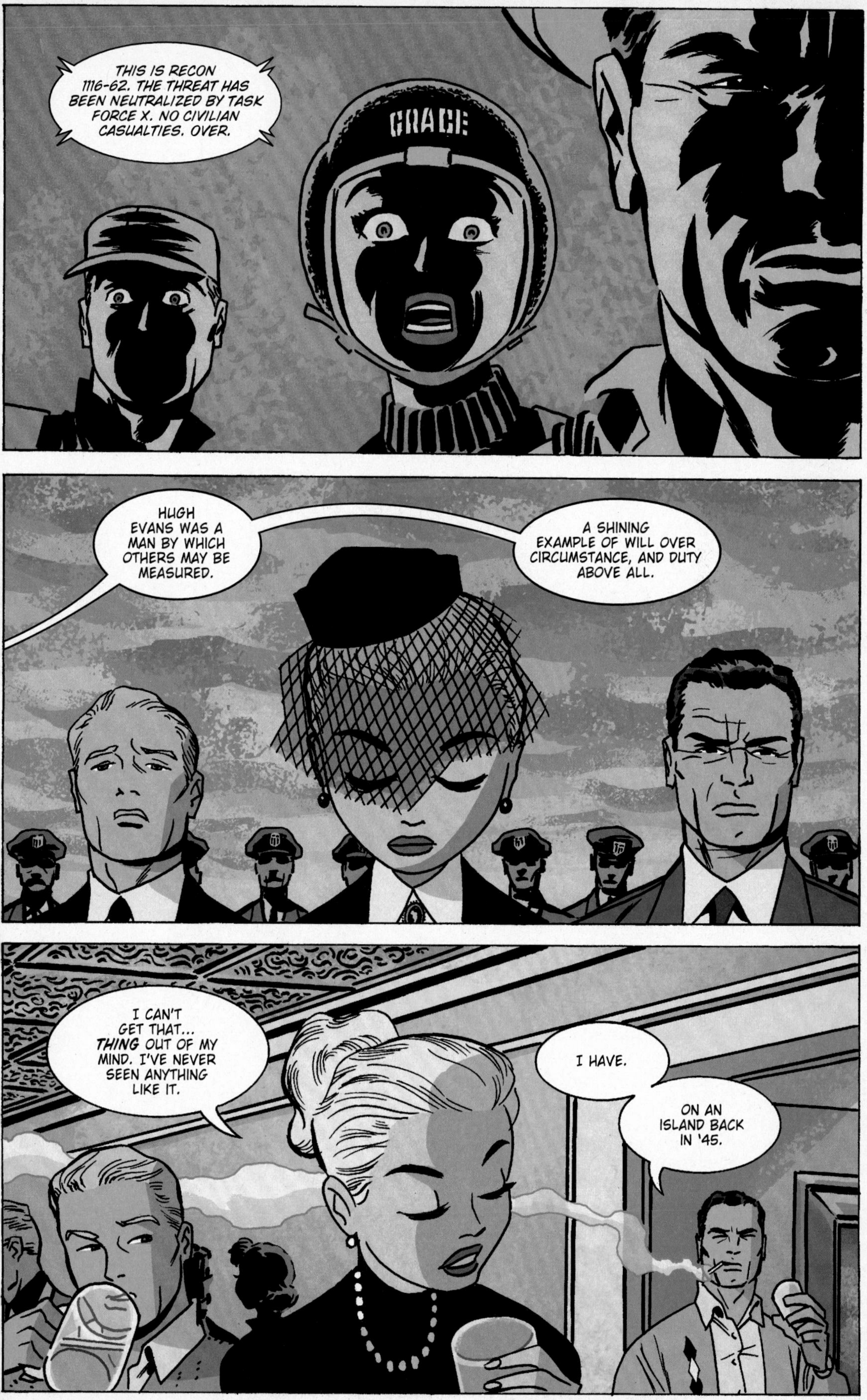
THIS IS RECON 1116-62. THE THREAT HAS BEEN NEUTRALIZED BY TASK FORCE X. NO CIVILIAN CASUALTIES. OVER.
GRACE
HUGH EVANS WAS A MAN BY WHICH OTHERS MAY BE MEASURED.
A SHINING EXAMPLE OF WILL OVER CIRCUMSTANCE, AND DUTY ABOVE ALL.
I CAN'T GET THAT... *THING* OUT OF MY MIND. I'VE NEVER SEEN ANYTHING LIKE IT.
I HAVE.
ON AN ISLAND BACK IN '45.

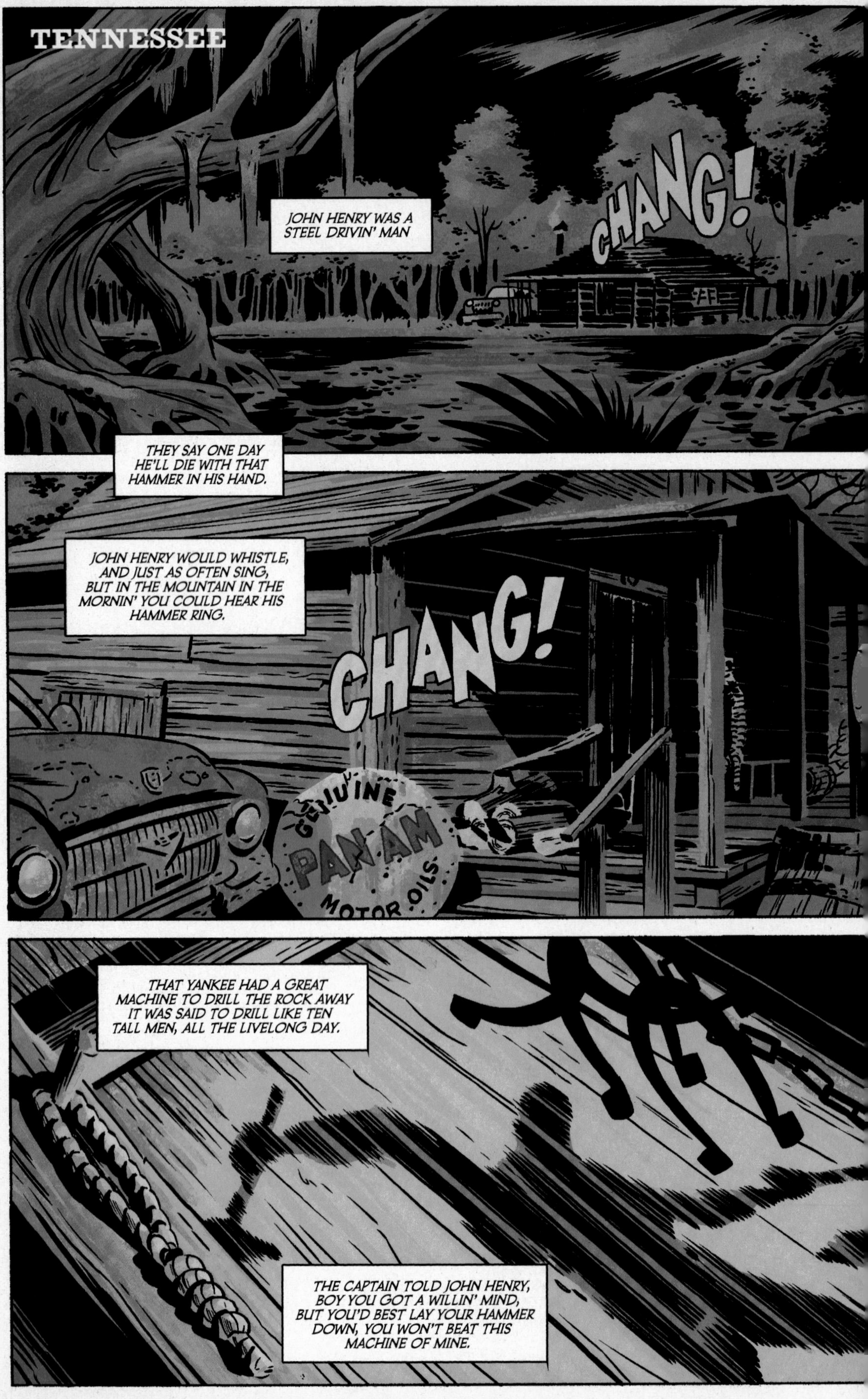
TENNESSEE
JOHN HENRY WAS A STEEL DRIVIN' MAN
CHANG!
THEY SAY ONE DAY HE'LL DIE WITH THAT HAMMER IN HIS HAND.
JOHN HENRY WOULD WHISTLE, AND JUST AS OFTEN SING, BUT IN THE MOUNTAIN IN THE MORNIN' YOU COULD HEAR HIS HAMMER RING.
CHANG!
GENUINE PAN AM MOTOR OILS
THAT YANKEE HAD A GREAT MACHINE TO DRILL THE ROCK AWAY IT WAS SAID TO DRILL LIKE TEN TALL MEN, ALL THE LIVELONG DAY.
THE CAPTAIN TOLD JOHN HENRY, BOY YOU GOT A WILLIN' MIND, BUT YOU'D BEST LAY YOUR HAMMER DOWN, YOU WON'T BEAT THIS MACHINE OF MINE.

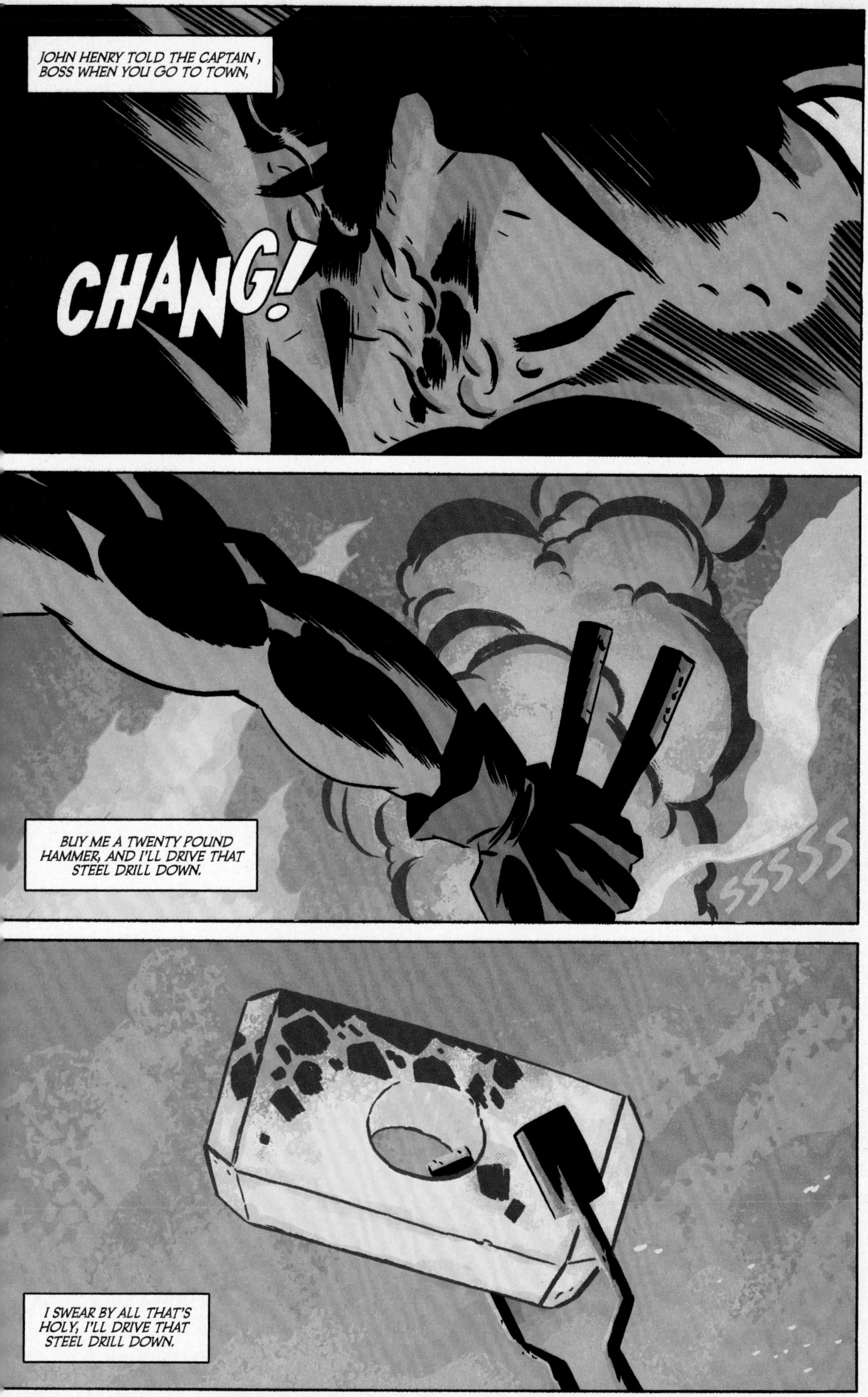
JOHN HENRY TOLD THE CAPTAIN , BOSS WHEN YOU GO TO TOWN,
CHANG!
BUY ME A TWENTY POUND HAMMER, AND I'LL DRIVE THAT STEEL DRILL DOWN.
SSSSSS
I SWEAR BY ALL THAT'S HOLY, I'LL DRIVE THAT STEEL DRILL DOWN.

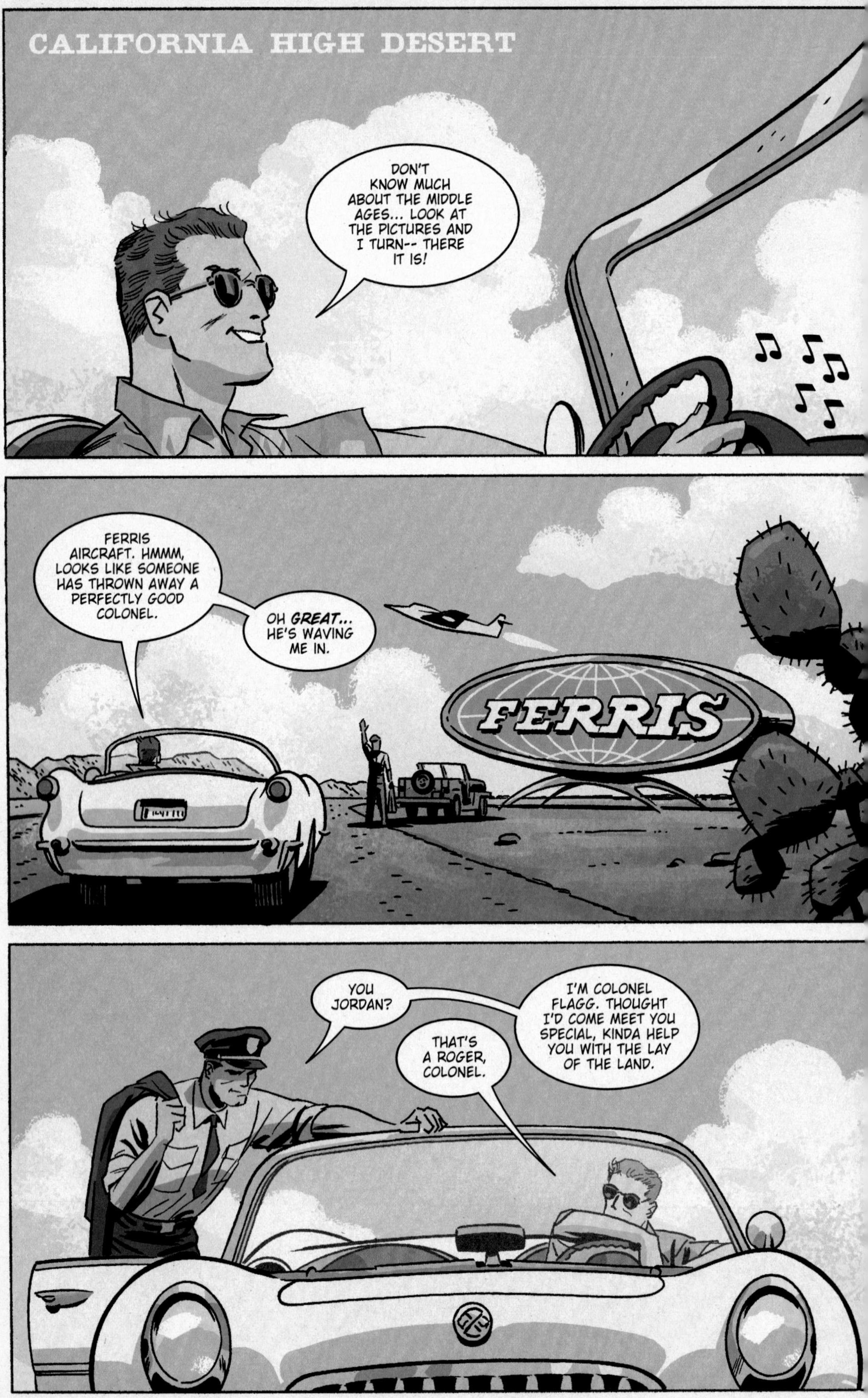
CALIFORNIA HIGH DESERT
DON'T KNOW MUCH ABOUT THE MIDDLE AGES... LOOK AT THE PICTURES AND I TURN-- THERE IT IS!
FERRIS AIRCRAFT. HMMM, LOOKS LIKE SOMEONE HAS THROWN AWAY A PERFECTLY GOOD COLONEL.
OH GREAT... HE'S WAVING ME IN.
FERRIS
YOU JORDAN?
THAT'S A ROGER, COLONEL.
I'M COLONEL FLAGG. THOUGHT I'D COME MEET YOU SPECIAL, KINDA HELP YOU WITH THE LAY OF THE LAND.

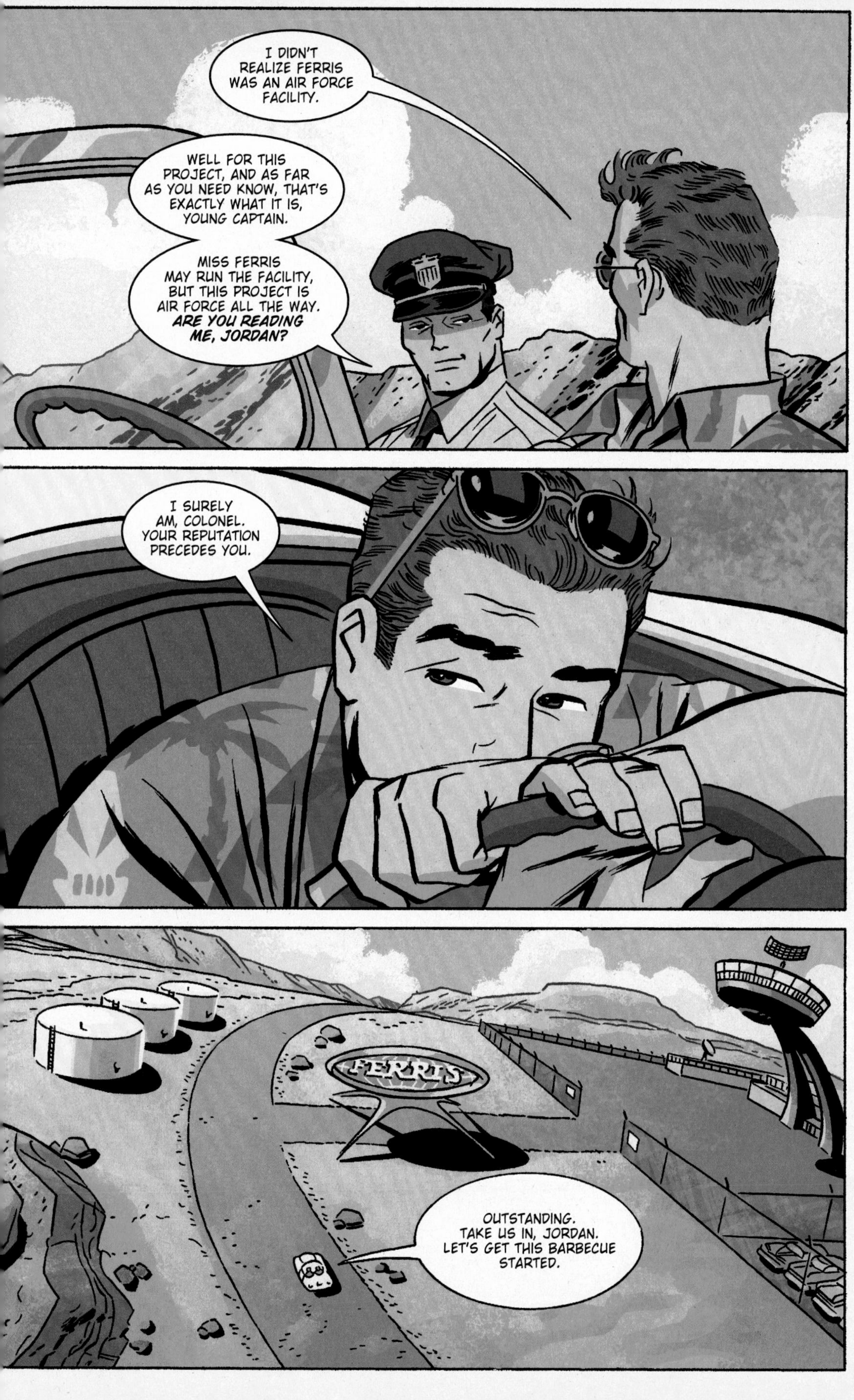
I DIDN'T REALIZE FERRIS WAS AN AIR FORCE FACILITY.
WELL FOR THIS PROJECT, AND AS FAR AS YOU NEED KNOW, THAT'S EXACTLY WHAT IT IS, YOUNG CAPTAIN.
MISS FERRIS MAY RUN THE FACILITY, BUT THIS PROJECT IS AIR FORCE ALL THE WAY. ***ARE YOU READING ME, JORDAN?***
I SURELY AM, COLONEL. YOUR REPUTATION PRECEDES YOU.
FERRIS
OUTSTANDING. TAKE US IN, JORDAN. LET'S GET THIS BARBECUE STARTED.

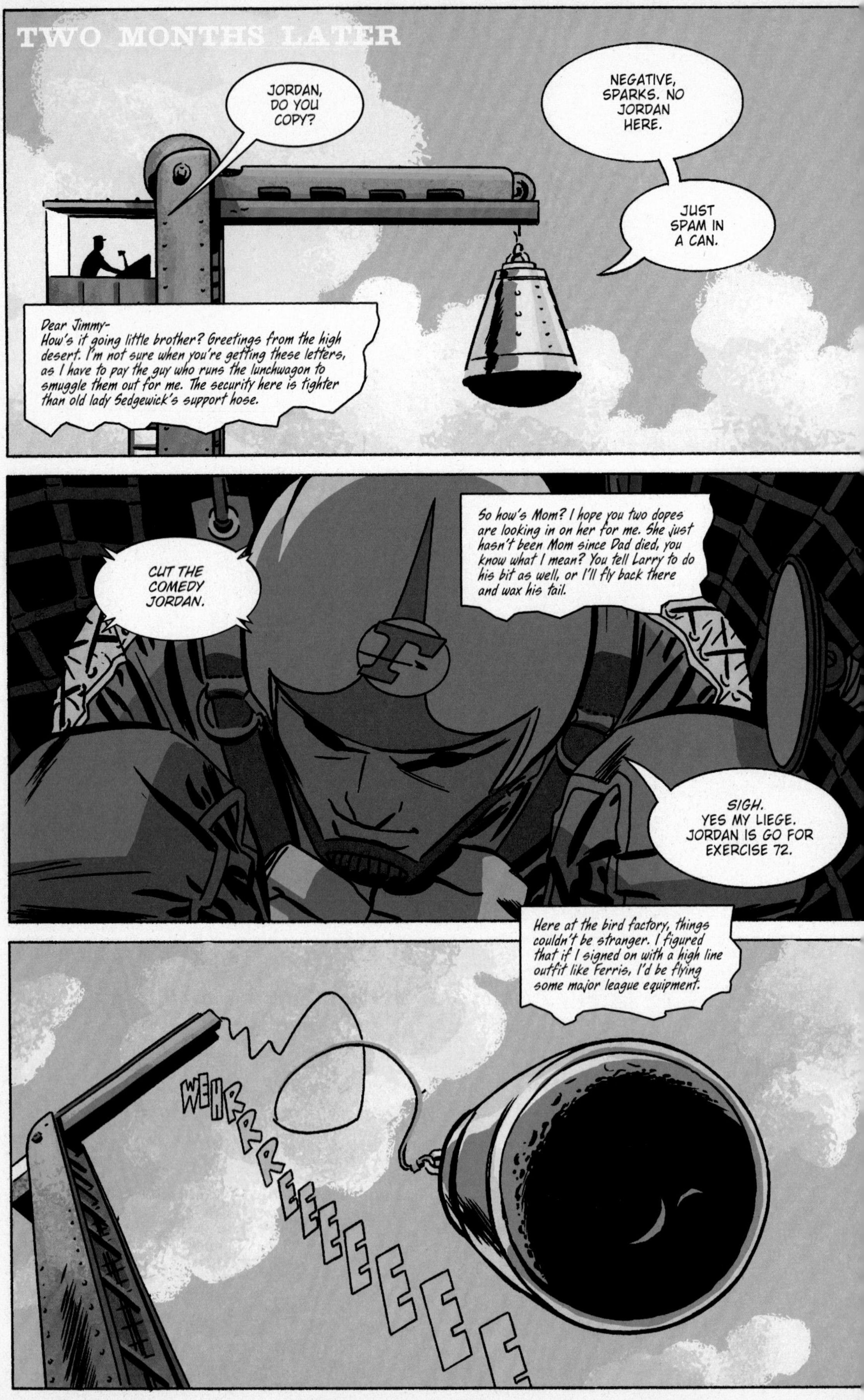
TWO MONTHS LATER
JORDAN, DO YOU COPY?
NEGATIVE, SPARKS. NO JORDAN HERE.
JUST SPAM IN A CAN.
Dear Jimmy-
How's it going little brother? Greetings from the high desert. I'm not sure when you're getting these letters, as I have to pay the guy who runs the lunchwagon to smuggle them out for me. The security here is tighter than old lady Sedgewick's support hose.
CUT THE COMEDY JORDAN.
So how's Mom? I hope you two dopes are looking in on her for me. She just hasn't been Mom since Dad died, you know what I mean? You tell Larry to do his bit as well, or I'll fly back there and wax his tail.
SIGH. YES MY LIEGE. JORDAN IS GO FOR EXERCISE 72.
Here at the bird factory, things couldn't be stranger. I figured that if I signed on with a high line outfit like Ferris, I'd be flying some major league equipment.
WEHRRREEEEEEEEE

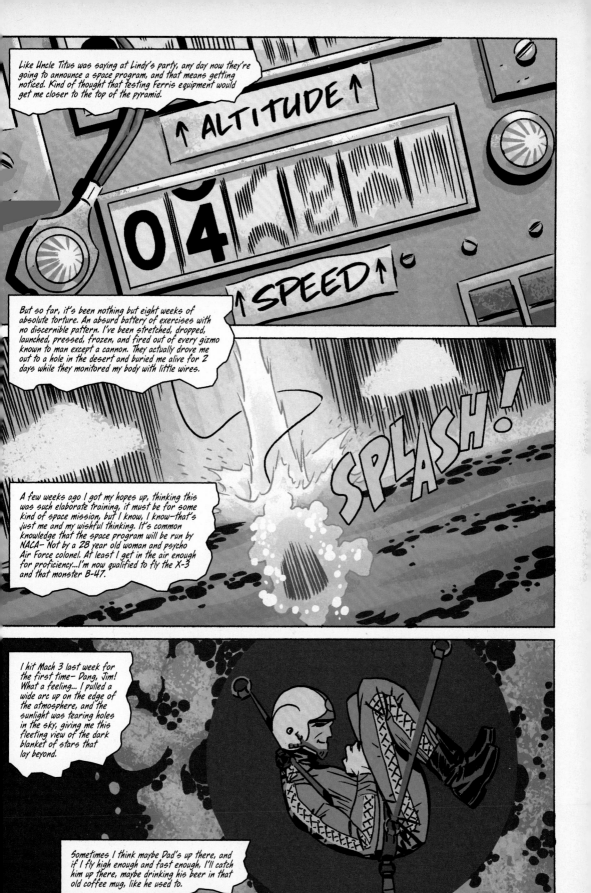

Like Uncle Titus was saying at Lindy's party, any day now they're going to announce a space program, and that means getting noticed. Kind of thought that testing Ferris equipment would get me closer to the top of the pyramid.

↑ ALTITUDE ↑

↑ SPEED ↑

But so far, it's been nothing but eight weeks of absolute torture. An absurd battery of exercises with no discernible pattern. I've been stretched, dropped, launched, pressed, frozen, and fired out of every gizmo known to man except a cannon. They actually drove me out to a hole in the desert and buried me alive for 2 days while they monitored my body with little wires.

SPLASH!

A few weeks ago I got my hopes up, thinking this was such elaborate training, it must be for some kind of space mission, but I know, I know—that's just me and my wishful thinking. It's common knowledge that the space program will be run by NACA— Not by a 28 year old woman and psycho Air Force colonel. At least I get in the air enough for proficiency...I'm now qualified to fly the X-3 and that monster B-47.

I hit Mach 3 last week for the first time— Dang, Jim! What a feeling... I pulled a wide arc up on the edge of the atmosphere, and the sunlight was tearing holes in the sky, giving me this fleeting view of the dark blanket of stars that lay beyond.

Sometimes I think maybe Dad's up there, and if I fly high enough and fast enough, I'll catch him up there, maybe drinking his beer in that old coffee mug, like he used to.

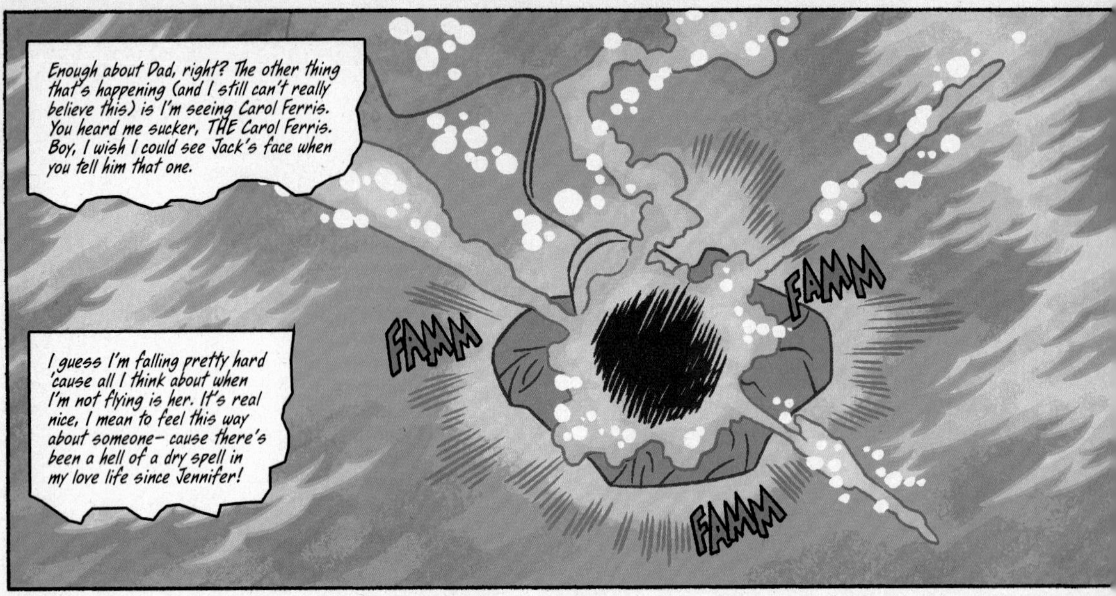
Enough about Dad, right? The other thing that's happening (and I still can't really believe this) is I'm seeing Carol Ferris. You heard me sucker, THE Carol Ferris. Boy, I wish I could see Jack's face when you tell him that one.
FAMM
FAMM
I guess I'm falling pretty hard 'cause all I think about when I'm not flying is her. It's real nice, I mean to feel this way about someone- cause there's been a hell of a dry spell in my love life since Jennifer!
FAMM

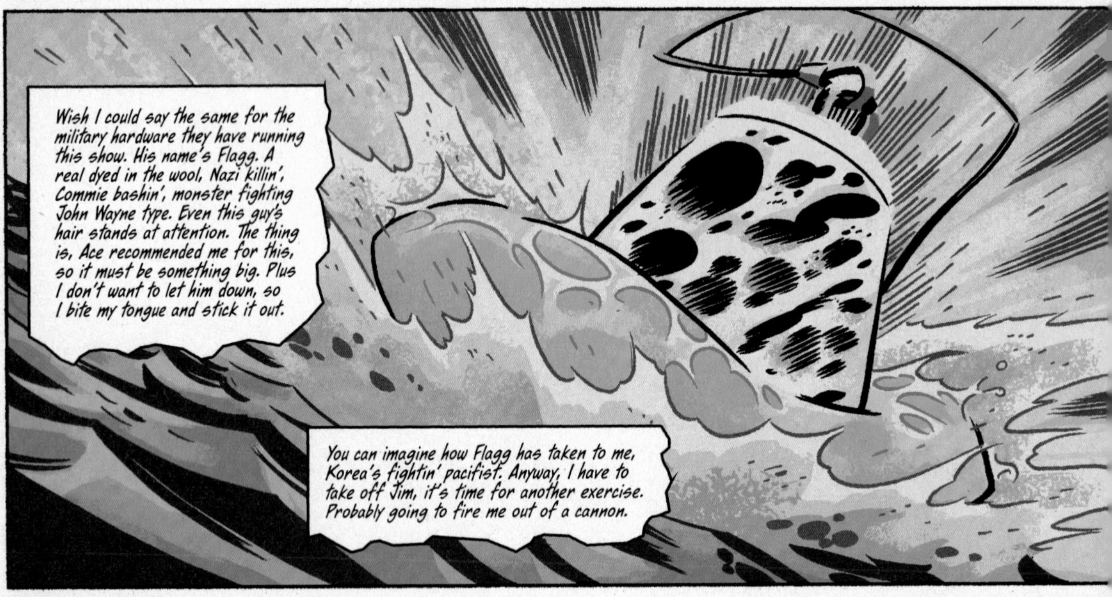
Wish I could say the same for the military hardware they have running this show. His name's Flagg. A real dyed in the wool, Nazi killin', Commie bashin', monster fighting John Wayne type. Even this guy's hair stands at attention. The thing is, Ace recommended me for this, so it must be something big. Plus I don't want to let him down, so I bite my tongue and stick it out.
You can imagine how Flagg has taken to me, Korea's fightin' pacifist. Anyway, I have to take off Jim, it's time for another exercise. Probably going to fire me out of a cannon.

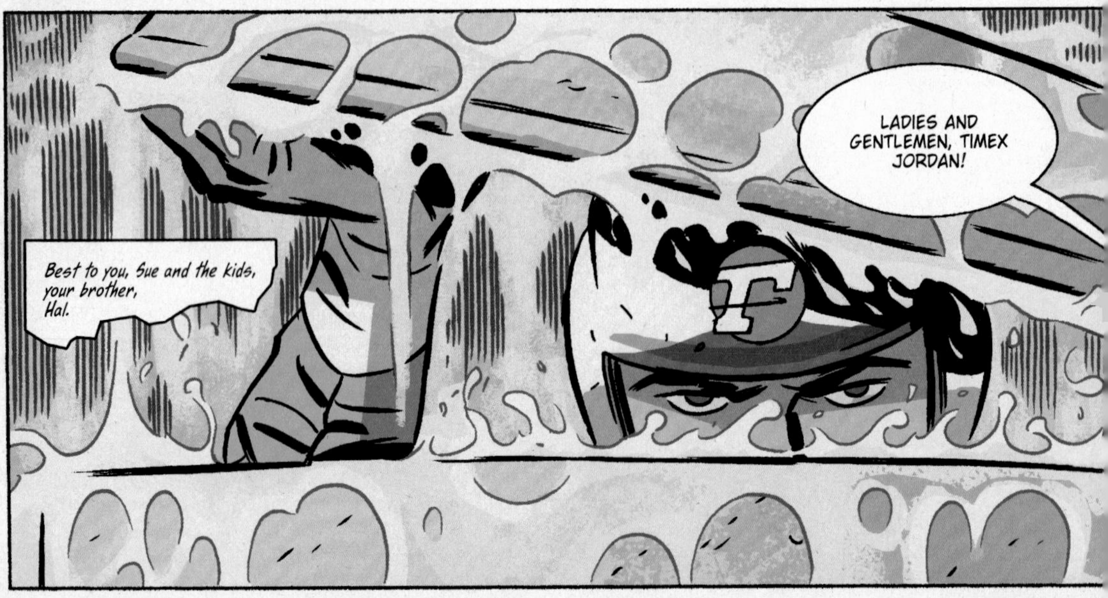
LADIES AND GENTLEMEN, TIMEX JORDAN!
Best to you, Sue and the kids, your brother, Hal.

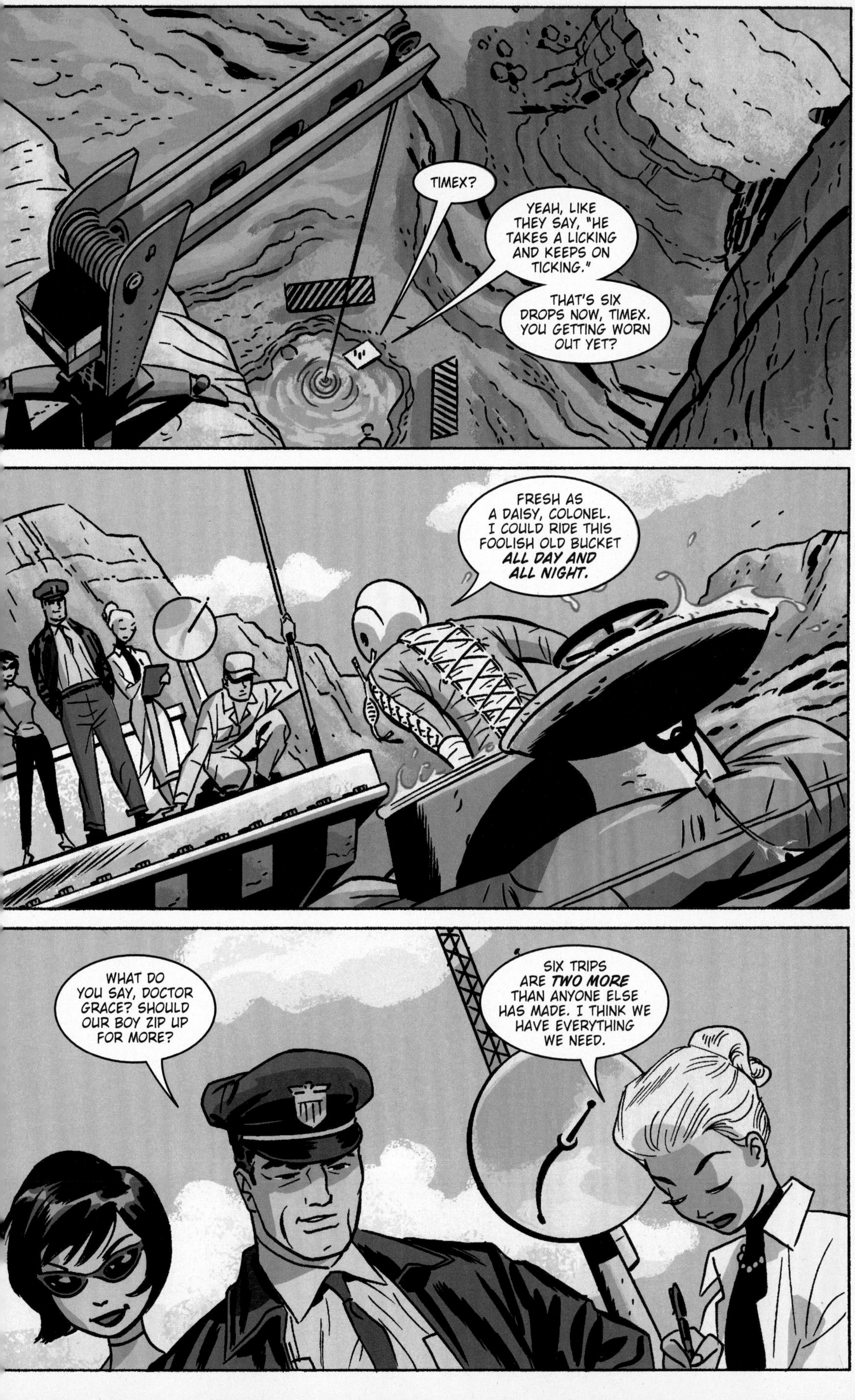
TIMEX?
YEAH, LIKE THEY SAY, "HE TAKES A LICKING AND KEEPS ON TICKING."
THAT'S SIX DROPS NOW, TIMEX. YOU GETTING WORN OUT YET?
FRESH AS A DAISY, COLONEL. I COULD RIDE THIS FOOLISH OLD BUCKET ***ALL DAY AND ALL NIGHT.***
WHAT DO YOU SAY, DOCTOR GRACE? SHOULD OUR BOY ZIP UP FOR MORE?
SIX TRIPS ARE ***TWO MORE*** THAN ANYONE ELSE HAS MADE. I THINK WE HAVE EVERYTHING WE NEED.

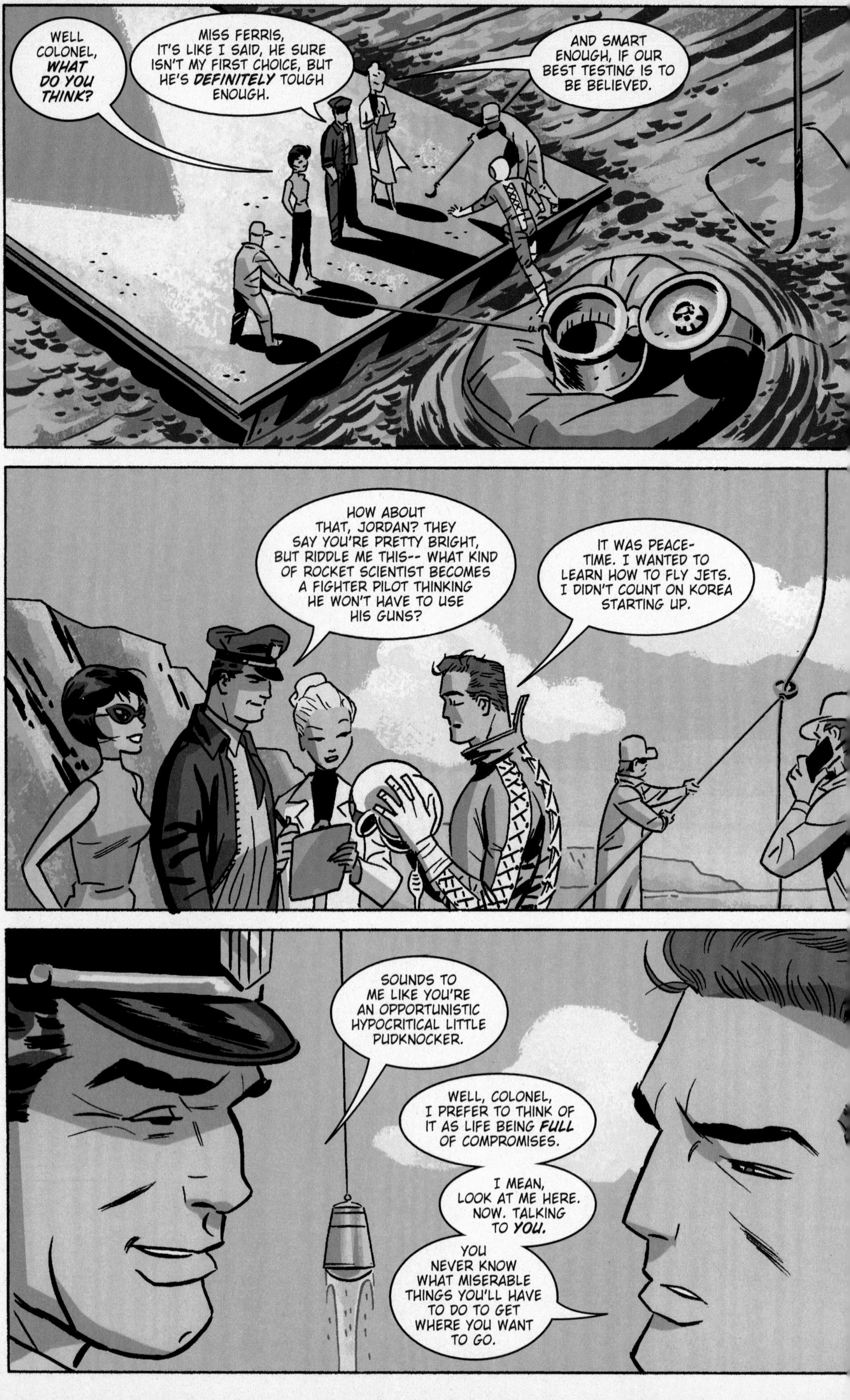

WELL COLONEL, WHAT DO YOU THINK?
MISS FERRIS, IT'S LIKE I SAID, HE SURE ISN'T MY FIRST CHOICE, BUT HE'S DEFINITELY TOUGH ENOUGH.
AND SMART ENOUGH, IF OUR BEST TESTING IS TO BE BELIEVED.
HOW ABOUT THAT, JORDAN? THEY SAY YOU'RE PRETTY BRIGHT, BUT RIDDLE ME THIS-- WHAT KIND OF ROCKET SCIENTIST BECOMES A FIGHTER PILOT THINKING HE WON'T HAVE TO USE HIS GUNS?
IT WAS PEACE-TIME. I WANTED TO LEARN HOW TO FLY JETS. I DIDN'T COUNT ON KOREA STARTING UP.
SOUNDS TO ME LIKE YOU'RE AN OPPORTUNISTIC HYPOCRITICAL LITTLE PUDKNOCKER.
WELL, COLONEL, I PREFER TO THINK OF IT AS LIFE BEING FULL OF COMPROMISES.
I MEAN, LOOK AT ME HERE. NOW. TALKING TO YOU.
YOU NEVER KNOW WHAT MISERABLE THINGS YOU'LL HAVE TO DO TO GET WHERE YOU WANT TO GO.

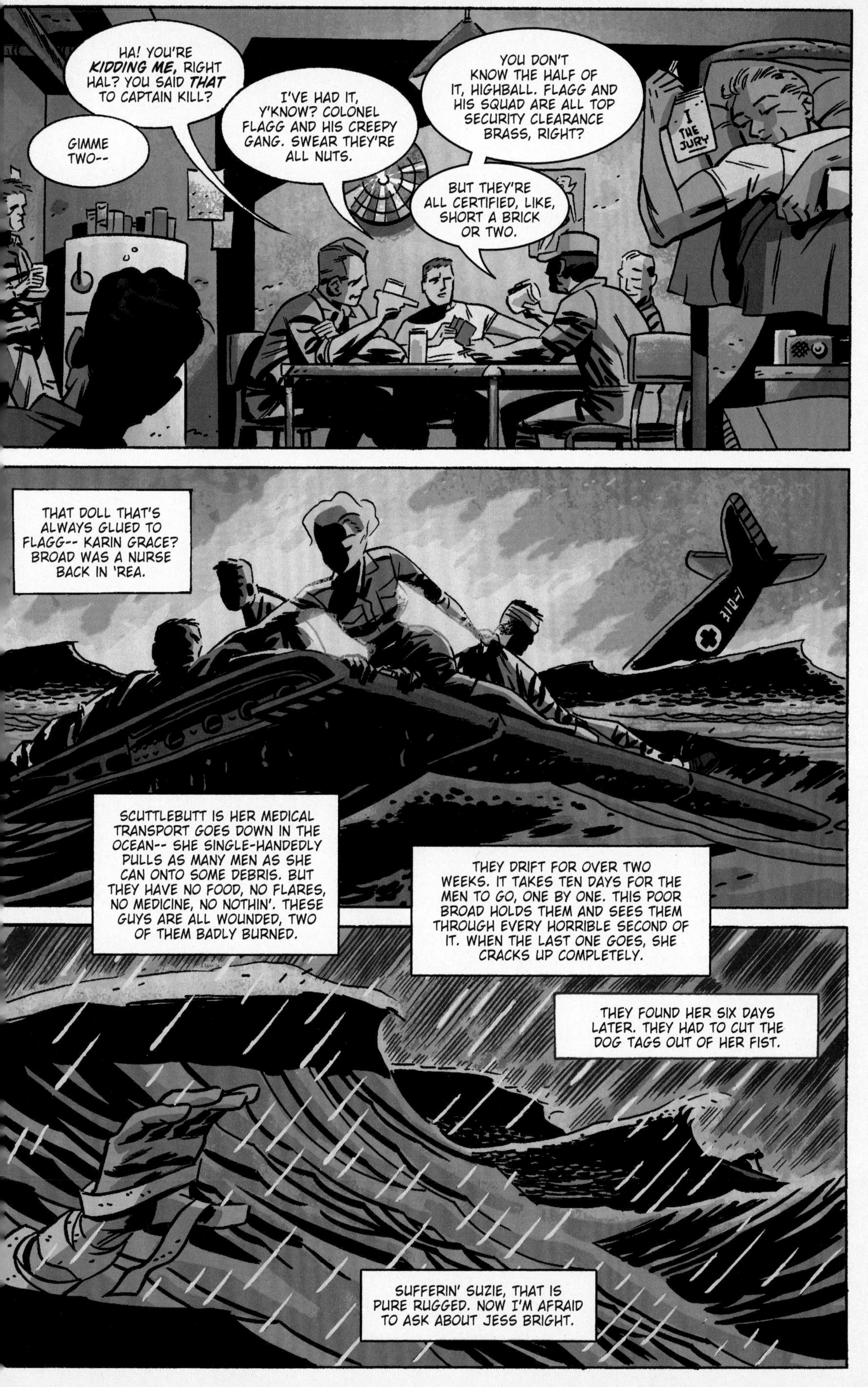
HA! YOU'RE *KIDDING ME,* RIGHT HAL? YOU SAID *THAT* TO CAPTAIN KILL?
GIMME TWO--
I'VE HAD IT, Y'KNOW? COLONEL FLAGG AND HIS CREEPY GANG. SWEAR THEY'RE ALL NUTS.
YOU DON'T KNOW THE HALF OF IT, HIGHBALL. FLAGG AND HIS SQUAD ARE ALL TOP SECURITY CLEARANCE BRASS, RIGHT?
BUT THEY'RE ALL CERTIFIED, LIKE, SHORT A BRICK OR TWO.
I THE JURY
THAT DOLL THAT'S ALWAYS GLUED TO FLAGG-- KARIN GRACE? BROAD WAS A NURSE BACK IN 'REA.
SCUTTLEBUTT IS HER MEDICAL TRANSPORT GOES DOWN IN THE OCEAN-- SHE SINGLE-HANDEDLY PULLS AS MANY MEN AS SHE CAN ONTO SOME DEBRIS. BUT THEY HAVE NO FOOD, NO FLARES, NO MEDICINE, NO NOTHIN'. THESE GUYS ARE ALL WOUNDED, TWO OF THEM BADLY BURNED.
THEY DRIFT FOR OVER TWO WEEKS. IT TAKES TEN DAYS FOR THE MEN TO GO, ONE BY ONE. THIS POOR BROAD HOLDS THEM AND SEES THEM THROUGH EVERY HORRIBLE SECOND OF IT. WHEN THE LAST ONE GOES, SHE CRACKS UP COMPLETELY.
THEY FOUND HER SIX DAYS LATER. THEY HAD TO CUT THE DOG TAGS OUT OF HER FIST.
SUFFERIN' SUZIE, THAT IS PURE RUGGED. NOW I'M AFRAID TO ASK ABOUT JESS BRIGHT.

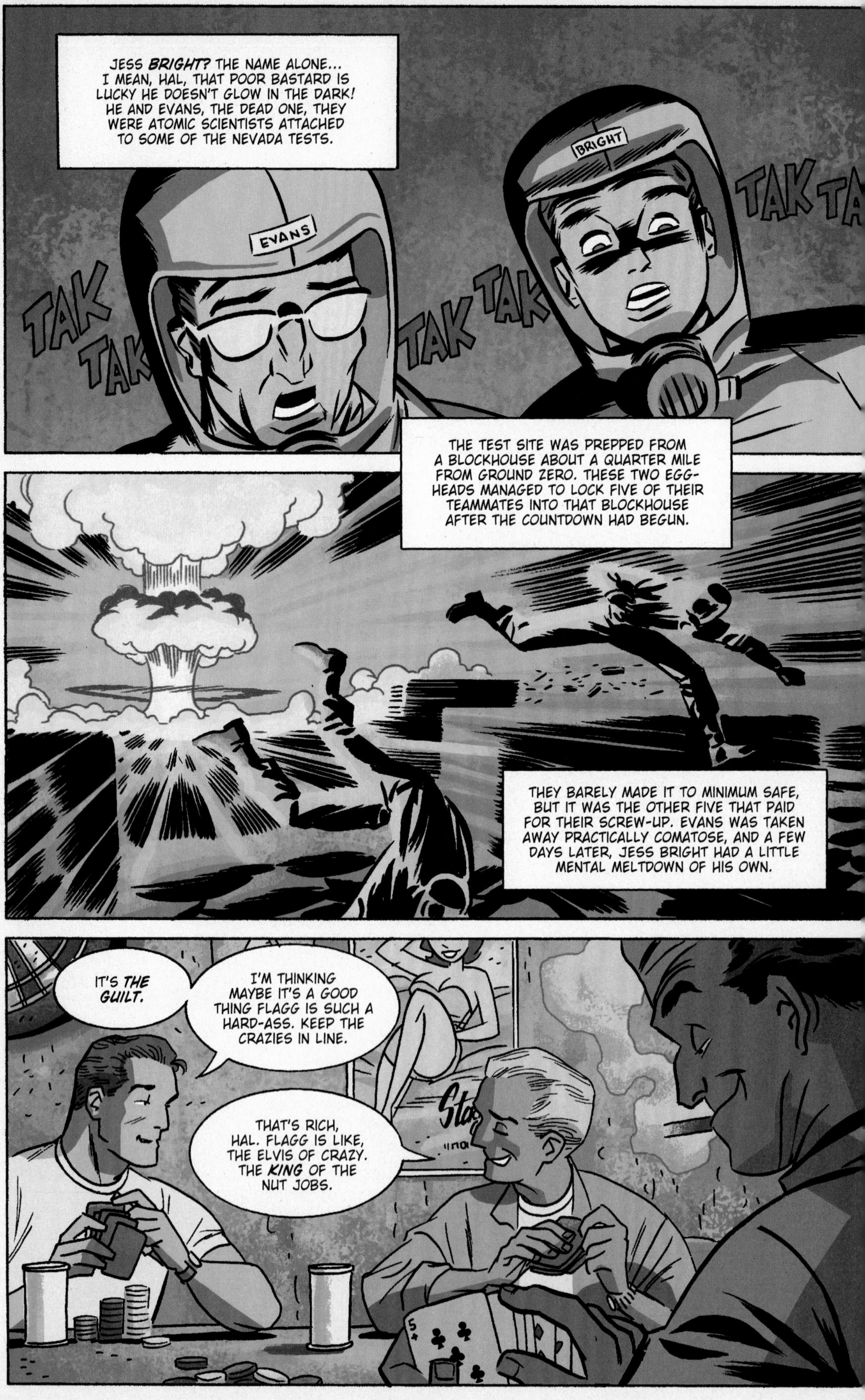
JESS *BRIGHT?* THE NAME ALONE... I MEAN, HAL, THAT POOR BASTARD IS LUCKY HE DOESN'T GLOW IN THE DARK! HE AND EVANS, THE DEAD ONE, THEY WERE ATOMIC SCIENTISTS ATTACHED TO SOME OF THE NEVADA TESTS.
BRIGHT
TAK TA
EVANS
TAK TAK
TAK TAK
THE TEST SITE WAS PREPPED FROM A BLOCKHOUSE ABOUT A QUARTER MILE FROM GROUND ZERO. THESE TWO EGG-HEADS MANAGED TO LOCK FIVE OF THEIR TEAMMATES INTO THAT BLOCKHOUSE AFTER THE COUNTDOWN HAD BEGUN.
THEY BARELY MADE IT TO MINIMUM SAFE, BUT IT WAS THE OTHER FIVE THAT PAID FOR THEIR SCREW-UP. EVANS WAS TAKEN AWAY PRACTICALLY COMATOSE, AND A FEW DAYS LATER, JESS BRIGHT HAD A LITTLE MENTAL MELTDOWN OF HIS OWN.
IT'S *THE GUILT.*
I'M THINKING MAYBE IT'S A GOOD THING FLAGG IS SUCH A HARD-ASS. KEEP THE CRAZIES IN LINE.
THAT'S RICH, HAL. FLAGG IS LIKE, THE ELVIS OF CRAZY. THE *KING* OF THE NUT JOBS.

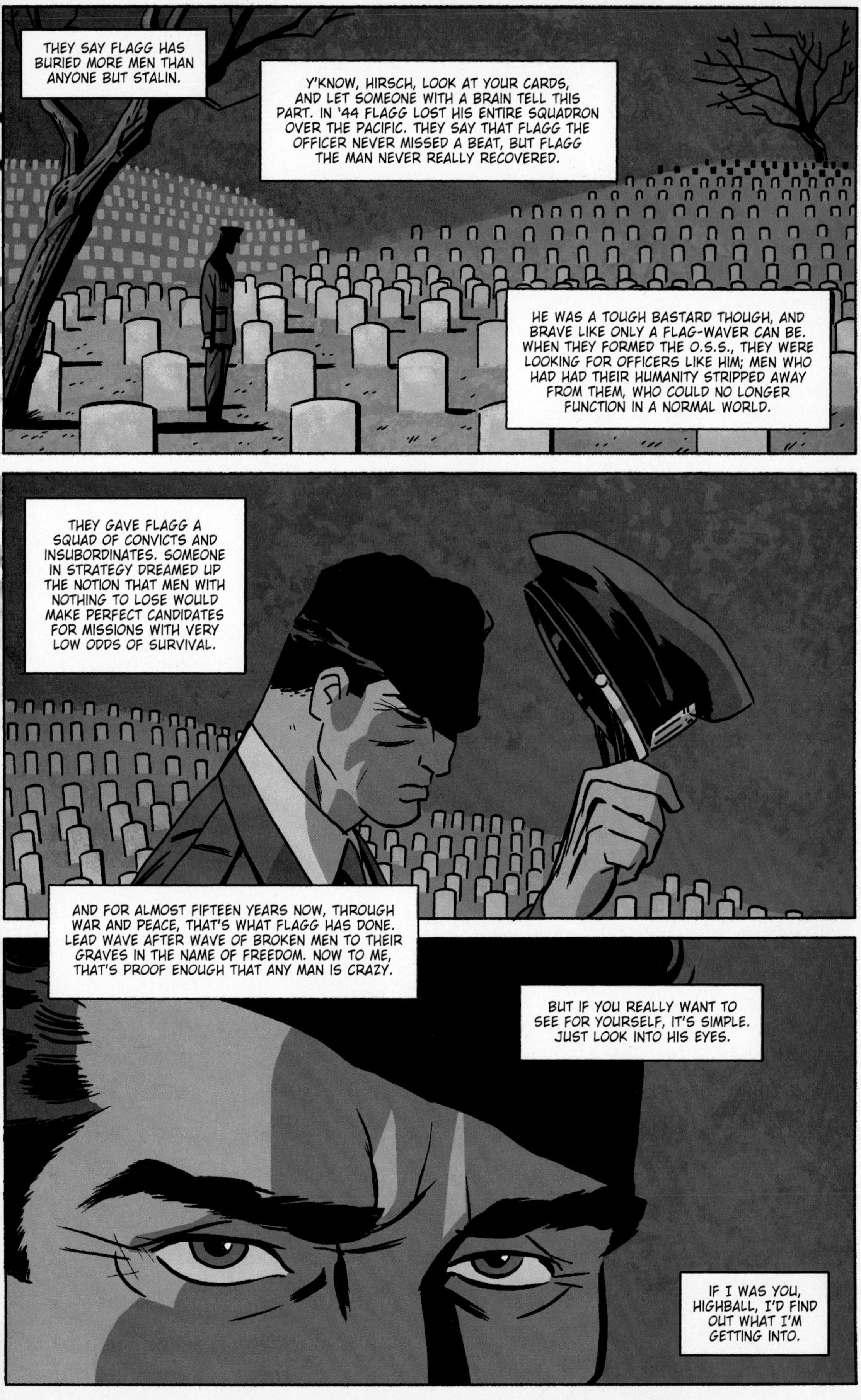
THEY SAY FLAGG HAS BURIED MORE MEN THAN ANYONE BUT STALIN.
Y'KNOW, HIRSCH, LOOK AT YOUR CARDS, AND LET SOMEONE WITH A BRAIN TELL THIS PART. IN '44 FLAGG LOST HIS ENTIRE SQUADRON OVER THE PACIFIC. THEY SAY THAT FLAGG THE OFFICER NEVER MISSED A BEAT, BUT FLAGG THE MAN NEVER REALLY RECOVERED.
HE WAS A TOUGH BASTARD THOUGH, AND BRAVE LIKE ONLY A FLAG-WAVER CAN BE. WHEN THEY FORMED THE O.S.S., THEY WERE LOOKING FOR OFFICERS LIKE HIM; MEN WHO HAD HAD THEIR HUMANITY STRIPPED AWAY FROM THEM, WHO COULD NO LONGER FUNCTION IN A NORMAL WORLD.
THEY GAVE FLAGG A SQUAD OF CONVICTS AND INSUBORDINATES. SOMEONE IN STRATEGY DREAMED UP THE NOTION THAT MEN WITH NOTHING TO LOSE WOULD MAKE PERFECT CANDIDATES FOR MISSIONS WITH VERY LOW ODDS OF SURVIVAL.
AND FOR ALMOST FIFTEEN YEARS NOW, THROUGH WAR AND PEACE, THAT'S WHAT FLAGG HAS DONE. LEAD WAVE AFTER WAVE OF BROKEN MEN TO THEIR GRAVES IN THE NAME OF FREEDOM. NOW TO ME, THAT'S PROOF ENOUGH THAT ANY MAN IS CRAZY.
BUT IF YOU REALLY WANT TO SEE FOR YOURSELF, IT'S SIMPLE. JUST LOOK INTO HIS EYES.
IF I WAS YOU, HIGHBALL, I'D FIND OUT WHAT I'M GETTING INTO.

TENNESSEE

BAM

JOHN HENRY LOOKED AT THE MOUNTAIN, AND HE GOT IN THE LEAD TO DRIVE;

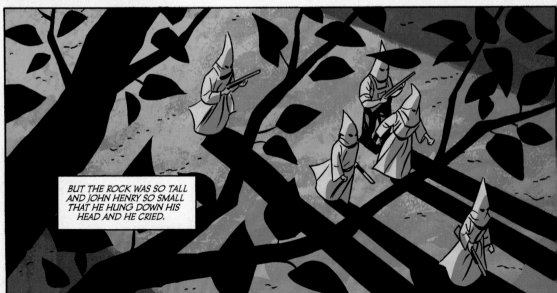

BUT THE ROCK WAS SO TALL AND JOHN HENRY SO SMALL THAT HE HUNG DOWN HIS HEAD AND HE CRIED.

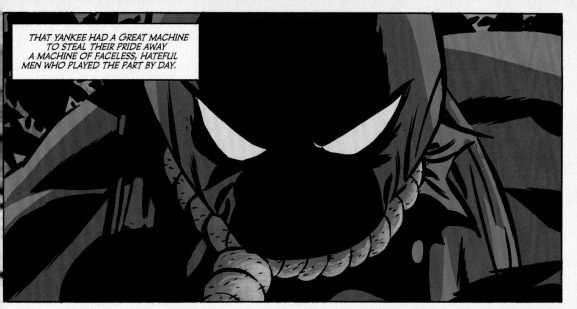

THAT YANKEE HAD A GREAT MACHINE
TO STEAL THEIR PRIDE AWAY
A MACHINE OF FACELESS, HATEFUL
MEN WHO PLAYED THE PART BY DAY.

THE CAPTAIN TOLD JOHN HENRY,
SON YOU GOT A WILLIN' MIND,
BUT YOU'D BEST LAY YOUR HAMMER
DOWN, YOU WON'T BEAT THIS
MACHINE OF MINE.

JOHN HENRY TOLD THE CAPTAIN
THAT A MAN IS JUST A MAN,
BUT BEFORE THAT MACHINE CAN
BEAT ME DOWN I'LL DIE WITH
MY HAMMER IN HAND.

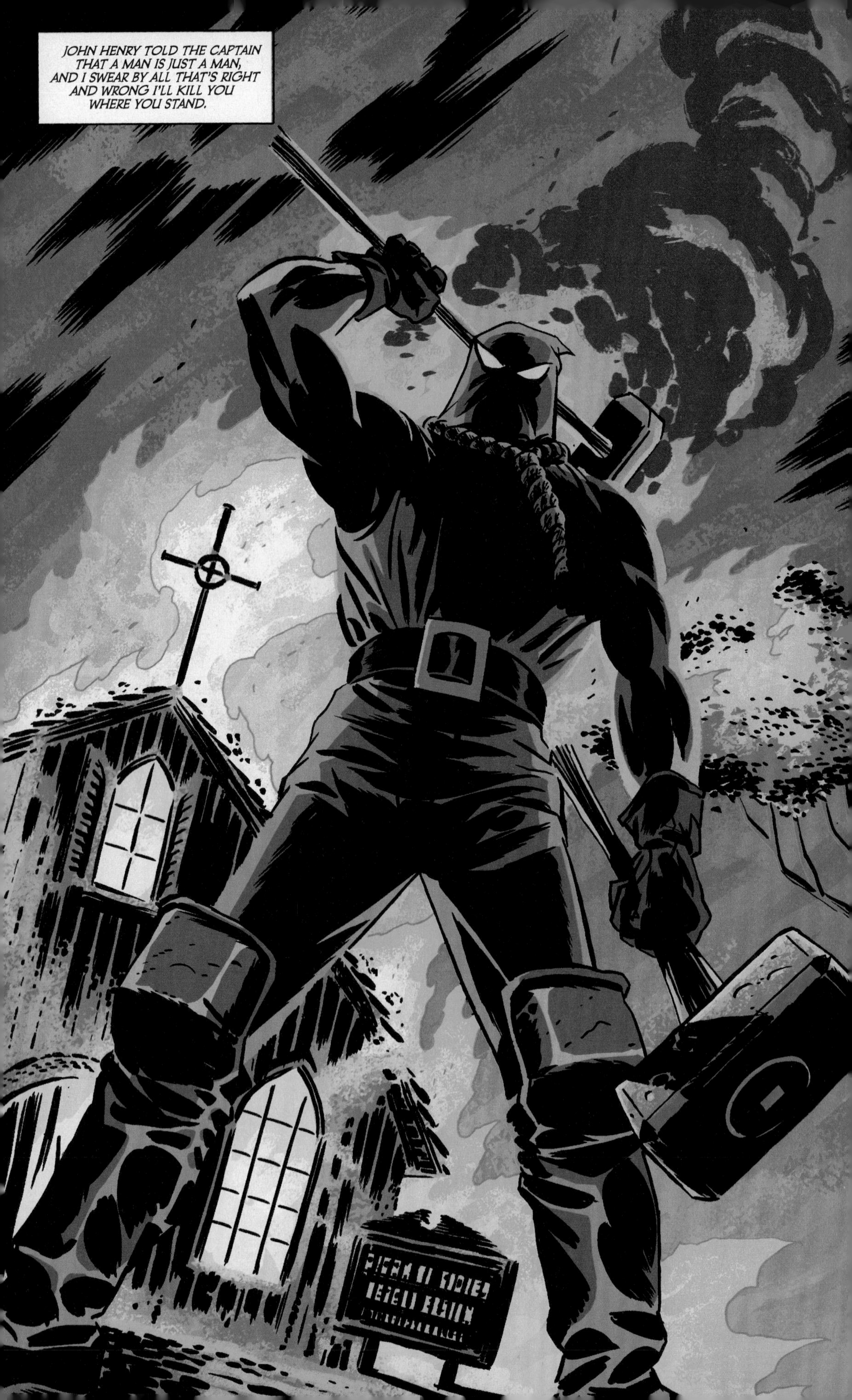
JOHN HENRY TOLD THE CAPTAIN THAT A MAN IS JUST A MAN, AND I SWEAR BY ALL THAT'S RIGHT AND WRONG I'LL KILL YOU WHERE YOU STAND.

CHAPTER SEVEN

PARANORMAL PARANOIA

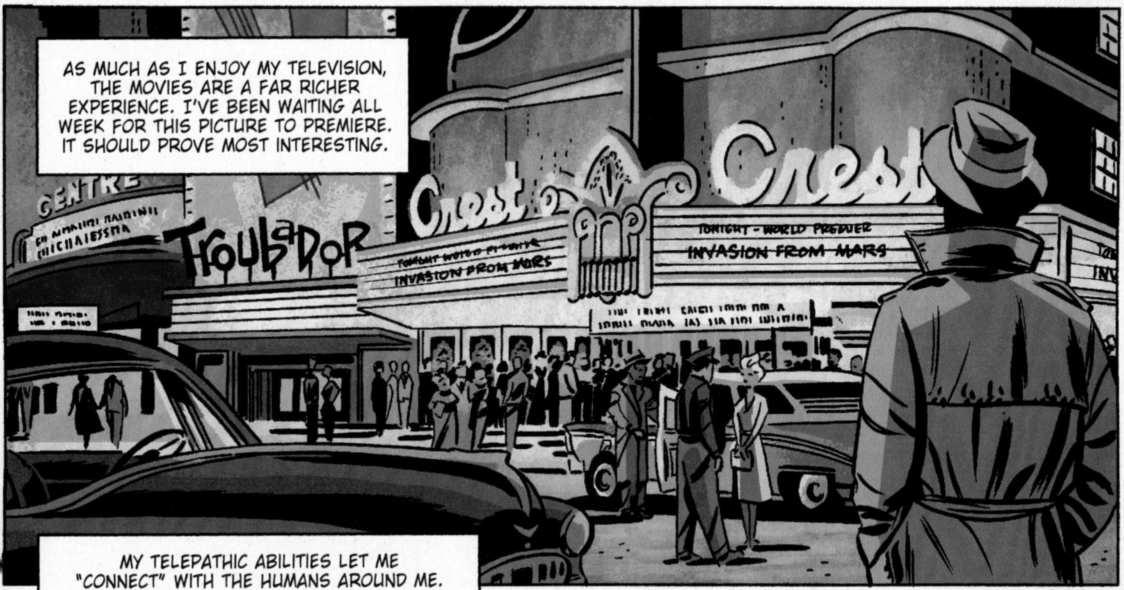

AS MUCH AS I ENJOY MY TELEVISION, THE MOVIES ARE A FAR RICHER EXPERIENCE. I'VE BEEN WAITING ALL WEEK FOR THIS PICTURE TO PREMIERE. IT SHOULD PROVE MOST INTERESTING.
CENTRE
TROUBADOR
Crest
INVASION FROM MARS
Crest
TONIGHT - WORLD PREMIER
INVASION FROM MARS

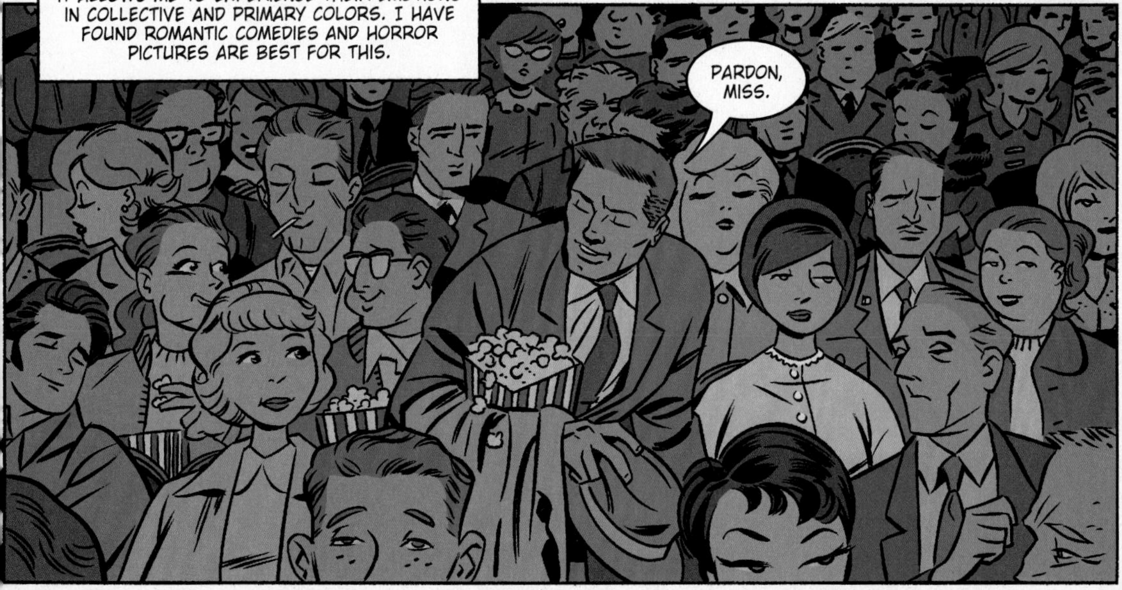

MY TELEPATHIC ABILITIES LET ME "CONNECT" WITH THE HUMANS AROUND ME. IT ALLOWS ME TO EXPERIENCE THEIR EMOTIONS IN COLLECTIVE AND PRIMARY COLORS. I HAVE FOUND ROMANTIC COMEDIES AND HORROR PICTURES ARE BEST FOR THIS.
PARDON, MISS.

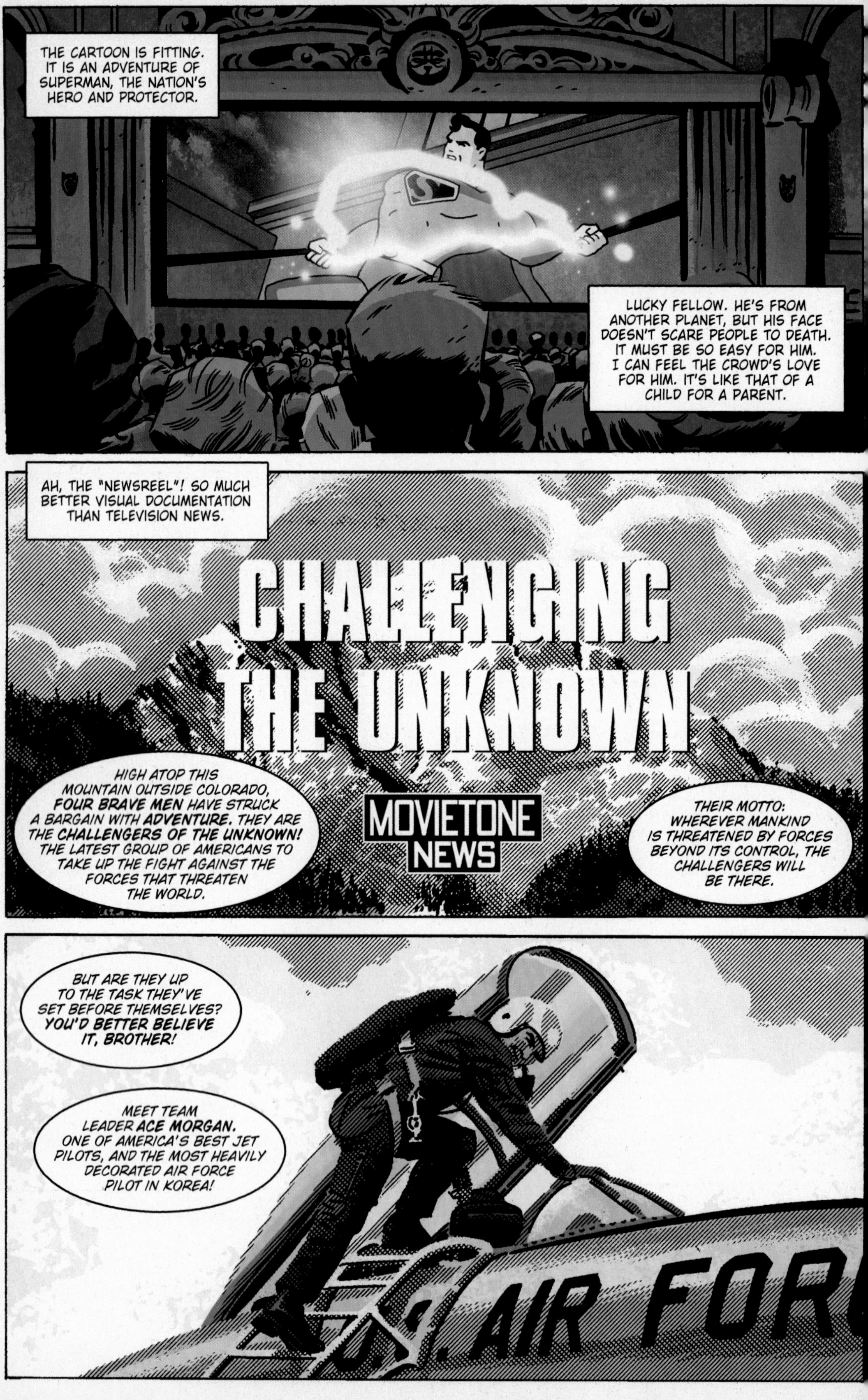
THE CARTOON IS FITTING. IT IS AN ADVENTURE OF SUPERMAN, THE NATION'S HERO AND PROTECTOR.
LUCKY FELLOW. HE'S FROM ANOTHER PLANET, BUT HIS FACE DOESN'T SCARE PEOPLE TO DEATH. IT MUST BE SO EASY FOR HIM. I CAN FEEL THE CROWD'S LOVE FOR HIM. IT'S LIKE THAT OF A CHILD FOR A PARENT.
AH, THE "NEWSREEL"! SO MUCH BETTER VISUAL DOCUMENTATION THAN TELEVISION NEWS.
CHALLENGING THE UNKNOWN
HIGH ATOP THIS MOUNTAIN OUTSIDE COLORADO, FOUR BRAVE MEN HAVE STRUCK A BARGAIN WITH ADVENTURE. THEY ARE THE CHALLENGERS OF THE UNKNOWN! THE LATEST GROUP OF AMERICANS TO TAKE UP THE FIGHT AGAINST THE FORCES THAT THREATEN THE WORLD.
MOVIETONE NEWS
THEIR MOTTO: WHEREVER MANKIND IS THREATENED BY FORCES BEYOND ITS CONTROL, THE CHALLENGERS WILL BE THERE.
BUT ARE THEY UP TO THE TASK THEY'VE SET BEFORE THEMSELVES? YOU'D BETTER BELIEVE IT, BROTHER!
MEET TEAM LEADER ACE MORGAN. ONE OF AMERICA'S BEST JET PILOTS, AND THE MOST HEAVILY DECORATED AIR FORCE PILOT IN KOREA!
AIR FOR

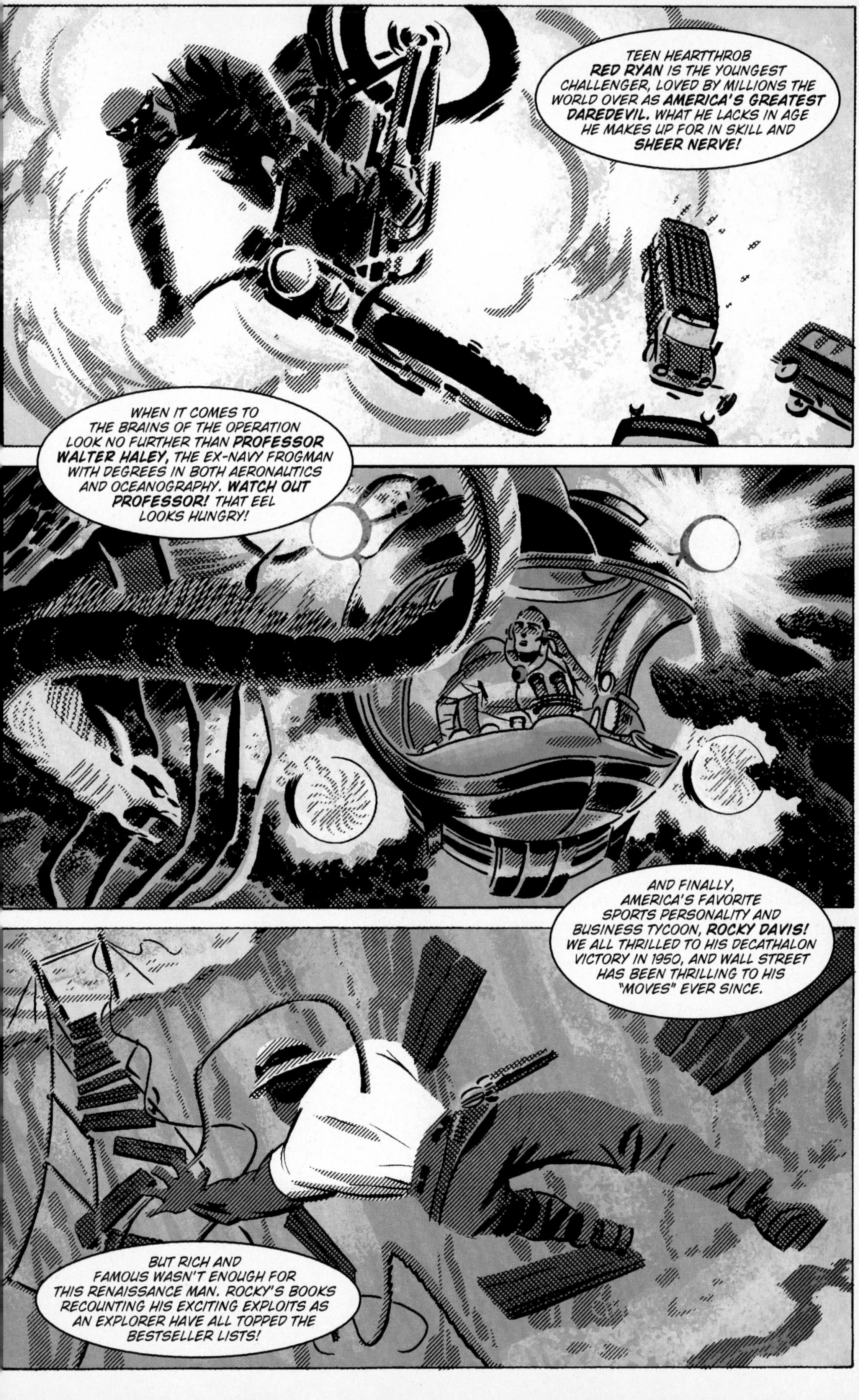
TEEN HEARTTHROB **RED RYAN** IS THE YOUNGEST CHALLENGER, LOVED BY MILLIONS THE WORLD OVER AS **AMERICA'S GREATEST DAREDEVIL.** WHAT HE LACKS IN AGE HE MAKES UP FOR IN SKILL AND **SHEER NERVE!**
WHEN IT COMES TO THE BRAINS OF THE OPERATION LOOK NO FURTHER THAN **PROFESSOR WALTER HALEY,** THE EX-NAVY FROGMAN WITH DEGREES IN BOTH AERONAUTICS AND OCEANOGRAPHY. **WATCH OUT PROFESSOR!** THAT EEL LOOKS HUNGRY!
AND FINALLY, AMERICA'S FAVORITE SPORTS PERSONALITY AND BUSINESS TYCOON, **ROCKY DAVIS!** WE ALL THRILLED TO HIS DECATHALON VICTORY IN 1950, AND WALL STREET HAS BEEN THRILLING TO HIS "MOVES" EVER SINCE.
BUT RICH AND FAMOUS WASN'T ENOUGH FOR THIS RENAISSANCE MAN. ROCKY'S BOOKS RECOUNTING HIS EXCITING EXPLOITS AS AN EXPLORER HAVE ALL TOPPED THE BESTSELLER LISTS!

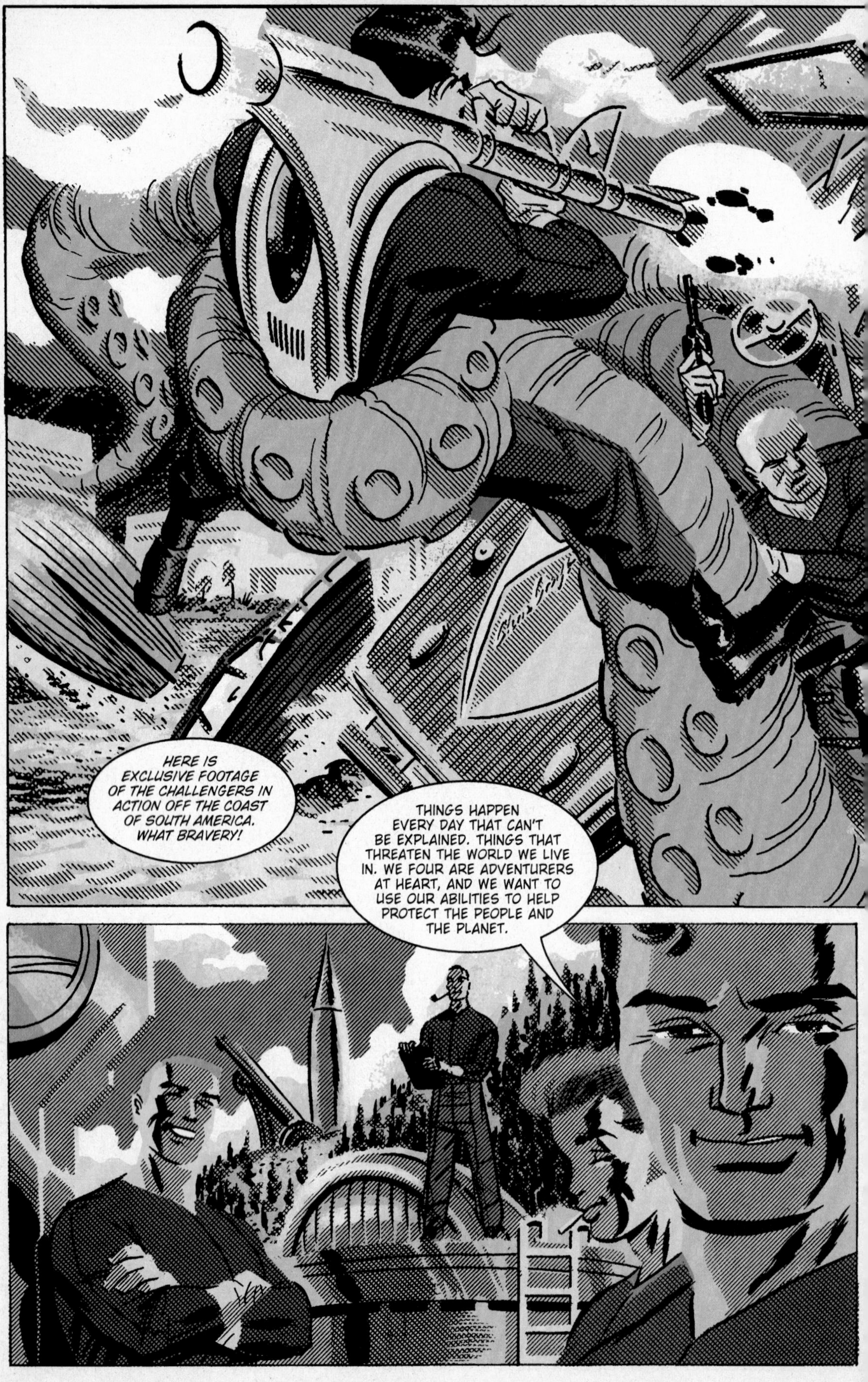
HERE IS EXCLUSIVE FOOTAGE OF THE CHALLENGERS IN ACTION OFF THE COAST OF SOUTH AMERICA. WHAT BRAVERY!
THINGS HAPPEN EVERY DAY THAT CAN'T BE EXPLAINED. THINGS THAT THREATEN THE WORLD WE LIVE IN. WE FOUR ARE ADVENTURERS AT HEART, AND WE WANT TO USE OUR ABILITIES TO HELP PROTECT THE PEOPLE AND THE PLANET.

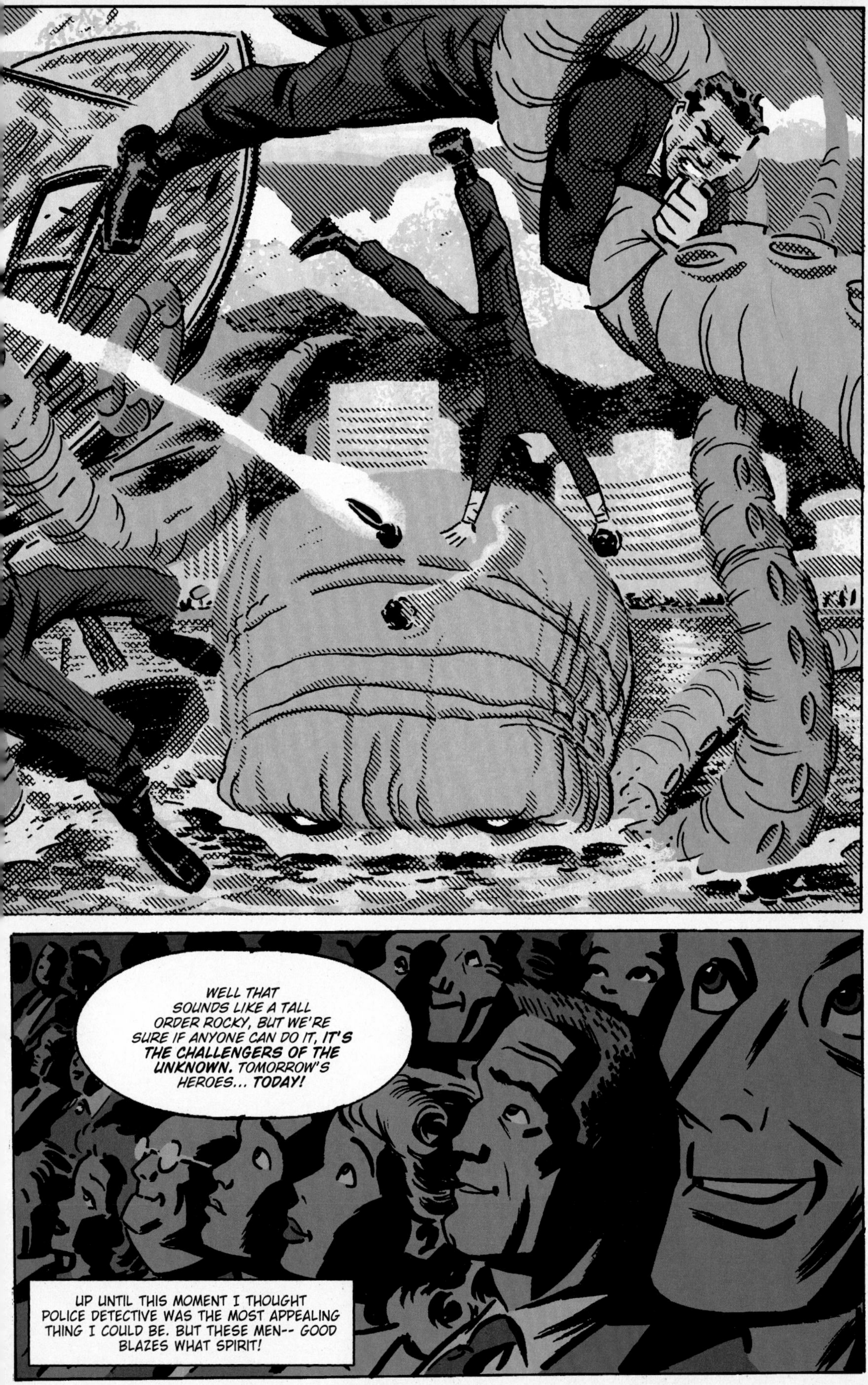
WELL THAT SOUNDS LIKE A TALL ORDER ROCKY, BUT WE'RE SURE IF ANYONE CAN DO IT, IT'S THE CHALLENGERS OF THE UNKNOWN. TOMORROW'S HEROES... TODAY!
UP UNTIL THIS MOMENT I THOUGHT POLICE DETECTIVE WAS THE MOST APPEALING THING I COULD BE. BUT THESE MEN-- GOOD BLAZES WHAT SPIRIT!

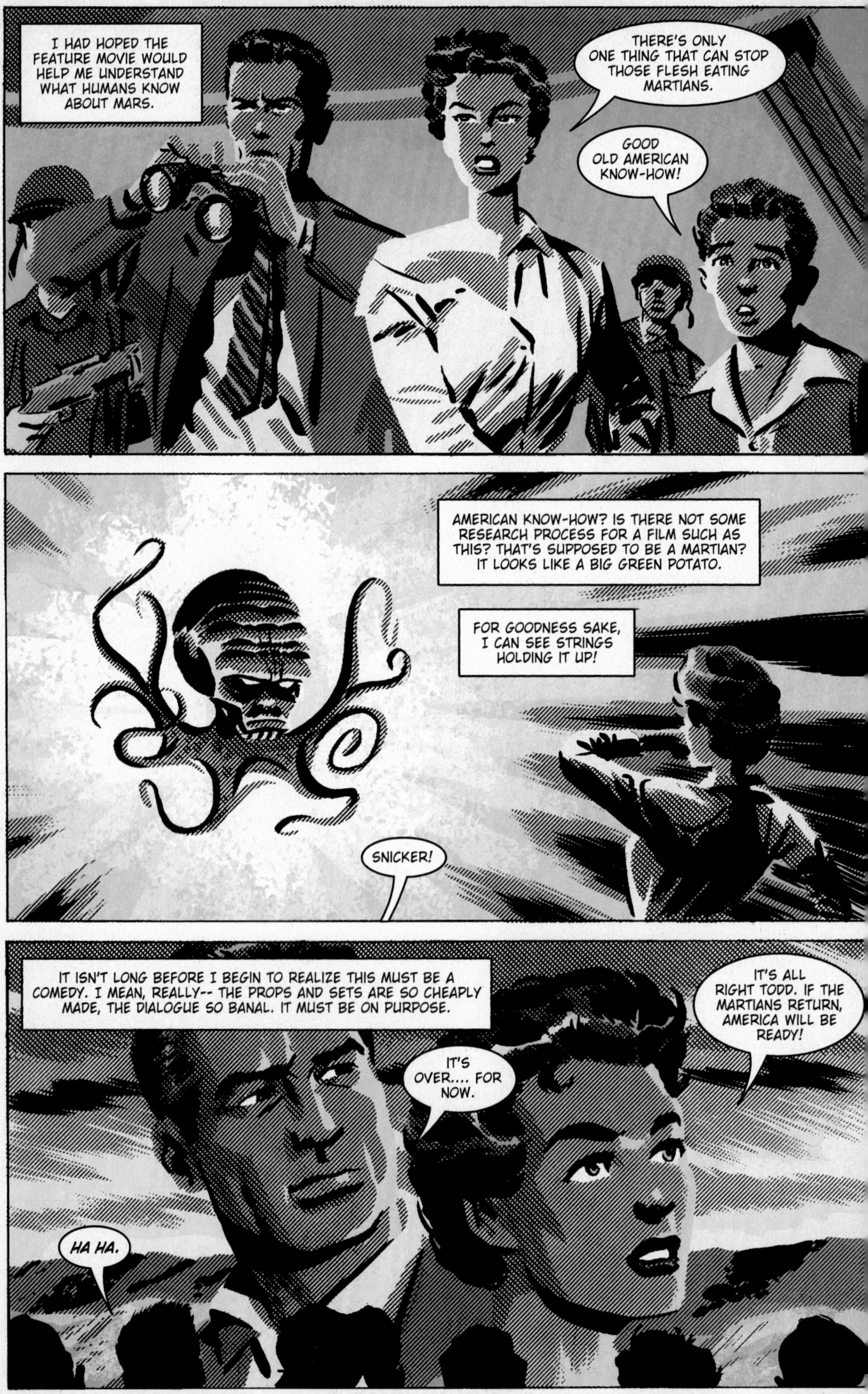
I HAD HOPED THE FEATURE MOVIE WOULD HELP ME UNDERSTAND WHAT HUMANS KNOW ABOUT MARS.
THERE'S ONLY ONE THING THAT CAN STOP THOSE FLESH EATING MARTIANS.
GOOD OLD AMERICAN KNOW-HOW!
AMERICAN KNOW-HOW? IS THERE NOT SOME RESEARCH PROCESS FOR A FILM SUCH AS THIS? THAT'S SUPPOSED TO BE A MARTIAN? IT LOOKS LIKE A BIG GREEN POTATO.
FOR GOODNESS SAKE, I CAN SEE STRINGS HOLDING IT UP!
SNICKER!
IT ISN'T LONG BEFORE I BEGIN TO REALIZE THIS MUST BE A COMEDY. I MEAN, REALLY-- THE PROPS AND SETS ARE SO CHEAPLY MADE, THE DIALOGUE SO BANAL. IT MUST BE ON PURPOSE.
IT'S OVER.... FOR NOW.
IT'S ALL RIGHT TODD. IF THE MARTIANS RETURN, AMERICA WILL BE READY!
HA HA.

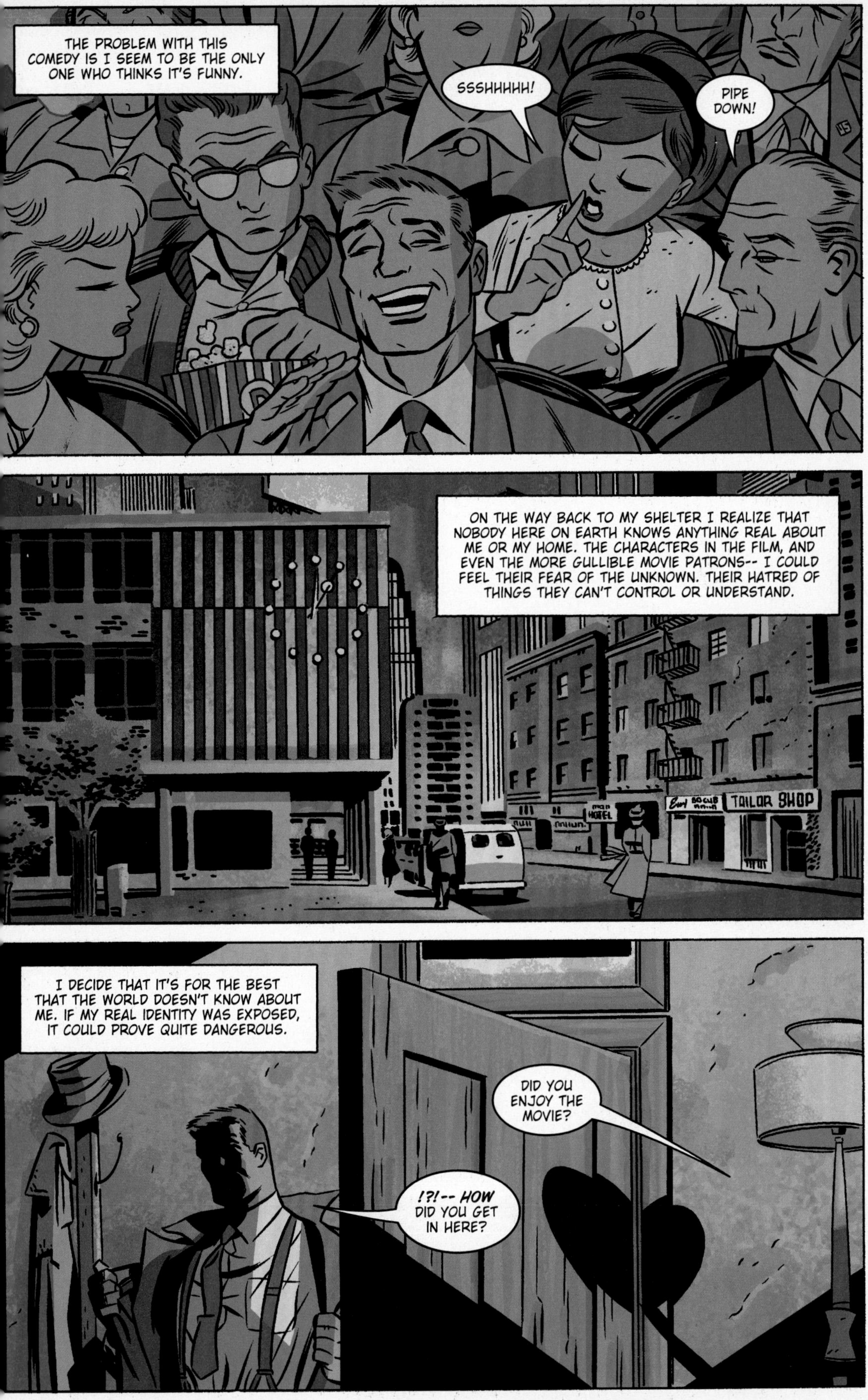
THE PROBLEM WITH THIS COMEDY IS I SEEM TO BE THE ONLY ONE WHO THINKS IT'S FUNNY.
SSSHHHHH!
PIPE DOWN!
ON THE WAY BACK TO MY SHELTER I REALIZE THAT NOBODY HERE ON EARTH KNOWS ANYTHING REAL ABOUT ME OR MY HOME. THE CHARACTERS IN THE FILM, AND EVEN THE MORE GULLIBLE MOVIE PATRONS-- I COULD FEEL THEIR FEAR OF THE UNKNOWN. THEIR HATRED OF THINGS THEY CAN'T CONTROL OR UNDERSTAND.
HOTEL
TAILOR SHOP
I DECIDE THAT IT'S FOR THE BEST THAT THE WORLD DOESN'T KNOW ABOUT ME. IF MY REAL IDENTITY WAS EXPOSED, IT COULD PROVE QUITE DANGEROUS.
DID YOU ENJOY THE MOVIE?
!?! -- HOW DID YOU GET IN HERE?

CUT THE PRETENSE. DON'T YOU MEAN "WHY DIDN'T I SENSE HIS PRESENCE? WHY CAN'T I READ HIS MIND?"

THAT'S MY SECRET. AND TONIGHT, I'M HERE TO TALK ABOUT YOURS.

THIS'LL GO HARD FOR YOU, VIGILANTE. I'M NOT SOME ROOKIE--

STOW THE ACT, MISTER JONES.

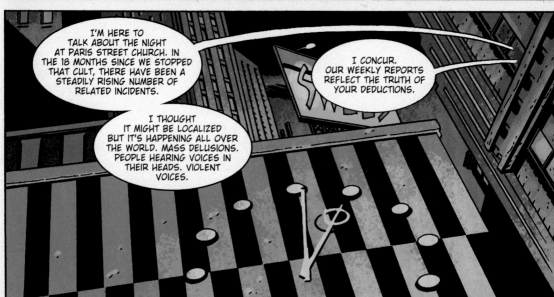

I'M HERE TO TALK ABOUT THE NIGHT AT PARIS STREET CHURCH. IN THE 18 MONTHS SINCE WE STOPPED THAT CULT, THERE HAVE BEEN A STEADILY RISING NUMBER OF RELATED INCIDENTS.

I CONCUR. OUR WEEKLY REPORTS REFLECT THE TRUTH OF YOUR DEDUCTIONS.

I THOUGHT IT MIGHT BE LOCALIZED BUT IT'S HAPPENING ALL OVER THE WORLD. MASS DELUSIONS. PEOPLE HEARING VOICES IN THEIR HEADS. VIOLENT VOICES.

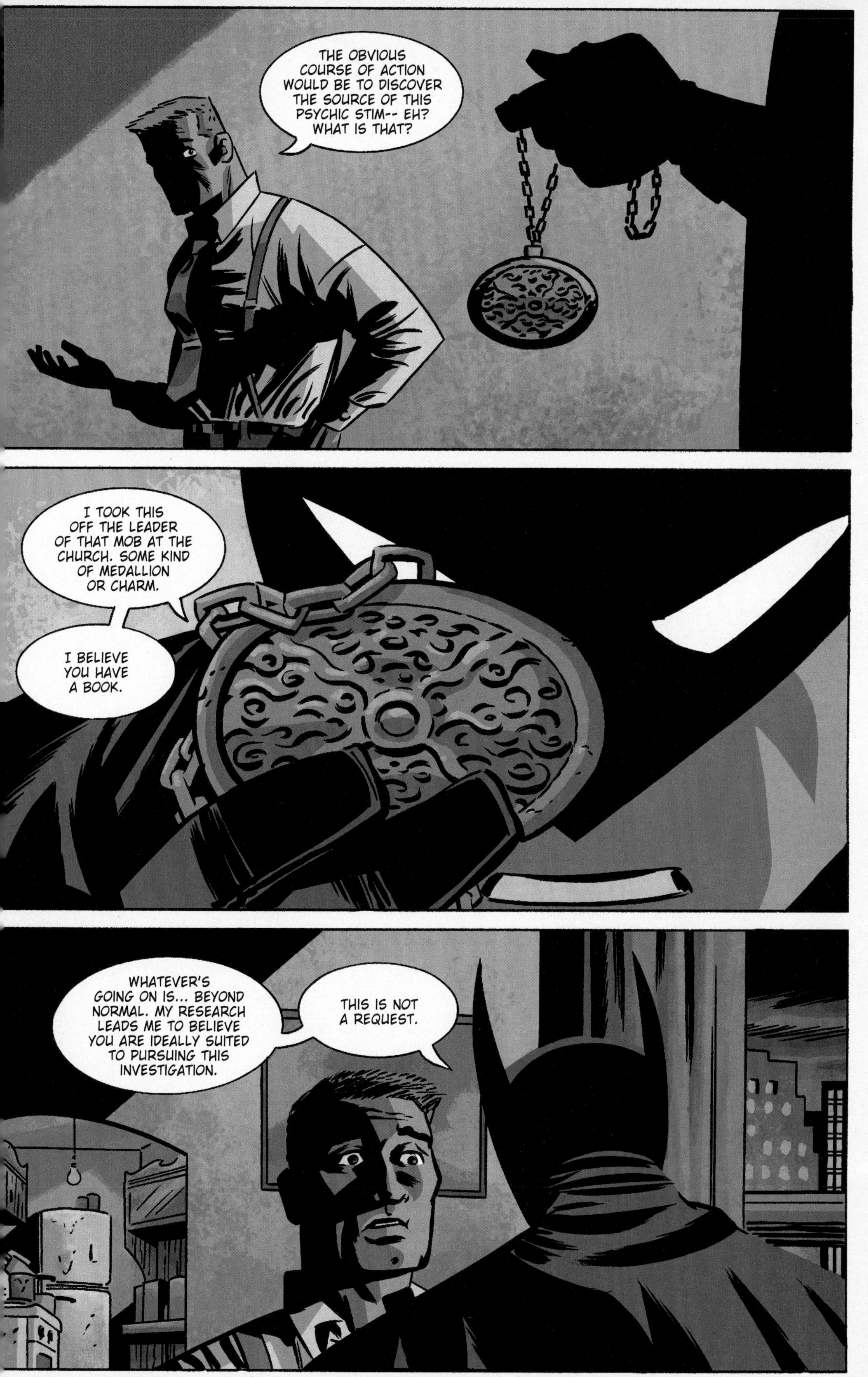
THE OBVIOUS COURSE OF ACTION WOULD BE TO DISCOVER THE SOURCE OF THIS PSYCHIC STIM-- EH? WHAT IS THAT?
I TOOK THIS OFF THE LEADER OF THAT MOB AT THE CHURCH. SOME KIND OF MEDALLION OR CHARM.
I BELIEVE YOU HAVE A BOOK.
WHATEVER'S GOING ON IS... BEYOND NORMAL. MY RESEARCH LEADS ME TO BELIEVE YOU ARE IDEALLY SUITED TO PURSUING THIS INVESTIGATION.
THIS IS NOT A REQUEST.

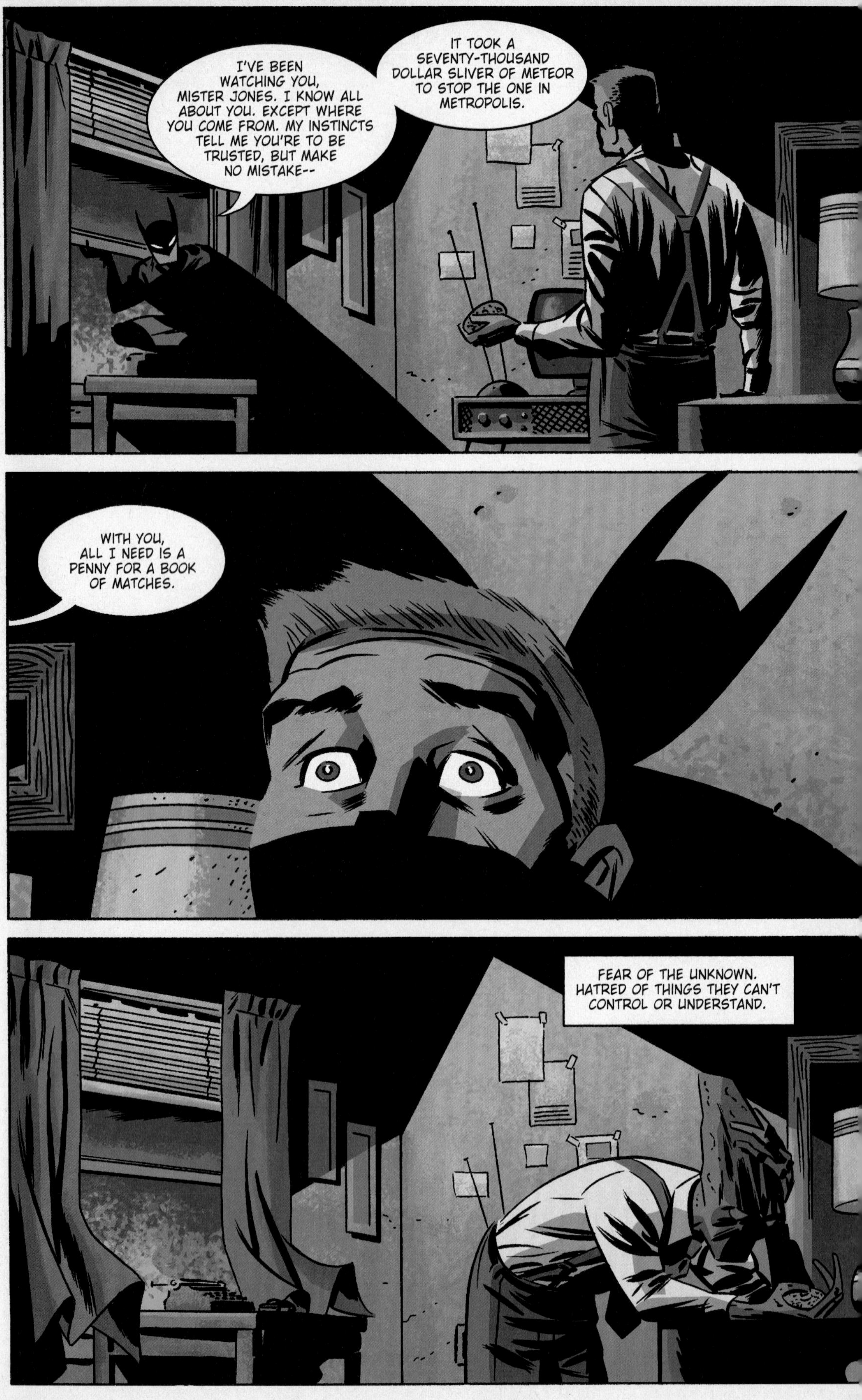
I'VE BEEN WATCHING YOU, MISTER JONES. I KNOW ALL ABOUT YOU. EXCEPT WHERE YOU COME FROM. MY INSTINCTS TELL ME YOU'RE TO BE TRUSTED, BUT MAKE NO MISTAKE--
IT TOOK A SEVENTY-THOUSAND DOLLAR SLIVER OF METEOR TO STOP THE ONE IN METROPOLIS.
WITH YOU, ALL I NEED IS A PENNY FOR A BOOK OF MATCHES.
FEAR OF THE UNKNOWN. HATRED OF THINGS THEY CAN'T CONTROL OR UNDERSTAND.

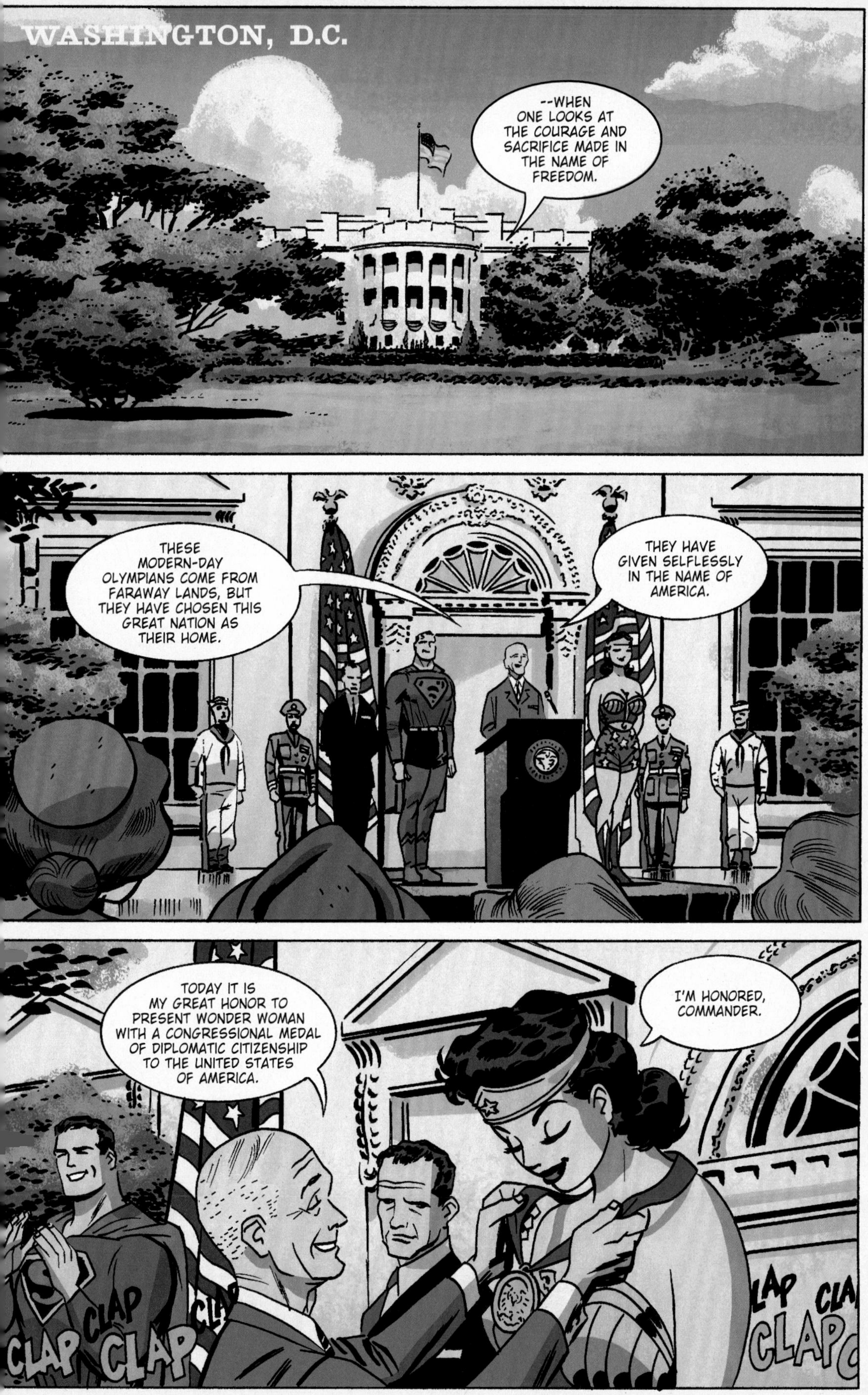
WASHINGTON, D.C.
--WHEN ONE LOOKS AT THE COURAGE AND SACRIFICE MADE IN THE NAME OF FREEDOM.
THESE MODERN-DAY OLYMPIANS COME FROM FARAWAY LANDS, BUT THEY HAVE CHOSEN THIS GREAT NATION AS THEIR HOME.
THEY HAVE GIVEN SELFLESSLY IN THE NAME OF AMERICA.
TODAY IT IS MY GREAT HONOR TO PRESENT WONDER WOMAN WITH A CONGRESSIONAL MEDAL OF DIPLOMATIC CITIZENSHIP TO THE UNITED STATES OF AMERICA.
I'M HONORED, COMMANDER.
CLAP CLAP CLAP
CLAP CLAP

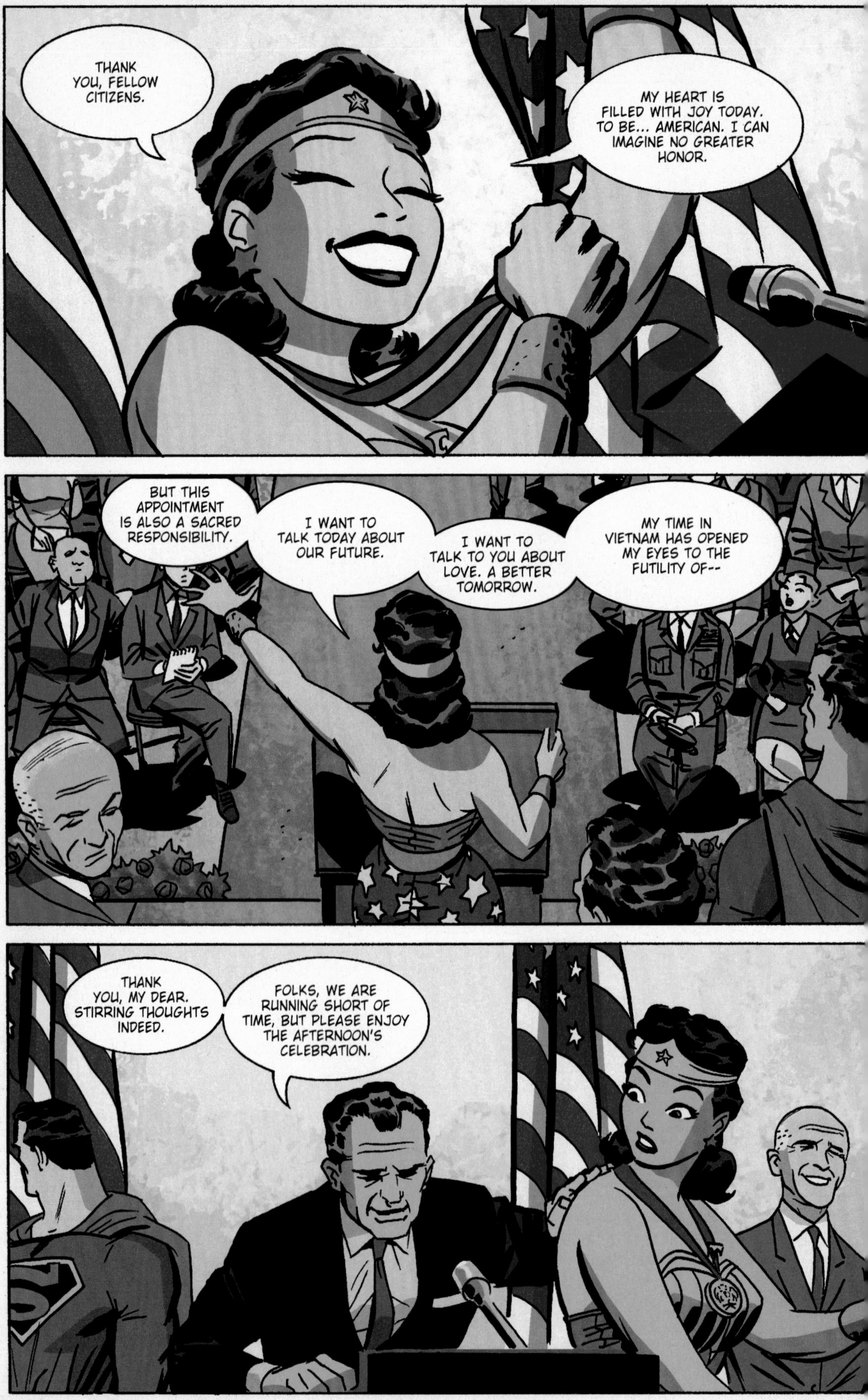
THANK YOU, FELLOW CITIZENS.
MY HEART IS FILLED WITH JOY TODAY. TO BE... AMERICAN. I CAN IMAGINE NO GREATER HONOR.
BUT THIS APPOINTMENT IS ALSO A SACRED RESPONSIBILITY.
I WANT TO TALK TODAY ABOUT OUR FUTURE.
I WANT TO TALK TO YOU ABOUT LOVE. A BETTER TOMORROW.
MY TIME IN VIETNAM HAS OPENED MY EYES TO THE FUTILITY OF--
THANK YOU, MY DEAR. STIRRING THOUGHTS INDEED.
FOLKS, WE ARE RUNNING SHORT OF TIME, BUT PLEASE ENJOY THE AFTERNOON'S CELEBRATION.

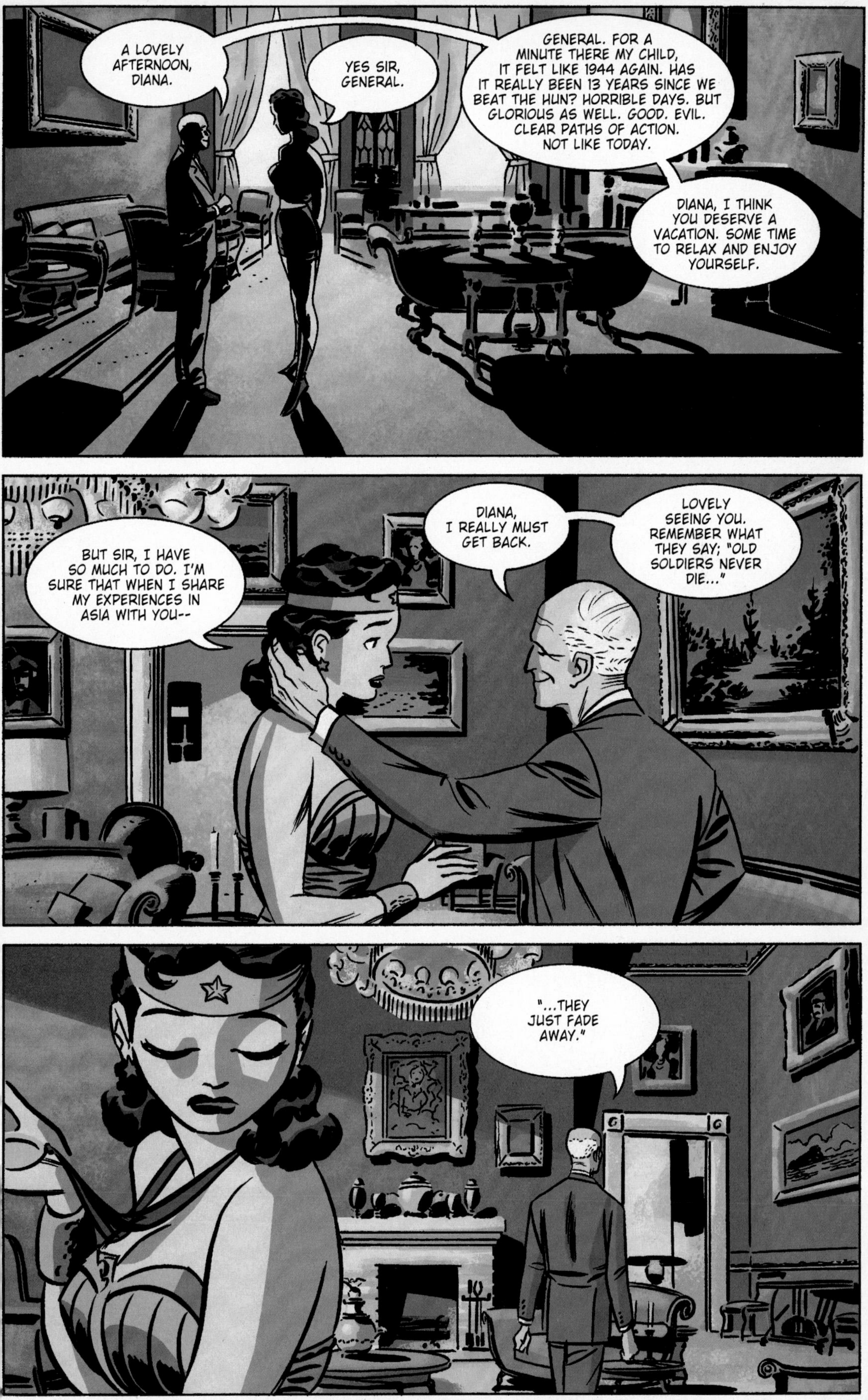
A LOVELY AFTERNOON, DIANA.
YES SIR, GENERAL.
GENERAL. FOR A MINUTE THERE MY CHILD, IT FELT LIKE 1944 AGAIN. HAS IT REALLY BEEN 13 YEARS SINCE WE BEAT THE HUN? HORRIBLE DAYS. BUT GLORIOUS AS WELL. GOOD. EVIL. CLEAR PATHS OF ACTION. NOT LIKE TODAY.
DIANA, I THINK YOU DESERVE A VACATION. SOME TIME TO RELAX AND ENJOY YOURSELF.
BUT SIR, I HAVE SO MUCH TO DO. I'M SURE THAT WHEN I SHARE MY EXPERIENCES IN ASIA WITH YOU--
DIANA, I REALLY MUST GET BACK.
LOVELY SEEING YOU. REMEMBER WHAT THEY SAY; "OLD SOLDIERS NEVER DIE..."
"...THEY JUST FADE AWAY."

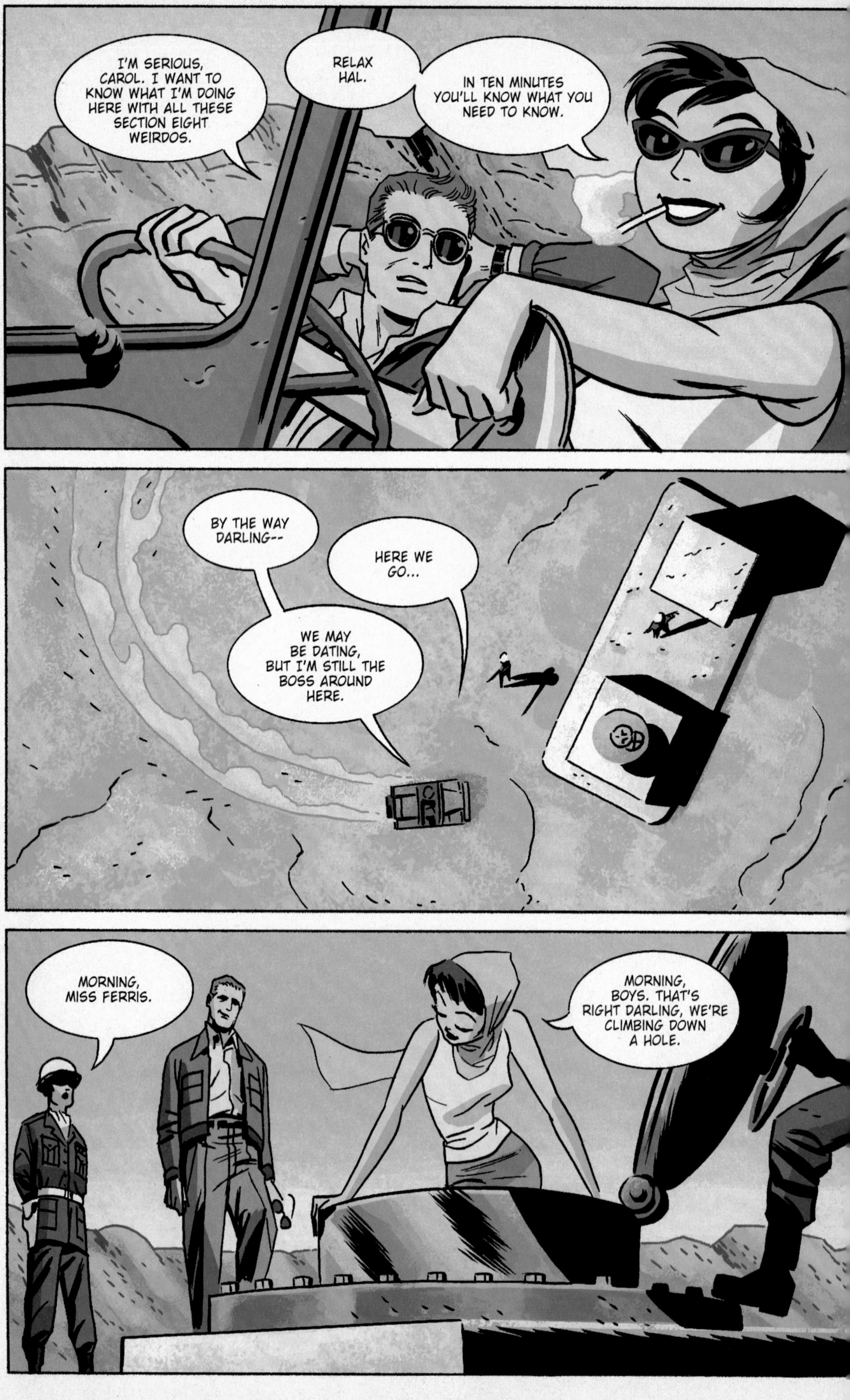
I'M SERIOUS, CAROL. I WANT TO KNOW WHAT I'M DOING HERE WITH ALL THESE SECTION EIGHT WEIRDOS.
RELAX HAL.
IN TEN MINUTES YOU'LL KNOW WHAT YOU NEED TO KNOW.
BY THE WAY DARLING--
HERE WE GO...
WE MAY BE DATING, BUT I'M STILL THE BOSS AROUND HERE.
MORNING, MISS FERRIS.
MORNING, BOYS. THAT'S RIGHT DARLING, WE'RE CLIMBING DOWN A HOLE.

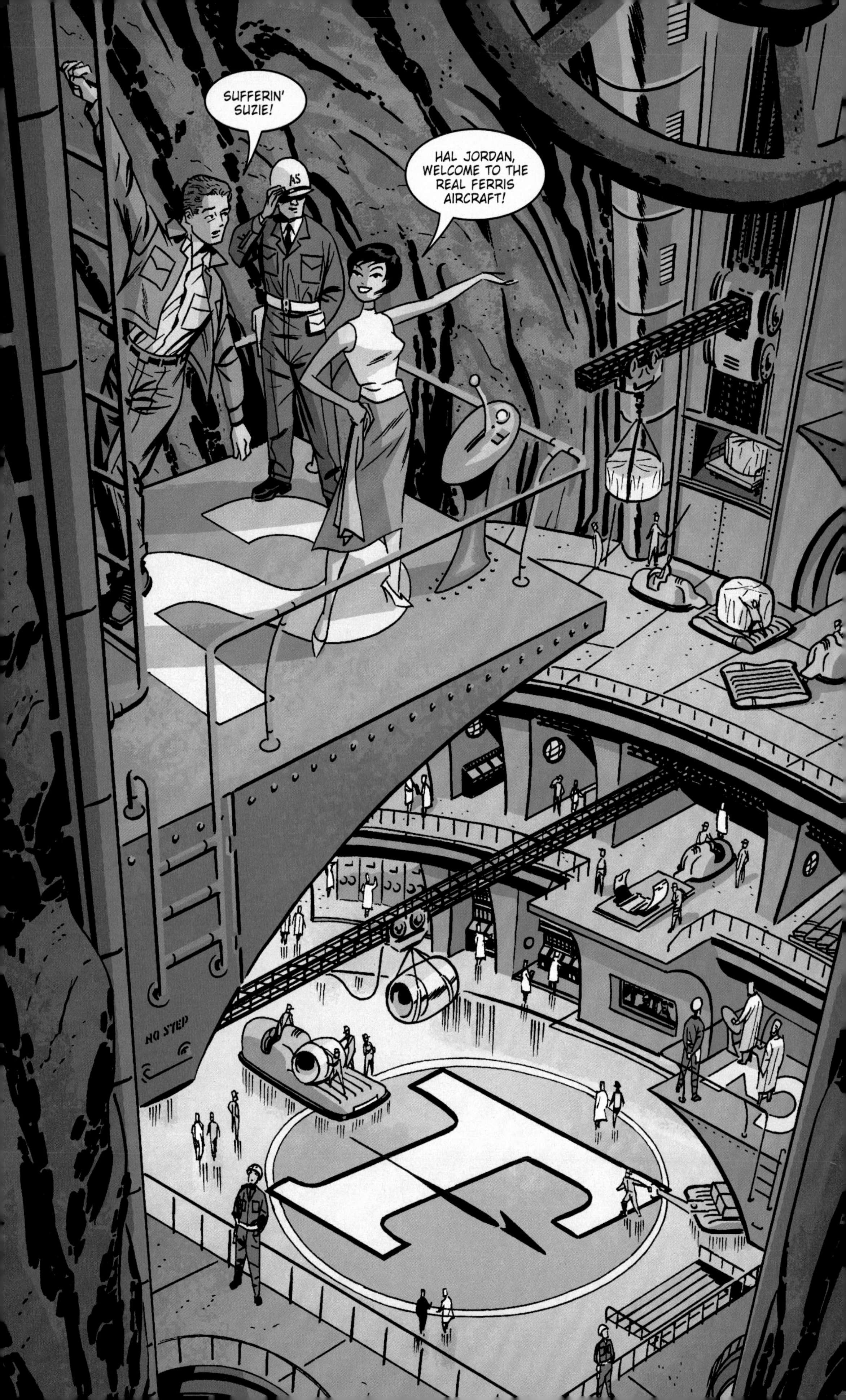
SUFFERIN' SUZIE!
HAL JORDAN, WELCOME TO THE REAL FERRIS AIRCRAFT!
AS
NO STEP

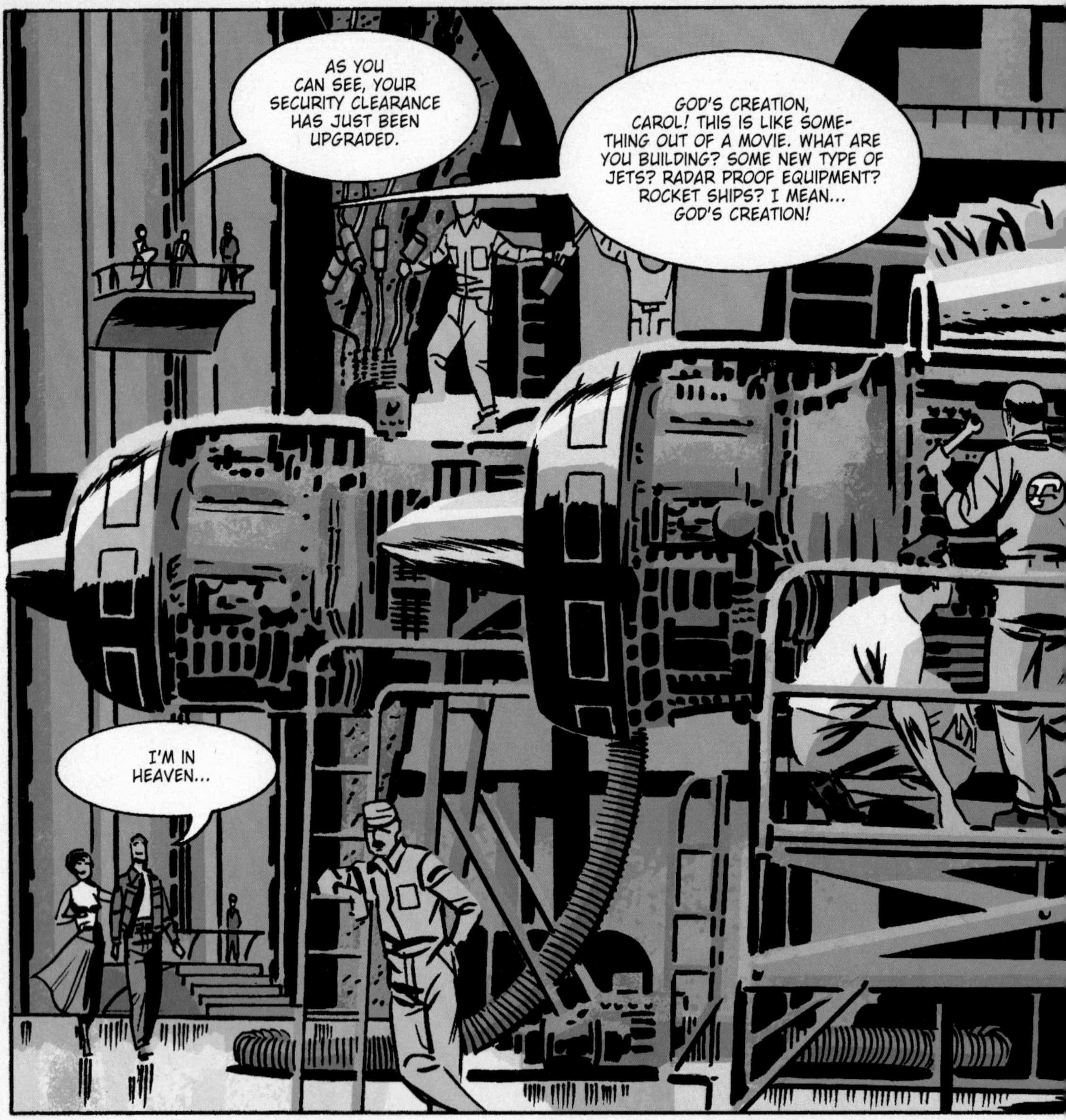
AS YOU CAN SEE, YOUR SECURITY CLEARANCE HAS JUST BEEN UPGRADED.
GOD'S CREATION, CAROL! THIS IS LIKE SOMETHING OUT OF A MOVIE. WHAT ARE YOU BUILDING? SOME NEW TYPE OF JETS? RADAR PROOF EQUIPMENT? ROCKET SHIPS? I MEAN... GOD'S CREATION!
I'M IN HEAVEN...

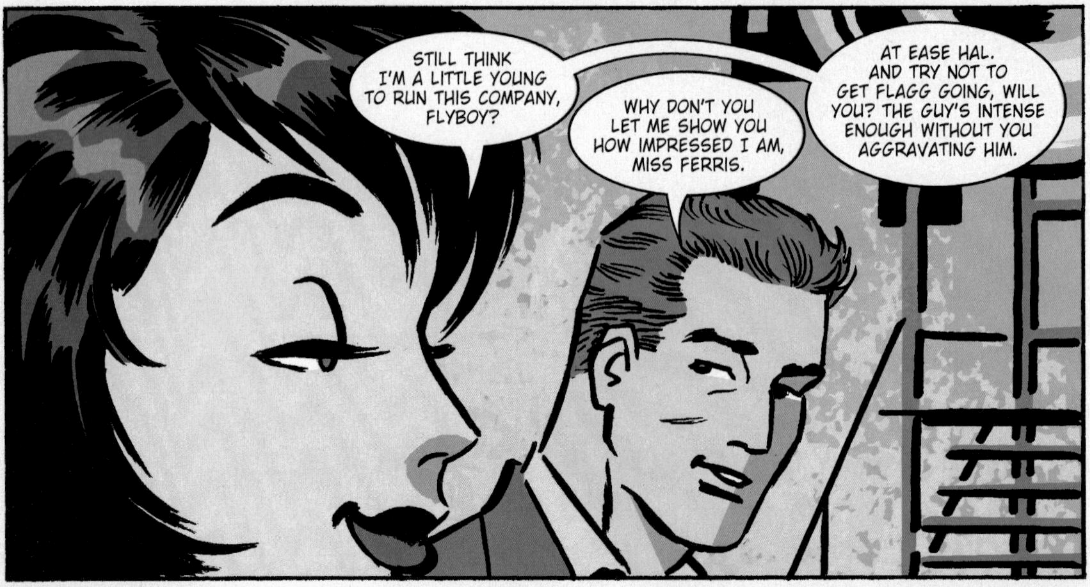
STILL THINK I'M A LITTLE YOUNG TO RUN THIS COMPANY, FLYBOY?
WHY DON'T YOU LET ME SHOW YOU HOW IMPRESSED I AM, MISS FERRIS.
AT EASE HAL. AND TRY NOT TO GET FLAGG GOING, WILL YOU? THE GUY'S INTENSE ENOUGH WITHOUT YOU AGGRAVATING HIM.

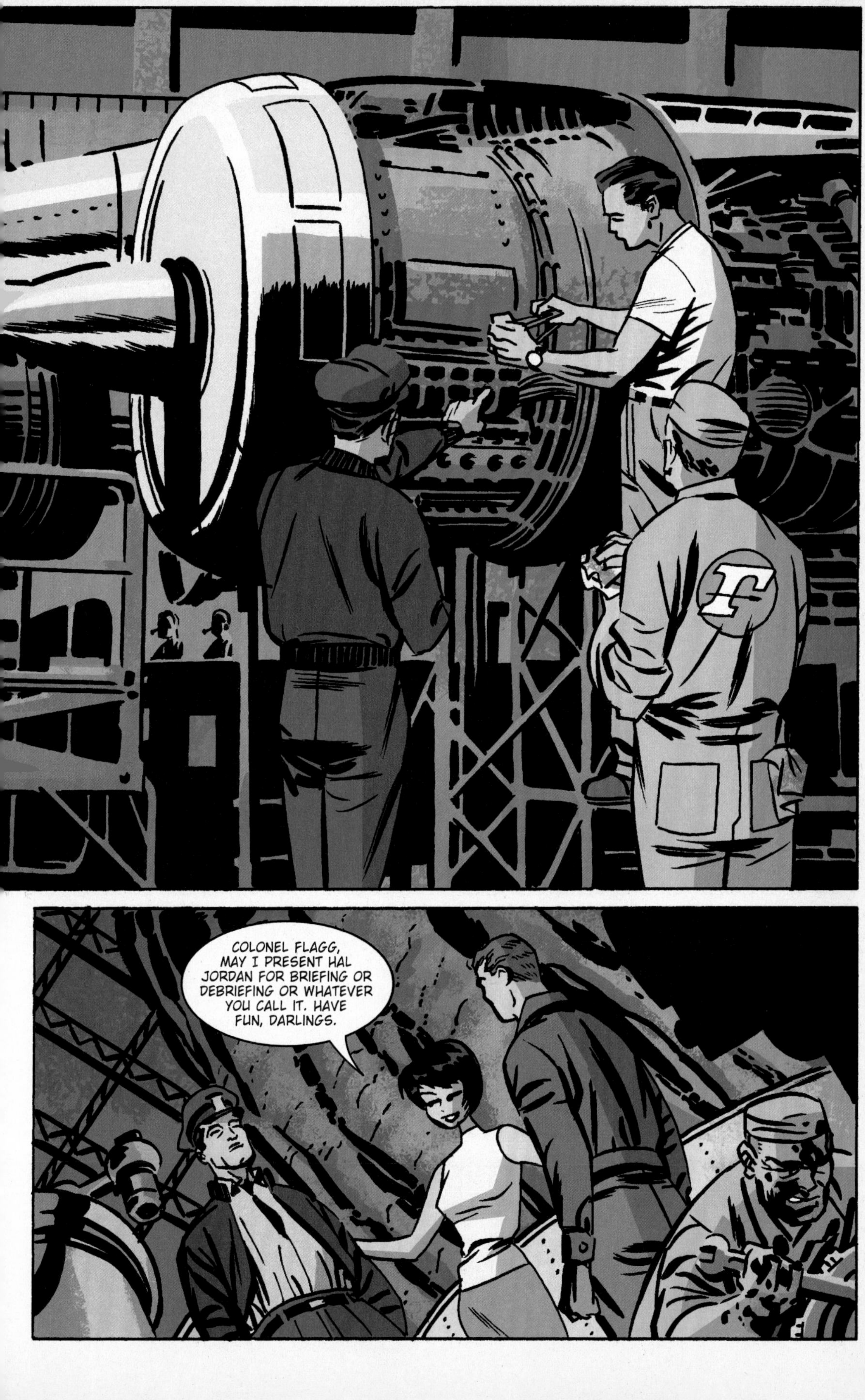
COLONEL FLAGG, MAY I PRESENT HAL JORDAN FOR BRIEFING OR DEBRIEFING OR WHATEVER YOU CALL IT. HAVE FUN, DARLINGS.

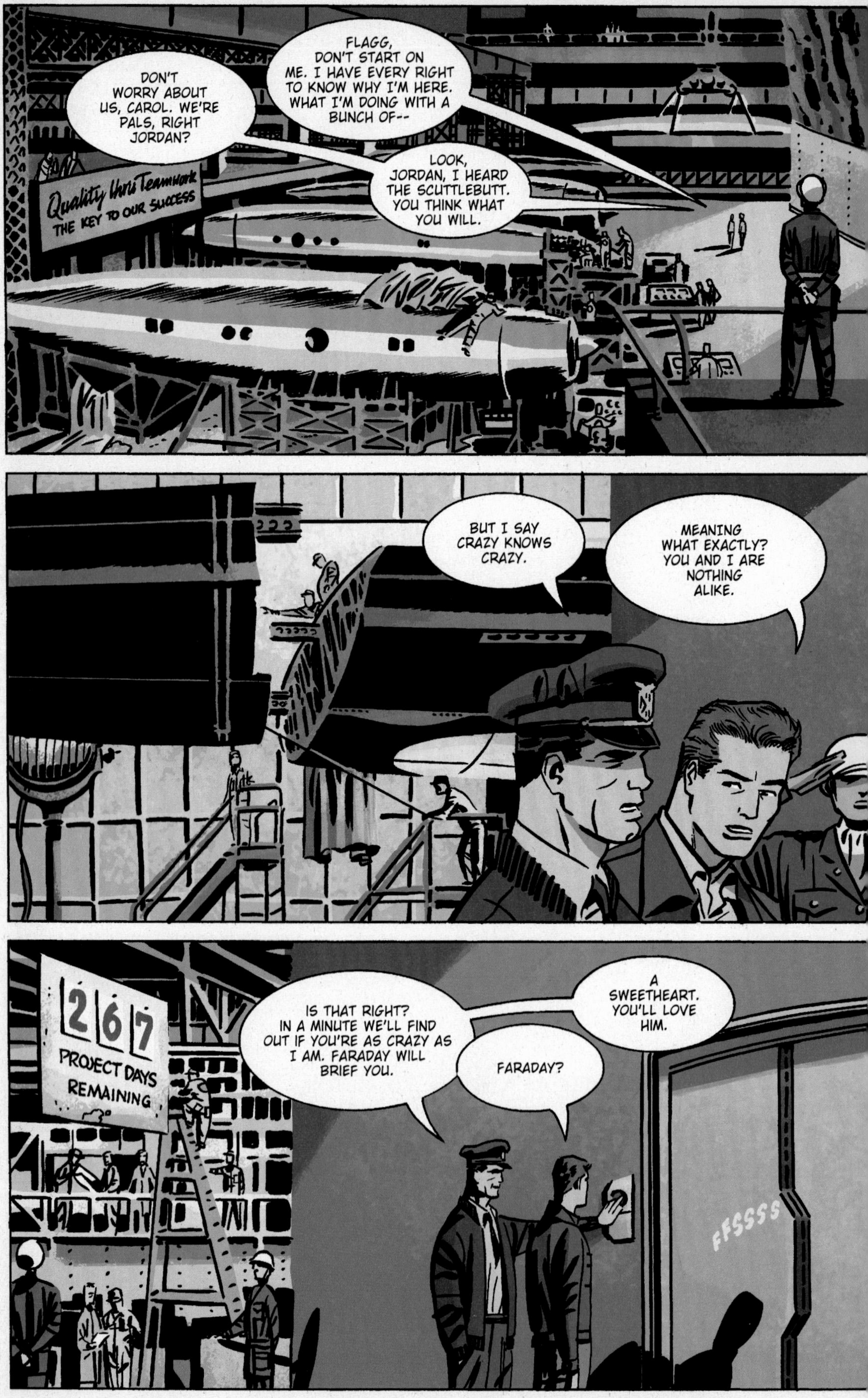
DON'T WORRY ABOUT US, CAROL. WE'RE PALS, RIGHT JORDAN?
FLAGG, DON'T START ON ME. I HAVE EVERY RIGHT TO KNOW WHY I'M HERE. WHAT I'M DOING WITH A BUNCH OF--
LOOK, JORDAN, I HEARD THE SCUTTLEBUTT. YOU THINK WHAT YOU WILL.
Quality thru Teamwork
THE KEY TO OUR SUCCESS
BUT I SAY CRAZY KNOWS CRAZY.
MEANING WHAT EXACTLY? YOU AND I ARE NOTHING ALIKE.
267
PROJECT DAYS REMAINING
IS THAT RIGHT? IN A MINUTE WE'LL FIND OUT IF YOU'RE AS CRAZY AS I AM. FARADAY WILL BRIEF YOU.
FARADAY?
A SWEETHEART. YOU'LL LOVE HIM.
FFSSSS

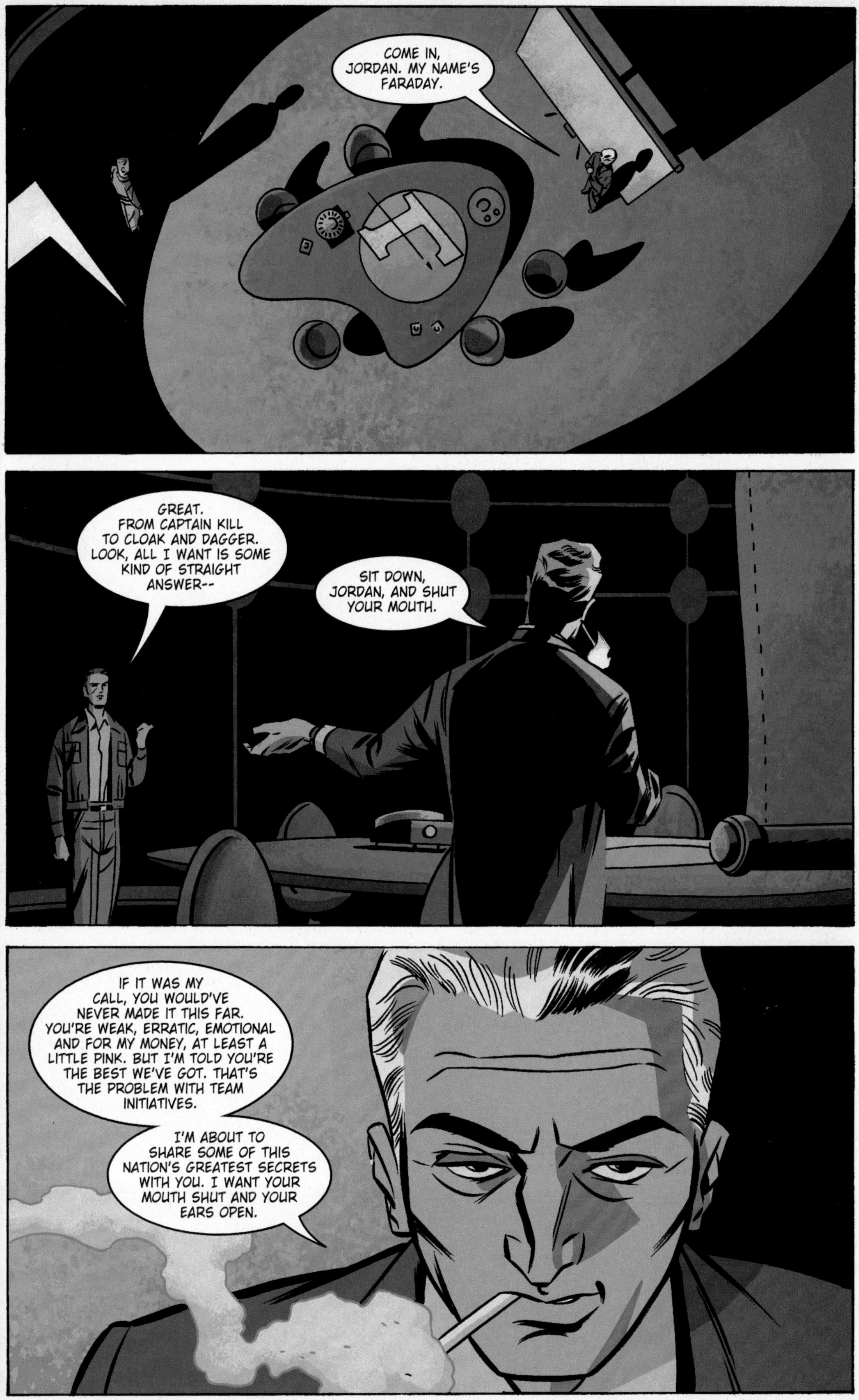
COME IN, JORDAN. MY NAME'S FARADAY.
GREAT. FROM CAPTAIN KILL TO CLOAK AND DAGGER. LOOK, ALL I WANT IS SOME KIND OF STRAIGHT ANSWER--
SIT DOWN, JORDAN, AND SHUT YOUR MOUTH.
IF IT WAS MY CALL, YOU WOULD'VE NEVER MADE IT THIS FAR. YOU'RE WEAK, ERRATIC, EMOTIONAL AND FOR MY MONEY, AT LEAST A LITTLE PINK. BUT I'M TOLD YOU'RE THE BEST WE'VE GOT. THAT'S THE PROBLEM WITH TEAM INITIATIVES.
I'M ABOUT TO SHARE SOME OF THIS NATION'S GREATEST SECRETS WITH YOU. I WANT YOUR MOUTH SHUT AND YOUR EARS OPEN.

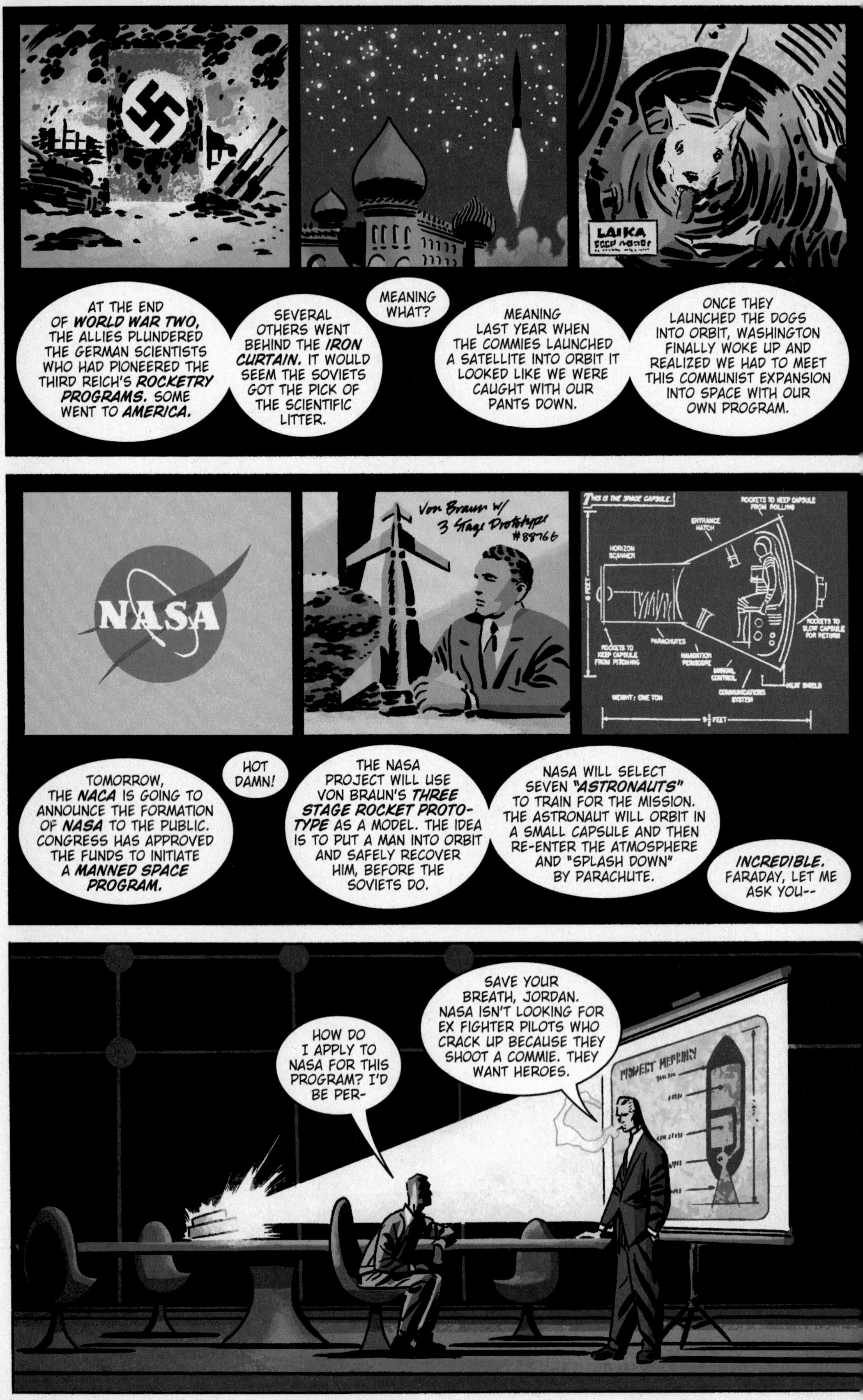
LAIKA
AT THE END OF WORLD WAR TWO, THE ALLIES PLUNDERED THE GERMAN SCIENTISTS WHO HAD PIONEERED THE THIRD REICH'S ROCKETRY PROGRAMS. SOME WENT TO AMERICA.
SEVERAL OTHERS WENT BEHIND THE IRON CURTAIN. IT WOULD SEEM THE SOVIETS GOT THE PICK OF THE SCIENTIFIC LITTER.
MEANING WHAT?
MEANING LAST YEAR WHEN THE COMMIES LAUNCHED A SATELLITE INTO ORBIT IT LOOKED LIKE WE WERE CAUGHT WITH OUR PANTS DOWN.
ONCE THEY LAUNCHED THE DOGS INTO ORBIT, WASHINGTON FINALLY WOKE UP AND REALIZED WE HAD TO MEET THIS COMMUNIST EXPANSION INTO SPACE WITH OUR OWN PROGRAM.
NASA
Von Braun w/ 3 Stage Prototype #88766
THIS IS THE SPACE CAPSULE.
ROCKETS TO KEEP CAPSULE FROM ROLLING
ENTRANCE HATCH
HORIZON SCANNER
ROCKETS TO SLOW CAPSULE FOR RETURN
PARACHUTES
ROCKETS TO KEEP CAPSULE FROM PITCHING
NAVIGATION PERISCOPE
MANUAL CONTROL
HEAT SHIELD
COMMUNICATIONS SYSTEM
WEIGHT: ONE TON
$9\frac{1}{2}$ FEET
TOMORROW, THE NACA IS GOING TO ANNOUNCE THE FORMATION OF NASA TO THE PUBLIC. CONGRESS HAS APPROVED THE FUNDS TO INITIATE A MANNED SPACE PROGRAM.
HOT DAMN!
THE NASA PROJECT WILL USE VON BRAUN'S THREE STAGE ROCKET PROTOTYPE AS A MODEL. THE IDEA IS TO PUT A MAN INTO ORBIT AND SAFELY RECOVER HIM, BEFORE THE SOVIETS DO.
NASA WILL SELECT SEVEN "ASTRONAUTS" TO TRAIN FOR THE MISSION. THE ASTRONAUT WILL ORBIT IN A SMALL CAPSULE AND THEN RE-ENTER THE ATMOSPHERE AND "SPLASH DOWN" BY PARACHUTE.
INCREDIBLE. FARADAY, LET ME ASK YOU--
HOW DO I APPLY TO NASA FOR THIS PROGRAM? I'D BE PER-
SAVE YOUR BREATH, JORDAN. NASA ISN'T LOOKING FOR EX FIGHTER PILOTS WHO CRACK UP BECAUSE THEY SHOOT A COMMIE. THEY WANT HEROES.
PROJECT MERCURY

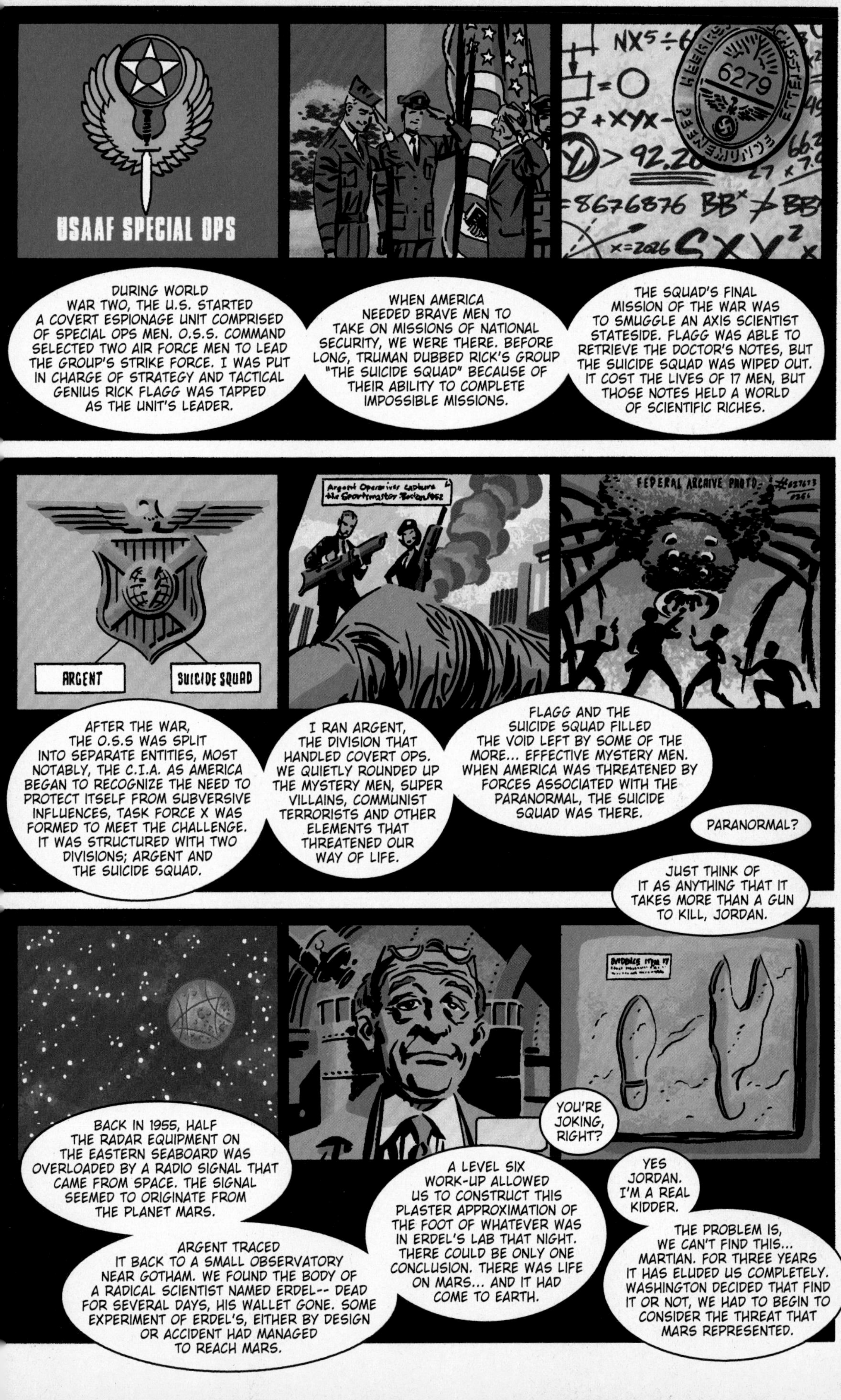
USAAF SPECIAL OPS
DURING WORLD WAR TWO, THE U.S. STARTED A COVERT ESPIONAGE UNIT COMPRISED OF SPECIAL OPS MEN. O.S.S. COMMAND SELECTED TWO AIR FORCE MEN TO LEAD THE GROUP'S STRIKE FORCE. I WAS PUT IN CHARGE OF STRATEGY AND TACTICAL GENIUS RICK FLAGG WAS TAPPED AS THE UNIT'S LEADER.
WHEN AMERICA NEEDED BRAVE MEN TO TAKE ON MISSIONS OF NATIONAL SECURITY, WE WERE THERE. BEFORE LONG, TRUMAN DUBBED RICK'S GROUP "THE SUICIDE SQUAD" BECAUSE OF THEIR ABILITY TO COMPLETE IMPOSSIBLE MISSIONS.
THE SQUAD'S FINAL MISSION OF THE WAR WAS TO SMUGGLE AN AXIS SCIENTIST STATESIDE. FLAGG WAS ABLE TO RETRIEVE THE DOCTOR'S NOTES, BUT THE SUICIDE SQUAD WAS WIPED OUT. IT COST THE LIVES OF 17 MEN, BUT THOSE NOTES HELD A WORLD OF SCIENTIFIC RICHES.
ARGENT
SUICIDE SQUAD
FEDERAL ARCHIVE PHOTO
AFTER THE WAR, THE O.S.S WAS SPLIT INTO SEPARATE ENTITIES, MOST NOTABLY, THE C.I.A. AS AMERICA BEGAN TO RECOGNIZE THE NEED TO PROTECT ITSELF FROM SUBVERSIVE INFLUENCES, TASK FORCE X WAS FORMED TO MEET THE CHALLENGE. IT WAS STRUCTURED WITH TWO DIVISIONS; ARGENT AND THE SUICIDE SQUAD.
I RAN ARGENT, THE DIVISION THAT HANDLED COVERT OPS. WE QUIETLY ROUNDED UP THE MYSTERY MEN, SUPER VILLAINS, COMMUNIST TERRORISTS AND OTHER ELEMENTS THAT THREATENED OUR WAY OF LIFE.
FLAGG AND THE SUICIDE SQUAD FILLED THE VOID LEFT BY SOME OF THE MORE... EFFECTIVE MYSTERY MEN. WHEN AMERICA WAS THREATENED BY FORCES ASSOCIATED WITH THE PARANORMAL, THE SUICIDE SQUAD WAS THERE.
PARANORMAL?
JUST THINK OF IT AS ANYTHING THAT IT TAKES MORE THAN A GUN TO KILL, JORDAN.
BACK IN 1955, HALF THE RADAR EQUIPMENT ON THE EASTERN SEABOARD WAS OVERLOADED BY A RADIO SIGNAL THAT CAME FROM SPACE. THE SIGNAL SEEMED TO ORIGINATE FROM THE PLANET MARS.
ARGENT TRACED IT BACK TO A SMALL OBSERVATORY NEAR GOTHAM. WE FOUND THE BODY OF A RADICAL SCIENTIST NAMED ERDEL-- DEAD FOR SEVERAL DAYS, HIS WALLET GONE. SOME EXPERIMENT OF ERDEL'S, EITHER BY DESIGN OR ACCIDENT HAD MANAGED TO REACH MARS.
A LEVEL SIX WORK-UP ALLOWED US TO CONSTRUCT THIS PLASTER APPROXIMATION OF THE FOOT OF WHATEVER WAS IN ERDEL'S LAB THAT NIGHT. THERE COULD BE ONLY ONE CONCLUSION. THERE WAS LIFE ON MARS... AND IT HAD COME TO EARTH.
YOU'RE JOKING, RIGHT?
YES JORDAN. I'M A REAL KIDDER.
THE PROBLEM IS, WE CAN'T FIND THIS... MARTIAN. FOR THREE YEARS IT HAS ELUDED US COMPLETELY. WASHINGTON DECIDED THAT FIND IT OR NOT, WE HAD TO BEGIN TO CONSIDER THE THREAT THAT MARS REPRESENTED.

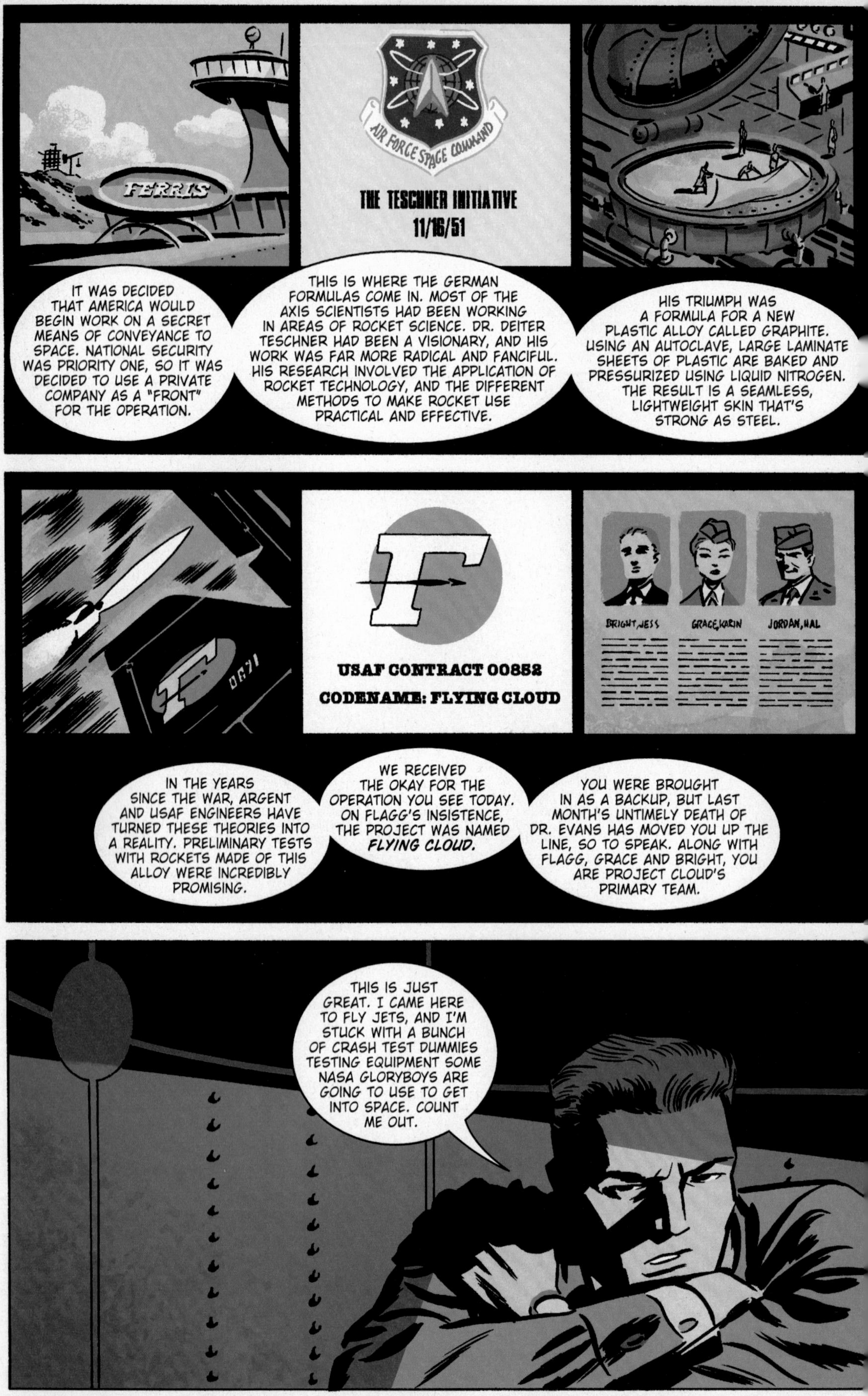

FERRIS
AIR FORCE SPACE COMMAND
THE TESCHNER INITIATIVE
11/16/51
IT WAS DECIDED THAT AMERICA WOULD BEGIN WORK ON A SECRET MEANS OF CONVEYANCE TO SPACE. NATIONAL SECURITY WAS PRIORITY ONE, SO IT WAS DECIDED TO USE A PRIVATE COMPANY AS A "FRONT" FOR THE OPERATION.
THIS IS WHERE THE GERMAN FORMULAS COME IN. MOST OF THE AXIS SCIENTISTS HAD BEEN WORKING IN AREAS OF ROCKET SCIENCE. DR. DEITER TESCHNER HAD BEEN A VISIONARY, AND HIS WORK WAS FAR MORE RADICAL AND FANCIFUL. HIS RESEARCH INVOLVED THE APPLICATION OF ROCKET TECHNOLOGY, AND THE DIFFERENT METHODS TO MAKE ROCKET USE PRACTICAL AND EFFECTIVE.
HIS TRIUMPH WAS A FORMULA FOR A NEW PLASTIC ALLOY CALLED GRAPHITE. USING AN AUTOCLAVE, LARGE LAMINATE SHEETS OF PLASTIC ARE BAKED AND PRESSURIZED USING LIQUID NITROGEN. THE RESULT IS A SEAMLESS, LIGHTWEIGHT SKIN THAT'S STRONG AS STEEL.
USAF CONTRACT 00852
CODENAME: FLYING CLOUD
BRIGHT, JESS
GRACE, KARIN
JORDAN, HAL
IN THE YEARS SINCE THE WAR, ARGENT AND USAF ENGINEERS HAVE TURNED THESE THEORIES INTO A REALITY. PRELIMINARY TESTS WITH ROCKETS MADE OF THIS ALLOY WERE INCREDIBLY PROMISING.
WE RECEIVED THE OKAY FOR THE OPERATION YOU SEE TODAY. ON FLAGG'S INSISTENCE, THE PROJECT WAS NAMED *FLYING CLOUD.*
YOU WERE BROUGHT IN AS A BACKUP, BUT LAST MONTH'S UNTIMELY DEATH OF DR. EVANS HAS MOVED YOU UP THE LINE, SO TO SPEAK. ALONG WITH FLAGG, GRACE AND BRIGHT, YOU ARE PROJECT CLOUD'S PRIMARY TEAM.
THIS IS JUST GREAT. I CAME HERE TO FLY JETS, AND I'M STUCK WITH A BUNCH OF CRASH TEST DUMMIES TESTING EQUIPMENT SOME NASA GLORYBOYS ARE GOING TO USE TO GET INTO SPACE. COUNT ME OUT.

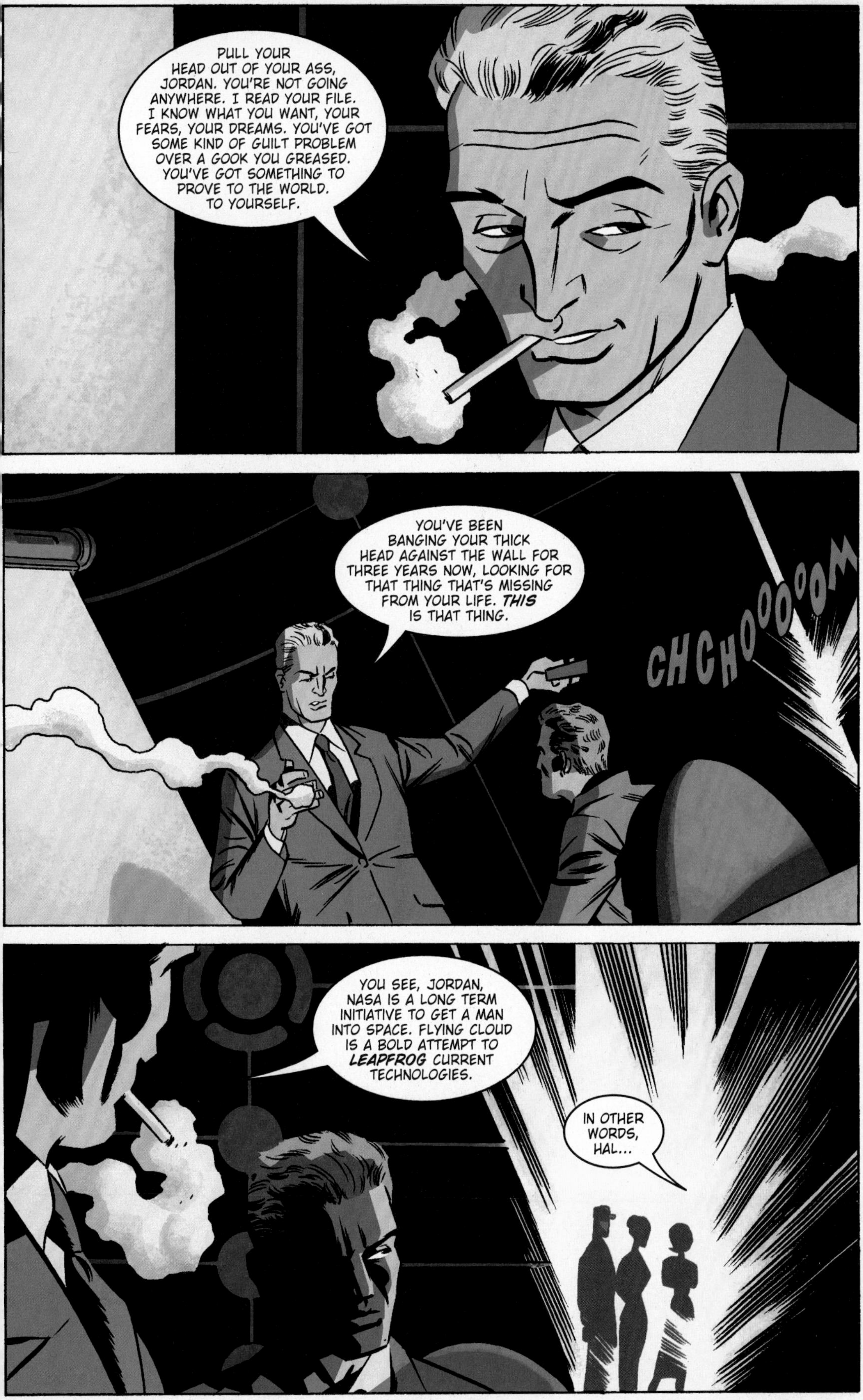
PULL YOUR HEAD OUT OF YOUR ASS, JORDAN. YOU'RE NOT GOING ANYWHERE. I READ YOUR FILE. I KNOW WHAT YOU WANT, YOUR FEARS, YOUR DREAMS. YOU'VE GOT SOME KIND OF GUILT PROBLEM OVER A GOOK YOU GREASED. YOU'VE GOT SOMETHING TO PROVE TO THE WORLD. TO YOURSELF.
YOU'VE BEEN BANGING YOUR THICK HEAD AGAINST THE WALL FOR THREE YEARS NOW, LOOKING FOR THAT THING THAT'S MISSING FROM YOUR LIFE. THIS IS THAT THING.
CHCHOOOOOOM
YOU SEE, JORDAN, NASA IS A LONG TERM INITIATIVE TO GET A MAN INTO SPACE. FLYING CLOUD IS A BOLD ATTEMPT TO LEAPFROG CURRENT TECHNOLOGIES.
IN OTHER WORDS, HAL...

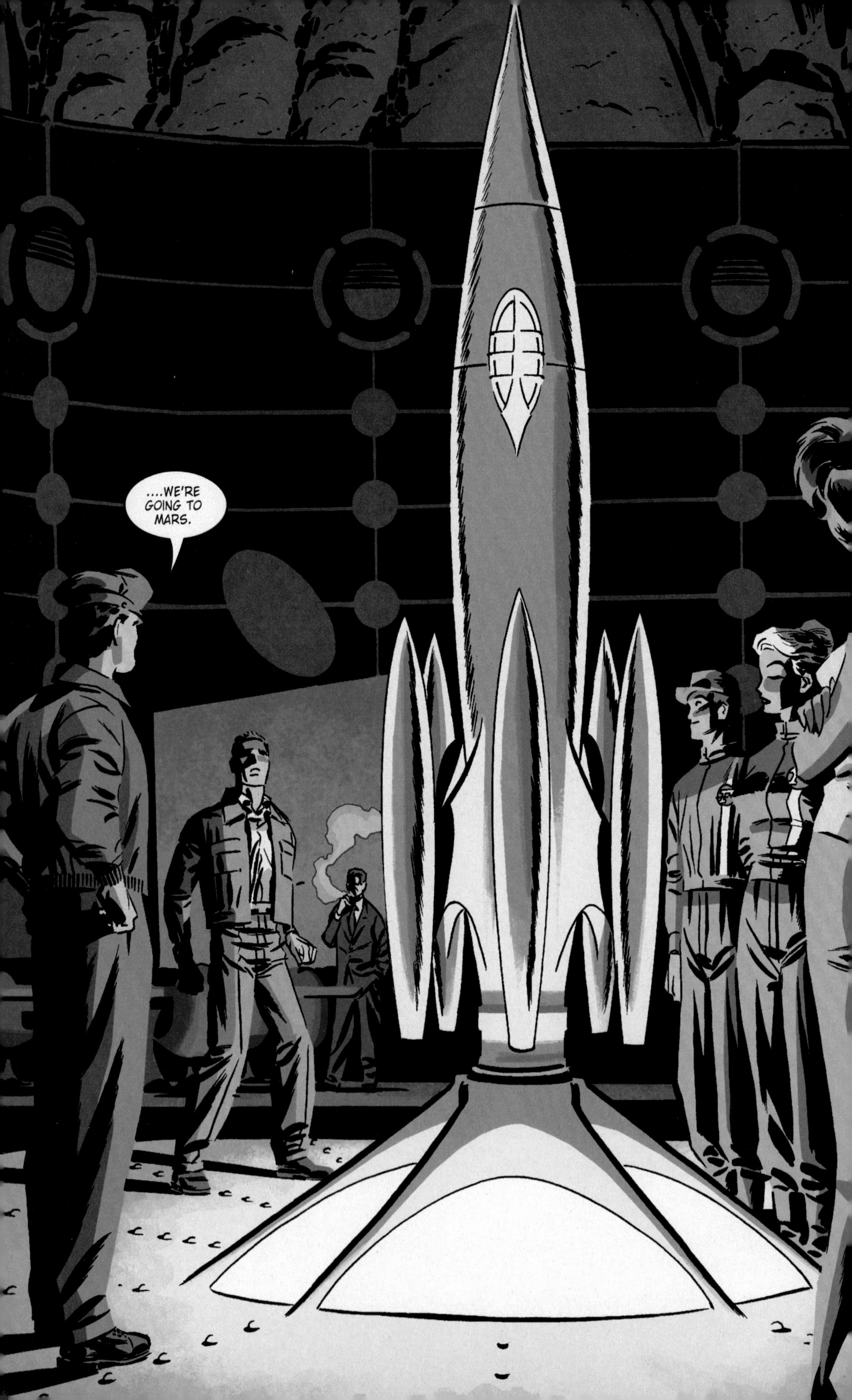
....WE'RE GOING TO MARS.

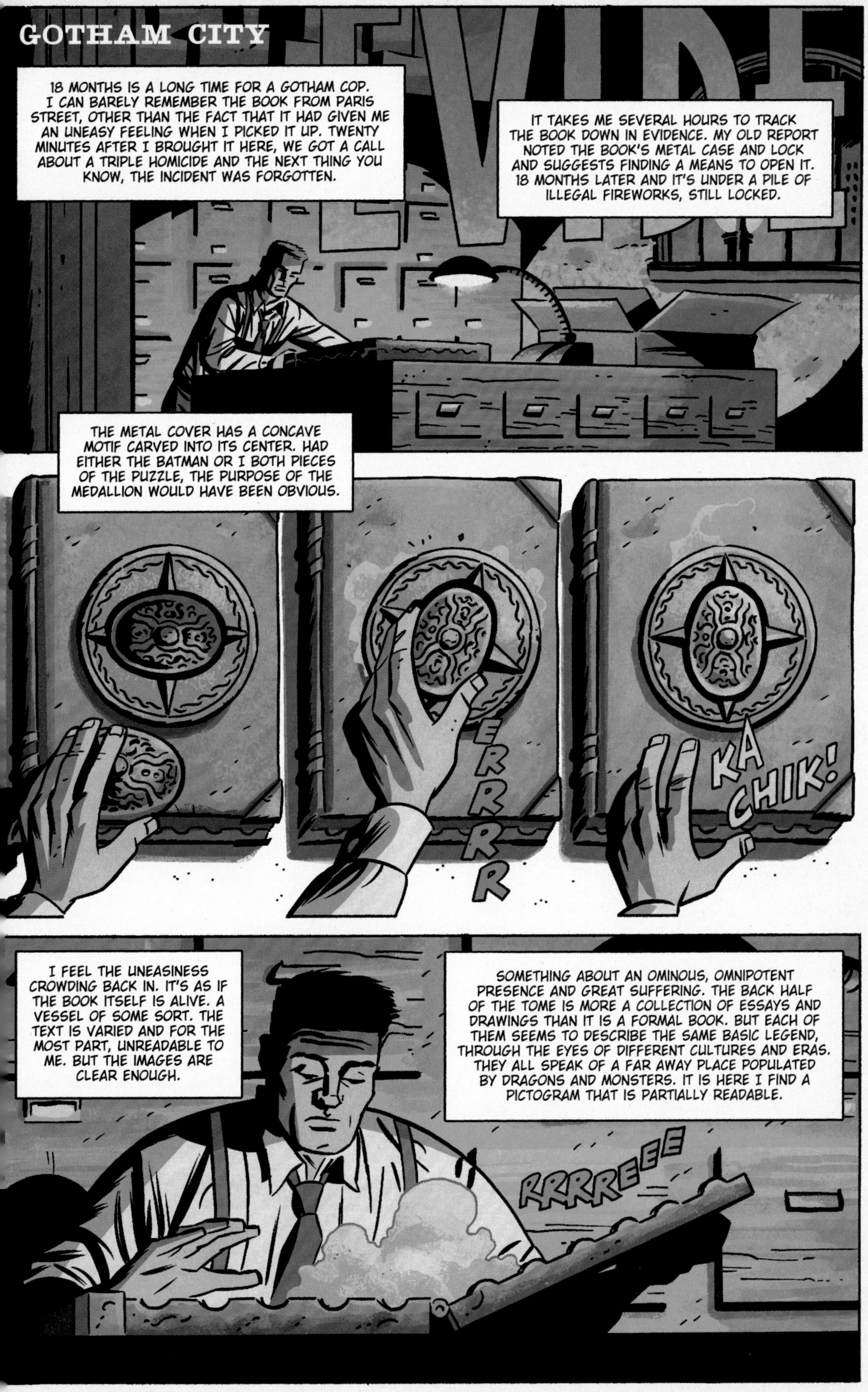
GOTHAM CITY
18 MONTHS IS A LONG TIME FOR A GOTHAM COP. I CAN BARELY REMEMBER THE BOOK FROM PARIS STREET, OTHER THAN THE FACT THAT IT HAD GIVEN ME AN UNEASY FEELING WHEN I PICKED IT UP. TWENTY MINUTES AFTER I BROUGHT IT HERE, WE GOT A CALL ABOUT A TRIPLE HOMICIDE AND THE NEXT THING YOU KNOW, THE INCIDENT WAS FORGOTTEN.
IT TAKES ME SEVERAL HOURS TO TRACK THE BOOK DOWN IN EVIDENCE. MY OLD REPORT NOTED THE BOOK'S METAL CASE AND LOCK AND SUGGESTS FINDING A MEANS TO OPEN IT. 18 MONTHS LATER AND IT'S UNDER A PILE OF ILLEGAL FIREWORKS, STILL LOCKED.
THE METAL COVER HAS A CONCAVE MOTIF CARVED INTO ITS CENTER. HAD EITHER THE BATMAN OR I BOTH PIECES OF THE PUZZLE, THE PURPOSE OF THE MEDALLION WOULD HAVE BEEN OBVIOUS.
ERRRRR
KA CHIK!
I FEEL THE UNEASINESS CROWDING BACK IN. IT'S AS IF THE BOOK ITSELF IS ALIVE. A VESSEL OF SOME SORT. THE TEXT IS VARIED AND FOR THE MOST PART, UNREADABLE TO ME. BUT THE IMAGES ARE CLEAR ENOUGH.
SOMETHING ABOUT AN OMINOUS, OMNIPOTENT PRESENCE AND GREAT SUFFERING. THE BACK HALF OF THE TOME IS MORE A COLLECTION OF ESSAYS AND DRAWINGS THAN IT IS A FORMAL BOOK. BUT EACH OF THEM SEEMS TO DESCRIBE THE SAME BASIC LEGEND, THROUGH THE EYES OF DIFFERENT CULTURES AND ERAS. THEY ALL SPEAK OF A FAR AWAY PLACE POPULATED BY DRAGONS AND MONSTERS. IT IS HERE I FIND A PICTOGRAM THAT IS PARTIALLY READABLE.
RRRREEE

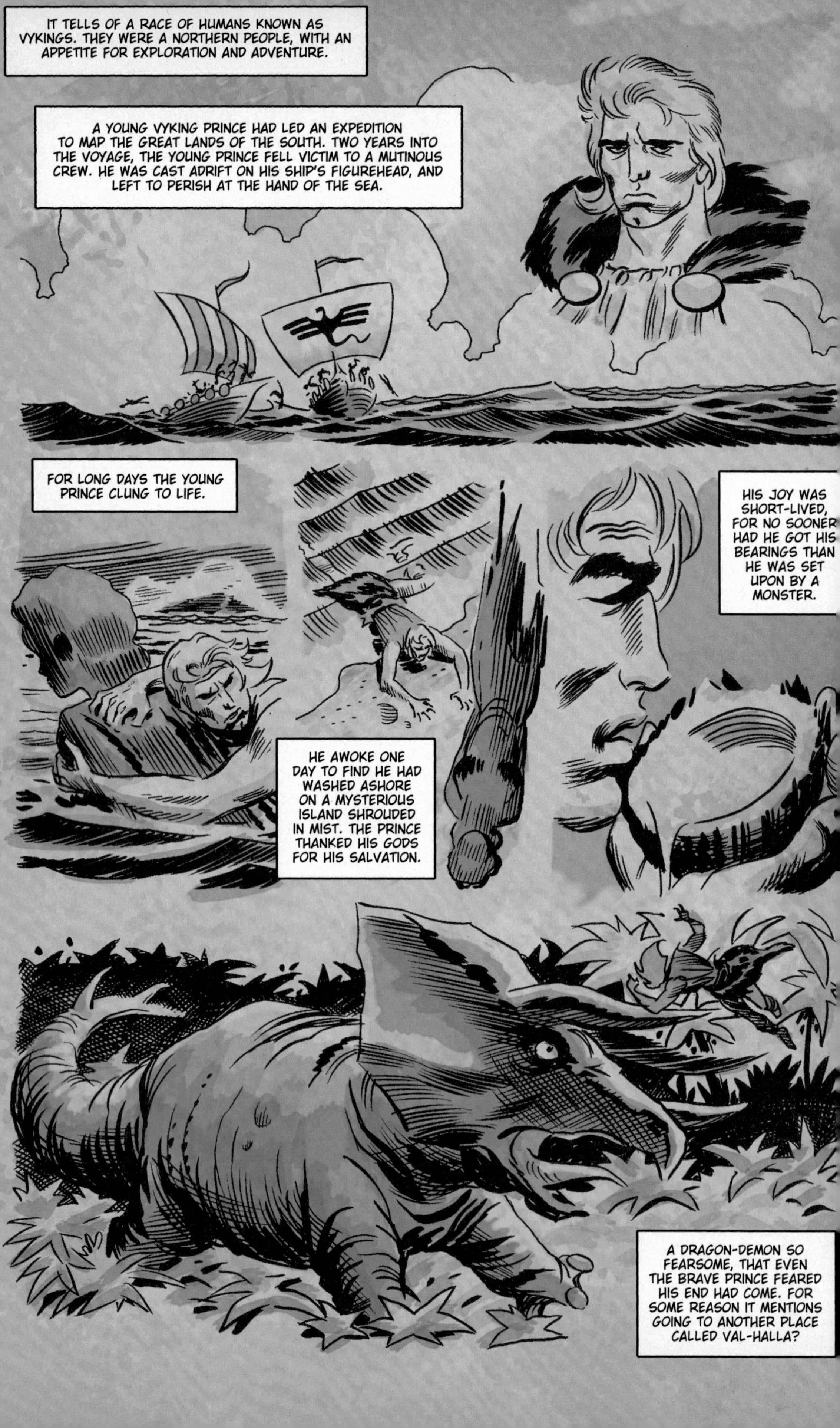
IT TELLS OF A RACE OF HUMANS KNOWN AS VYKINGS. THEY WERE A NORTHERN PEOPLE, WITH AN APPETITE FOR EXPLORATION AND ADVENTURE.
A YOUNG VYKING PRINCE HAD LED AN EXPEDITION TO MAP THE GREAT LANDS OF THE SOUTH. TWO YEARS INTO THE VOYAGE, THE YOUNG PRINCE FELL VICTIM TO A MUTINOUS CREW. HE WAS CAST ADRIFT ON HIS SHIP'S FIGUREHEAD, AND LEFT TO PERISH AT THE HAND OF THE SEA.
FOR LONG DAYS THE YOUNG PRINCE CLUNG TO LIFE.
HE AWOKE ONE DAY TO FIND HE HAD WASHED ASHORE ON A MYSTERIOUS ISLAND SHROUDED IN MIST. THE PRINCE THANKED HIS GODS FOR HIS SALVATION.
HIS JOY WAS SHORT-LIVED, FOR NO SOONER HAD HE GOT HIS BEARINGS THAN HE WAS SET UPON BY A MONSTER.
A DRAGON-DEMON SO FEARSOME, THAT EVEN THE BRAVE PRINCE FEARED HIS END HAD COME. FOR SOME REASON IT MENTIONS GOING TO ANOTHER PLACE CALLED VAL-HALLA?

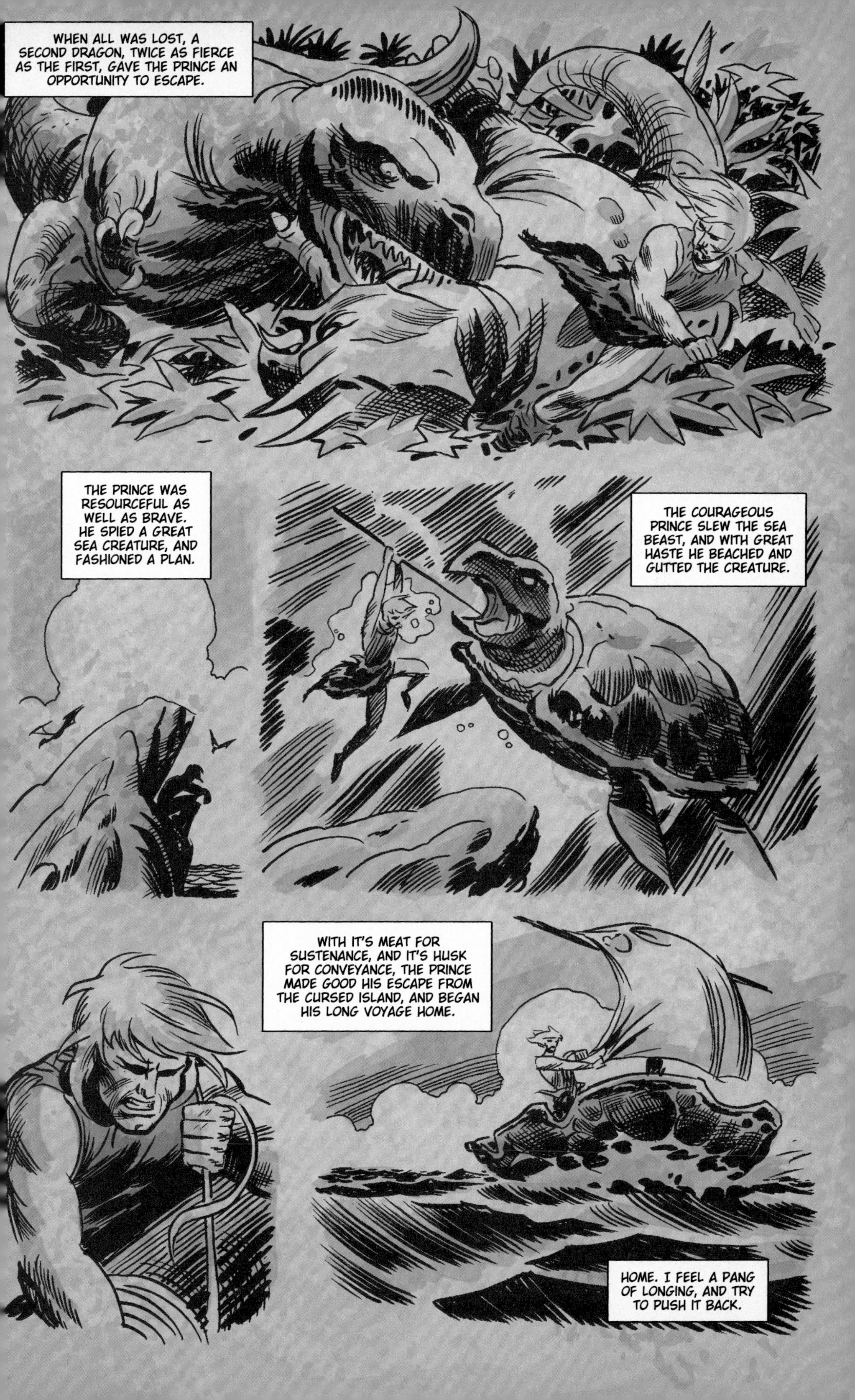
WHEN ALL WAS LOST, A SECOND DRAGON, TWICE AS FIERCE AS THE FIRST, GAVE THE PRINCE AN OPPORTUNITY TO ESCAPE.
THE PRINCE WAS RESOURCEFUL AS WELL AS BRAVE. HE SPIED A GREAT SEA CREATURE, AND FASHIONED A PLAN.
THE COURAGEOUS PRINCE SLEW THE SEA BEAST, AND WITH GREAT HASTE HE BEACHED AND GUTTED THE CREATURE.
WITH IT'S MEAT FOR SUSTENANCE, AND IT'S HUSK FOR CONVEYANCE, THE PRINCE MADE GOOD HIS ESCAPE FROM THE CURSED ISLAND, AND BEGAN HIS LONG VOYAGE HOME.
HOME. I FEEL A PANG OF LONGING, AND TRY TO PUSH IT BACK.

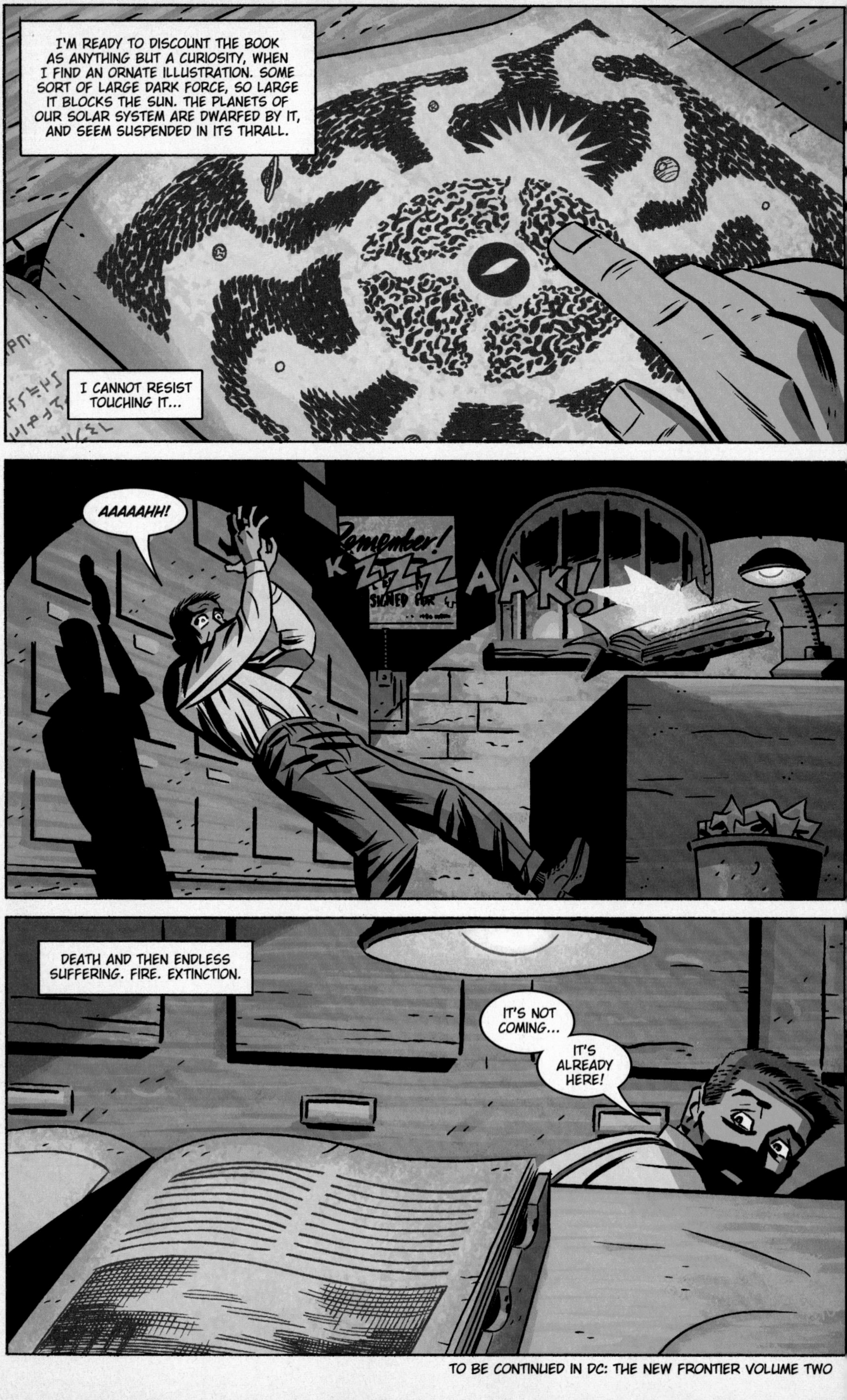
I'M READY TO DISCOUNT THE BOOK AS ANYTHING BUT A CURIOSITY, WHEN I FIND AN ORNATE ILLUSTRATION. SOME SORT OF LARGE DARK FORCE, SO LARGE IT BLOCKS THE SUN. THE PLANETS OF OUR SOLAR SYSTEM ARE DWARFED BY IT, AND SEEM SUSPENDED IN ITS THRALL.
I CANNOT RESIST TOUCHING IT...
AAAAAHH!
Remember!
KZZZZAAK!
DEATH AND THEN ENDLESS SUFFERING. FIRE. EXTINCTION.
IT'S NOT COMING...
IT'S ALREADY HERE!

TO BE CONTINUED IN DC: THE NEW FRONTIER VOLUME TWO

COVER GALLERY

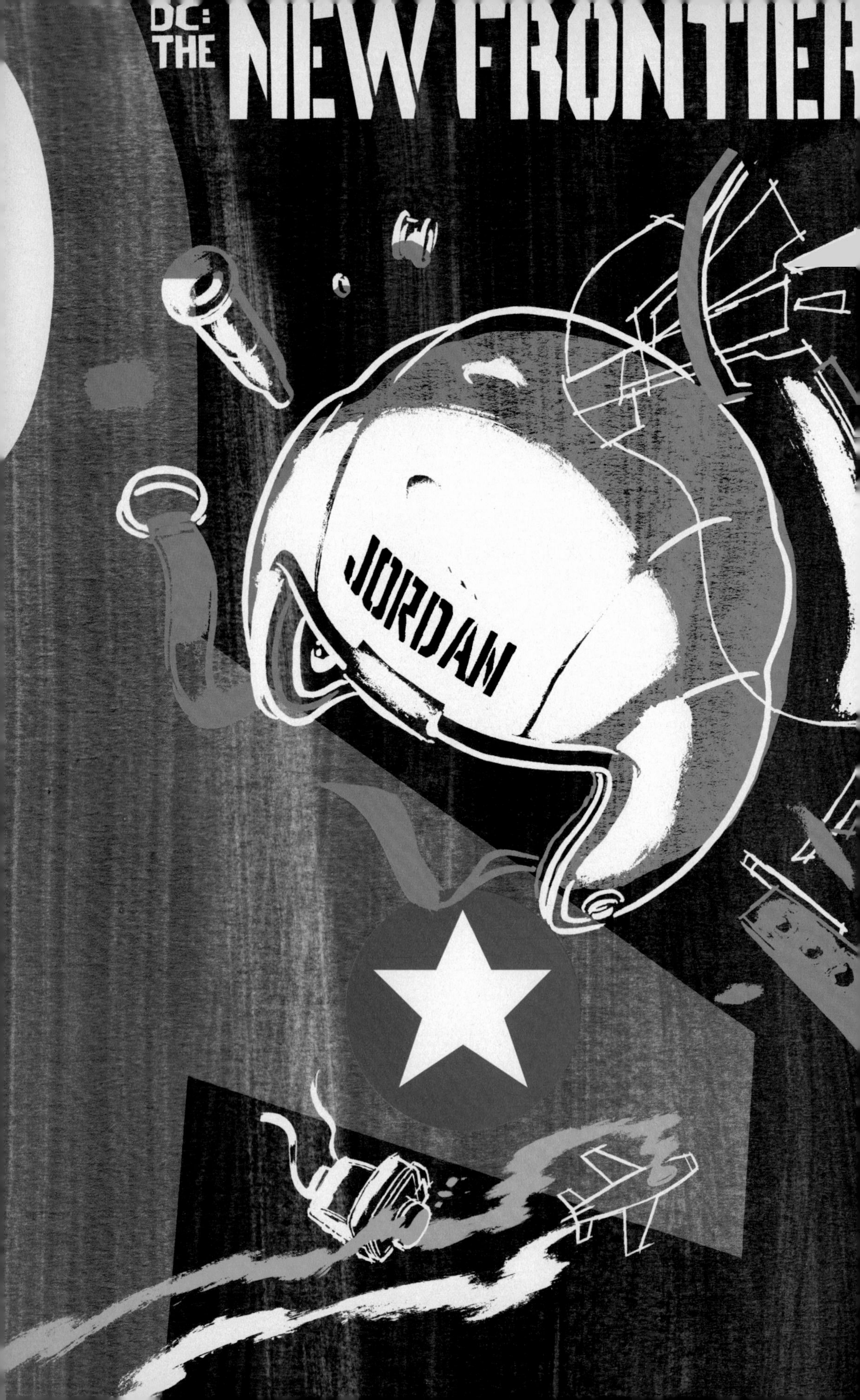
DC: THE
NEW FRONTIER
JORDAN

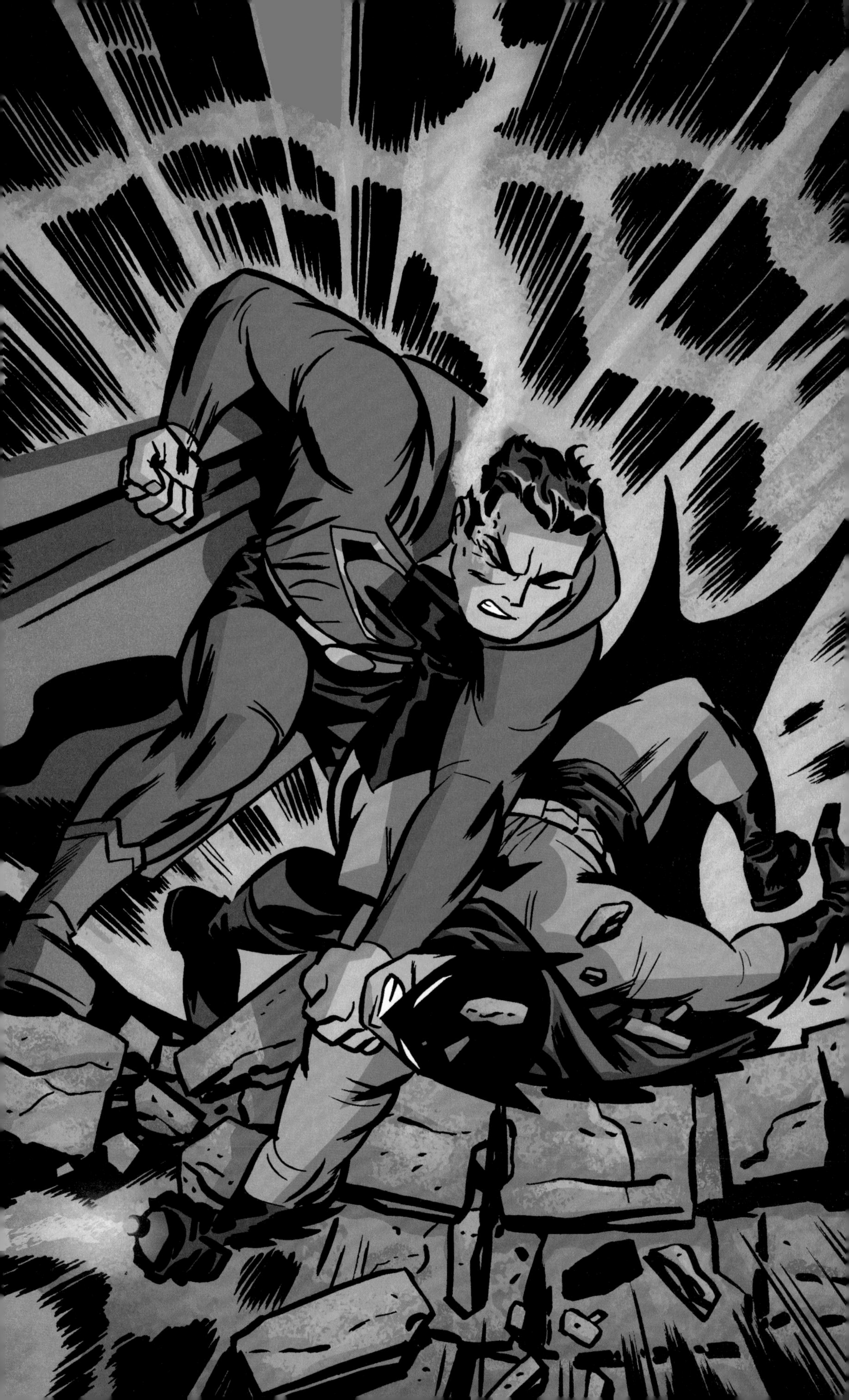

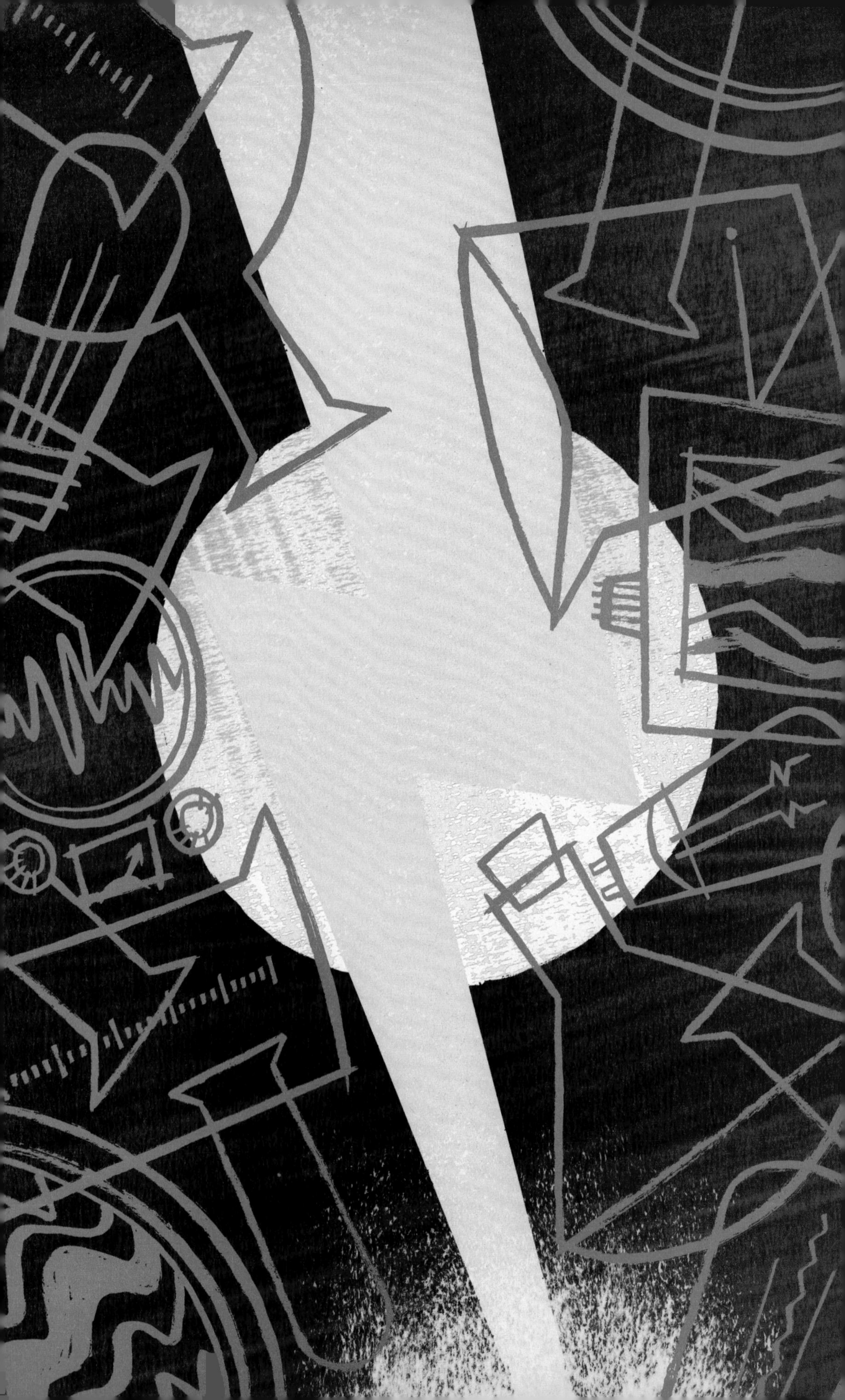

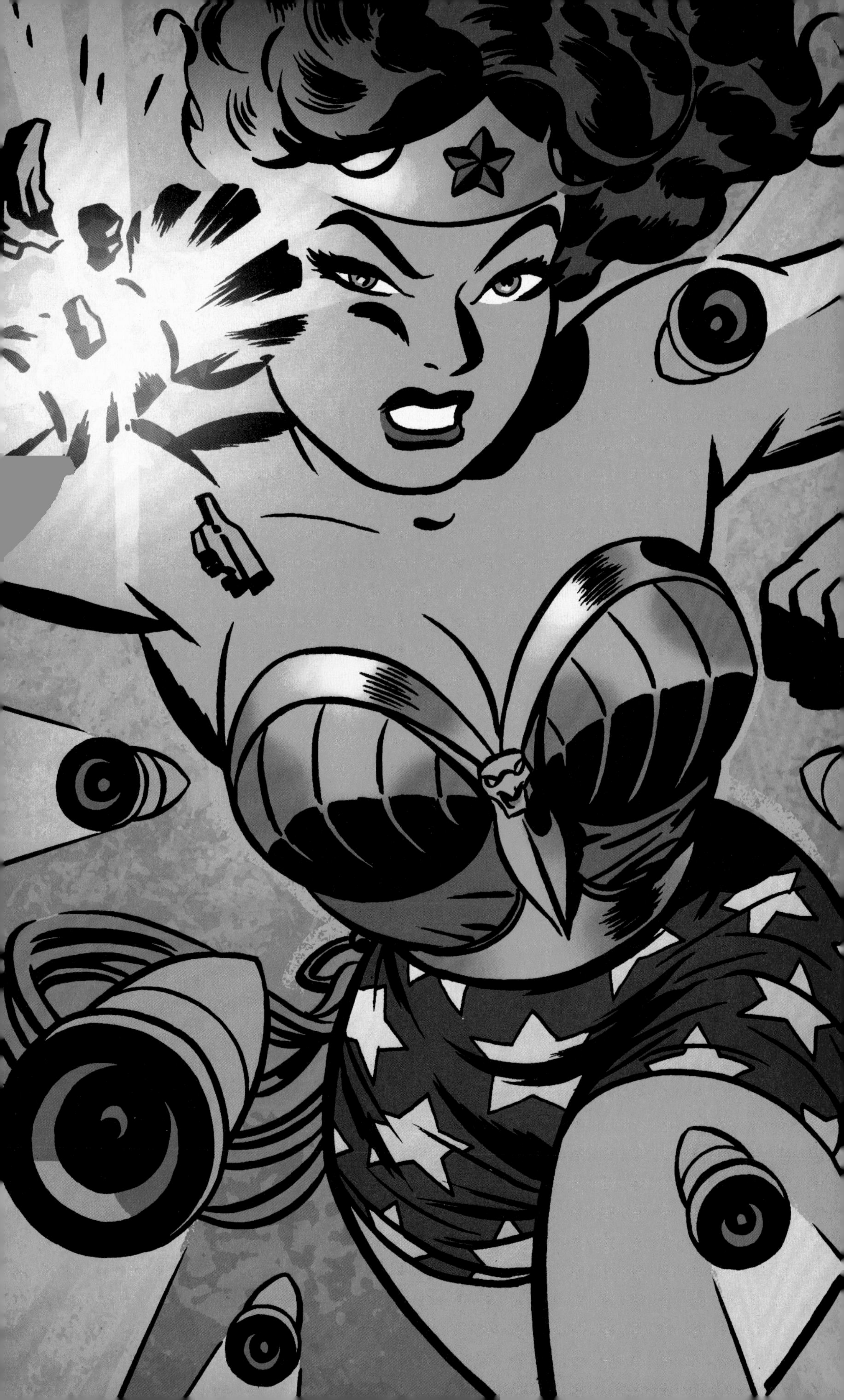

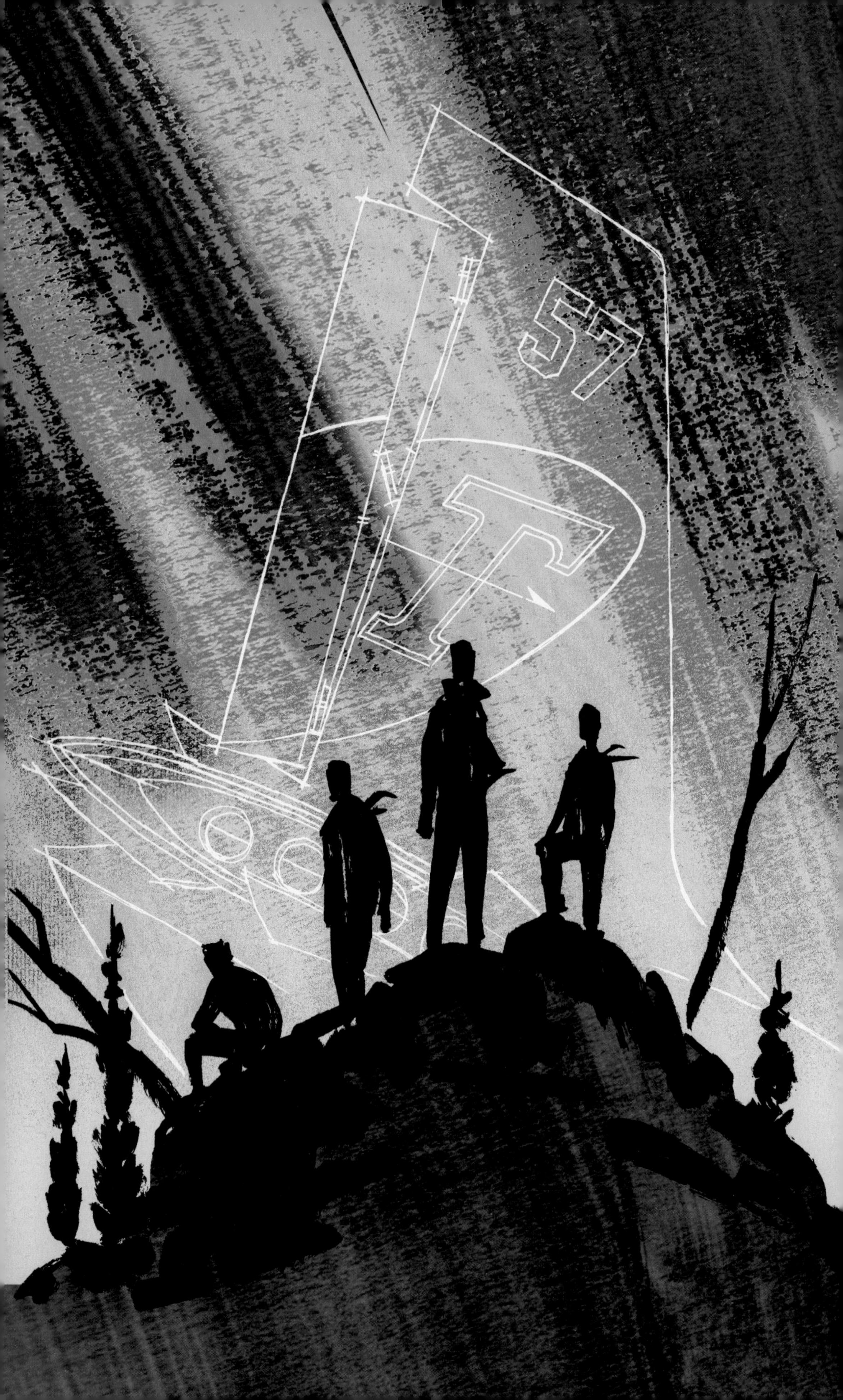
57

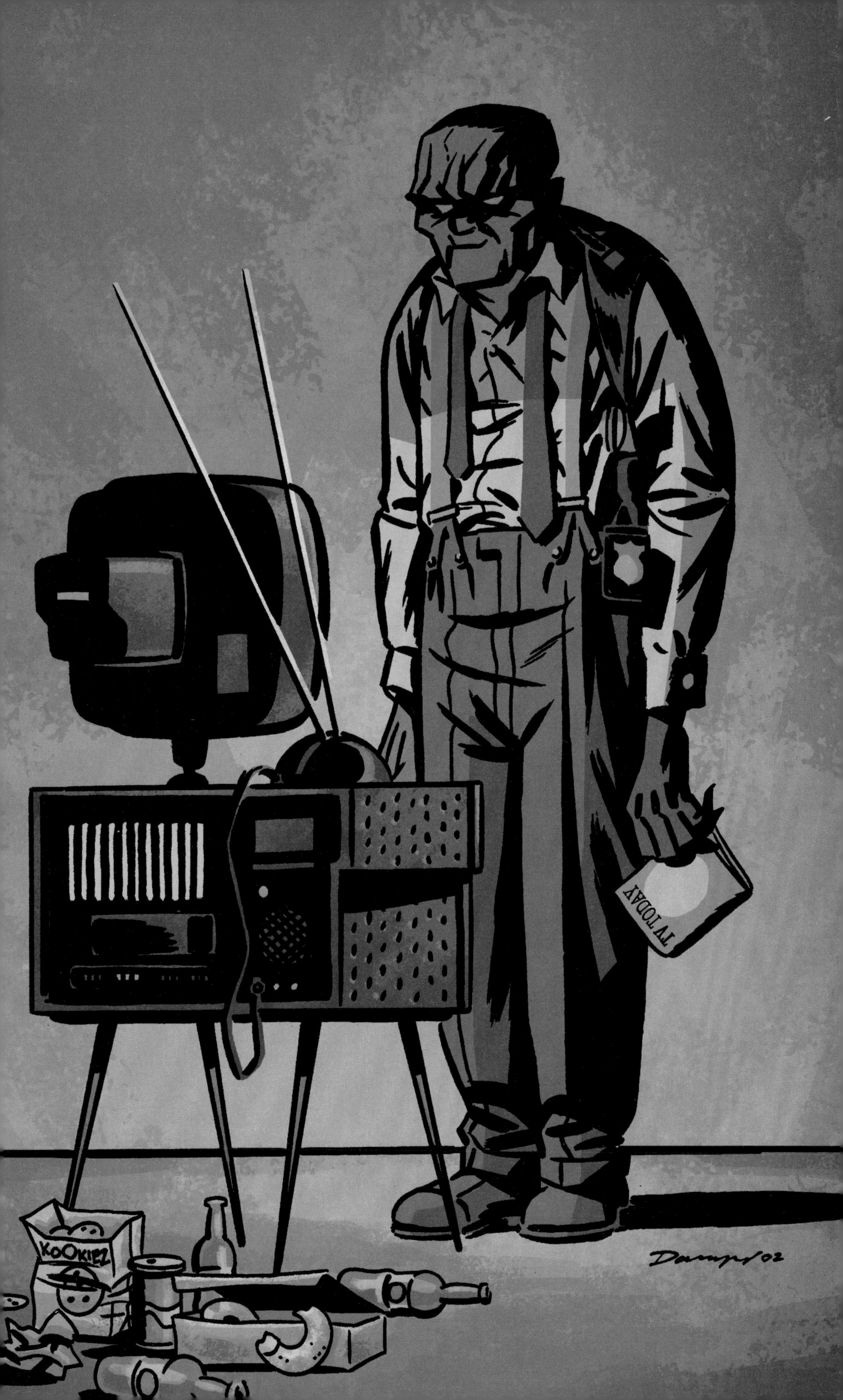
KOOKIEZ
TV TODAY

THE STARS OF THE DC UNIVERSE CAN ALSO BE FOUND IN THESE BOOKS: